Doug Van
Valkenburgh
1 4 85

NEW YORK
THE WONDER CITY

1932

NEW YORK
THE WONDER CITY

1932

W. PARKER CHASE

With a new Introduction by

Paul Goldberger

Architecture Critic of *The New York Times*

New York Bound / New York

Introduction copyright © 1983 by Paul Goldberger.

First published in 1932 by the Wonder City Publishing Co. in New York City.

This facsimile edition published in 1983 by New York Bound, 43 West 54th Street, New York, N.Y. 10019.

Distributed by Kampmann & Company, 9 East 40th Street, New York, N.Y. 10016.

The cover illustration is by Vernon Howe Baily from *Empire State: A Pictorial Record of Its Construction,* 1931.

Printed in the United States of America.

Library of Congress Cataloging in Publication Data

Chase, W. Parker.
 New York, the wonder city, 1932.

 Reprint. Originally published: New York: Wonder City Pub. Co., c1931.
 1. New York (N.Y.)—Description.   2. Architecture—New York (N.Y.)   3. New York (N.Y.)—Buildings.   I. Title.
 F128.5.C48   1983   974.7'1042   83-19388
 ISBN 0-9608788-3-1
 ISBN 0-9608788-2-3 (pbk.)

INTRODUCTION

No one today seems quite sure who W. Parker Chase was—city directories show him as residing at 301 East 21st Street in 1931, and no more—but wherever he came from and whatever his intentions, he produced an extraordinary document of a brief moment in New York's history. *New York: The Wonder City* is part encyclopedia, part social register, part architectural guide, part history, and part business directory of the city as it existed in 1932; but more important than any of these parts is the whole, and the whole is an altogether unabashed work of civic boosterism. It was a low moment in the Depression when the book was conceived and written, and it is difficult not to think that W. Parker Chase's hope was to awe the reader with New York's glory and in so doing somehow help the city to recapture some of the self-confidence, if not the prosperity, that it had lost. In his Foreword he says that he expected the book to sell three million copies, and he urged readers to impress their friends with the knowledge of the city they could glean from its pages.

To Parker Chase—and here we must quote, since no paraphrase could do justice to his own words—New York was a "synonym for big, great, astounding, miraculous." He went on: "NEW YORK—mecca which lures the brightest minds, the most brilliant writers, the most masterful artisans to its gates! NEW YORK—home of the world's greatest captains of industry, the world's most stupendous structures, the world's richest business institutions—veritable center of our country's wealth, culture and achievement! NEW YORK—!!! What visions of magnitude, variety and power the name New York conjures up for human comprehension."

This is not the sort of prose that generally calls for serious analysis; it is written without irony, though not without humor, and though it talks constantly of the sophistication of New York, it is perhaps the least blasé book about the city ever written. Parker Chase never takes anything for granted, except of course the fact that everything in New York is the biggest and the best; he is as amazed at the accomplishments of Douglas Elliman as at those of John D. Rockefeller, as impressed with the buildings of the garment center as with the Woolworth Building. The unrelenting optimism and utterly uncynical tone could not be less characteristic of New York, of course, and this provides a pleasing, if altogether unintended, degree of irony to the entire book. It is a view of New York that, for all its pretense of complete intimacy with the city, is very much that of the outsider.

Chase begins with a page defining the meaning of the term New Yorker—and a curious definition it is. "Merely *moving* to New York does not make one a New Yorker!" he exclaims. "In order to be a *real* New Yorker, one must have been *born* in New York, or else have lived in New York for *ten full years!*" Then, as if to answer the obvious question, Chase tells us that "although the above qualifications are neither the result of legislative enactment nor aldermanic decree, they represent what is required by *genuine* New Yorkers from those who migrate here....New Yorkers are proud of New York. They are unwilling to permit strangers who merely *move* to the city to declare themselves as New Yorkers until they have lived here sufficiently long to have achieved something or done their bit in adding to New York's prestige."

The tone is not a little like Helen Gurley Brown here, gushing and full of italics, though if that is true of this passage, the book overall might be said to be more Helen Gurley Brown crossed with Horatio Alger. There is a sense here that New York is an exclusive club, but a club whose membership rolls are theoretically open to all who earn their place. So it is, too, with foreigners, who, Chase tells us, comprise a significant percentage not only of the city's total population, but also of its "leaders." Hard work and good values will prevail in New York, fear not—despite the "large Bolshevik and criminal element" which Chase tells us lurks in the city's nether reaches, the good, solid folk of the city, backed up by their fine police force, manage to keep order.

Indeed, much of *New York: The Wonder City* is a kind of morality play, a chronicle of the forces of good triumphing over the forces of evil. Though New York has more poor than any other city, social service agencies bring more help than anywhere else; though there is gangsterism and corruption, the political system has somehow managed to rise above it. A page devoted to "The Working Girls of New York"—four pages after "The Millionaires of New York"—tells us that "no city in the world is more philanthropic, more generous or more sincerely concerned about its future mothers than is New York." But "on the other hand there is no place on the map offering more temptation, more pitfalls or more discouragement. It depends on the *girl herself*," Chase concludes, and goes on to tell the story of two girls who came to New York from a small town out west. One worked hard and soon became a high-ranking secretary; the other, sad to say, fell prey to liquor and men, and is now a hostess in a cheap dance hall.

The values of this book could not at this point be more clear—what W. Parker Chase is trying to tell us is that the city is full of evil temptation, but also full of goodness and reward, and that it is not so different from other places underneath. It is only bigger, more glorious, and more decadent. Thus a page in this chronicle is called "Home life in New York," and it tells us that despite the fact that most New Yorkers live in "towering apartments" or crowded tenements, there is still congenial neighborhood life—that the sense of community of a small town does not disappear altogether, but can be recreated on the scale of the apartment building, the tenement block, or whatever.

It is a not unsophisticated point so far as urban planning is concerned. But it was not Chase's intent, I think, to foreshadow Jane Jacobs; his real purpose is to sell the city as an environment for business, and here he pulls out all the stops. After an introductory page in which he exhorts his Depression-conscious readers to recall the lasting values of New York real estate ("New York real estate is *good* real estate. No matter how much of a burden it may be at present to carry it!"), he goes on to list virtually every office tower, hotel, apartment building, club, church, school, university, hospital, bank, movie theater, department store, and park in the city, each of these complete with photograph, cost, architect, and enough other vital statistics to stretch this section out to 200 pages.

Here, too, almost everything is described as the best and the grandest—"Almost as High as the Woolworth" shouts the headline atop the page devoted to the City Bank Farmers Trust Building at 22 William Street, a fine but not exceptional skyscraper from 1931. "One of the Sights of New York. Everything in connection with this monumental building expresses beauty, completeness and grandeur," says the listing, and this building is by no means special for Chase. His real enthusiasm is reserved for such as the Waldorf-Astoria—"Nothing has ever approached the magnitude, daring, ingenuity and achievement in hotel construction that is exemplified in the new Waldorf-Astoria just completed. Words convey but a faint impression of the stupendity [*sic*], the grandeur, and the magnificence of this wonder hotel." Or the New York Central Building, which sits astride the railroad tracks leading to Grand Central Terminal: "The construction of this mammoth building *over* the great cavern beneath it is one of the most remarkable engineering achievements of the age."

What is it that prevents all of these superlatives finally from blurring together into something that numbs us more than it impresses us? Perhaps it is Chase's amiable, earnest, and perpetually eager stance, so much that of the outsider striving to convince us that he knows as much, if not more, than the insiders. This is a deeply ingenuous book, with considerable charm almost in spite of itself, and that charm survives intact over the half-century since original publication. And of course *New York: The Wonder City* contains a torrent of information that continues to be of value to us even today; it is important not to underestimate this part of the book's appeal. What better reference for obscure architects' names, building dates, and so on? There is an occasional error, but the information by and large still holds.

But ultimately, the attraction of *New York: The Wonder City* to us today, in the New York of the 1980s, is that of innocence. It is the least jaded compendium on the most jaded city in the world, and its love for New York, earnest and fresh, cannot but communicate itself to us.

Paul Goldberger
New York
July 1983

NEW YORK
THE WONDER CITY

AN ILLUSTRATED STORY of NEW YORK
with statistics and general data concerning
NEW YORK'S VASTNESS, NEW YORK'S PEOPLE
NEW YORK'S ACTIVITIES AND NEW YORK'S

INTIMATE INSIDE LIFE

IN THE YEAR
1932

Compiled and written by
W. PARKER CHASE
With special contributions by
prominent New Yorkers

WONDER CITY PUBLISHING CO., INC.
NEW YORK CITY

FOREWORD

We hope the folks who read this book will like it.

We love New York and want everybody, everywhere, to know what a truly *wonder city* New York really is.

On a trip we took over the country some time ago, we visited the cities of practically every state in the Union. Everywhere, daily papers featured New York, picture shows devoted the larger part of their pictorial review to New York, and *everybody, everywhere* seemed interested in New York, and what was going on in New York.

In the practically 300 pages which follow are found 851 half-tone illustrations of buildings, people, and views of New York; short life-sketches of New York's outstanding men; articles and stories concerning New York's streets, its various activities, and even its intimate inside life, etc.

There are close to 2,000,000 foreign born citizens in New York. This book is the first comprehensive illustrated story of New York ever published that covers every phase of the city's buildings, people and activities. It is the first opportunity that this vast army of people has ever had of sending to "their folks at home" a complete showing of the great city in which they live.

There is another million who live in New York who have come to the city from all over America. They too will likely want to send copies to *their* folks—marking the buildings in which they live or in which they work.

Close to 5,000 strangers daily visit the city's sight-seeing towers, patronize sight-seeing buses, etc. where this book is on sale. Most of them will likely want to take a copy home with them.

Some time ago when the "dummy" was in the rough, we called on one of the heads of one of New York's $100,000,000 corporations and asked him how "daffy" he considered us if we made the statement that 3,000,000 copies of this book would be sold. He replied, "You're not daffy, you're crazy"! He then went on to emphasize that the bible and dictionary were the only two books ever printed that had reached such a circulation. We made a wager that we would pass the 3,000,000 mark before July 1st, 1932. Later, when he saw the completed "dummy" he wanted to call off the bet.

We hope to break all book-sales records with "NEW YORK—THE WONDER CITY," so—, *tell your friends about it.* Make 'em ashamed of their ignorance about the greatest city in the world, by the exploitation of your own knowledge concerning its buildings, its achievements and its people—after you have absorbed the pages following.

We feel safe in stating that nine out of ten figures quoted herein are absolutely accurate. But we cannot guarantee this, nor do we assume any responsibility for entire accuracy of statement. Over 10,000 pieces of material had to be collected, allocated and copied, and being human, a few mistakes have undoubtedly crept in. However, we have collected our data from reliable sources, used extreme care in both compilation and printing, and believe the figures and facts given are as nearly correct as is possible in a book of this kind with its almost endless detail.

NEW YORK—THE WONDER CITY

NEW YORK—synonym for big, great, astounding, miraculous!

NEW YORK—mecca which lures the brightest minds, the most brilliant writers, the most masterful artisans to its gates!

NEW YORK—home of the world's greatest captains of industry, the world's most stupendous structures, the world's richest business institutions—veritable center of our country's wealth, culture, and achievement!

NEW YORK—! ! ! What visions of magnitude, variety and power the name New York conjures up for human comprehension.

MILLIONS and BILLIONS instead of hundreds and thousands are the figures constituting the basis for calculation nowadays in this wonder city! Banks and corporations with resources of $250,000,000, $500,000,000 and even billions are becoming more and more common. Buildings that house whole cities in themselves, such as the Empire State, Graybar, Chrysler, Lincoln, and a score of others, keep going up in almost every part of the huge city.

Note statistics on following pages showing the vastness of New York's wealth, New York's business, and New York's activities generally. Observe the startling and surprising totals on pages 11 and 12. In fact, all through this volume will be found information, data and pictures quite confirming New York's indisputed supremacy as the wonder city of the world.

Airmap Corp. of America Inc.

NEW YORKERS

Merely *moving* to New York does not make one a New Yorker!

In order to be a *real* New Yorker, one must have been *born* in New York, or else have lived in New York *ten full years!*

Although the above qualifications are neither the result of legislative enactment nor aldermanic decree, they represent what is required by *genuine* New Yrokers from those who migrate here and claim the right to be classed as New Yorkers.

It is permissible for newcomers to mention the fact that they *reside* in New York, and when they travel, they may register at hotels as *from* New York, but under no circumstances may they claim to *be* New Yorkers, until they have served their full ten years of apprenticeship.

New Yorkers are proud of New York. They are unwilling to permit strangers who merely *move* to the city, to declare themselves as New Yorkers until they have lived here sufficiently long to have achieved something or done their bit in adding to NewYork's prestige.

New York is more than a wonder city—it is the miracle city that has broken every known municipal record.

New York has grown so rapidly that even those most active in city development can scarcely comprehend it all. Those whose interests confine them to Wall Street, know little of the big operations going on in the Central Park, and East River areas. Even "42nd Streeters" have but slight conception of the continual developments in the Seventh, Eighth and Ninth Avenue sections, etc.

Everywhere—even in the outlying districts, old landmarks, tenements, and one, two, and three story shacks are being demolished to make place for big apartment house projects. The excavations recently begun for the $250,000,000 Radio City to be built by John D. Rockefeller Jr. inaugurate the most gigantic single building enterprise in world history.

Is it any wonder New Yorkers are a bit squeamish about the indiscriminate adoption of the name and prestige of the Wonder City they have built, and refuse to strangers the right to *call* themselves New Yorkers (merely because they *move* here)' until they have *done* something entitling them to the distinction!

Famous Old New Yorkers

KEY TO PICTURES OF OLD NEW YORKERS

1—Daniel C. Robbins
2—Alfred Van Santvoord
3—Benjamin H. Field
4—Gustav Schwab
5—Jeremiah P. Robinson

6—Elliott F. Shepherd
7—Frederick A. Conkling
8—Joseph Frances
9—Samuel B. Ruggles
10—Thomas B. Coddington
11—Edward K. Collins

12—Shephard Knapp
13—Richard Irvin
14—William F. Havemeyer
15—James S. T. Stranahan
16—Ambrose Snow

4

EARLY DAYS OF NEW YORK

New York's history begins with the discovery of the Hudson River by Hendrik Hudson in 1609—some 320 years ago.

Although Hendrik Hudson was of English descent, he was in the employ of the Dutch East India Co.—a very enterprising institution those days, which in 1610 sent ships to America to engage in the fur business with Indians.

The settlement which later developed became known as "New Amsterdam."

In 1613 the first four buildings ever erected on Manhattan Island, were constructed by Adrian Block whose ship caught fire and burned to the waters edge, thus forcing him and his crew to seek shelter. The land on which Block built his cabins was in the direct vicinity of what is now Bowling Green, the value of which at that time could be reckoned by a few strings of beads, as thirteen years later (1626) Peter Minuit brought over two ship loads of immigrants and purchased the entire island of Manhattan from the Indians for $24.00!

During the following years, the colony grew slowly but substantially—being maintained largely by the Dutch East India Co. In 1664, however, Charles II. granted "New Netherlands"—(as the district was at first called,) and the entire surrounding country, to his brother, the Duke of York. On September 2nd, Richard Nichols sailed into the harbor and took possession of the Community in the name of the Duke of York.

Notwithstanding that Peter Stuyvesant (who for a number of years had been Governor of the Island) protested vigorously, English rule was established, and later the name of the settlement was changed to New York.

The old stockade at Wall St.

All through the years leading up to the American revolution, the colonists, as a whole, quarrelled with the English Governors, and at one time a German merchant by the name of Jacob Leisler, seized control while England was embroiled with troubles at home, resulting in his being hanged on the very spot where the *World* building now stands. In fact, the early settlers of New York maintained a difficult existence up to the very close of the American Revolution itself. Foreign injustice, heavy taxation, Indian massacres as well as internal troubles made their life a strenuous one.

At the close of the American Revolution, New York had a population of a little over 22,000, and from 1785 until 1790, Congress met in the old Federal Hall—where the Sub-treasury building now stands at the Northwest corner of Wall and Nassau Streets. In 1790 this corner was valued at around $5,000. Today it is worth in excess of $5,000,000.

The history of New York—from the time of Hendrik Hudson, right up to date, has been that of a wonder City. Since New York became "GREATER NEW YORK," the community's growth and prosperity has been unparalleled in the history of the world.

It was on January 1, 1898—34 years ago, that Manhattan, the Bronx, Brooklyn, Long Island and Richmond, became GREATER NEW YORK. New York County was christened "*Manhattan* borough." That part of Manhattan just north of the Harlem River, became "BRONX borough." Kings County became "BROOKLYN borough." Queens County of Long Island, became "QUEENS borough," and Staten Island, became "RICHMOND borough." The various County Supervisors were merged into a Board of Aldermen, thus constituting the Lower Branch of Greater New York's Municipal Assembly—the Upper Branch consisting of the Board of Estimate and Apportionment. It is doubtful if any city in the world is better governed—notwithsanding some very bitter feeling against Tammany's power.

THE FOREIGNERS OF NEW YORK

America is called the "melting pot" of the world!

But the "fire" that seems to keep the pot boiling seems to be mostly in New York.

Statisticians claim there are 516,792 *foreign born* Russians and 429,830 Italians in New York alone.

Their children born in this country (first generation) bring this total up to an enormous figure.

Of New York's 7,000,000 population, *over* 2,000,000 are Jewish.

Altogether, there are only about 5,000,000 Hebrews in the entire United States. Therefore, close to 50 per cent. of all the Jews in the country are located in New York. Many of the city's greatest philanthropists, wealthiest capitalists, and most public spirited citizens are of Jewish descent.

New York boasts of over 400,000 Italians, among whom are many *leaders* in the city's various activities.

The approximate foreign born population of Greater New York, according to recent compilation, is as follows:

Russian	517,000	Polish	160,000
Italian	405,000	Austrian	139,000
Irish	223,000	English	78,000
German	213,000	Hungarian	70,000

French, Swedish, Norwegian, Scottish, Roumanian and other European countries have also contributed their thousands. The balance of New York's foreign born is made up of those coming mostly from Japan, China, Syria, Greece and various colonies from over the world.

New York has a Negro population of close to 300,000.

Nowhere on the map has the Negro the advantages he has in the wonder city. In upper Harlem (Lenox Avenue, Seventh Avenue and contiguous streets all the way from 110th up to 150th) approximately the entire district is peopled by them. Many New York Negroes are extremely wealthy, highly educated and occupy positions of greatest trust and importance in New York business life.

New York is the most cosmopolitan city in the world.

Practically every language known to civilization is spoken here. Newspapers printed in almost every tongue are published in New York. Churches and places of worship of practically every religion and creed are supported by New York's foreign element.

Entire districts are given over to various nationalities such as the Ghetto, Little Hungary, Chinatown, "Darktown," etc., etc.

A large portion of the alien immigrants admitted into the United States come in at the Port of New York.

The landing place of the immigrants is on Ellis Island, which is occupied by the Federal Government for this purpose. It is an interesting place to visit and is reached by a ferry at the foot of Whitehall Street and the Battery.

A good percentage of the immigrants coming to America have never left the neighborhood of the City of New York. The result is that the total foreign-born population of New York State is 2,783,773, and of these 1,989,216, or almost 75 per cent., reside in the metropolis. Over fifty nations are represented in the population of New York.

Although European and oriental countries have sent to America many undesirable members of society, New York owes to its foreign born, thousands of our most valued and respected citizens, and, as a whole, New York is extremely proud of its foreign population!

HOME LIFE IN NEW YORK

"There is no place like home!"

Especially is this true in New York.

Notwithstanding the general impression that there is but little real home life in the great city, and that the whole community is cold, unresponsive, unfriendly and unneighborly, there are just as many happy homes, ideal homes, and as much genuine home contentment in New York per square mile as in any other location in the entire country.

True, New Yorkers are "cliff dwellers"—most of them. The average family lives in two, three or four rooms in towering apartment buildings, with no yards, no gardens, no trees, no green grass, etc., such as characterizes the average home in small cities and towns, and yet in almost every part of New York's residential areas, beautiful parks, wide shady boulevards and countless breathing spots are found directly opposite, or are within short walking distance of these miles of homes.

Even in the tenement districts and most congested centers, the city fathers have, through foresight or frequent purchase, provided public squares with shade trees, cooling fountains and restful benches, which afford fresh air for both children and adults. And these crowded sections are no worse off than many of the tumble-down and disgraceful shanty districts of other communities.

Although New Yorkers live in more or less cooped up tenements and apartments, they have at their very doors breathing spots, and other outdoor advantages! But consider the other appeals New York offers!

New York presents everything that is *best* in life from the standpoint of *culture, education, entertainment, recreation,* and so on. No matter what particular penchant or bent one living in New York may have, whether it be music, art, literature, sport, the theatre, or the more serious considerations such as invention, science, business, etc., leaders in every vocation or activity come to New York to exploit their ambitions. New York leads the world and stands supreme in providing the greatest opportunities and possibilities for advancement, study, or achievement, as well as entertainment, recreation and gratification of desire.

THE CARNEGIE HOME

THE SCHWAB HOME

THE MORGAN HOME

It is true that New York is not "neighborly" in the small-town sense of the term. This is necessarily so because of the cosmopolitan population. A bootlegger and an evangelist, or a gambler and a reformer may live on the same floor of an apartment building, and not even meet in the hallways during a period of years! On the other hand, there may be a number of other families in the building disposed to be friendly, and chance meetings may bring about relationships that revelop into as sincere friendships and as desirable social intercourse as can be found *anywhere.* In other words, if one desires congenial neighbors, and wishes to make friends, one has more opportunity and a *greater field* from which to select, than in smaller communities—and without the detestable "gossip" and meddlesomeness which so invariably characterizes the intimacy of small town population.

Home life in New York can be just as ideal as one wants it.

REAL ESTATE IN NEW YORK

For the past half dozen years, one has been repeatedly asked the question, "HOW ARE THEY GOING TO FILL 'EM?"

The question was the natural sequence to the ever-increasing number of new business structures, gigantic office buildings, and towering skyscrapers being erected in every part of New York.

No matter in what part of the city one went, whether in the lower Wall Street section, up in Harlem, the Bronx, or in Brooklyn, the noise of steel riveters would mark another new building in construction!

Millions, tens of millions, yes, hundreds of millions were being invested in building activity. Down in lower Manhattan, fully fifty new skyscrapers of 25, 30, 40, and even 60-story towers were added to New York's famous skyline. Farther uptown in "Midtown New York," twice this number, including the Empire State, Chrysler, Lincoln and other huge structures discounted Wall Street and vicinity. Even up at 59th, in the Central Park area, a forest of new skyscrapers, staggering in their cost and immensity, were replacing old landmarks.

"HOW ARE THEY GOING TO FILL 'EM?" continued to be asked with increased curiosity.

Notwithstanding the Wall Street crash in the fall of 1929, and the general business depression that held for over a year and a half, the biggest and costliest structures ever erected by man were built in 1930—and more building permits are being granted by the City Building Department right along!

"How *are* they going to fill 'em?"

The answer *must* be that New York is growing so rapidly in population and wealth there is a *need* for all this construction. In spite of foreclosures, vacant space for rent, and the general calamity propaganda on the part of weak-kneed pessimists who insist that real estate is at a standstill and the country is on the way to the bow wows, there are many red-blooded real estate he-men still in New York. They have the horse sense and the foresight to recognize that "over-inflation" is fairly well adjusted, and normalcy is once more in the offing. It is only a question of time until we awaken to the fact that there is *just as much money* in the country *as there ever was.* Over $12,000,000,000 is on deposit in New York banks at this moment. *When* this miasma of fear, which seems to so completely control, will have been overcome, ending the temporary lull that has so depressed and partially paralyzed the business world in general, a sounder and more permanent prosperity will be experienced than has ever before been recorded in national history.

Real estate in New York has "sagged" many times. But it has always recovered and not long after the recovery increased surprisingly in value. During past depressions many who were "property poor" or impatient, and sold a plot or parcel, later regretted their shortsightedness. There is no "dirt" in all the world which has a more stable value than New York real estate.

New York real estate is *good* real estate. No matter how much of a burden it may be at present to carry it!

8

THE VASTNESS OF NEW YORK

In 1900 New York's population was 3,437,202, according to the Federal census.

In 1930 New York had more than doubled these figures—population 6,930,446.

We are commencing 1932 with a considerable number over 7,000,000—as New York is gaining several hundred thousand every year as the result of births (far exceeding the death rate), immigrants and new residents from all over the country.

New York is not only the largest city in America, but the wealthiest, most cosmopolitan and most stupendous in every way.

Everybody, everywhere, who has never visited New York, lives in hope that he or she may some day see its towering skyscrapers, its great art galleries and museums, its countless phases of business life, and experience its day and night thrills!

New York is supreme in practically every activity known to life. It is now the world's financial center, and in the mass and architecture of its buildings, no other community on the globe can compete with it. In volume of business done, in invention, art, science, education, music, literature, in every phase of human endeavor, New York leads.

Like every other large metropolitan center, New York has its criminals, its underworld, its speak-easies, its spasmodic exposure of political corruption, and its other sinful and iniquitous agencies which seem to be a part of every populous community. On the other hand no city anywhere has more churches, more missions, more philanthropic institutions, and more channels for the uplift, and welfare of mankind in general.

In no city on the map has there ever been manifested such generosity on the part of its prosperous citizens in the interest of fellow man. The generous benefactions of New York's men of wealth is estimated at over $3,000,000,000 during the past fifty years. New York has over 1,500 churches valued at more than $250,000,000, also the Salvation Army, Red Cross, Y.M.C.A., Y.W.C.A., and countless other organizations for the betterment of humanity.

New York is the pride of all America! Although rivalries and jealousies between local communities persist in various parts of the country, New York has forged so far ahead of any former rival for supremacy among the cities of the United States, that today, in every part of our land, there seems to be a feeling of national pride in the fact that the eyes of the world are focused on New York—"our New York," the American city that is now "ours" in the national sense!

As an example of the vastness of New York as compared with other American cities note tabulation at right—

Observe that the total population of *all cities* in the United States (of 500,000 or over) is less than double that of New York—and this group includes Chicago, Philadelphia, Detroit and Los Angeles—the four largest in the country.

New York's population exceeds that of the combined population of the following 13 states: Maine, New Hampshire, Vermont, Rhode Island, Delaware, North Dakota, Montana, Wyoming, Idaho, Utah, Nevada, Arizona and New Mexico.

1930 CENSUS	
Chicago	3,376,438
Philadelphia	1,950,961
Detroit	1,568,662
Los Angeles	1,238,040
Cleveland	900,429
St. Louis	821,960
Baltimore	804,874
Boston	781,188
Pittsburgh	669,817
San Francisco	634,394
Milwaukee	578,249
Buffalo	573,072
Total	13,998,084

(See next page)

9

(Continued from Page 9)

Those who travel will note that in each of our larger cities, outstanding office buildings and skyscrapers loom conspicuously in the local skyline, but these larger buildings are invariably confined to a more or less restricted area constituting the center of activities.

This is not so in New York. From lower Broadway, as far north as 175th Street, a distance of over ten miles, 20, 30, 40, and even 50 and 60 story buildings high spot the view all along the entire stretch of territory from the East River to the Hudson.

Fully fifty huge skyscrapers dot the skyline of lower Manhattan.

Scattered along the route up to Madison Square (23rd Street) other towering structures rise.

From Madison Square all the way up to 60th Street (which includes mid-town New York with its EMPIRE STATE, CHRYSLER, LINCOLN, CHANIN, 500 FIFTH AVENUE BUILDING, GRAYBAR and 200 other huge and imposing spires of the air) a picture is presented that discounts even the famous lower Broadway panorama.

And beginning at 59th Street, mammoth hotel and apartment buildings continue the spectacle all the way up to the forty story Broadway Temple at 175th Street, a combination of stores, offices, hotel and church. (See page 54.)

Even above 175th—in fact up to the northernmost part of Manhattan, building activity in every part of the island has been steadily going on. On the Grand Concourse, the Bronx, Washington Heights, and in all directions, beautiful new buildings have been replacing old shacks and eye-sores, in keeping with the "spirit of New York."

Over *three billions* were expended in building operations within three years in New York—from January 1, 1927 to December 31, 1930.

If President McKinley (who was assassinated *less than thirty years ago*) could come back to life today, and see New York as it is *now*, with its **7,000,000** population, its **637,527** buildings, its bank resources of over **$15,000,000,000**, its hundreds of miles of subways, its million motor cars, its airships and blimps, and its myriad other sensational and astounding evidences of progress and development, he would probably be more confused than was old Rip Van Winkle after *his* famous twenty years sleep!

To further appreciate the stunning and unparalleled figures which proves New York's vastness, note 100 SENSATIONAL TOTALS on following pages.

Airmap Corp. of America Inc.

100 SENSATIONAL TOTALS

Every figure given in the following has been gathered from reliable sources, although many of them have been necessarily approximated.

1—New York's area comprises 202,508 acres—316 square miles.
2—New York's public property is valued at $2,500,000,000.
3—New York has over 3,000 *miles* of *paved* streets.
4—New York has 637,527 buildings (January 1, 1931.)
5—New York has over 4,000 buildings of ten floors and more.
6—New York has over 500 buildings of twenty floors or more.
7—New York has 216 buildings ranging from 25 to 102 floors.

According to survey made by Thompson & Starrett Co. (building contractors) in 1929, *covering* 173 *cities* of the U. S. *of* 50,000 *population* or over, *less than* 50 *of them* had even *one* building as high as 21 stories.

8—New York has *over* 500 buildings valued at $1,000,000 each.
9—New York has 89 buildings valued at $5,000,000 each, or more.
10—New York has 76 buildings valued at $10,000,000 each, or more.
11—New York has 12 buildings valued at from $20,000,000 to $50,000,000 each!
12—New York's real estate is assessed at over $18,000,000,000.
13—N. Y. has 8,703 acres in park lands—194 parks, 82 playgrounds and 24 parkways.
14—New York has nearly $200,000,000 invested in bridges.
15—New York has $700,000,000 (city's money) invested in subways.
16—New York has over $500,000,000 invested in its water system.
17—New York has $331,151,000 invested in its school system.
18—N. Y. employs 37,000 teachers, etc., in its schools—wages $114,748,000.
19—New York has 1,118 schools—over 1,200,000 pupils attend N. Y. schools.
20—New York has $750,000,000 invested in public and civic buildings, etc.
21—N. Y. has five big City Markets—Bronx Market cost $16,000,000.
22—New York has 119,546 street lamps—cost to operate $5,000,000 yearly.
23—New York employs 17,780 policemen—wages $16,994,030 yearly.
24—New York employs 6,568 in its Fire Department—wages $6,562,500.
25—New York employs, all told, 131,667 help—wages $190,900,000.
26—New York's budget for "running the city" (1931) nearly $670,000,000.
27—New York has 100 legal courts in sessions daily.
28—New York has over a dozen air ports.
29—New York's banks have resources of $15,917,432,160 (Jan. 1, 1931).
30—Deposits in New York banks (Jan. 1, 1931) $12,684,808,730.
31—New York's bank clearings (1929) totaled $477,242,282,000.
32—Custom duties collected at port of New York (1930) $334,012,906.
33—New York's foreign commerce totals close to $4,000,000,000 yearly.
34—4,997 vessels landed at New York's piers and docks in 1930.
35—New York is the *terminal* of 89 navigation companies.
36—New York is the *terminal* of 9 railroads.
37—An average of 15,000 *car loads* of various freight arrive in N. Y. daily.
38—New York has 29,500 manufacturing plants, employing 560,000 workers.
39—New York's manufactured product (1930) totaled in excess of $6,000,000,000.
40—New York produces 60% of all the clothing manufactured in the U. S.
51—New York furnishes 75% of all the furs sold in the U. S.
42—Over 75,000,000 books are printed in New York yearly.
43—New York has over 3,000 printing plants, employing 57,000 actual printers.
44—80% of the magazines having national circulation, are published in N. Y.
45—New York prints over 5,000,000 copies of daily newspapers every week-day.
46—65% of the advertising of the U. S. is done in New York.
47—New York supports 121,727 *retail* dealers—121,727 places to "spend money!"
48—There are over 8,000 licensed "push cart peddlers" in New York.
49—The retail business in New York is estimated at over $3,000,000,000 annually.
50—New York's hotels have a combined total of over 130,000 guest rooms.
51—Estimated hotel receipts of New York hotels—close to $1,000,000 daily.

Continued on next page

(Continued from page 11)

52—New York consumed in 1930, 220,000 car loads of fresh fruits and vegetables, 10,432 car loads of butter, 148,315 car loads of milk, and uses daily 7,000,000 eggs. Other foods in proportion.

53—It requires 1,000,000,000 gallons of water daily to keep New York "wet."

54—New York mails 70,000,000 letters every 24 hours.

55—New York has 2,925,648 telephones—almost 3,000,000!

56—New York has over 12,000,000 telephone calls daily. Company owns 13,821,739 miles of wiring, and has assets of $816,490,000. See page 194.

57—Close to 10,000,000 fares are collected daily by New York's surface, elevated, subway and bus traffic lines.

58—3,358,701,237 "nickels" were spent for car fare in New York in 1930—over $167,000,000 —nearly half a million dollars daily.

59—New York spends in excess of half a million a day for taxi fares.

60—An average of 568,420 *commutors* pay daily railroad fare to New York.

61—It is estimated that over 300,000 strangers are in New York constantly.

62—Holland Tunnel tolls range from 50 cents to $2.00. An average traffic of 1,000,000 cars per *month* are now patronizing this tube under the Hudson. See page 197.

63—New York has a motor registration of nearly 800,000—value estimated at over $500,000,000.

64—Over 35,000 men are employed as chauffers in New York.

65—New York supports 11,000 attorneys, 12,000 physicians and surgeons, 4,000 clergy, 8,000 artists, sculptors and painters, 16,000 musicians, 6,000 authors and writers, nearly 11,000 actors, 12,500 trained nurses, 87,000 stenographers, 163,000 waiters and servants. 236,000 clerk, etc.

66—150,000 alien immigrants arrive in New York annually—a very considerable percentage of whom remain in the city.

67—New York has over 2,000,000 Hebrews, 430,000 Italians, 225,000 Germans, 385,000 Slavic and Lettic, 350,000 English, Irish and Scotch, etc.

68—New York has the largest negro section in the world—253,000 in Harlem alone!

69—Births in New York have averaged about 50,000 a year over deaths the past two or three years.

70—New York had 29,723 fires in 1930. Loss $16,994,030.

71—New York is the largest insurance center in christendom. Insurance carried by New York, fire and life companies, totals up in the *billions*.

72—It is estimated that over 3,000,000,000 electric light globes are in use in New York.

73—The elevators of New York are capable of transporting 10,000 people 75,000 miles daily!

74—There are close to 350,000 dogs in New York—230,000 being licensed.

75—Over 17,000 married couples in New York have "pet dogs" in place of children.

76—New York has a valuable tract of land devoted to a "dog cemetery."

77—There are *yet* 22,740 horses in New York.

78—New York supports 30 different museums—several of which are the largest and most complete in the entire world.

79—New York supports 252 "legitimate" theatres, 22 ("million dollar") moving picture palaces, 669 movie houses, and numerous concert halls and other places of amusement.

80—New York's amusement institutions seat over 1,000,000.

81—New York spends more than $11,000,000 weekly on amusements.

82—New York has 137 hospitals, including three of the largest in the universe.

83—New York has 122 homes and asylums for unfortunates.

84—New York has 1,584 churches, valued at $251,000,000 and 3,000,000 members.

85—New York has nearly 1,000 clubs, a number of which own their own club homes, some of them costing up in the millions.

86—New York prints 43 daily newspapers, and close to 600 weekly or monthly periodicals.

87—New York is headquarters of most of the gigantic business corporations of the country. The A. T. T. Co., for instance, have assets of 5,000,000,000.

88—Stocks listed on the New York Stock Exchange represent $65,000,000,000 value.

89—In the vaults of the New York Federal Reserve Bank is stored a considerable percentage of all the gold in the world.

90—One of New York's huge department stores hauled 26,000 passengers an hour in their elevators during a "bargain sale." 223,000 actual sales were made in one day.

91—The "Bush" Terminal in Brooklyn has $50,000,000 invested—35,000 employees in the various buildings. See page 262.

92—The New York Edison Co. have an investment of $900,000,000, and employ nearly 37,000 workers.

93—New York has 578 miles of water front and New Jersey—directly opposite—has 192 miles —770 miles all told.

94—The CHASE NATIONAL BANK is the largest financial institution in the world. The NEW YORK GUARANTY & TRUST and THE NATIONAL CITY BANK rank next.

95—New York's tobacco bill is enormous. It is estimated that since women have learned to smoke, there are 17,000,000 cigarettes consumed daily in the big city.

96—But tobacco is not the only thing New York burns—the inhabitants of the community consume 21,000,000 tons of coal a year.

97—18 New Yorkers pay taxes on INCOMES of from $4,000,000 to $10,000,000.

98—Over 650 New Yorkers pay taxes on *incomes* of $250,000 or more.

99—New York has close to 7,000 millionaires (see page 31).

100—New York is so vast, its wealth so fabulous, its activities so strenuous, that even those born and raised in the city themselves have but little conception of its true magnitude. The above figures and data, however, convey a fair impression of its supremacy—the wonder city that has astounded the world!

NEW YORK IN 1982 A LA BELLAMY
A WORD PICTURE OF NEW YORK FIFTY YEARS HENCE

Along in the eighties, when Edward Bellamy wrote his famous book "Looking Backward," and presented his picture of life fifty years hence, he was considered "crazy" and a dreamer, as he referred to sitting in a room on Sunday morning and distinctly hearing a sermon being preached in a church miles away!

But—, what will happen by 1982!

M. P. C. Co.

In 1982 New York will likely have so expanded that, if the same ratio of growth in population continues for the coming fifty years as has held for the past fifty, its census will show a community of close to 50,000,000; and its boundary limits including a goodly share of Long Island, as well as absorbing White Plains, Yonkers, and other contiguous territory northward. East River will have been filled in, and hundreds of acres of the Hudson River bed reclaimed.

Buildings will possibly be from 200 to 250 stories in height. Triple-deck elevators, vacuum-tube escalators, and other vertical travel will be so improved as to whisk tenants upwards at a speed surpassing all imagination at this time.

Traffic arrangements will no doubt have provided for several tiers of elevated roadways and noiseless railways—built on extended balconies flanking the enormous skyscrapers, or passing directly through them, as shown in picture, so as to keep the streets cleared for "*air-taxi*" ships.

Note Arrow Pointing to the Tower of one of the *low* buildings—only 200 stories high.

The picture shows only the top 100 stories of the 1982 Wall Street District.

It may be a simple matter for one to eat breakfast in New York and attend the Follies Bergere in Paris that evening. Those who for *some* reason still prefer to *sleep* in Chicago, may be included among New York commuters.

New York in 1982 will probably be fed on concentrates—pills at so much per box or bottle. Restaurants, cafes and dining places generally, will probably be passé. Meals will largely consist of various pellets according to the taste and hunger of the masses.

The same principle of concentrates applying to foods, meats, etc. will likely be applied to alcoholic concoctions; pellets or pills furnishing "buns" and doing away with cumbersome bottles.

In 1982 ladies will likely have discarded skirts altogether—wearing something on the order of the present day bathing suit.

Marriage will undoubtedly still be an institution but provisions for incompatibility and restoration of liberty to henpecked husbands will be incorporated in the ceremony.

Politics in 1982 will probably be idealistic as by 1940 some young high school genius, (who generally knows more than anybody else) will have discovered a serum which perpetuates life and the country will be saved because Will Rogers will be among us. This dope will also have prolonged our beloved Calvin Coolidge, so that the Republican party will always have an ace up the sleeve.

Business depressions, Wall Street crashes, Communistic upheavals and other disturbances will be a thing of the past by 1982, as with the tens of thousands of brilliant young college graduates with which our Universities are blessing us, there will be no problem of either a financial, social or other nature, that this esteemed young gentry will not have solved.

So cheer up everybody, and try and peg along as best you can until about 1940, when that serum thing is perfected. From then on even Ghandi and his goat should be satisfied with life, as probably by 1982 transportation lines will operate hourly air ships between New York and Heaven itself.

BANKING, MANUFACTURING and GENERAL BUSINESS IN NEW YORK

The greatest and wealtiest banking institutions in the world are located in New York.

The Bank of New York and Trust Co. is the oldest bank in America.

The Chase National is the wealthiest bank in America.

In resources, the twelve largest banks in New York are as follows:

	Resources	Chairman
Chase National Bank	$2,697,328,855	Albert H. Wiggin
Guaranty Trust Co.	2,022,425,111	Charles H. Sabin
National City Bank	1,944,244,523	Charles E. Mitchell
Irving Trust Co.	881,366,821	Lewis E. Pierson
Bankers' Trust Co.	848,967,289	Seward Prosser
Central Hanover Bank & Trust Co.	835,128,026	William Woodward
First National Bank	564,428,180	George F. Baker
Bank of Manhattan	552,085,686	Stephen Baker
Bank of America National Ass'n	487,402,426	A. H. Giannini
Chemical Bank & Trust Co.	478,635,357	John W. Platten
New York Trust Co.	416,241,223	Mortimer N. Buckner
Chatham Phenix National Bank & Trust Co.	344,172,204	Louis G. Kaufman

New York banks not only have connections with practically every city, town and hamlet in America, but with every important city or town on the globe.

New York banks are largely responsible for the distinction our country holds as the richest country on the map.

It was American dollars that won the world war.

It is American dollars that is saving Europe from bankruptcy.

The buildings housing New York banks are more magnificent than palaces pictured in stories of the Arabian Nights. Six New York banks (Irving Trust, Bankers Trust, Bank of Manhattan Trust, Equitable Trust, Chase National and City Bank Farmers Trust) occupy buildings assessed at over $96,000,000—and all six within three square blocks!

In close proximity to these towering palaces are the $8,800,000 National City Bank, the $7,500,000 Bank of America, the $16,000,000 Continental Bank, the $7,000,000 Morgan Bank, the $7,400,000 Bank of New York and Trust Co., and other regal buildings housing other powerful banking institutions.

New York banks transact business in millions daily.

New York banks carry deposits approximating $12,000,000,000.

New York's yearly clearings have reached the astounding total of $477,242,282,-000 (1929)!

In the $14,500,000 granite citadel of the United States Federal Reserve Bank are stored $1,007,123,000 in bullion—not to mention other millions in securities.

New York supports 29,500 manufacturing establishments. The manufactured products of New York's factories in a single year have totaled the immense sum of $6,000,000,000; over 560,000 workers employed, and $1,134,000,000 paid out in wages.

New York manufactures 60 per cent. of all the women's clothing worn in the United States. 75 per cent. of the fur trade of the country is done in New York. Nearly 70 per cent. of the 110,000,000 books printed in the United States are turned out by New York publishers. Men's clothing, boots and shoes, hats, neckwear and practically every item known to wearing apparel is manufactured in New York in enormous totals, besides the thousands of items in almost every other field.

Department stores, shops, and retail establishments of all kinds, do an annual business in New York approximating $5,500,000,000.

Even during the business depression of 1930-31, there were comparatively few failures among New York banks, manufacturers and business concerns generally. New York's enormous population, its unmatchable wealth, and its great national and international commerce always insure "business"—no matter how hard the times or how "depressed" the conditions 7,000,000 persons have to eat, have to wear clothes, have to pay rent (or taxes) and *will* be entertained. If the average expenditure were but $5 per capita per day, the huge sum of $35,000,000 would be in constant circulation!

Yes, *business in New York is always possible*. And *good business* for those who cater to the wants and necessities of 7,000,000 people.

CHAMBER of COMMERCE
OF THE STATE OF NEW YORK
65 Liberty St.   N. W. Cor. Nassau St.

THE PRIDE OF THE CITY

The first and oldest institution of its kind in all the world.

Organized April 5th, 1768.

Building of handsomely carved marble. The interior is beautiful—the Grand Hall as sumptuous as any palace in Europe.

Cost over $1,500,000 without the land.

The New York Chamber of Commerce is the foremost commercial body in America with a limit of 2,000 members comprising New York's most prominent and influential citizens.

Nearly every great New Yorker back to the days of John Cruger and Hugh Wallace have been members of this great organization—many of whose pictures appear on pages 118 and 119 of this book.

THIS CHAMBER HAS BEEN FUNCTIONING FOR OVER 163 YEARS!

The organization was founded for the promotion and encouragement of commerce, the support of industry, and the adjustment of disputes relative to trade and navigation, as well as the procuring of such laws and regulations as might be helpful to business in general.

The work of the Chamber is carried on largely by Committees formed of business men whose vocations especially qualify them for securing effective results. The great strides New York has made in almost every phase of its astounding progress is largely due to the unselfish devotion of members of the Chamber. They have been instrumental in making huge gains for the city by their tireless efforts—such as the launching of the great New York Subway System, the building of New York's world-famed Water System, etc. Harmonious settlement of many serious arbitration cases, and the delightful relationships enjoyed by New York with various Foreign Business Organizations, are among the Chamber's great achievements.

It is a positive distinction to belong to New York's Chamber of Commerce. The membership is limited to 2000 as above stated, and there is always a full waiting list.

Ever since the Chamber was organized, the names of New York's respected and outstanding citizens have graced its roster. Note the names of a few of its past Presidents and Vice Presidents:

John D. Rockefeller	J. Pierpont Morgan
James J. Hill	Andrew Carnegie
William H. Webb	Irving T. Bush
Alexander E. Orr	Morris K. Jessup
Seth Low	Jacob H. Schiff
John Sloan	Alfred E. Marling

Pirie MacDonald

Blank & Stoller, Inc.

THE TWO MEN WHO ARE SO ABLY GUIDING THE CHAMBER'S DESTINIES AT THE PRESENT TIME

Herewith note pictures of Mr. J. BARSTOW SMULL the present President, and Mr. CHARLES T. GWYNNE the Executive Vice President, who have been doing a great work in the Chamber the past year. Notwithstanding the business depression that has been world wide, these two dynamic workers have not only upheld the great traditions of this august body, but have had the foresight and aggressiveness to make one of the best showings in the many years of the Chamber's activities.

Mr. J. BARSTOW SMULL

Mr. CHAS. T. GWYNNE

NEW YORK'S WATER SYSTEM

Not one in ten thousand of those residing in New York, has any conception of the magnitude of *New York's* water system or of the enormous quantity of water consumed—(nearly one billion gallons daily). Nor do they appreciate the tremendous problem constantly confronting the City Fathers to keep the ever growing metropolis supplied with pure water.

Concrete work on Kensico Dam during construction.

New York's water system is not only the largest and most extensive in the world, but the most *costly*.

The Croton and Catskill systems are the principal sources from which the city gets its supply. Tremendous reservoirs such as the Ashokan, the Carmel, the Muscot, and the Croton basins alone have a capacity of over 90,000,000,000 gallons. The total available storage of all reservoirs provides for over 130,000,000,000 gallons.

Over 24,000 acres (37 square miles) represent the area of these reservoirs exclusive of the enormous acreage constituting their water sheds.

At Storm King Mountain, the Hudson River is crossed by a tunnel bored through solid granite at a depth of over 1,000 feet below sea level. At Ashokan and also at Kensico reservoirs, gigantic aerators have been built containing thousands of nozzles through which the water is sprayed in the air, thus admitting oxygen at the same time it removes undesirable gases and other matter which might cause tastes or odors. Within the giant aqueducts down stream, chlorine is introduced for the destruction of germ life, so that the water is thoroughly sterilized before reaching the distribution pipes. No city in all christendom has purer or better water than Father Knickerbocker furnishes New Yorkers.

The cost of the Catskill system alone totaled over $187,000,000. An additional $42,000,000 was appropriated in 1928 for improving and safeguarding the present Catskill supply. And bear in mind the Catskill system provides only something over half of New York's water needs. Over $500,000,000 is invested in New York's water wagon!

Entrance to one of the huge tunnels from 200 to 1,214 feet underground.

The huge tunnel through which water is brought to New York varies from four to five and a half feet in diameter and is from 200 to 750 feet below the surface of the streets, thus avoiding interferences with big building operations, subways and sewers, etc. The total length of the delivery system in the city is over 55 miles!

A new tunnel is in course of construction—extending from Hill View reservoir through the Bronx, the estimated cost of which is over $42,000,000.

Showing the completed Kensico Dam after an expenditure of tens of millions.

The city sells over $25,000,000 worth of water yearly, so, if New York ever stops growing faster than the building of new reservoirs, the city has a chance some day of "breaking even." In the meantime the Water Commission is kept busy trying to keep pace with the ever increasing demand. In April 1931 there was a serious shortage, but May rains replenished the big "tanks." The shortage emphasized the necessity of "preparedness"!

New York's water system is one of its most amazing wonders.

NEW YORK'S SUBWAYS

AND TRANSIT SYSTEM

For nearly quarter of a century, discussion, investigation, and negotiation ensued before New York's subways became a reality.

To New York's famous Chamber of Commerce, largely belongs the credit for whipping into shape the solution which gave to the city its first subway—work on which was formally begun March 24, 1900, and the opening of which to the public occurred October 27, 1904.

Mr. Alexander E. Orr (President of the Chamber from 1894 to 1899) and Mr. Abram S. Hewitt were two outstanding factors in this great achievement— involving millions of outlay and an engineering undertaking considered little short of miraculous.

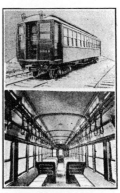

Thirty-five years ago, New York was growing so rapidly something drastic had to be done to cope with the transportation problem. Transit facilities were so inadequate that subways offered the only remedy. The cost and risks involved, however, were so tremendous and other considerations so weighty, it required both wisdom and foresight to perfect sound and practical plans which provided for financing, construction, and engineering the gigantic enterprise. But Mr. Orr, Mr. Hewitt and their fellow members of the Chamber unraveled the tangles, and the world-famous New York Subway System was launched. New York's subway system is now recognized as one of the greatest achievements of the present age with its subterranean

Showing a subway car, also interior of car.

tunnels bored for miles through solid rock—winding its underground course directly beneath the enormous tonnage of towering skyscrapers, amid the network of water and gas mains, electric wire conduits, sewers, etc., which underlie the streets.

This first subway extended from City Hall to 59th Street and Broadway—extensions being added later. Wm. Barclay Parsons was the engineer, John B. McDonald the contractor, and the operating company "The Rapid Transit Subway Co.," of which August Belmont was President.

Today the investment in New York subways already completed and planned totals the staggering sum of nearly $1,000,000,000.

On January 1, 1931, New York had 650 miles of subway tracks in operation, 80 additional miles in construction, and plans accepted which total *close to* 1000 *miles!*

In addition to its subways, New York has 1114 miles of *surface* lines, close to 650 miles of *elevated* railway tracks and a large number of *motor bus* lines networking the entire community.

And yet, with all this seemingly adequate transportation, congestion is becoming

more and more acute every year, demanding constantly increasing facilities for travel. In 1930, 3,358,701,237 fares were paid for "five cent" transportation. New York is the only large city in the country which still enjoys a "nickel" carfare.

New York spends nearly half a million dollars *daily* for taxicabs! Transportation continues as one of the principal problems of this wonder city!

Showing two, three and four track tunnels.

TRAFFIC CONDITIONS in New York

By Phillip D. Hoyt

1st Deputy Police Commissioner of New York.

Every year, *congestion* is becoming a more and more serious problem in "THE WONDER CITY." New York has 5,043 miles of streets. From every block of this enormoue mileage traffic leads to Broadway and the streets contiguous to Broadway comprising the great financial and business sections of Manhattan. The day time population of the city is largely concentrated between the Battery and Columbus Circle.

The actual *resident* population of New York City is only around 6,000,000, but it is estimated that this number is increased by *close to* 2,000,000 additional persons whose homes are in the suburban districts—who come to the city daily for business, education or recreation. Traffic regulation is therefore a task demanding the most detailed study, careful planning and skillful direction.

Many factors contribute to the complexity of the problem of moving traffic smoothly and safely. The millions of people; the great automobile registration; the physical barriers which divide and surround the city; the concentration of population and activity in various districts; the extreme height of buildin, with their thousands of tenants; and the over-demand upon street facilities, are among them. Although there are only between 700,000 to 750,000 actual automobile registrations, the number of cars and trucks rolling into New York from nearby districts and from practically every state in the country, bring the total up to over a million! Three times the total registration of motor vehicles in New York in 1912 cross Queensboro Bridge every twenty-four hours!

Courtesy City Administration.

The concentration of traffic in the financial and business sections of Manhattan is intensified by the staggering height of new skyscrapers constantly being erected. Ten buildings alone in the Grand Central zone have a population of tenants and visitors of *over one hundred thousand daily.*

The street facilities of New York were for the most part laid out before the advent of the automobile. Changes in the physical structure of a number of these streets have been made in the way of widening some of them, etc., but the expense has been prodigious and the only way that this program could be continued would be by introducing engineering projects requiring the acquisition of valuable property and the expenditure of huge sums for construction work. Note picture above of the new Elevated Express Highway (starting on West Street at Canal Street)—which is to extend north all the way to 72nd Street. The city voted $4,500,000 for initial work for this huge undertaking which should be a big help towards alleviating future traffic conditions. This highway has already been completed to almost 23rd Street and when finished will permit of close to 10,000 cars an hour traveling at a 35-mile speed. There are two thirty-foot roadways (one north bound and one south bound) and the structure varies from 70 to 80 feet wide. When completed, it will be 21,800 feet long, approximately four miles. If the increase of motor traffic continues at the pace it has been growing the past few years, in 1950 New York will likely have to build these elevated highways in leading lanes of travel throughout the city.

A group of engineering experts and those conversant with traffic needs are more or less constantly devoting their energies to figuring out ways and means for solving the ever increasing traffic demands. New York will cope with the situation as it has always done with every other civic problem.

MUNICIPAL GOVERNMENT IN NEW YORK

By MARTIN GREEN
Nationally known writer and authority on New York

NEW YORK'S CITY HALL
See page 81

One, out of every eleven inhabitants of the United States, lives in the metropolitan district of New York, which takes in an area twice as large as the State of Rhode Island. Included in the metropolitan district is the city of Newark, Jersey City and other populous communities, all so closely linked with the metropolis proper as to be classified by the United States Census Bureau as essentially part of it.

The suburban population of the metropolitan district is about half that of what is recognized as New York, and about half of this suburban population commutes to New York and their families and trade people largely depend upon New York for a livelihood.

New York is second only to the Federal government in the matter of receipts and expenditures, as well as the number of employees engaged in the municipal machinery which operates the city. It takes in, and distributes more money than any state in the union, in fact more than that of many groups of states, and more than many nations throughout the world.

The credit of New York is the highest of any municipality in the world. The city borrows vast amounts at interest as low as that paid by the Federal government. Its tangible resources insure this stability of credit for years to come—no matter what may happen to the rest of the country or the rest of the world.

Despite the growth elsewhere of the automobile, rubber and associated industries, New York remains the premier manufacturing city of the union.

The State of New York pays 25% of the vast amount of Federal income taxes and the City of New York pays between 75% and 80% of this huge sum—close to 20% of the entire revenue of the nation from income tax sources. New York pays in taxes 70% of the expenses of the State government and much more than that percentage of the State income tax.

The existing form of New York City government dates back to January 1, 1898, when as the result of a referendum, following the adoption by the Legislature of a Charter, the City of Greater New York was assembled. Prior to that time the present city was made up of New York City,—which embraced Manhattan Island and what is now Bronx County, the City of Brooklyn, and a scattered group of towns in Queens County and Richmond County (Staten Island).

Under the new dispensation Greater New York was divided into five boroughs—Manhattan, Brooklyn, Bronx, Queens and Richmond. Each of these boroughs included a county with the exception of the Bronx, which did not achieve county independence until 15 years later.

NEW YORK'S MUNICIPAL BUILDING
See page 81

(Continued on next page)

19

(Continued from page 19)

The budget of the city in 1900, which then had approximately one-third of its present population, was $90,778,000. The budget for 1931 was close to $670,000,000. The population in three decades tripled while the expense of government increased nearly eight fold.

The heaviest single item of expenditure in New York City budget is for education. This amounts to about $140,000,000 annually. There are 1,250,000 children in New York's day and evening schools.

In addition, there are 42 high schools. The College of the City of New York (supported by the municipality) is one of the largest in the country, ranking up toward Columbia University, which cares for more students the year round than any other American institute for advanced learning.

About 40 per cent. of the money paid out by the City of New York annually is for the protection of life, property and health. The Police Department requires about $62,500,000, with the demand constantly growing; the Department of Sanitation spends about $40,000,000; the Department of Health & Hospitals about $26,000,000; and the Fire Department some $40,000,000.

There are 20,000 men in the Police Department alone. The Fire Department musters nearly 8,000. The Department of Education gives employment to nearly 45,000—men and women. These three classifications account for more than one-half the total number of city employees on the regular pay roll lists, amounting to 136,000.

The Police Department is the most up to date in the country. The training for policemen takes up a term of three months and only the best physical types are accepted. The entire emergency reserve force of the Police Department can be concentrated at any point in the five boroughs in thirty minutes.

Despite widespread reports of graft in the Police Department, the morale and morality of the force is as high as that of any large city in the world. In 1930 and 1931 about 40 policemen were involved in scandals in connection with the enforcement or non-enforcement of the laws against vice, and yet on October 6, 1931, the United Press ditpatch reported that an inspector and 26 officers of the police force of London had been dismissed for grafting.

New York is the greatest hospital center in the world with two medical centers, which are acknowledged to be the finest in the country. In the city there are five Class A medical schools, 82 general hospitals, 57 special hospitals and 120 asylums and homes, in addition to numerous private proprietary hospitals.

The hospitals of New York have a daily capacity for 36,000 patients and treat on an average of 1,250,000 dispensary patients a year.

The health rate of New York ranks far above the average of American cities. The infant mortality rate is very low due to the careful inspection of milk and food. Opportunities for summer seashore and mountain recreation within easy reach by cheap transportation are not exceeded anywhere. Coney Island, America's greatest playground and bathing beach, is only 45 minutes from the heart of Manhattan and the fare only five cents.

At the close of 1931, there were 650 miles of subway in operation, 80 miles additional under construction and plans have been made which will extend the system to 1,000 miles. A five cent fare holds on all transport lines in New York, with the exception of one omnibus route, on which the fare is ten cents.

The harbor of New York, with nearly 600 miles of water front, is the most spacious and accessible in the world. In may lack the scenery of Naples in Italy, Rio de Janeiro in Brazil, and San Francisco on the west coast, but what it lacks in natural scenic investiture it more than makes up with the vista of skyscrapers which is the wonder of all time.

The fall of 1931 witnessed the opening of the George Washington Memorial Bridge over the Hudson between New York City and the New Jersey Palisades. A picture of this wonderful bridge and the four enormous bridges over the East River will be found on page 45.

In addition to the Holland Tube under the North River, there is to be another vehicular tunnel under the Hudson.

A detailed description of the government of the City of New York and its numerous ramifications would require pages of this size but it is safe to say that the people of the United States are almost as familiar with what is going on in New York in its government, as well as in its developments of its many sided feverish activities, because almost everything that happens in New York becomes front page news in the average paper printed throughout America.

This is one of eight most interesting articles concerning New York or New York's activities written by men who are authorities on their subjects, and the publishers of this volume wish to take advantage of this space to thank them, both for ourselves and the hundreds of thousands of readers who will be profited by such authentic information. We refer to Messrs. Martin Green, Philip D. Hoyt, Harold Keller, Robert G. Morris, Charles Frederick Stevens, Jack Alicoate, Howard Shiebler and Ray B. Bolton.

MUNICIPAL CORRUPTION, RACKETEERING, AND GANGSTER ACTIVITY GROSSLY EXAGGERATED

It is a deplorable fact that municipal corruption, graft, and crime are more or less prevalent in every part of our country. It is therefore only natural that New York should come in for its share.

Due to New York's enormous population and its vast area, it is only in keeping with the law of ratios that the big city should have more frequent occurrences of this unfortunate phase of civic life than other communities smaller in size. And yet corruption, racketeering and gangster activity in New York is very much exaggerated. Sensational newspapers make a specialty of glaring head lines on the front page, in featuring scandal, betrayal of trusts, or crime, in order to increase sales. Not only New York papers, but all over the country the public interest in New York is such that local sheets exploit even the *details*.

In a city of 7,000,000, and in this age of loose morals, plus the growing tendency to want to "get rich quick," it might be *expected* that here and there would develop a dishonest official, a greedy racketeer, and an unprincipled criminal. But why should the entire 131,000 employees of the city government be condemned because a *few* betray trust! Why should the city be called *racket-ridden* because a group of grafters take advantage of the spineless and force tribute. And why should New York be considered unsafe because an occasional feud between the denizens of the underworld, once every so often, terrorize a neighborhood by gun play.

Were it not for the sensational way in which papers over the country devote columns to details and pictorial accounts of these happenings there would be little more attention paid to these unfortunate occurrences than to similar misdeeds in Oshkosh, Kanakee, or Boise City.

There is no denying the fact that there *is* more corruption in New York, more racketeering in New York and more crime committed in New York just as it is true that there is more philanthropy in New York, more churches in New York, and *more of every thing else* in New York than in any other civic center in our nation.

The police have orders to "SHOOT TO KILL."

Taken all in all, New York is one of the very best governed cities in all the world. It is the most prosperous, and there is no city on the map in which it is *safer to live*, or in which citizens have *better protection*.

No where is there a more efficient police department, a better drilled fire department, more thorough provisions for the health and comfort of its residents, or a more all round consideration given by the City Fathers for the general welfare of its citizens and guests.

Mayor Walker has been criticised, condemned, and thoroughly maligned. Many of the city officials have been charged with gross misdeeds. Tammany Hall has been censured and damned for its political power, and yet during the past half dozen years there was never so much done in the way of tremendous achievement, such as miles of new subways and transportation facilities costing over $400,000,000; the erection of new schools and magnificent new college buildings,—being part of over $600,-000,000 spent on education; the building of the elevated express highway from Canal to 72nd Street already completed as far as 14th Street; and the hundred other expenditures of almost every phase for civic betterment.

There are countless reasons why living in New York is desirable. A careful perusal of this book is corroborative evidence of this fact.

Lower picture shows motor squad with both rifles and machine guns. Gansters do not fare well in New York, notwithstanding sensational newspaper reports over the country concerning their activities.

FEDERAL GOVERNMENT ACTIVITIES IN NEW YORK

By HAROLD KELLER . . . . Newspaper and Magazine Writer

With one-fifth of the nation's wealth concentrated in New York City, it is only natural that relatives should come flocking into Gotham-town to partake of its hospitality. Uncle Sam is the most prominent of these relatives. He is, in fact, perfectly at home in New York. He has brought along a good part of his possessions and evidently intends to stay around a long time.

Industrially, commercially and financially, New York is the capitol of the country. It might have been made the centre of governmental administration as well. Lacking only the social and historical significance of Washington in matters of state, it is largely the hub of the nation's public business.

Practically every department in Washington has its counterpart in New York. A considerable percentage of the Federal Government's 625,000 civil service employees work in New York. The wide range of their activities is amazing. While Uncle Sam reaches out one hand to collect our taxes, his other hand holds out to us the multifarious fruits of democracy—paternalistic benefits with which few ever come in direct contact and yet which play an important role in the daily lives of every one of us. These extend from the forecast of the weather to the inspection of the food we eat. In between is an assortment of activities—some technical, some dreary, some dramatic and spectacular—that throws an ironic light on that portion of the United States Constitution which reserves to the States all powers not expressly delegated to Congress.

These governmental functions are housed in various buildings. But the abandon with which the Japanese Beetle Quarantine Office and that of the Prohibition Administration are thrown under one roof, is suggestive of the need for Uncle Sam to continue erecting new structures in the big city. Many of the present ones are worse than obsolete.

However, Uncle Sam has a $10,000,000 Post Office Building on Eighth Avenue (see page 82) that compensates somewhat for the old out-of-date Federal Building at City Hall Park and other old landmarks he occupies.

There are 150 branch post offices throughout the city. In point of direct service to the public, Uncle Sam's postal activities are of chief importance. More than 30,000 persons are employed to handle the mail in New York. Nearly 30 miles of pneumatic tubes buried under the ground, rush more than 5,000,000 letters daily between the 25 chief stations. One of these subway carriers runs under the East River, connecting the main Brooklyn station with that of Manhattan. Others extend as far north as 125th Street, thus eliminating the delay that goes with truck transfer. New York's postal receipts in 1930 were $90,000,000, or one-eighth of the national total.

The famous Customs House at the foot of Broadway contains the offices of the Collector of Internal Revenue which handled nearly one-fifth of the nation's $2,410,-000,000 income taxes in 1929; the Collector of the Port of New York, the greatest customs collecting agency in the world; the Civil Service; the Secret Service of the Treasury Department; the Steamboat Inspection Service; the Public Health Service and the Tariff Commission.

The Barge Office at the Battery harbors the offices for various waterways departments; the meat inspection office of the Agriculture Department, responsible for the 2,000 tons of meat received daily for consumption in New York City, and the Coast Guard recruiting station. It also serves as a ferry slip for boats to Ellis Island, the Statue of Liberty and Governors Island.

The Shipping Board Building, 45 Broadway, houses the crew of public servants who perform their functions here. Besides the offices of the Shipping Board and the United States Lines, there are the narcotics agents, the Federal Trade Commission, the Veterans Bureau, the Federal Horticultural Board, the Grain Supervisor and the Plant Quarantine.

The Sub-Treasury Building, Broad and Wall Streets, is one of New York's great historic structures, where Washington took his oath of office as President, and is now less and less identified with fiscal matters. A band of special prohibition agents, the radio service, the State Department and the Passport Bureau have crowded their way in also.

The Federal Building, (referred to above) houses the City Hall (see page 42).

(Continued on page 42)

22

TAMMANY HALL

AND

POLITICS IN NEW YORK

TAMMANY HALL!!—revered by its constituents; feared by neutrals; hated by its opponents!

The New York Tammany Society was founded about 1786, and organized under a constitution in 1789 as a charitable and patriotic order. It has gradually developed into one of the most powerful political influences in the history of our nation.

Deriving its name from a sachem of the Delaware Indians (Tammany—one of the chiefs of the Algonquins, living on the banks of the Delaware River, who for years held undisputed sway over Eastern America) this great society, from its very organization became a dominating factor in the councils of the Democratic Party and has commanded such a power in local, state, and even national politics, that the name "Tammany" has become known world over.

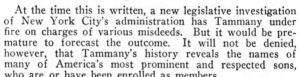

Tammany Hall is the shrine at which hundreds of thousands of loyal democrats worship, and point with pride to its achievements. On the other hand, its opponents damn Tammany Hall as the hellish headquarters for graft, corruption, and misused power!

Has any institution ever organized outside of fanatical religious circles, been so beloved or so hated; so lauded or so execrated; so eulogized or so condemned!

JOHN R. VOORHIS
102 Years of Age,
Born in July, 1829.
Elected Grand Sachem
of Tammany for 20th
term on May, 1931.

At the time this is written, a new legislative investigation of New York City's administration has Tammany under fire on charges of various misdeeds. But it would be premature to forecast the outcome. It will not be denied, however, that Tammany's history reveals the names of many of America's most prominent and respected sons, who are or have been enrolled as members.

Records also show that vast sums have been donated to charity or expended in relieving distress—not only in New York and America, but all over the world, such as generous contributions to Japan's earthquake sufferers, the Cuban Freedom Fund, the Irish Bond Issue, the Messina earthquake disaster, etc. Those who can see no good in Tammany insist that Tammany is an agency of Satan and that policy prompts these benefactions. They claim that all this is merely a part for a price paid for votes and popularity.

Therefore, any estimate of Tammany to be formed by a stranger, must be based largely on whether information or data concerning the institution is furnished by a Tammany supporter, or a Tammany opponent.

New York politics are so intimately identified with Tammany Hall it is said that the Democratic Party in New York City is so completely controlled by this powerful organization that no nominee has even a fighting chance for victory unless endorsed by Tammany.

In State politics, also, Tammany commands an influence which is widespread and generally conceded to be a power that must be thoroughly recognized.

The new Tammany Hall, facing Union Square at 17th Street and 4th Avenue. Built in 1929.

PROHIBITION IN NEW YORK

A discussion of the subject of "Prohibition in New York" brings to mind the reply of a recent American visitor from England, who when asked as he was departing for his native shore what he thought of prohibition in the United States, answered: "Show me where it is, and I'll tell you what I think about it."

New York has always very definitely been a "wet" city. Just as Boston, Philadelphia, Chicago, or any other large city with many industrial workers and large floating and foreign populations are "wet" cities.

If local option prevailed instead of national prohibition—or what is popularly referred to as prohibition—there is no doubt that New York City would still be wet, and "The Wonder City" would not be isolated in its self-proclaimed moistness, for many other cities and states in widely scattered sections of the country would be found in the wet column. By the same token, other cities and states, in keeping with the dictates of their citizenry, would be dry.

In as much as the publishers of this book are attempting to cover practically every phase of New York life and New York activity, not to mention prohibition would be a glaring omission, as New York's wetness has been noised abroad for many years. Therefore we feel that we are neither damning nor dimming the city's fair name by admitting what the world already knows and has known for a long time . . . that New York is a very wet city.

This, however, is not to be wondered at. In the first place it is the largest city in the world, and hundreds of thousands of visitors from all parts of America and all corners of the globe enter its gates every day. It is a known fact that a very considerable quantity of alcoholic beverages consumed daily and nightly in New York City goes down the throats of visitors from other sections of the country.

More than half of New York's great population are foreign born or of foreign descent. In addition, a large portion of the population are engaged in industrial employment. The foreign born citizen, or the Americanized foreigner, demand wine or beer as their right. If they cannot obtain it legally, they will obtain it *illegally*. The industrial laborer, likewise, considers a law that prohibits him from enjoying his wine and beer at home after a hard day's work, as an unwonted interference and an encroachment upon his personal liberty. Since these elements make up the greater portion of New York's voters, it is plain that this City is likely to always be in the wet column.

However, because New York is New York—the world's largest city, anything that happens here is heralded with emphasis in the newspapers of the nation. An event occurring in a mid-Western or Southern city seldom ever receives the same attention from newspaper editors as is accorded events transpiring in New York. Why? Because it *is* New York, and the entire nation is *interested* in New York. Of course, New York has its speakeasies, plenty of them, perhaps more than any other city in the country with perhaps one or two exceptions. But *proportionately speaking*, there are no more speakeasies in New York than any other city in the country having a population upwards of 50,000. Except in dives and lower type speakeasies, beer is 25 cents a glass, and high-balls, cocktails and other decoctions range in price from 50 cents to $1.50,—proprietor charging what he finds the traffic will bear.

And this is practically the standard price charged in dozens of cities all over the country for the same assortment of drinks.

Prohibition officials, and the police department, have endeavored with but scant success to enforce the Prohibition Law. The Federal Government maintains a veritable handful of enforcement agents in New York, which is comparable to hunting wild animals with an air-rifle. The police are too busily engaged in maintaining law and order and protecting the lives and property of more than 8,000,000 people to undertake the enforcement of a Federal law in serious fashion. Many places are padlocked, but the padlock is soon removed, or the proprietor begins business the next day at a new location. So New York, (not as wet as it is painted but still quite wet nevertheless), will probably continue to be wet, in company with other cities and municipalities in the West, the East, the North and the South.

24

LABOR UNIONS IN NEW YORK

By **ROBERT G. MORRIS,** Labor Editor of the New York Evening Journal

Organized labor, taken as a whole, is more firmly entrenched in New York City than in any other city of the country. True, New York has been the scene of many a hard fought struggle between employer and laborer with resultant rioting causing much damage to property, and, during some strikes, even the loss of life. The details of these strikes cannot be gone into in this limited space. We will attempt however, to outline briefly some of the reasons for organized labor's strength in this city, which has steadily increased during the past twenty years.

Despite the fact that more different forms of industry are centered in New York than in any other equal area in the world, organized labor and industrial leadership have had comparatively few serious clashes during the last quarter of a century. This is due largely to the fact that the leaders of organized labor and the masters of industry have come to a better understanding of each other's rights as well as being affected by public opinion. No strike or lockout has been called in this city during the past decade that has not followed weeks and sometimes months of negotiation between the employers and the unions in an effort to adjust their difficulties.

This attitude, on the part of the leaders of unionism and industry can be better understood when it is realized that *more than* 10 % of New York's more than 7,000,000 population are members of organized labor. Based on the government's estimate of four in a family this means that nearly 50 % of the city's entire population is directly or indirectly affiliated with the trade union movement in this city. Naturally, a strike involving any large portion of a union is serious, not only to the immediate employer but to the community at large; for unlike other sections of the country where there are large group of union members, the workers here are not housed in company owned dwellings nor do they have to go to company owned stores to make their purchases. Therefore a strike in New York City, that is of any duration, is felt by others not directly involved, especially property owners, and pressure is soon brought to bear on those responsible to see that a settlement is arrived at and business resumed while a basis for a new agreement is worked out.

A notable example of this was the action of Governor Franklin D. Roosevelt during the garment workers strike of 1929. The strike had been called, following weeks of fruitless negotiation between the officials of the International Ladies' Garment Workers' Union and the New York Cloak and Suit Council, of which the employers were members. The Governor immediately summoned both sides to Albany and had them agree to the appointment of a commissioner to settle the dispute. By this step a costly strike was averted.

The needle trade is one of the greatest industries in the city doing a business of more than $750,000,000 yearly, which means that 98 % of all the women's garments made in the State are manufactured in this city.

During the same year another disastrous strike was called off when the Building Trades Employers Association agreed with public opinion and rescinded a "lockout order" that had been issued against the Building Trades Council and which would have directly involved more than 100,000 men.

Another outstanding example of the changed attitude is the long reign of peace existing between the steamship companies and the longshoremen's union. For more than a decade new contracts have been arrived at by mutual agreement between parties who in the past fought some of the most bitterly contested labor wars in the country. These strikes often resulted in the city authorities being compelled to step in and see that the necessary foodstuffs and coal were moved, under police escort, to hospitals and other municipal institutions.

The above may give an idea of the strength of organized labor, as well as the changed attitude of the employer. In very isolated cases old methods of "knock down and drag out" may occur in New York, but only by the minor unions. This is due largely to the fact that a newer type of labor leader and business man have taken over the control of union and industry.

An idea of the actual strength of unionism in New York is shown by the fact that in the Central Trades and Labor Council of this city, which represents the American Federation of Labor, there are some 750,000 trade unionists. Then there is the Amalgamated Clothing Workers of America, an independent union with a membership of about 65,000 workers employed in the men's clothing trade. There also are some half dozen other organizations built on trade union lines but not affiliated with the American Federation of Labor, which have a membership totalling another 50,000 or 75,000 workers, all employed in earning their livelihood in the wonder city of the world.

Mr. Robert G. Morris is not only a leading authority on the labor situation in New York, but in the above brief article has presented one of the most comprehensive word pictures on the subject that has ever come to our notice in so few words. Labor unions are strong in New York and Mr. Morris has explained why in a lucid and interesting way—Thank you, Mr. Morris.

THE "REDS" AND BOLSHIVISM IN NEW YORK

If the augmented gatherings of "Reds" at Union Square signify anything, the cause of Bolshivism has been helped very materially during the past two years by the world business depression.

People out of work are more inclined to listen to propaganda than when employed.

But the average American citizen pays little attention to communistic arguments, he is too occupied in his own activities. If he does give them a thought he finds it difficult to understand their reasoning when he pauses to consider the status of their condition in America as compared with what they experienced in the countries from which they came.

Nine out of ten of the communist hoard suffered the extreme of poverty at home. Arriving in the United States with its freedom from every national restraint, and with opportunity at every turn, it would seem that they would be grateful for the change afforded them. But perversely, a number of them attempt the upheaval of our laws, customs, and provisions for industry which have made our nation the greatest on the globe, and undertake to influence all who will listen, to their Bolshivistic fanaticism.

Of every hundred immigrants coming to America however, fully 97% or more *conform* to our methods, learn our language, and busy themselves in trying to better their lot in life. Many thousands of our very best citizenry have developed from these more or less poverty stricken unfortunates who migrated to this country from Russia, Poland, Italy, the Balkans and other foreign parts.

But go down to Union Square on a Saturday afternoon and you will find the soap box orator, the sidewalk specialist, etc., haranguing the crowds who gather there, beligerently condemning capital, and trying to excite opposition to existing laws and conditions.

Bolshivistic Russia and all agencies of communism, anarchism and socialism work overtime in New York.

But an analysis of the communistic element will reveal that the rank and file of their number comprise those who do not *want* to work, who *shirk* responsibility, or are *incapable* of competing with their fellows.

New York, as in every other field of human activity, leads in the number of its communists, anarchists and socialists, and yet the police have adopted methods which prevent any serious demonstrations or attempts at violence.

Communism in New York may be a menace, but the city fathers are taking good care that this "menace" does not become a serious one.

The picture below shows a noon time crowd on the street in one of New York's congested districts. This will give an idea of the masses which assemble in Union Square on "May Day" and at other "Red" demonstrations—the difference being that about every tenth "Red" will be carrying a banner denouncing the wealthy or else waving a red flag.

Courtesy "P. & A. Photo" Inc.   Copyrighted Pacific & Atlantic Photos, Inc.

THE UNDER-WORLD OF NEW YORK

Every big city has its underworld.

In *one* phase of its underworld, New York leads all other cities.

We refer to the 340,000 people engaged in various activities *under the streets* of New York.

Scores of enormous office and business buildings in the big metropolis have from two to even six basement floors under their huge construction. Cafes, tonsorial parlors, arcades and almost every conceivable kind of retail establishments are operated in the sub-floors because of lower rentals, and the hundreds of thousands patronizing the subways with which entrances of many are connected.

In addition to the thousands of *subway attendants* who spend their working day underground, there tens of thousands of *laborers, mechanics, etc.*, working on tunnels and other subterranean activities.

The visitor in New York will be surprised at finding underground passage ways *four* and *even five blocks long* (for pedestrians), which connect the various large office buildings, hotels, etc. with subway stations.

Unfortunately, however, New York has its *other* underworld:—

Some years ago, the district west of 10th Ave. from 34th St. almost up to 51st, was termed "Hell's Kitchen."

There are *extremely* few hold-ups in New York considering its enormous population — T H E STREETS ARE TOO WELL LIGHTED.

In this district lived about as lawless an element as ever operated in the United States. Hold-ups, murders, and gangster misdeeds became so frequent that one's life was not considered safe anywhere in this section after dusk.

But New York has always been able to cope with its problems—Today Hell's Kitchen is just as safe as Park Avenue.

The lower east side, with its poverty, its tremendous foreign element and its isolation from the better influences of more refined neighborhoods, also has had its criminals.

The population of New York is so large, its area so extended and social intercourse so confined to neighborhoods that one can live for years in the big city and seldom meet anyone he knows for days at a time. Therefore, it is very difficult to locate a wrong doer if he wants to hide himself.

Furthermore, the great wealth of New York attracts criminals to its gates, and yet New York's very able police department has kept crime at a minimum in a way that cannot be appreciated until the ratios of population are applied. With its enormous riches and its myriad population it is not to be expected that New York could be entirely free from crime. But there is in reality *less* of it in the big city in proportion to its number of residents *than any other city in the world*. Were it not that sensational newspapers play up crime in the way they do, there would never have to be any necessity to advertise the safety of New York as an ideal place to live.

Tens of thousands spend their time underground working on tunnel construction.

27

THE RADIO IN NEW YORK

By CHARLES FREDERICK STEVENS
Nationally known writer and radio authority

New York is the Radio Capital of the entire world. Practically all of the fine radio programs that are offered in the United States either originate in New York or are relayed to the key stations of the broadcasting chains in Manhattan.

There are two great radio chain systems in the United States:—the Columbia Broadcasting System and the National Broadcasting Company. The headquarters, executive offices, key stations, and main control rooms of both networks are in central Manhattan.

The Columbia Broadcasting System's building is at 485 Madison Avenue. Station WABC, (key station of the System:) W2XE, (the short wave station) and W2XAB, (the chain's television station) are all located here.

The National Broadcasting Company's building is at 711 Fifth Avenue. Here are located Stations WEAF and WJZ,—principal stations of the National's Red and Blue Networks. National also has a Times Square Studio in the Amsterdam Theatre Building from which stars of the theatre world broadcast on occasion.

Within a block or two of both network headquarters the site of the new Radio City may be seen. (See page 24). Here will rise a new broadcasting studio building, theatres, motion picture theatres, etc., under the magic hand of the Rockefeller fortune in collaboration with the broadcasting company—the most ambitious project of modern times.

One of the new buildings in the $250,000,000 Radio City. See page 249.

Welcome is extended to *visitors* by both the National and Columbia—especially those from out of town. Passes are obtainable for a tour through the studios, and even a visit *into a studio while a program is on the air.*

The visitor will doubtless be surprised at the vast extent of the studios, offices, lobbies, control rooms, etc. Both chains occupy many floors in their own sky-scraper buildings. Some of the studios are as large as theatres—two stories or more in height.

Large organizations are busy at each of these chain headquarters. Programs are conceived and executed here for seventeen or more hours every day in the week and relayed to stations in every one of the forty-eight states.

Departments, with a hundred or more employees, are devoted to the writing of continuities, the casting of programs, music arranging, the sending of programs and radio news to newspapers and magazines throughout the world. There are heavily staffed engineering departments—engineers to govern programs from control rooms, construction engineers, line engineers, traffic engineers, main control room engineers (who have the complicated job of keeping the programs flowing to the proper stations all over the country) and other engineering heads.

Hostesses and page boys are busy on each floor. A large staff of clerks in a separate department sort "fan" mail. Radio stars whose names are familiar in almost every home in the land hurry by, giving the last minute look at their scripts.—Morton Downey, Rudy Vallee, Kate Smith, Graham McNamee, Ted Husing, Amos and Andy, Miller and Lyles, Bing Crosby, Russ Columbo, The Street Singer, the Mills Brothers, the Gloom Chasers, etc. The visitor is sure to see some of these stars about, no matter what time of day it may be.

In a great studio, a program such as the "The March of Time" requires as many as a hundred musicians and performers in the studio simultaneously. Visitors on passes may number several hundred more, but most complete silence must prevail. Howard Barlow, his eye on the control room, lowers his baton; the theme song of the period sounds; the announcer speaks; a swift succession of players step to the microphone, then make way for others. The orchestra weaves in the musical themes throughout the program. The "atmosphere" players, sometimes as many as fifty, supply the noises or conversations they have been drilled in. The sounds of airplanes, machine guns, doors shutting, police sirens, or liquids pouring into glasses are supplied at the right moments by young women and men working at a high desk covered with all sorts of devices. Everybody works from scripts, and those scripts represent hours of careful rehearsal—everything times to the second, without exaggeration.

About 19,000 hours of entertainment, instruction and news comes each year from these stations that head the chains. There are probably 15,000,000 radio sets in the United States alone, and it is estimated each set is operated several hours per day.

These sets must be supplied with the best that art and science can devise. New York is indisputably the Radio Capital of the world.

AVIATION IN NEW YORK

Fairchild Aerial Surveys.

ROOSEVELT FIELD, MINEOLA.

Around the world in less than nine days! What would our forefathers have thought if some one had been such a wild dreamer as to have predicted such a thing as even a possibility! And yet, two daring Americans, Wiley Post and Harold Gatty, sponsored by one of Oklahoma's oil kings, performed the seeming miracle— making the circuit in 8 days, 15 hours and 51 minutes (June 23rd to June 30, 1931), actual flying time—4 days and 10 hours.

Colonel Charles A Lindbergh immortalized himself by making the first successful solo-flight across the Atlantic.

In the meantime, hundreds of aviators over the country have been establishing various records and accomplishing remarkable progress in flying—proving beyond all possible doubt that it is now only a question of time until air travel will be as safe and sane as either water or ground transportation.

When the Armstrong "floating islands" have been installed in the Atlantic, ocean flying should be as free from danger or mishap as traveling by steamship. And when experiments with centrifugal principles have been solved, vertical "take-offs" and other aviation problems have been mastered, new inventions and improvements will have brought the airship to the same stage of perfection the automobile has reached today.

New York is leading the procession in fostering, encouraging and exploiting aviation. Nearly every important airship company or organization in the country has its headquarters in New York, or else maintains offices in New York.

New York is the home of Captain Horace B. Wild—one of the pioneer aviators of the world. He holds the distinction of being the first navigator of a dirigible in America. Captain Wild has been interested in air travel for forty years— before aviation was even considered an actual possibility. It was at Captain Wild's "school" that Colonel Lindbergh learned to fly, and on a large percentage of the prominent flights either made or attempted, Captain Wild is called upon to inspect the "ship," consult and advise the pilot.

Courtesy City Administration

In New York there are over a dozen airports, 17 air-transportation lines, 12 aircraft manufacturers, 10 concerns which manufacture or furnish aircraft supplies, and a number of aircraft engineers, machinists, schools for the instruction of flying, etc.

FLOYD BENNET FIELD—Owned by the City of New York, 400 acres. Adjacent to Flatbush Avenue, Jamaica Bay.

RICHES and POVERTY IN NEW YORK
AND PICTURES OF A FEW MEN WHO HAVE ATTAINED FAME

The many pictures of regal homes and palatial business buildings shown and described in these pages, quite emphasize the fact that a vast number of very rich people reside in the wonder city.

Not elsewhere will be found such wealth.

In fact, the wealth of the world is *centered* in New York.

And those who *seek* wealth *come* to New York—they find that the best place to *get* wealth is where wealth *is*.

Although New York offers greater opportunity for riches than any other community on the globe, there are no bushes or trees growing in the parks where bags of gold can be plucked at will. On the contrary, the shrewdest, keenest, most expert and experienced business generals in all the world continually offer a competition that means the "gong" for those who lack in initiative, courage and genuine ability.

New York is often times condemned as cold, monopolistic, and heartless.

But isn't business being conducted along cold, monopolistic, and heartless lines *everywhere*—that is, *big* business!

Isn't business in *all* cities, merely a survival of the fittest!

"SUCCESS" in our present age, seems to be reckoned by the dollar mark.

Culture, breeding, "family" and old-school standards which meant so much in days gone by, seem to weigh but slightly in the scale in this year of our Lord 1932 as compared with a big "bank roll!"

Money today spells power, prestige, and even position.

In consequence, the rank and file of New York's 7,000,000 are bending every energy to securing money.

And New York is getting richer every twelve months!

New York has its *poor*,—just as every other city has.

Sickness, misfortune, unemployment, shiftlessness or one of the other forty causes which bring about poverty, contributes to a continual bread-line—the same as in other cities.

But New York has a thousand helpful and charitable agencies ever on the job to assit the really needy. Those who manifest a disposition to help themselves, and are worthy, can almost invariably "come back" if they will make an earnest effort.

The squalor and poverty of New York's old tenement districts is being gradually eliminated, and although there may still remain isolated remnants of what held in "Hell's Kitchen" and similar sections, modern housing conditions, philanthropic benefactions, and general welfare crusades have cleaned up most of the poorer districts. New York may justly claim to have an exceedingly small proportion of "poor" considering its enormous population.

Men who attain fame in New York almost invariably attain wealth along with it. Bud Fisher (No. 5 in picture) has amassed a fortune as a result of his clever cartoon work—"Mutt and Jeff" . . . . Babe Ruth (No. 6) has made a national name in baseball, as has Gene Tunney (No. 4) in boxing . . . . John Philip Sousa (No. 3) is known the world over as the "March King" . . . . Earl Carroll (No. 10) is famed as a writer of plays and as a theatrical producer . . . Jacob Ruppert (No. 2) as owner of the Yankees and John J. Raskob (No. 1) Chairman of the Democratic National Committee are known all over America . . . . Irvin S. Cobb (No. 7) humorist, Rex Beach (No. 8) novelist, and Owen Davis (No. 9) dramatist and author, are three of New York's great names in the literary field. There are a thousand famous men in New York whose pictures we could show had we the space—the above group are just a few of them.

30

THE MILLIONNAIRES OF NEW YORK

When a small town merchant, banker or other citizen of the rural sections amasses a respectable sum of money, he is inclined to want to move to Des Moines, Chicago or some other *city* where his opportunities for comforts, and the advantages large population affords, are greater.

And when those in the larger cities reach the seven figure mark, a considerable percentage of them move to New York for the same reason.

From all over America, those who attained wealth have located in the big city. But entirely aside from the many millionaires who have come to New York to live, New York has produced its own family of rich men—a number of whom count their wealth in a *score* of millions and more.

According to New York State tax returns, in 1929, 11 New Yorkers paid taxes on *INCOMES* above $5,000,000, 7 on *INCOMES* of between 4 and 5 millions, 46 between 2 and 3 millions, 167 on over $1,000,000, and 461 on *INCOMES* from ½ to 1 million.

A very large number of New York's wealthier population are extremely philanthropic, and donations, bequests, and gifts of various kinds total upwards of $150,000,000 annually.

As a class, New York millionaires are neither ostentatious nor prodigal. It seems that the richer a man becomes, the more modest he is in his tastes. Great wealth apparently has a tendency to arouse in the owner a keen desire to help others.

Fairchild Aerial Surveys, Inc.

Of course there is the more selfish type—the showy class, and the sporty element. The latter two groups will be found very much in evidence at the gilded cafes, fancy night clubs, the theatre, etc.

They are the ones who buy Rolls Royces, much jewelry and over-lavishly equip their offices and homes.

There is a much mistaken idea prevalent that rich men's sons are very likely to be wild and even degenerate, and although there are a few who accentuate this fallacy, the large majority of the sons and daughters of wealth are more carefully raised than those in the average home. New York millionaires as a whole are refined, and a highly respected element. The old song says that the "rich are getting richer and the poor are growing poorer." But there is at least the consolation that the average New Yorker of wealth is considerate of his fellow beings, and much inclined to distribute a generous portion of his accumulations for their betterment and general welfare.

Where but in New York with its Multi-Millionaires could this be possible

According to carefully compiled estimates, New York can boast of

7,000 who are worth $1,000,000 or over

22,000 who are worth $500,000 or over

93,000 who are worth $250,000 or over.

MOVING PICTURES IN NEW YORK

By JACK ALICOATE
Editor and Publisher of "The Film Daily"*

Photos by Pach Bros.

MISS ALICE JOYCE   MISS CLAIRE WINDSOR
Two Great Favorites in New York

Although the general public almost unanimously associates motion pictures with Hollywood, the City of New York actually plays the leading role in the destinies of the film industry.

Production of pictures, of course, is concentrated in Hollywood, with only Paramount, Vitaphone and a few smaller studios now operating in the east. But most of the presidents, other officials and directing heads of the big film companies all have their offices in New York.

The offices of Will H. Hays, head of the Motion Picture Producers & Distributors of America, Inc., and the official organization of the major film companies, are also located in New York.

Pictures are made mostly in Hollywood, but they are financed from New York and sold to the world from New York.

From a movie theatre standpoint, New York may well be called the "Wonder City" of the world—see pages 69 to 71. "First-run" houses on Broadway charge as high as $2.00. On the other hand, at the Bowery theatres, one can see three and four features on one bill for 10 cents. There are many houses devoted to talkies in German, French, Italian, Yiddish, Swedish, Spanish, etc. One German film operetta, "Two Hearts in Waltz Time," ran for 50 weeks at the same house.

Box-office receipts of the 10 principal Broadway movie theatres aggregate more than half a million dollars weekly. More than a million persons weekly attend *these 10 theatres* alone.

Because pictures run longer in New York than in the average city and town, and since it is the policy to show all the first-run attractions at one of the important Times Square houses before releasing them anywhere else in New York, many pictures are not presented in New York until sometime after they are released throughout the country. This explains why so many visitors to New York find theatres here showing pictures that they saw several weeks before in their home town.

Story material, books, magazine yarns and stage plays which are converted into motion pictures, are practically all acquired in New York. The Broadway stage is being drawn upon continually for most of the new acting talent that can be utilized on the screen.

In the embryonic days of the industry, motion pictures were produced entirely in the east. D. W. Griffith and Mack Sennett had their start at the old Biograph Studio on East 14th Street. Mary Pickford, Lillian and Dorothy Gish, John Bunny, Mabel Normand, Maurice Costello, Flora Finch, Wallace Reid, Norma Talmadge, Clara Kimball Young, Mae Marsh, Francis X. Bushman, Beverly Bayne and Blanche Sweet are only a few of the stellar names who did their early screen work around New York in the industry's beginning.

At present, Paramount is making all of its short subjects and some of its features at the Astoria studios. Among the stars and leading players who have worked there in the past season are Nancy Carroll, Gary Cooper, Clive Brook, Tallulah Bankhead, Maurice Chevalier, Claudette Colbert, Miriam Hopkins, Fredric Marsh, Carole Lombard, Irving Pichel and Charles Starrett, Smith and Dale, Karl Dane and George K. Arthur, and others. Vitaphone is making only shorts at its Brooklyn studios, and among the big names appearing in these are Harry Richman, Helen Morgan, Mr. and Mrs. Jack Norworth, Ruth Etting, Robert L. Ripley, Fanny Watson and Thelma White, Joe Frisco, Primo Carnera, et al.

It is worth noting that, while movie houses have climbed in number, New York legitimate theatres have dropped to nearly a third—many of them have become "movies."

All the above illustrates to what a very important extent New York figures in the movie world.

---

*The film industry is such a factor in New York that a *daily* paper is published, known as "The Film Daily" —leading trade paper of the film field founded 14 years ago and regarded among motion picture executives as "the Bradstreet of Filmdom." One of the best moving picture magazines is "Film Fun".

THE SPORTS OF NEW YORK

Boxing, Golf, Tennis, Base Ball, Foot Ball, Racing, and every other known sport has its devotees in New York. No city on the map patronizes sports in their every phase so generously, so enthusiastically, and so consistently.

It is estimated that 60,000 New Yorkers either belong to golf clubs or patronize the public links at Pelham Parkway, Van Cortlandt, and other courses.

Boxing bouts at the Polo Grounds, Yankee Stadium, Madison Square Garden and other large arenas draw crowds of 30,000 and upward at a single contest.

Forest Hills has one of the most ideal tennis courts amphitheatre in all the world where the great tennis stars from all nations compete for championships.

In no city of America is baseball patronized as in New York. The combined seating capacity of the Yankee Stadium, Polo Grounds, and Ebbetts Field is nearly 135,000 and on scores of occasions standing room only has been obtainable.

New York Base Ball Clubs have produced some of the greatest players the game has ever known. Everybody has heard of Christy Matthewson, and Babe Ruth!

Many of the great games of foot-ball are played in New York. The Army and Navy contests are held in the big city every fall. Columbia College, Fordham, and various other College and High School teams draw enormous crowds.

Racing at Belmont Park, Acqueduct Park and other tracks; Seven day Bicycle Grinds at Madison Square Garden, Yachting, Sailing, Motor Boating, Swimming, Skating, Hockey, Rook, Hand Ball, Cricket, Polo, and every kind of athletic and sporting activity or game in the category of exercise or contest has its thousands of enthusiastic followers in New York.

A juggler in statistics has figured out that New York spends over $270,000,000 annually for indulgence in or the patronage of games and athletics. Most of New York's Captains of Industry attend gymnasiums, play games, or make it a point to engage in *some* form of recreation, fully appreciating that to keep fit for business, one should keep fit physically.

New Yorkers as a class, are the greatest patrons of sports and athletics of any civic body in our nation.

Madison Square Garden was formerly at the corner of 26th St. and Madison Ave. and was for many years the chief arena for the big hippodrome events of the city such as trade exhibitions, conventions, horse shows, Ringling Bros. Circus, etc. It was on the roof theatre of Madison Square Garden that Stanford White was shot. The late "Tex" Rickard promoted the new Madison Square Garden shown herewith. Assessed at $3,740,000.

THE HUGE NEW MADISON SQUARE GARDEN
8th Ave. from 49th to 50th Sts.
The arena seats....................18,000
Built.............................1925

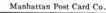
Manhattan Post Card Co.

POLO GROUNDS
8th Ave. & 155th St.
Ass'd Val............$1,175,000
Seats..................40,000

YANKEE STADIUM
161st St. & River Ave.
Est'd Cost..........$2,000,000
Seats...................60,000
Largest stadium in America.

CITY COLLEGE STADIUM
138th St. to 140th St. on
Amsterdam Ave.
Ass'd Val............$600,000
Accommodates over......30,000
Presented to the city by the beloved Adolph Lewisohn.

THE SIDEWALKS OF NEW YORK AND AL SMITH

"East Side, West Side, all around the town,
The tots sing ring-a-rosy, London Bridge is falling down!"

The above two lines are the start of a song chorus referring to the sidewalks of New York, which over thirty years ago spread all over the country, and which even today is almost as well known as our national anthem.

When Al Smith ran for President of the United States in 1928, this tune was played wherever he appeared. The Hon. Alfred E. Smith was a product of the East Side and his name so linked with the sidewalks of New York, that the little ditty has become a part of his introduction to any gathering in which he functions.

HON. ALFRED E. SMITH
a Product of the Sidewalks
of New York.

The sidewalks of New York have developed some great characters in the Wonder City. In no place on the globe is there such a cosmopolitan mixture of all races as mingle on the streets of the Big Town. Every nation is represented.

And in the lower East Side, the sidewalks are thronged with kids.

Kids from eight to fifteen seldom draw any lines at color, race or creed. With them there is no "Who's Who."

From the day a little shaver is able to get along without his mother, the young kids of the lower East Side spend most of their time on the sidewalks of their particular neighborhoods. They soon become accustomed to dodging traffic and the seething maelstrom of city life, busying themselves in playing, selling papers and absorbing wisdom.

Is it any wonder that as they grow up, they become independent, fearless, daring, and quite able to take care of themselves! No school or college curriculum can ever teach life as the sidewalks of New York teach it. And it might be a very good thing if some of the pampered children of the avenues and aristocratic sections generally, could be thrown on their own resources as was little "Al."

By referring to pages 86 to 117, it will be noted that of the 100 OUTSTANDING NEW YORKERS selected from the various fields of the city's activities, a very large percentage of them are self-made men who have risen from the ranks of either obscure parentage or actual poverty.

The sidewalks of New York have produced some of the grandest men in our entire nation—*he* men in every meaning of the term. The late Dwight Morrow was so poor when a young man he walked *miles* because he could not afford car fare. Poverty is no disgrace if one doesn't *stay* poor. Furthermore poverty seems to be a foundation for success.

———————●———————

In showing pictures of buildings, people, etc., throughout this book, we have ried very earnestly to give credit to each photographer who took same—thus the names above or below cuts throughout the volume, on several hundred, however, we could find no name of photographer, as many reproductions were made from black and white impressions.

THE WORKING GIRLS OF NEW YORK

No city in all the world offers young women who have ability and strength of character, greater opportunity than New York.

On the other hand there is no place on the map offering more temptation, more pitfalls or more discouragement.

It depends on the *girl herself*.

Without friends, "pull," or initiative, she may find New York cold, unresponsive and almost heartless.

If she has had no business training, does not know how to manipulate a typewriter, take shorthand, keep books or qualify in other office positions, or, if she is not a musician, manicurist, or experienced in *some* capacity, she must take her chances as a clerk, waitress, housemaid, or some other "small pay" position.

Of course there are chorus girl jobs for attractive girls, opportunities to act as hostesses at dance halls, etc., but the girl who has ambition, self-respect, character and a desire to be somebody *can* be somebody if she will make the effort. She does not have to depend solely upon good looks, dress or feminine charm to get somewhere in New York. New York is not nearly as cold, unresponsive and heartless as many of those who *start* wrong so insistently assert.

On the contrary, no city in the world is more philanthropic, more generous, or more sincerely concerned about its future mothers than is New York.

Y. W. C. A.'s, Church Guilds and Societies, Welfare Organizations and Clubs (Hotel Clubs, Social Clubs and School Clubs) all work earnestly to secure employment and extend assistance to any worthy young woman who *wants* work and will do her part to make good in whatever position she obtains.

It is up to the girl herself!

Two young girls came to New York three years ago from a small town out west. Both were young, good looking and full of western pep and ambition. They had little money and did not know a soul in the big town. Both had read about New York and had thrilled at the screen pictures of New York life, shown at the movies. It was all grand! But after being in the city three weeks their money was gone. They suddenly found themselves hungry. The older one had already found a "boy friend," but the younger (aged 20) awoke to the seriousness of the situation and commenced to *think*. The next morning she called at one of the Y. W. C. A. branches and told her story. She secured a position as filing clerk in an office and applied herself assiduously to the tasks given her. She made friends of the other employees and induced one of the typists to teach her how to use a typewriter. During evenings she studied shorthand. Today, she is secretary to one of the managers drawing $40.00 a week. Her friend "kidded" her, sponged on her and abused her, Finally they separated. The other girl followed the primrose path and at present is a hostess in a cheap dance hall.

New York can claim that she affords bigger and better opportunities and more of them for the right kind of working girls than any other metropolis.

But—it's up to the girl herself.

Courtesy N. Y. Times Studios

LOWER NEW YORK

MIDTOWN NEW YORK

UPTOWN NEW YORK

ONLY IN A CITY OF BILLIONS COULD SUCH SKY LINES BE POSSIBLE

BILLION DOLLAR ORGANIZATIONS IN NEW YORK

It wasn't so many years ago that a billion dollars was considered about "all the money there was in the world."

Today, in 1932, New York has a number of individual institutions—each with assets or resources in excess of a billion dollars, among which are the American Telephone & Telegraph Co., the Chase National Bank, the Guaranty Trust Co., the National City Bank, the Edison Light & Power Co., etc.

The assets of American Telephone & Telegraph Co. are *more than* $5,000,000,000.

The resources of the Chase National Bank over $2,500,000,000, and so on.

There are hundreds of banking and commercial institutions in New York who have reached the *multi*-million figure in calculating assets, and many have even passed the $50,000,000 and $100,000,000 mark. But the amassing of a "billion" is something that has never been accomplished until within recent years. With the exception of Henry Ford of Detroit, there is no other individual or organization in America (outside of New York) that has ever even *approached* this figure—all of which goes to prove that New York is not only the financial center of the universe but the only city in the world where (with rare exceptions) this *could* be accomplished.

And this is the reason why the picture on this page is possible. Just note the three sky-lines: One is that of lower Broadway—the middle view is that of "Mid-town"—three miles north. The bottom picture is the "Up-town" section, a mile or so further north.

New York as a *city*, is also included in the "billion" class. One may imagine the municipality's wealth when confronted with the fact that New York's bonded debt is **over two billion.** And yet no city in the world has better credit. New York can borrow *any* sum desired at as low a rate as the United States Government itself.

THE WONDER AIR VIEWS OF NEW YORK

It is doubtful if any city on earth has been photographed from the sky as often and in as many different ways as has New York and we are greatly indebted to a number of the city's splendid aerial photographers for the various air views shown in this book. We want to call especial attention to several of the pictures shown herein taken by the Air Map Corporation of New York which are outstanding in their clearness and detail. Note picture taken of lower New York and Battery Park on page 3. Also the "Air Map of Manhattan Island" on Page 10. This picture of "Knickerbockerville" is one of the most masterful achievements in photography ever taken with a camera. Note the bare looking space in about the center of cut. This is Central Park—three miles long and yet notwithstanding the picture as a whole covers nearly an area of twenty miles the details are such that even individual buildings can be recognized. This is just a sample of the work the Air Map Corporation of America does.

36

NEW YORK'S GREAT WHITE WAY

No street in all the world compares with New York's Great White Way!

Even the night life of "Gay Paree" cannot compete with it.

Hundreds of thousands of revelers, pleasure-seekers, sightseers, and some on business bent, throng the brilliantly lighted half mile leading from Times Square to the hundred theatres, moving picture palaces, dance halls, and cafes for which the district is famous.

More people parade the Great White Way at *midnight* than can be found on the streets in most cities at *high noon!*

A quarter million of them every pleasant evening!

Thousands come merely to see the crowds. Thousands pack the "million dollar" picture houses. Other thousands ride in motor cars through the scintillating thoroughfare blazing with countless electric lights, adding the honking of their horns to the din of music, loud speaking ballyhoos, traffic-cop whistles and the general diapason of noise created by the hordes of people themselves.

Gaiety, good nature, and the Bohemian spirit generally characterize the vast throng. The crowded jostling of those in a hurry doesn't seem to interfere with the easy-going, happy-go-lucky masses—out to have a good time.

Shortly after half past seven, arrivals from every direction seem to spring from the very ground itself. By eight o'clock the street is full, and notwithstanding a hundred thousand enter the theatres and other places of amusement, additional arrivals take their place and mix in with the surging strollers.

Barnum in his palmiest days could never draw such hosts as assemble on the Great White Way every clear evening. Even when it rains, there is never less than a hundred thousand or more—taxicabs and motor cars discharging revelers at theatres, cafes, dance halls, etc.

Enormous electric signs on facades and roofs of great buildings provide dazzling light all along the way—not content to glare, but keyed up to motion picture flashes appropriate to the moving human panorama of the streets below.

The Great White Way is almost as "wet" as before Mr. Volstead became famous. Although the better class of hotels and restaurants display cards on their tables requesting the public to confine their thirsts to soft drinks and co-operate with the

management in obeying the law, thousands of flasks are toted down to the Great White Way which, in addition to the plentiful supply of contraband carried in stock by the speak-easies in the roaring forties, furnish all the thrills deemed necessary to "get going."

From midnight until dawn, the night clubs, dance halls, and cafes contribute to the general excitement and *keep* the crowd going. Even at four and five o'clock in the morning thousands are still on the streets. Broadway never sleeps—that is, that section of Broadway included in New York's famous "Great White Way."

Chorus girls, hostesses from dance halls, and night-club performers constitute a considerable factor in New York's night life. Venturesome young girls from the country, wayward young girls from the city itself, and scarlet women from the sporting circles of all parts of the huge metropolis, form a considerable share of the after-midnight crowds, all bent on either making a living or following the primrose path.

There is "sin" in the precincts of the Great White Way. There are plenty of wild oats sown, and plenty of "headaches" and bitter remorse "the morning after," and yet—each night new arrivals head for Times Square, and new faces mingle with the crowds.

International News Photo, Inc.

New York's Great White Way and Theatrical District
From the top of the Empire State Building.

BRIDGE POKER and PINOCHLE in NEW YORK

Bridge, poker, and pinochle are just *games*—games of cards, and yet New York is surely one huge card playing city. "All work and no *play,* doesn't get Jack anywhere." So, the majority of New Yorkers play. They are great patrons of *card* games.

The game of Bridge has become *more* than a pastime, it has become a most lucative business. Many Bridge "Instructors" are netting thousands of dollars a year by teaching. A dozen or more have written two and three hundred page books on the subject.

The hand every bridge player dreams about, but never gets!

Sidney Lenz, Milton Work, Ely Culbertson, E. V. Shepard, George Reith, the late Wilbur Whitehead, and practically all the outstanding Bridge authorities of America, belong to New York.

No one will attempt to dispute the fact that no game of *any* kind has ever so completely aroused national interest as has Bridge.

In 50,000 different homes, clubs, etc., in and around New York during the cooler months, a game of Bridge will be found going on every evening. Doubtless this is true all over the country in the same ratio to population.

The Knickerbocker Whist Club, at 270 Park Avenue, has for over thirty years held weekly "duplicate auction" contests (and more recently "Contract"). On the following afternoon the Card Committee would go over the boards, analyzing the play from scores recorded. From their findings, the various "conventions" that now largely hold, have been developed.

The Whitehead System, Work System, Culbertson System, and so on, are all more or less based on the studied and scientific analysis of the Knickerbocker Club's activities. However, each of these "systems" more or less differs in reference to sound bidding, proper finesse, the various ramifications of distribution, interpretation of values, and how to secure "information." But *playing the game itself* is the only way one will ever learn to become really proficient. Few players ever become consistent winners from studying or depending on instruction books. It generally requires from two to three years of *more or less constant patronage of the game* to become an adept.

The game of *Poker* is almost as old as Adam. But there are at present so many deviations of this diversion, that scarcely any standardized form of Poker is recognized any more. Jack Pot, Deuces Wild, "Omaha," Seven Card Peet, Spit in the Ocean, and a score of other variations of the old classic, have so debased the play on which Hoyle was supreme authority, that when one is asked to "sit in," a discussion almost invariably follows as to "what's what." However, Pairs, Three of a kind, Straights, Flushes, Full Houses, and so on, will always remain the fundamentals of every form of "poker."

Those who have experienced the thrill of holding "Fours" against a "Full House" can appreciate why even Bridge cannot wean over poker fans to its ranks.

Pinochle is the favorite game of Germans, Hebrews and "Commuters" in New York. Many of them are past-masters at it. There is no greater joy to any card player than the melding of "450" in one hand affords a pinochle player.

There are over a half million commuters who come to New York daily from their homes in outlying suburbs, Long Island, New Jersey, etc. Fully half this number travel by train or boat.

Nearly every smoking car is equipped with a dozen lap-boards, and a two-bit piece tendered the porter can secure the loan of one of these boards—including a passably clean deck of cards. On the boats, tables are supplied. Many a "pinochle shark" has developed from this "morning and evening play."

The sale of playing cards in New York averages over 10,000 decks daily. New Yorkers by and large are indefatigable card players.

THE DANCE HALLS OF NEW YORK

Vernon and Irene Castle earned a fortune and gained a world wide reputation for graceful dancing. It was they who started the "dance craze" which struck the country similar to that of the bicycle craze in the early nineties.

Everybody caught the fever and learned to dance—even white haired old patriarchs and grandmothers of seventy learned to fox-trot!

Dance hall proprietors made fortunes. Dinner Dances, Dansants, and Afternoon Tea Dances became the rage. Hotels, cafes, restaurants, and even clubs had polished hard wood floors laid in the center of their dining halls so that patrons could dance between courses.

But like all other fads, the dance craze came to an end.

And then came Roseland, Clover Garden and other palatial ball rooms with such magnificent appointments, such grand orchestras, and such bewitching lighting effects that, even though the "craze" was over, thousands continued to dance.

Clover Garden, which occupies the entire floor in the huge Grand Central Palace Building, is like fairyland. It is stated that the cost in fitting up, decorating and furnishing the place totaled over $100,000.

"ROSELAND" at 1658 Broadway however, is said to be the most artistic and beautiful dancing ball room in New York—as regal and gorgeous as any Fifth Avenue home. Neither garishness nor ostentation mars its exquisite furnishings, and an atmosphere of genuine refinement permeates the whole institution—even to the hostesses themselves.

There is continuous dancing at Roseland every night from 8 to 1 A.M., and tea dances every afternoon from 2:30 to 6. Two orchestras play constantly and on Thursday nights high grade vaudeville entertainment is offered. On Friday nights and Sunday afternoons dance contests are held and cash prizes awarded. Every Tuesday and Thursday the delightful dance music of the Roseland orchestras is broadcasted over the radio (WABC) at 1:30 A.M.

Interior Views of "ROSELAND"

There are many other high class ball rooms in New York but unfortunately there are too many public *dance halls*, similar to those of other large cities, that are hot beds of immorality and require more or less constant police surveilance. One of the greatest curses of city life today is the cheap "dance hall," and it is time that the forces which rid New York of its red light district should get busy in a similar crusade against these dens of iniquity.

But dancing is an art. Youth, just like the elder element who are enthusiasts on golf, must have recreation and as long as time lasts dancing will always be popular. Even some churches are now introducing dancing in their recreation halls to interest young people.

Although the "craze" is over, tens of thousands still dance in New York and New York supports a number of the most beautiful dance palaces in America.

39

THE NIGHT CLUBS IN NEW YORK

Back in the gay nineties, when Delmonico's, Rector's, Sherry's, Churchill's and the other "gay cafes" of Broadway and vicinity were operating full swing, night life in New York was quite different from what it is today. True, there were no cabarets, no squared, highly-polished dance floors, no girl shows and other divertissements characteristic today, but there was good food, the best of liquors, and *real fellowship*.

There is no comparison of the gayer cafes of the 90's with the present-day New York night clubs. Along about 1908, the "Turkey Trot," originated on the Barbary Coast of San Francisco—and a little later, the cabaret. Within a year or two the turkey trot, and a dozen other alleged dances requiring movement of every part of the body except the feet, spread all over the country with the cabaret in their wake. By slow but noticeably steady degrees the proprietors of cafes, particularly those catering to night life, have introduced various fads and finally brought into being the "night club," to the accompaniment of the fox trot, the semi-nude ballet, the jazz orchestra, and "ginger ale and ice." Theoretically, the night club patron is supposed to furnish any supplement to the ginger ale and ice.

While such cafes as Delmonico's and Rector's cannot be compared with the New York night club of 1931, there is one important point of contrast. Patrons of the aforementioned cafes were mainly *New Yorkers*—members of the best families. In those good old days, New Yorkers would gather in such places for "the feast of reason and the flow of soul." The preponderance of patronage in the New York *night clubs* is made up largely of out-of-towners, buyers for department stores, business men, tourists, etc. Oddly enough, the out-of-towner expects to "see New York and New Yorkers" in Gotham's night clubs, but they see mainly their fellow out-of-town people. A visit to six of the most pretentious night clubs in one evening revealed that the great majority of patrons were from out of the city.

The fact of the matter is, there are so many other and less expensive attractions and forms of entertainment in the city that New Yorkers prefer to patronize the less expensive cafes, etc. There is a disposition on the part of visitors to New York to want to see its "sin palaces," and they seem willing to pay the price. However, the lovely beauties who indulge in Terpsichorean contortions in semi-nude abadon are no more alluring than the girls who dance in the cabarets or on the stage of the average American city of metropolitan size.

The New York visitor, however, seems "sold" on the idea that the night club is an integral and deliciously wicked part of New York life, and this desire and willingness to "pay the piper," makes the night clubs a most flourishing activity in Manhattan.

Texas Guinan, the most widely publicized of the New York night club proprietors, set the pace and wrote the motto for the whole melange of New York night clubs in the greeting which she extended to all visitors—"Come on sucker!" The sucker comes on and likes it, while the New Yorker smiles and is pleased that his out-of-town cousin is enjoying himself, or at least appearing to.

THE COST OF LIGHTING NEW YORK

In 1826 New York had less than eight miles of lighted streets and possessed some 2,748 lamp posts. In Greater New York today the eight miles have been extended to more than 4,200 miles, and the 2,748 posts have been multiplied to over 120,000. The total cost of lighting the city annually is over $5,000,000. But this sum is less than 1 per cent. of the total tax budget.

New Yorkers today may claim the best lighted city in the world. Yet their pride is not greater than that of their forebears, who, in 1826, winessed 120 brand new gas lamps flickering on Broadway from the Battery to Grand Street.

THE CHORUS GIRLS OF NEW YORK

Of course they're pretty, shapely, gorgeously gowned, or else—, they wear little more than a fetching smile!

And most of them have the appeal of youth.

All showmen who know their business select from the hundreds of young girls who apply for positions, only those who have looks, figure and personality.

In the show business a girl does not have to be of gentle birth, have any particularly brilliant intellect, or be possessed of any specific capacity. She may be ignorant, common, and even *illiterate,* but if she has beauty, good looking legs, and plenty of "IT," she will be booked as quickly as a contract can be drawn!

Her morals are seldom questioned. Her past means nothing. Her whole stock in trade is that which conforms to standards demanded by the show-going public.

The public at large who attend the theatre demand good looking girls.

They also demand that they display their female charms.

A modest girl in any other vocation would thoroughly resent any suggestion that she show herself in a semi-nude condition, and yet a chorus girl must appear before a host of strangers nightly as nearly nude as the law will allow.

Raw as certain stage requirements may seem—it is all *business.*

It is up to the girl herself as to whether she will *consider* same as strictly business, or whether she loses all sense of decency, poise, and character and let the stage ruin her.

And yet, notwithstanding all the above, there are proportionately just as many fine, clean, virtuous young ladies in musical comedy, cabaret work, and other ramifications of theatrical life, as there are in almost any other business.

The writer speaks from experience as he has been the owner of several companies in which a large number of show girls were employed. In one company alone there were 32 chorus girls. Three-fourths of the number were ladies in morals as well as in other phases of the term.

New York's chorus girls are a very superior type of young womanhood.

The attractive salaries paid by high grade producers, influence a very much better class of girls to take to the stage than in years gone by.

It is quite true that many of them are wild, reckless and even "sporty," but don't condemn the fraternity as a whole simply because some of them don't seem to be able to withstand the lure of gay night life.

Many of New York's greatest stars of Musical Comedy started their careers as chorus girls. Is it any wonder that the fame and fortune attained by stage favories like Billie Burke, Julia Sanderson, Mitzie Hajos, Irene Bordoni and scores of others, should lure young girls to the footlights!

No city—even in Europe—offers greater opportunity to make good in the Musical Comedy field than New York offers.

Federal Government activities in New York—Continued from page 22

houses the City Hall Post Office, the offices of the United States Attorney, United States Marshal and the Naturalization Bureau, and the Federal Courts. These courts, incidentally, handle one-seventh of the nation's prohibition cases, obtain conviction or pleas of guilt in one for every eleven such results elsewhere and collected only $325,000 of the $6,922,491 paid for prohibition fines in the United States in 1930—all of which is cited as an indication of the brand of prohibition enforcement New York wants—*and gets!*

The Customs Warehouse, 201 Varick Street, is the only new building owned by the Government in New York. In it are the customs storerooms, containing unclaimed and contested imports; the Customs Court, and the laboratories of the Food and Drug Administration.

In the Government Warehouse, 641 Washington Street, are storage rooms for property confiscated by the Government, and the offices of the Prohibition Administrator, who denies there are 36,000 speakeasies in New York, although that is the figure given by his predecessor in office; the Bureau of Industrial Alcohol; the Interstate Commerce Commission; the Panama Canal store; the Navy Department; and, —we almost forgot—the Japanese Beetle Quarantine.

The Army offices are at 39 Whitehall Street. In or near New York there are a dozen Army forts and several arsenals. The Navy Yard in Brooklyn is important both as a shipbuilding plant and as a berth for battleships in New York waters. Scattered in various parts of the city are other minor functionaries of the Government, who help cater to the public needs of this metropolitan nation called New York. Even to the point of Federal servants, the city is self-sufficient, combining the best features of a capital city and still at a safe distance from Congress.

PHOTOGRAPHY IN NEW YORK

Photography has become an actual art in the Wonder City. New York has a number of studios devoted to the taking of pictures and the making of portraits not excelled anywhere in the world. A great many of the 784 half tone plates shown in this book were taken from photographs kindly furnished us by the New York TIMES, New York SUN, etc., Manhattan Post Card Co., Aerial View Companies, owners of buildings, and others. Wishing to extend the courtesy of credit to each of the photographers who took same, we called on a number of them to ascertain which were taken by their respective houses, and were surprised to note the elaborate and very interesting establishments many of the higher class New York photographer maintain. Underwood & Underwood, Kaiden Studios, Irving Underhill, Pach Bros., Wurts Bros., Brown Bros., Blank & Stoller, Guild-Photos, White Studios, and we could name dozens of others) not only have most beautiful and artistic quarters, but at Pach Bros., Mr. Albert Pach, the proprietor, showed us photographs his firm had taken of every president from General Grant to Herbert Hoover. He also exhibited personal letters from not only the presidents but many from the most prominent characters in national life, including Joseph Jefferson, James Russell Lowell, J. P. Morgan, James J. Hill, and countless others. It was interesting to note that Pach Bros. was organized in 1867 by three brothers—Mr. Albert Pach being the son of one of them and successor to the business. His picture of the late Thomas Edison working over his first talking machine is a masterpiece of photographic skill. We wish we had room to make reference to each of the others but space forbids. But those who want the best photographs the world offers, will find that New York photographers can furnish them.

ALBERT PACH
Owner of Pach Bros.

Air Map Corp. of America, N. Y.

Here is a sample of Aerial photography taken by the Air Map Corporation of America.

Many other air views are shown throughout the book taken by Fairhild Aerial Surveys Inc., International News Photos Inc. and others.

Other views by the Pacific Atlantic Photos Inc., Ewing Galloway, Irving Underhill, "Wide World," Orrin R. Louden, Browning Studios, etc., etc., all are gems of photographic skill.

101 POINTS OF INTEREST

WHICH EVERY STRANGER SHOULD VISIT

LISTED IN CONTINUTY ORDER

NO.

43

(Continued from Page 43)

JUMEL MANSION

Built in 1866 for which the City of New York paid over $225,000 in 1903, as a museum for relics of the Revolutionary War etc. This home was used as Gen. Geo. Washington's headquarters in 1876.

DYCKMAN HOUSE

Another famous old house that has been preserved because of great historical interest. During the Revolution there was "more doing" in this vicinity than in any other part of the revolting colonies.

ROOSEVELT HOME and MUSEUM

On the second floor of this building, Theo. Roosevelt was born Oct. 27, 1858. The Womens' Roosevelt Association and Roosevelt Memorial Association maintain the building as a Roosevelt Museum.

Man. Pst. Card Co.

Courtesy of
N. Y. Sun

Fairchild Aerial Surveys, Inc.

"ELLIS ISLAND"

All immigrants coming to America are first landed here and examined. Criminals, paupers, discarded and contract laborers, etc. are deported at the expense of steamship companies. Visitors take boats at the Battery

"STATUE OF LIBERTY"

Stands on Bedloe's Island 1¾ miles southwest of the Battery.

Presented to us by the French nation in 1884. 151 ft. high.

"FRAUNCES TAVERN"

S. E. Cor. Broad & Pearl Streets

Erected 1719. Chamber of Commerce founded here in 1768 — Where Washington bade farewell to his troops in 1783. Building sustained by Sons of the Revolution.

Copyrighted by Irving Underhill
Manhattan Post Card Co., etc.

Fairchild Aerial Survey's Inc.

"NEW WASHINGTON BRIDGE"

Crossing the Hudson River—connecting New York and New Jersey.

Now under construction, to be opened to the public 1932.

Extends from 178th Street in Manhattan to Fort Lee, New Jersey.

GREATEST ENGINEERING FEAT OF ANY AGE

The huge suspension span 3,500 feet long! Estimated cost of Bridge over $60,000,000.

"EAST RIVER BRIDGES"

1—"BROOKLYN BRIDGE"

    Cost $21,000,000   Opened 1883
                                      6,537 feet long

2—"MANHATTAN BRIDGE"

    Cost $20,000,000   Opened 1901
                                        6,855 feet long

3—"WILLIAMSBURG BRIDGE"

    Cost $23,000,000   Opened 1903
                                      7,200 feet long

4—"QUEENSBORO BRIDGE"

    Cost $25,000,000   Opened 1909
                                      7,636 feet long

Courtesy Manhattan Post Card Co.

"GRANT'S TOMB"

Riverside Drive at 123rd St.

Built in 1897
$600,000 contributed by 90,000 donors.

"HISTORIC CLAREMONT"

Riverside Drive and 125th St.

Situated just north of Grant's Tomb, a block north. Famous in Revolutionary days also as a residence of Joseph Bonaparte—late King of Spain. Claremont is now a high type restaurant.

EDUCATION IN NEW YORK

By Howard Shiebler

One of New York's Leading Authorities on Education

Not even the great educational centers of Europe can compare with New York schools and institutions of learning.

There are in the public schools of New York City approximately 1,250,000 students and some 37,000 teachers and principals. Classes are held in more than 1,000 school buildings, with more than 25,500 classrooms having a total seating capacity in excess of the number of students in attendance.

The City of New York spends approximately one million dollars every school day for educational purposes. The total cost of the school plant is approximately half a billion dollars.

Education is provided not for children alone but for adults as well. Adults who wish to take courses in Americanization, also adults who wish to be trained for a vocational pursuit.

Schools are conducted all the year around. There are summer sessions for those who wish to do advanced work and for those who have fallen behind. Evening schools of elementary and secondary grade carry on for those who cannot attend school in the day time. Continuation schools for those who have not reached their seventeenth birthday but who cannot attend regular school (because they are employed) have a registration of 70,000.

New York adopts unusual tactics to provide education: There are classes in hospitals, free transportation for crippled children who wish to attend school and also for normal children whose parents cannot afford to pay their carfare. Teachers, principals and supervisors contribute monthly from their salaries to a fund for needy children in the public schools, insuring that no child shall go hungry and none be without adequate clothing.

Out of the total amount spent by the City for all education purposes $86 out of every $100 goes directly to the instruction of the children. This is unusually high and is indicative of efficiency and economy in the matter of administration.

The schools of New York have about 650 gymnasiums, nearly 700 auditoriums, about 140 roof playgrounds, more than 500 other playgrounds, some 330 school gardens, and nearly 300 libraries. The newer school buildings have swimming pools, museums and miniature zoos for nature study.

The curriculum is modern to the point of embracing courses of study in airplane engine repair, television, radio broadcasting and maintenance, and repair of electric iceboxes. The girls may learn everything from beauty culture and tea room management to Latin and Greek.

Visitors to New York City are most impressed by the size of the system as a whole and by the size of its individual school buildings and organizations. Each of these high schools is a small democracy, student governed.

One of the newest bureaus in the New York schools is the Bureau of Child Guidance, a bureau organized for the purpose of making more adequate provision for the so-called problem child. The hope is to eliminate failures by adjusting the schools to meet the individual needs of pupils.

The school system is administered by a Board of Education of seven members. Dr. George J. Ryan is president of the Board. He has served as president since 1922, and his long administration has been one of the most successful in the history of public education in the city of New York.

The Superintendent of Schools is Dr. William J. O'Shea, a man who has given the greater part of his life to the city school system. He is beloved by all, and the period of his superintendency has been marked by many notable achievements, virtually all of which are a direct result of Dr. O'Shea's efforts.

The public *high schools,* which have grown by leaps and bounds to a registration of 202,000 boys and girls, are under the direction of Dr. Harold G. Campbell, Deputy Superintendent of Schools. Dr. Campbell has brought the high schools to a high state of efficiency. Under his guidance the high school pupils of New York City have for years led the entire State of New York in the matter of passing Regents examinations.

"DEWITT CLINTON HIGH SCHOOL"

Mosholu Parkway and Navy Ave., Bronx

"DeWitt Clinton" is reputed to be the largest high school in the world. It is certainly the most complete in its scope of activity. The purpose of DeWitt Clinton is to prepare FUTURE LEADERS for New York by encouraging fullest individual development of talent. It prepares students for any college and teaches trustworthiness, cleanliness, ethics, etc., as well as the academic.

Enrollment for 1931 over 10,000.

The building cost $4,000,000 and was dedicated in the fall of 1929. Most admirably equipped with Library, Gymnasium, Lockers, Swimming Pool, Firing Gallery and Rifle Range, Printing Room, Wood and Metal Workshop, Laboratory, General Store, Bank, Laundry, Band Practice Room, Pool Room, Hand Ball Court, Radio Room, Auditorium and Stage for Theatrical, etc., etc.

Some of the Courses taught at DeWitt Clinton:—

Commercial, French, German, Italian, Spanish and the Languages, Chemistry, Economics, Civics, Mathematics, General Science, Biology, Physics, History, Art, Music, Elocution, etc., etc.

The very able Principal of DeWitt Clinton is Mr. A. Mortimer Clark. Assistant Principal, Mr. Oscar W. Anthony. Architect, Wm. H. Gompert, Builders, Gibbs & Rice Co.

ROOSEVELT HIGH SCHOOL

"Roosevelt High" is another of the 45 wonderful high schools of New York, where carefully selected instructors of the highest type are engaged in teaching young men and women the usual courses constituting modern high school curriculum.

PUBLIC SCHOOL No. 152

One of the 1,118 school houses scattered all through the area of Greater New York where young boys and girls are given the rudiments of learning.

The growth of New York in recent years has been such that the city fathers have faced the serious problem of building school houses to keep pace with the constantly increasing army of youths applying for admittance. It will require a volume of more pages than this book to illustrate and adequately outline the stupendous cost and conduct of these institutions. Tens of thousands of teachers must be secured of the right type to inculcate in the juvenile mind proper ethics and the up-building of character, as well as the academic.

New York is proud of its wonderful school system.

COLUMBIA UNIVERSITY
Broadway to Amsterdam Ave.—114th St. to 120th St.

AERIAL VIEW OF COLUMBIA UNIVERSITY'S IMMENSE ACREAGE
(As seen from the West)

VALUE OF PROPERTY AND BUILDINGS—NEARLY $50,000,000
NUMBER STUDENTS 1931—OVER 40,000
FOUNDED 1754. PRESIDENT—DR. NICHOLAS MURRAY BUTLER

This enormous institution was originally founded in 1754 as King's College and the original location was at Broadway and Barclay Street. In 1857, just prior to the Civil War, the college moved "way out in the country" to what is now Madison Ave. and E. 49th St. In 1892, however, the college had outgrown this location. By 1902, 26 acres had been secured to the present location and from that time to the present, the college has grown steadily, both in wealth and importance. The generous endowments of successful graduates and public spirited citizens made it possible to erect the magnificent buildings shown in the picture above. The beautiful domed structure shown directly across the street from the Athletic Field, is the stately Low Library costing $1,200,000 and donated by the Hon. Seth Low—one of New York's former mayors.

The group of buildings to the right and left are the various "halls" containing class rooms, lecture auditoriums, study and recitation quarters and the various specific libraries and equipment used in connection with the several branches of learning to which the particular building may be devoted. There are "Furnald Hall", "Hall of Journalism", "Livingston Hall", "Hartley", "Hamilton", "Havemeyer" and "Earl" Halls, also "Hall of Mines", "Students Hall", "Kent Chapel", "Teachers College", etc. Directly across Broadway to the left are the buildings of Barnard College—exclusively for women students. Directly north of the Barnard buildings, is the Theological group of buildings.

Airview, as seen from the South—

Columbia University is not only a leading institution of higher learning, but one of the largest and most important in existence.

NEW YORK UNIVERSITY
ONE OF THE GREATEST UNIVERSITIES IN AMERICA

Just *100 years ago*, a small group of public spirited citizens in New York determined to organize a new type of University, deviating from the scheme of higher education in vogue at that time. While still clinging to classical lines, it should reach out into more practical fields not touched by University influence.

And thus—New York University!

As the college grew, it expanded—not all in one area, but in various parts of the city where students could be in closer touch with the activities in which they were interested.

Photo by Henry Sihler

This is a night scene of several of the buildings in the "Washington Square Center" of New York University

179th to 181st Streets—Sedgwick to Aqueduct Ave.
Showing the world renowned "Hall of Fame" in the "University Heights Center" of New York University

ALL OVER TOWN

At Washington Square are located various large buildings—and the imposing new "School of Education" shown in lower left hand corner of this page, is just around the corner, on 4th and Green Streets.

In the Wall Street district are the courses of Commerce and Business in the University's own building.

Over near Tudor City in east 43rd St. is the School of Fine Arts and Architecture.

An entire floor in the immense new New York Life Ins. Building has just been leased for the overflow of young men and women in the liberal arts and pre-professional classes.

But the principal University buildings occupy the forty acres

SCHOOL of EDUCATION BUILDING of NEW YORK UNIVERSITY, recently erected (1930) at the N. W. Cor. of Green and Fourth Streets

of beautiful rolling land at University Heights where are located the Colleges of Art, Engineering, Aeronautics, and the great "Hall of Fame." Schools of Medicine, Dentistry, etc., are located in the vicinity of Bellevue Hospital.

Thus the University grips the life of the city at many points, radiating its influence at these various University Centers.

FOUNDED 1831.

NUMBER OF STUDENTS (1931)—OVER 30,000.

PRESIDENT—
CHANCELLOR ELMER ELLSWORTH BROWN.

FORDHAM UNIVERSITY

Situated about nine miles from Grand Central Station on the New York Central Railroad, a short distance from beautiful Bronx Park.

Fordham University occupies 75 acres of ground purchased in 1841 by Bishop Hughes for a seminary. Later a college was started independent of the seminary, and by 1900 four hundred students were enrolled. From that time to the present, the growth of "Fordham" has been almost phenomenal.

In addition to the magnificent buildings comprising the Fordham group near Bronx Park, the University occupies the entire 28th floor of the Woolworth Building for the Law Department. It also has other downtown branches.

On November 1, 1931, there was only a few lacking of a roster of 10,000 students.

The President of Fordham University is J. Hogan, S.J.

Vice-President and dean—Rev. Charles J. Deane, S.J.

Fordham University is the largest Catholic institution of learning in America.

Administration Bldg.

HUNTER COLLEGE

Occupying a beautiful tract of 45 acres on the Jerome Ave. reservoir site in the Bronx.

Under the Walker administration, an appropriation of $3,900,000 was made for the erection of new buildings for Hunter College, which formerly was located between 68th and 69th Streets, from Park to Lexington Avenue.

The growth of Hunter College has been so remarkable that necessity demanded a drastic expansion in both buildings and facilities.

In 1926, Hunter College had an enrollment of 3,985. In 1928, Hunter College had an enrollment ment of 22,710.

Two of the new buildings recently completed.

Hunter College is the largest institution of learning exclusively for women, in the world, and the beautiful buildings shown herewith have all been erected within the past few years.

THE COLLEGE OF THE CITY OF NEW YORK

Amsterdam Avenue to St. Nicholas Terrace—West 138th Street to 140th Street

Familiarly known as

CITY COLLEGE

Aeroplane view, copyrighted by Fairchild Aerial Surveys Inc.

Originally named as

FREE ACADEMY OF NEW YORK

In 1866, name was changed as above.

"City College" is owned by the City of New York and consists of main building (tower structure with circular front), Chemistry Building, Engineering Building, Townsend Harris Hall, Gymnasium, Stadium and the big Athletic Field shown in picture.

Front view of main college building

A "three year preparatory" department fits young pupils for the four year collegiate course, and practical as well as classic instruction is furnished.

The College covers practically every branch of practical learning that the average college aspirant could ask. The arrangement of grounds and buildings makes a most imposing view of the institution as a whole and many of the tens of thousands of graduates who have received their degrees from the very superior seat of education have developed into powerful leaders in New York City's life and elsewhere.

A magnificent new 18 story brick and stone building has just been completed at 23rd Street and Lexington Avenue (on the site where the original home of the College was first built) for a "down town" branch of the institution.

Founded 1847
Value of Property and Buildings—over $20,000,000
Number of Students (1931) over 20,000
President—Dr. Frederick B. Robinson

NEW "COMMERCE" BUILDING
23rd Street & Lexington Avenue

Wide World Studios

DR. FREDERICK B. ROBINSON

President of the College of the City of New York.

Dr. Robinson was born in Brooklyn, N. Y. Oct. 16th, 1883. He worked his way through college, graduating from the College of the City of New York in 1904. After teaching in the public schools in Brooklyn, he returned to the College of the City of New York as tutor in 1906. Dr. Robinson's career from that time on, was one of steady progress, becoming president of the college in 1927. Among the many high positions held by him in the meantime was that of President of the Association of Colleges and Universities of the state of New York, and chairman of The American Council on Education. He advocated, created, and organized many important innovations in educational, administrative and economic fields of activity, expressing his views on the public platform and as author and editor. Dr. Robinson is an enthusiastic supporter of art, outdoor life, welfare work, good government, and municipal integrity, and never loses an opportunity to serve in any capacity in which he can be of help.

51

FAMOUS NEW YORK CHURCHES

New York is religious—despite its many channels for sin.

Nowhere in the country are there more magnificent church buildings.

Nowhere in the world are there more eloquent and eminent Divines.

Whether Jewish, Catholic or Protestant, whether Christian Scientist, Episcopalian or Methodist, one can find a church home in New York where one can worship God according to one's own particular creed.

Even the Hindu, the Chinese, and the Moslems have their own places of worship in New York.

There are 1,588 churches in New York.

More than $250,000,000 is invested in church property.

Brooklyn alone has 587 churches.

In the following pages, we show only a few of the best known or outstanding churches.

Courtesy N. Y. Sun

Courtesy N. Y. Central Lines

CATHEDRAL OF ST. JOHN THE DIVINE

(Protestant Episcopal)

Amsterdam Avenue—from 111th to 113th Sts.

A MONUMENT TO ART, ARCHITECTURE, AND RELIGION

Third largest place of worship in the world.

Only exceeded by St. Peters at Rome, (area 227,069 sq. ft.) and Seville Cathedral at Seville, Spain (128,570 sq. ft.).

Front View

Side View

This monumental edifice, when completed, will be one of the most costly cathedrals in the world. It was begun on St. John's day, 1892. The nave of the church was almost completed in 1929 and under the aggressive leadership of Bishop Wm. T. Manning (see page 103) $13,000,000 has been raised during the past five years. It is estimated that the total cost will be over $30,000,000.

ST. PATRICK'S CATHEDRAL

(Roman Catholic)

Fifth Avenue—From 50th to 51st Streets.

Ass'd Val............$15,250,000

ONE OF THE MOST BEAUTIFUL CHURCHES EVER ERECTED BY MAN BUILT IN 1859

©Irving Underhill

A remarkable example of Gothic architecture and one of the world's famous cathedrals. It is estimated that over 25,000,-000 people have passed through its doors. Seating capacity, 2,500. Rectory and Cardinal's residence in the rear. Beneath the sanctuary (near the altar), is a crypt for the entombing of the archbishops of New York. The two spires are 330 feet high.

The cathedral has 37 most picturesque windows depicting the saints and scriptural subjects. The huge altar is of purest Italian marble inlaid with alabaster and precious jewels.

We are indebted to the N. Y. Evening Sun and N. Y. Central R. R. for pictures of St. John the Divine and to the Manhattan Post Card Co. for many pictures all through the book.

GRANDEST SYNAGOGUE IN AMERICA

Indescribably beautiful

Cost....................$6,000,000

Congregation Emanu-El is the result of a merging of Emanu-El and Temple Beth El, in 1927.

Congregation Emanu-El was organized in 1845, using as their first synagogue, the parlor floor of a house on Clinton St. In 1865 the corner of 5th Ave. and 43rd St. was purchased and occupied until 1927, the Lefcourt National Building replacing the old structure.

The Rabbis of Temple Emanu-El are the Reverend Dr. H. G. Enlow, Nathan Krauss and Samuel Schulman.

TEMPLE EMANU-EL (Jewish)
Fifth Avenue—N. E. Cor. 65th St.

RIVERSIDE CHURCH (Baptist)

Riverside Drive from 122nd to 123rd Streets.
Pastor, HARRY EMERSON FOSDICK (see page 102).
First Service held Sunday, October 5, 1930.

The conspicuously beautiful church that John D. Rockefeller, Jr., made possible. Two years were required to build it, as a fire during early construction necessitated extensive rebuilding. Riverside church cost over $4,000,000. The main entrance and interior will command attention for generations. The carillon of 72 bells is the largest in the world. Seats 2,500; 392 feet high; modern throughout.

ST. BARTHOLOMEW'S CHURCH
(Episcopal)
Park Avenue—50th St. to 51st St.

Approximate Cost, $5,400,000
Organized 1835—nearly 100 years ago.
St. Bartholomew's has an extreely wealthy congregation and does an institutional work that is far reaching in both scope and effectiveness.

ST. THOMAS' CHURCH (Episcopal)
Fifth Ave.—N. W. Cor. 53rd St.

Cost.........$2,225,000
Built...............1906
Founded...........1824

Incorporated 1824 — 108 years ago. Its first building was at Broadway & Houston St. The cornerstone of the original church on the present site was laid in 1868. In 1905 the building was destroyed by fire and the magnificent edifice now gracing the site was erected. Many fashionable weddings have been held here — a number of which included members of the English nobility. 1,800 pews.

FIRST CHURCH OF CHRIST SCIENCE
96th St. & Central Park West—N. W. Cor.
(Christian Science)

Cost over..$1,000,000
Built............1903
Church founded..1908

This exquisite building of granite and steel (costing far in excess of a million dollars) is only one of 25 Christian Science Churches in New York comprising the army of grateful beneficiaries who have been restored to health and happiness as a result of following the teachings of Mrs. Mary Baker Eddy.

It is most interesting to attend the Wednesday evening testimony meetings at 8 o'clock. Thousands joyfully testify to their deliverance from all kinds of so-called incurable diseases. All are welcome at these gatherings.

BROADWAY TEMPLE
(Methodist)
Broadway—From 174th to 175th Streets

Est. Cost........$6,000,000
725 ft. High   41 Stories

When completed, the Broadway Temple will rank as one of the greatest achievements in all church history.

The dynamic Dr. Christian F. Reisner—pastor of Broadway Temple not only conceived this stupendous undertaking but has been the prime mover in raising over $3,000,000 with which to start construction and a considerable portion of the huge building is already done.

Broadway Temple will be 41 stories in height with an immense church auditorium—seating several thousand. There will also be a social hall seating 1200, various Sunday School rooms, a gymnasium, swimming pool, billiard hall and other church-club features.

As a means of producing revenue, there will be over 450 rooms devoted to hotel and apartment use, also ground floor store rooms. Broadway Temple will be a small city in itself.

BROADWAY TABERNACLE
(Congregational)
211 W. 56th—N. E. Cor. Broadway

Valued at over $2,000,000
Founded in 1840

One of the largest and oldest Congregational Churches in America.

Built along French Gothic architectural lines, this imposing edifice ranks with the most beautiful churches in the city.

Photo by Hiram Myers

CHURCH OF THE HEAVENLY REST
(Liberal)
2 E. 90th St. & Fifth Ave.—S. W. Cor.
Directly across the street from beautiful Central Park.
Ass'd Val. $3,000,000.

One of the most magnificent churches in the country. The pastor—Dr. Henry Darlington (note picture) ranks with the most eloquent, most forceful and most respected Divines of the age. He preaches to the masses without regard to race, color or creed. His church is growing rapidly.

TEMPLE BETH EL
(Jewish)
15th Ave. & 48th St., Brooklyn

Cost.....................$500,000
Year Built....................1921
Seats.........................1872
Archts ....Shampan & Shampan

The most beautiful of the synagogues of Brooklyn and attended by Brooklyn's highest type Hebrews.

Notwithstanding the Jew and Gentile differ in many points of religious views, the rabbi's of Temple Beth El are most cordial in their welcome to those of all creeds, emphasizing that we all worship the same God and that we should not allow our differences in methods to make us narrow.

54

MANHATTAN CONGREGATIONAL CHURCH
AND HOTEL
MANHATTAN TOWERS
2166 Broadway at
76th St. N. E. Cor.

Built............1930
Cost over...$2,000,000

The Manhattan Congregational Church solved their problem of taxes by building the imposing skyscraper shown herewith.

The "Church" occupies the central portion of the main floor. The HOTEL MANHATTAN rents the balance of the building—600 rooms.

ST. PAUL THE APOSTLE
(Roman Catholic)
9th Avenue—59th to 60th Streets
Valued at over $1,000,000
Another famous old landmark and one of the oldest of the many interesting Catholic churches of New York.

ST. MARK'S
IN THE BOUWERIE
(Episcopal)
Tenth St. at 2nd Ave.

Valued at..$500,000
OLDEST CHURCH IN NEW YORK

In 1660, services were begun in a chapel built by Gov. Stuyvesant on this site and the cornerstone of the present building was laid in 1795. As time passed, however, and New York commenced to grow, a shiftless and slovenly element located in the neighborhood and St. Mark's faced serious problems. In 1911, the Rev. William N. Guthrie accepted

TRINITY CHURCH
(Episcopal)
Broadway—at the
head of Wall Street.

RICHEST CHURCH IN AMERICA

Ass'd Value $25,000,000

Trinity Church dates back to 1697 having been granted a charter at that time by King William III of England.

ST. PAUL'S CHAPEL
(Episcopal)
Broadway—Between
Fulton & Vesey Streets.

Ass'd Val....$6,600,000

On Oct. 31, 1931, St. Paul celebrated its 165th anniversary.

George Washington, the Prince of Wales, and many other notables of older days attended services in this famous old chapel.

a call to the church and things commenced to happen. Under his magnetic influence and aggresive leadership, St. Mark's has been brought to the fore as a power in church circles again. The neighborhood has been cleansed, and with beautiful new apartment buildings already erected, the district is becoming one of the most desirable residential sections of the city. It is unnecessary to add that Dr. W. N. Guthrie continues to be Pastor at St. Marks.

COMMUNITY CHURCH
and
APARTMENT BUILDING

10 Park Avenue—
N. W. Cor. 34th St.

Owned by the Community Church whose church home occupied this valuable corner for many years.

Instead of having the church auditorium within the building proper, as is the custom with church organizations who demolish their old structures and erect business buildings, the Community Church acquired land in the rear and erected an "annex" for their church activities. See Page 213 for details of 10 Park Avenue building.

NEW RAILROAD Y.M.C.A. BLDG.

To be completed in 1932.

Including 2 basements and pent house, this magnificent new home of New York's Railroad Y. M. C. A. will have 12 floors.

Equipped with every convenience and attraction known to modern Y. M. C. A. requirements, this will be one of the most ideal institutions of its kind in America. The former Railroad Y. M. C. A. building was on Park Avenue.

WEST SIDE Y.M.C.A.

5 West 63rd Street. Extends thru block to 64th St. Just a few steps west of Central Park.

Ass'd Val...$2,160,000

A 14 story palace with social rooms, 4 innovation rooms: (Log Cabin Room, Pirates Den, Farm House Attic and Totem Room), "little theatre," billiard hall (10 tables) 6 hand ball courts, gymnasium, swimming pool, 8,000 locker space, 600 sleeping rooms, and cafeteria.

SLOANE Y.M.C.A. HOUSE

356 W. 34th Street. Extends thru block to 33rd St. Between 8th & 9th Avenues.

Valued at.......$2,500,000

One of the most magnificent Y. M. C. A. buildings in all America. Made possible by gifts of the generous William Sloane who wished to erect a memorial for the benefit of young men, newly arrived in the city and members of the Army, Navy and Marine Corps.

Beautiful Modern, Complete—social rooms, gymnasium, baths, etc. The 12 upper floors are devoted to dormitories.

Y.W.C.A. CENTRAL HEADQUARTERS

610 Lexington Ave. Cor. 53rd St.

Ass'd Val. $3,450,000
Established 1870.

Principal buildings of Y. W. C. A. in New York:—

610 Lexington Ave.
341 E. 17th St.
124th & Lenox Ave.
501 W. 50th Ave.
179 W. 137th St.

Also 6 residences at
14 E. 16th St.
138 E. 38th St.
607 Hudson St.
175 E. 137th St.
210 E. 77th St.
132 E. 45th St.

Y.M.H.A.

Cor. 92nd St. and Lexington Ave.

Ass'd Val......$1,900,000

The Young Men's Hebrew Ass'n is to Hebrews what the Y. M. C. A. is to Gentiles—a club for young men, with influence for good as the outstanding objective of the directors.

Completed in 1930, and equipped with a wonderful gymnasium, bowling alleys, billiard rooms, library, cafeteria, dormitories, etc., also an auditorium (seating 900) pipe organ, stage for theatricals, etc.

Educational Departments offer courses in stenography and commercial. The Employment Department has secured positions for thousands.

THE SALVATION ARMY IN NEW YORK

120 West 14th Street—Extends through block to 13th Street

The picture at right shows one of the group of grand new buildings erected by the Salvation Army in New York.

COST $2,500,000

On the 13th Street front is the John and Martha Markle Memorial Residences for young business women accommodating 325 young women with an age limit of thirty-five, and a salary not exceeding $35.00 per week. Building is 17 stories high, equipped with a gymnasium, swimming pool, etc. The building facing 14th Street is used entirely for executive purposes as National and Territorial headquarters for the Army's activities. In this building however there is the beautiful "Centennial Memorial Temple," the main floor and balcony of which seats 1700. The stage seats 300 extra. A grand organ has just been installed by the Estey Organ Co. Architects—Voorhees Gmelin & Walker.

The Salvation Army—founded by General William Booth, has become one of the most powerful agencies for good in all the world. Non-sectarian, and not discriminating against race or color, its aim has been to preach the simple gospel of Jesus Christ, reclaim the sinner, help the needy, and reclaim the human derelict. They make a specialty of working in the streets ,the slums and the areas which the churches fail to reach and tens of thousands of those who were on the downward path or actually down and out have been helped to come back and are now well to do and respected members of society.

Any donation or benefaction to the Salvation Army is absolutely one of the BEST INVESTMENTS any one can make in life. The GOOD that this wonderful organization achieves is incalculable.

(Continued from page 3C)

WHAT ONE LONE MAN CAN ACCOMPLISH

The magnificent $4,000,000 building shown herewith, is only one of over 20 structurese rected in New York, involving close to $125,000,000 for which one man is responsible—Mr. A. E. Lefcourt, who from a newsboy on the street rose to the head of an organization in command of tens of millions of dollars and gave to New York a score of regal buildings. His right hand associate was Mr. Arthur Tarshis.

Ass'd Val........$4,000,000	
310 ft. high........27 F .oors	
Rent Area....410,000 sq. ft.	
Housing.............6,000	
Completed............1927	
Archt.Firm Ely Jacques Kahn	
Builder. .Lefcourt Realty Co.	

See Index showing a dozen of these Lefcourt palaces.

Mr. A. E. Lefcourt
(Photo by Mishkin)

LEFCOURT CLOTHING CENTER—275 Seventh Ave.

THE HOSPITALS OF NEW YORK

New York takes excellent care of its sick.

There are over 100 high-class hospitals on Manhattan Island alone (not counting Brooklyn, Queens or Richmond), capable of providing for nearly 150,000 patients at one time.

The hospitals of New York are not equalled elsewhere in all the world. Not only for size and completeness of appointment are these institutions famous, but also for the eminent surgeons and physicians who are connected with them. A great many of the larger hospitals have an ambulance service in constant readiness to answer calls for help. Training schools for nurses are also maintained. Many dispensaries and infirmaries are also located in various parts of the city for the treatment of the sick. It is the custom in the majority of these to charge a fee varying from ten cents in some to fifty cents in others. Of course this fee is waived if the patient is not able to pay. In fact, about 47% of those who avail themselves of New York's hospitals receive free treatment. This of course does not include work done in the dispensaries.

Medical Center, East Side Medical Center, and Bellevue Hospitals are three of the largest in the world.

In addition to the few hospital buildings shown here, and on following pages, there are many splendid Catholic, Jewish and other sectarian hospitals, maintained by the adherents of various religious faiths.

Photo by Underwood & Underwood

PRESBYTERIAN HOSPITAL OF NEW YORK

which combined with other hospital organizations, constitutes the great

NEW YORK MEDICAL CENTER

From Broadway to Riverside Drive, between 165th to 168th St.

Covers 21 acres. Cost $25,000,000. Most colossal hospital project in the world. "Medical Center" is a combination of eleven units including the Presbyterian Hospital (founded for the poor of New York without regard to race, color or creed and supported by voluntary contributions) the College of Physicians and Surgeons of Columbia University, Sloan Hospital for Women, Squier Urological Clinic, Harkness Private Pavilion, Vanderbilt Clinic, Maxwell Hall School of Nursing, Babies' Hospital, Neurological Institute, N. Y. State Psychiatric Institute and Hospital, and Columbia School of Surgery.

This gives to the world an unparalleled center for healing, teaching and research. At left in the picture is the N. Y. State Psychiatric Institute. In the center is the Neurological Institute and at the right are the huge buildings comprising the enormous Presbyterian Hospital and other units of the "Center"—several of which are hidden from view in the photo but which group alone cost over $15,000,000!

MEDICAL CENTER IS ONE OF THE BIG SIGHTS OF NEW YORK

NEW YORK-CORNELL HOSPITAL

Occupying 3 full squares 68th to 71st Streets.
Between York Ave. and Exterior Streets—
overlooking East River.

Also known as
EAST SIDE MEDICAL CENTER

Photo by Ritt~ce

COST
NEARLY
$15,000,000

A
GROUP
OF 14
MODERN
BUILDINGS

Main building is 26 stories—400 feet high. Has several ten-story wings which afford vast areas of space. Ground broken in June, 1929. Grand opening November, 1932.

In August, 1929, the City ceded East 69th St. between York and Exterior to the hospital for $250,000, which land became part of the building site. The bulk of the land was acquired thru gifts and bequests of the late Harry Payne Whitney, John D. Rockefeller, Jr., and others. J. P. Morgan, Vice-President of the Lying-in Hospital (one of the institutions to be removed to the center), gave $2,000,000 to endow the maternity work. Sunken gardens, roof gardens, nurses' homes, various subway tunnels and a dozen innovations and features all combine in what will be one of the world's most stupendous hospital organizations. Coolidge, Shipley & Bullfinch, Architects. Marc Eidlitz & Son, Builders.

---

4 OTHER MAGNIFICENT BIG HOSPITALS
Each of them costing up in seven figures

BELLEVUE HOSPITAL
Foot of E. 25th St. Covers nearly four squares.
City owned. Ass'd Val..........$10,125,000

MT. SINAI HOSPITAL
1 East 100th Street.
Ass'd Val., $4,125,000.............671 beds

ST. LUKE'S HOSPITAL
Amsterdam Ave. from 113th to 114th Streets.
Extending through to Morningside Drive.
Cost $5,575,000....................614 beds

ROOSEVELT HOSPITAL
9th Avenue, 58th to 59th Sts.
Ass'd Val., $4,450,000....... .....400 beds

M. Rosenbluth

BETH ISRAEL HOSPITAL
Stuyvesant Park—East
Cost $5,500,000
Founded 1889
501 beds

LYING-IN HOSPITAL
2d Ave. 17th to 18th Sts.
Cost $1,680,000
156 beds for mothers
127 beds for babies

FIFTH AVENUE HOSPITAL
5th Ave. and 105th St.
Cost $3,000,000
37,000 patients yearly
310 Beds

LENOX HILL HOSPITAL
Lexington to Park Ave.
76th to 77th St.
Main unit in new buildings costing $5,000,000.

POST GRADUATE HOSPITAL
2nd Ave. from 20th to 21st Sts.

Assd. Val. $1,100,000
Founded 1882
Ten operating rooms with an average of 30 operations daily. 400 beds.

OTHER LARGE OR VERY EFFICIENT HOSPITALS

Babies' Hospital of the City of New York
167th St. and Broadway. (Inc. 1887).
Broad Street Hospital, Broad and South Sts.
Brooklyn Hospital, Raymond and De Kalb Avenues
City Hospital (Welfare Island)
Coney Island Hospital, Ocean Parkway and Avenue Z.
Cumberland Hospital, 109 Cumberland Street, Brooklyn.
Doctors Hospital, East End Ave. and 87th St.
French Hospital and Dispensary, 324 West 30th St.
Jewish Hospital, Classon and St. Marks Aves., Brooklyn.
Kings County Hospital, Clarkson Avenue, Brooklyn.
Long Island College Hospital, Henry and Pacific Sts., Bklyn.
Manhattan Maternity and Dispensary, 327 East 60th St.
Manhattan State Hospital on Ward's Island.
Midtown Hospital, formerly New York Throat, Nose and
Lung Hospital, 315 East 49th St.
Neurological Institute of New York, Haven Ave. and 168th St.
New York Dispensary, (Org. 1790), 34-36 Spring St.
New York Ear and Eye Infirmary, 218 *Second Avenue.*
New York Nursery and Child's Hospital, 161 West 61st Street
New York Skin and Cancer Hospital, cor. 19th St. & 2d Ave.
Radium Institute of New York, 323 Riverside Drive
St. Vincent's Hospital, Seventh Ave. and 11th St.
Woman's Hospital in the State of New York, 141 W. 109th St.

FLOWER HOSPITAL
450 East 64th St. at York Ave.

Cost $2,000,000
228 Beds
Founded 1890

HOSPITAL FOR RUPTURED AND CRIPPLED CHILDREN
321 E. 42nd St.
As'dVal. $2,300,000

One of the *great* hospitals of New York.
250 Beds

A FEW OF NEW YORK'S PHILANTHROPIES

New York is famed for the generous benefactions of its wealthy citizens and the many philanthropic institutions and organizations founded for the welfare and general betterment of mankind.

In no place in the entire world have such enormous sums been donated or such zeal manifested in considering our fellowmen, as in New York. John D. Rockefeller, Edward Harkness, Adolph Lewisohn, James Speyer, Cornelius Bliss, August Heckscher, Felix Warburg, and scores of other successful men of the wonder city have donated vast sums of money and unlimited time to alleviating distress, or creating endowments for the furtherance of education, science, art, research, improved living conditions, more ideal social relationships and better civic conditions.

Here are two outstanding philanthropic institutions of the Wonder City.

"THE RUSSELL SAGE FOUNDATION"
S. W. Cor. Lexington & 22nd Street—Estimated Cost $1,000,000.

New Annex

Founded in 1907 as a result of a $15,000,000 benefaction of Mrs. Margaret Olivia Sage to be used for the improvement of social and living conditions in the United States. In addition to the very laudable work the Foundation has done, schools for the training of social workers, the placing of orphan children in good homes, and the agitation for better facilities in public education, constitute activities wherein great good has already been accomplished. The Foundation maintains a library of more than 120,000 books and pamphlets on the subject of social studies which is free to all.

SCOPE OF WORK

Prevent infant mortality.
Improvement of child health.
Re-unite or prevent broken families.
Encourage ideal home life.
Improve conditions of women's work.
Stimulate idea of employees representation in management.
Discourage and prevent strikes.
Provide for public recreation.
Prevent crime and more effective care of delinquents.
Stop the "loan shark" evil.
Encourage every reform for the betterment of mankind.

The Foundation also maintains a publishing department and issues in book or pamphlet form the results of investigation and findings which every citizen interested in the public welfare should read. Write to them for a list of same. The Russell Sage Foundation is doing a grand work, and is one of the most outstanding agencies for good in the entire city.

During 1932, the magnificent new granite and brick Annex shown at left was completed, adding much needed extra space for the helpful activities of the institution.

ROCKEFELLER INSTITUTE
York Avenue to Exterior Street—at 66th Street

ROCKEFELLER FOUNDATION
(General Offices at 61 Broadway)

Both of these great institutions were made possible by the generous donations of John D. Rockefeller.

Untold benefit to the world at large has resulted from the great research work carried on by the "Foundation" and the "Institute's" activities have been far reaching also.

Mr. Rockefeller's original endowment was $100,000,000. To date, donations have been increased to $75,000,000— just to the Foundation alone.

Above—Main Building of the Rockefeller Institute.
Below—Air view of group of buildings devoted to research work, training of doctors and nurses, etc.

Here are only a few of the achievements:
   Control of malaria in vast sections.
   Eradication of yellow fever in vast sections.
   Control of hook worm diseases.
   Tuberculosis combatted with wonderful results,
   Etc., etc., etc.

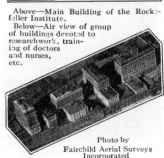

Photo by
Fairchild Aerial Surveys
Incorporated

A FEW OF NEW YORK'S POPULAR CLUBS

There are over 1,000 recognized clubs listed in the telephone directories of New York—in addition to the innumerable private, social and business clubs.

New Yorkers attach tremendous importance to friendly intercourse.

It has been said that the most miserable man in the world is one who has no friends.

There are few "miserable men" in New York—if gauged by the number of its clubs and their colossal combined memberships.

Nearly all New York clubs have a limited membership—consequently many of them have long waiting lists.

The Union Club pictured on next page, has recently sold its old home, and is building a magnificent new club house on Park Avenue at 69th Street, costing over $850,000.

It is reported that no two clubs in the world equal the New York Athletic Club (pictured below), and the Down-town Athletic Club (shown on next page), either in cost, equipment, membership or size. Both of these buildings are modern palaces.

The Union League Club is reputed to be the most famous club in all America. It is certainly one of the most modern and beautiful.

Mere membership in the Union League Club, the Metropolitan Club, the University, Union, and New York Yacht Clubs, as well as several other similarly aristocratic club organizations, carries with it both prestige and distinction.

It is very difficult to secure entry into many New York clubs, as a censorship of strictest discrimination is exercised, and closest investigation of a prospect's character, standing and general ethics employed.

Fully a hundred New York clubs own their own homes.

New York is unquestionably the greatest "Club" city in Christendom.

NEW YORK ATHLETIC CLUB

7th Avenue and 59th Street—N. E. Cor. between 6th and 7th Avenues.

Ass'd Val. $5,350,000
Completed, 1930   22 floors

Reputed to be the most sumptuous, most thoroughly equipped and most generously patronized athletic club in the world.

In this magnificent new club house opened in 1930 (having outgrown its former quarters at 59th St. near Sixth Avenue), will be found space or equipment for all forms of athletic exercise or diversion known. Here is the last word in gymnasium apparatus, hand ball courts, squash courts, boxing ring, etc., all the way to its immense and beautiful swimming pool.

At "Travers Island" (on Long Island Sound), the Club maintains its own "Country Club" where an enormous Club House, with yacht landing and spacious grounds for baseball teams and other outdoor sports, afford ideal facilities for every branch of athletic and social activities.

We are indebted to the Edison Co. of N. Y. for picture of N. Y. Athletic Club.

DOWN TOWN ATHLETIC CLUB

18 West Street—Just north of the Battery.

Ass'd Val. $4,000,000
534 feet high....... 40 Floors
Completed 1930
Arch., Starrett & Van Vleck
Bldrs., Thompson-Starrett Co., Inc.

The only way to realize the grandeur, the completeness and the varied range of equipment and provision for every kind of athletic activity and social entertainment is to visit this structure from basement to tower and inspect the various floors devoted to the specific sports or forms of exercise patronized by its members.

Within three minutes of the Wall Street district and only half a block from Battery Park with its delightful sea breezes and commanding view, the 20 floors devoted to living quarters for members make the Down Town Club an ideal home for men who are free from family cares and in a position to enjoy the last word in luxurious living.

The Union Club has sold this property and is building a grand new home on Park Ave. and 69th

UNION LEAGUE CLUB

Park Ave. at 37th St.—S. W. Cor.

Ass'd Val. $1,750,000
Founded 1863
Membership Fee $300
Annual Dues $175
About 750 men.bers

One of the most famous clubs in America. Organized for the purpose of encouraging genuine patriotism. Republican in politics. The magnificent new club house shown above was opened Feb. 1931—the club's old home at 37th and Fifth Ave. having been sold to make way for another business skyscraper.

There are few clubs in the world as well known as the Union League, or more highly respected.

UNION CLUB

Fifth Ave.—60th St.—N. E. Cor.

Ass'd Val. $3,000,000
Founded in 1836
Membership Fee $300
Annual Dues $200
About 300 members

Organized by the descendants of the Knickerbocker family. The oldest and most exclusive club in New York. The above building was erected in 1902 and has been the center of the club's activities for 30 years. Membership in this aristocratic organization is very difficult to secure and is very highly prized.

METROPOLITAN CLUB

Fifth Ave. & 60th St. N. E. Cor.

Ass'd Val. $3,250,000
Founded 1891
Membership Fee $300
Annual Dues $225
About 300 members

Frequently called the "Millionaires Club." Its exclusive membership is c a r e f u l l y guarded, and membership in the Metropolitan Club is esteemed most highly.

The building is of white marble, a n d magnificently furnished. McKim, Mead and White are the architects. Few clubs in the world compare with the Metropolitan in point of wealth, distinction, and clientele.

UNIVERSITY CLUB
1 West 54th Street
N. W. Cor. Fifth Ave.

Ass'd Val............$4,700,000
Organized in..............1865
Membership Fee..........$200
Annual Dues.............$100
Building completed........1900
Archts...McKim, Mead & White

Club maintains a very valuable library and one of its aims is the encouragement of good literature.

Only those who have University degrees are eligible to membership.

Chas. T. Wells, builder.

NEW YORK YACHT CLUB
37 W. 44th Street
Just west of Fifth Avenue

Ass'd Val.............$645,000
Organized................1844

Built on land donated by J. Pierpont Morgan.

Oldest yacht club in America. Has limited membership, and noted for its aristocratic exclusiveness, yet liberal patronage of any worthy movement.

The names of many of New York's most famous men will be found on both old and present rosters.

NATIONAL ARTS CLUB
15 Gramercy Park
Half block east of 20th St. and Fourth Avenue.

Ass'd Val.............$525,000
Organized................1898
Membership over.........1600
Membership Fee..........$100
Dues.....................$80

The club purchased this magnificent old home of Samuel J. Tilden and acquired the property in the rear—through to 19th Street, on which they erected an annex of 12 stories thus permitting its members to have studios right in the club building.

Organized to encourage art in all its phases—painting, sculpture, literary work, music, etc. Membership however is not confined to artists, many prominent business men belong.

CENTURY ASSOCIATION
7 W. 43rd Street
Just a step from Fifth Avenue

Ass'd Val.............$900,000
Organized in.............1847
Membership fee........$115.00
Annual dues.............$90.00
Building completed........1919
Archt...McKim, Mead & White

Club maintains library, picture gallery and restaurant.

Encourages literature and art. Members consist largely of literary men, painters, and sculptors. The Century Association has many men of national reputation on its roster.

LOTOS CLUB
110 W. 57th Street

Ass'd Val.............$850,000

Founded in 1870 with a membership consisting largely of literary men.

House built in 1909.

Many elaborate social functions are held at the Lotos Club and the ladies who attend insist that the "Lotos is the nicest club in town."

RACQUET & TENNIS CLUB
370 Park Ave.—at 52nd St.

Ass'd Val...........$2,775,000

One of the most beautiful club buildings in the city with a most aristocratic membership interested in tennis, racquet and other sports.

Architects, McKim, Mead & White.

THREE COLLEGE CLUBS

YALE CLUB
44th St. & Vanderbilt Ave.—
N. W. Corner

Ass'd Val..........$2,000,000

Home of Yale College Alumni. Membership over 1,700. Initiation fee $30. Annual dues $50. Attractive Club Rooms, Library, etc., plus the old Yale spirit. Many "Old Eli" graduates make their homes in the huge building.

HARVARD CLUB
27 W. 44th St.—near 5th Ave.

Ass'd Val..........$1,700,000

Founded Nov. 3, 1865. Incorporated 1887. Supported by the Harvard Alumni. Over 6,400 members. Property on which club building is erected was purchased in 1892, additional ground was bought and now extends through block to 43rd St.

FRATERNITIES CLUB
22 E. 38th St.—S. E. Cor. Madison Ave.

Ass'd Val..........$1,500,000

This palatial structure known as the "Fraternity Club Building," is also the home of Cornell Alumni. Card rooms, a well stocked library and excellent cafe insure a generous attendance of members at all times.

ENGINEERS CLUB
32 W. 40th St.—near 5th Ave.

Es't Val..........$1,200,000

Organized Feb. 3, 1888.

Initiation fee $200, annual dues $80.

Membership largely confined to legitimate engineers and those interested in engineering.

An excellent cafe, also living quarters for members.

B. P. O. E.—ELKS CLUB
108 W. 43rd St.—East of Bway.

Ass'd Val..........$1,250,000

One of the finest lodge homes in all Elkdom. New York headquarters of "Benevolent Protective Order of Elks" always has its latch string open to visiting brothers from other lodges where a cordial welcome awaits them.

LAMBS CLUB
128 W. 44th St.—East of Bway.

Ass'd Val.......... $630,000

The club home of the most famous actors of the American stage. This popular club is known the world over for its cheery hospitality and the many "good times" so continually had here. Building was completed 1905. Architects—McKim, Mead & White.

ADVERTISING CLUB

23 Park Ave.
N. E. Cor. 35th St.

Ass'd Val. $345,000

Club home of New York's leading advertising men. Membership however is not confined to those actually engaged in the advertising business. Many of the city's most prominent men, including a number of national advertisers, have their names on the roster and are frequent attendants.

AMER. WOMEN'S ASSOCIATION

CLUB HOUSE 353 W. 57th St.
Cor. 9th Avenue
Extends thru block to 58th St.

Cost $8,000,000

30 floors — Built in 1929

In building this magnificent structure New York women have established one of the most charming and ideal club homes for "members" in all the country.

From the fully-equipped gymnasium in the basement to the airy roof gardens atop, it meets every demand of the modern woman for ideal living quarters and club life.

COSMOPOLITAN CLUB'S NEW HOME

at 122 to 124 E. 66th St.

The Cosmopolitan Club is one of the most delightful social organizations in New York, and as its name implies, has members from all parts of the world. Their new home (pictured above) will be one of the most beautiful in the city when completed.

THE BARBIZON

140 E. 63rd St.
S. E. Cor. Lexington Ave.

A residence for students of Art, Music, Drama or Business Women.

Cost $4,000,000
22 Floors.........Built 1927
Archt...Laurence Emmons Inc.

TWO MAGNIFICENT RESIDENCE - HOTELS FOR WOMEN.— WITH CLUB ADVANTAGES.

THE BARBIZON has delightful bed-sitting rooms, spacious lounges, Recital Hall with stage and organ, Swimming P o o l, Gymnasium, Squash Courts, Solarium, etc. etc. —Very moderate rates.

THE PANHELLENIC appeals especially to college women. Has grand ball room (stage and balcony) with 600 seats, a roof garden, a laundry on each floor provided with tubs, dryer, electric irons (where one may do one's own wash). Every room an "outside" room. In Panhellenic Annex apartments for men and women both.

VISITORS ALWAYS WELCOME

PANHELLENIC TOWER

3 Mitchell Place
Cor. 1st Ave. & 49th St.

Cost $1,600,000
293 ft. high....28 Floors
Built 1928
Archt. John Mead Howell
Bldr. ..Hegeman Harris

66

NEW YORK THEATRES
MOVING PICTURE PALACES, ETC.

New York is the amusement center of the world. Even the Ringling circus starts its season in New York. It "shows" a full month every spring at Madison Square Garden.

Nearly all successful musical comedies, dramas and moving picture productions have their premieres in New York.

Over 1,000,000 people can be seated in New York's amusement places at one time.

It is said that the New York Theatre Market is composed of 17,500,000 persons who spend over 63 millions of dollars annually for theatrical and moving picture entertainment.

The Commissioner of the Department of Licenses showed *two years* ago a total of 815 theatres with a seating capacity of 962,280. 243 licensed theatres, seating 415,682, and 572 licensed motion picture houses, seating 546,598.

METROPOLITAN OPERA HOUSE
Broadway from 39th to 40th Sts. through to 7th Avenue. Covers entire square.

Ass'd Val............$6,900,000
Completed...............1883
Seats............... ...3,366

BELASCO THEATER
115 W. 44th St.—Just east of Broadway.

Ass'd Val.............$780,000
Completed...............1907
Seats...................1,000

New York's grand old Metropolitan Opera House (shown above) was opened in 1883 and is exclusively devoted to Grand Opera. Practically every great singer of the world for the past 48 years has sung before its immense audiences. The wealth and elite of the city, and lovers of classical music generally, have supported the great institution liberally, season after season. "The Metropolitan" is famous the world over.

Immediately below the "Metropolitan" is shown the famous Belasco Theatre. In this building, the lamented David Belasco had his studio and general offices.

The Belasco has been the Mecca to which histrionic talent has aspired, and from which many of America's most prominent actors and actresses started on their road to fame. Here is the scene of many of Mr. Belasco's greatest triumphs as a producer, which won for him the title of "Dean of the American stage."

The picture shown at bottom of page is the home of the famous Ziegfeld Productions, one of the most modern and beautiful theatres in New York. Built, 1927. Here is where "Rio Rita," the "Show Boat," and other big Ziegfeld hits played to capacity houses for months running. Here is where Mr. Ziegfeld selects his beautiful girls and prepares them for "glorification." Ziegfeld productions are always as gorgeous as money and skill can provide.

We are indebted to the Manhattan Post Card Company for pictures of the Metropolitan and Belasco, and many other pictures in this book.

©American Photo Service, Inc.

ZIEGFELD THEATER
1341 Sixth Ave.—
N. W. Cor. 54th St.

Ass'd Val..........$1,530,000
Completed...............1927
Seats...................1,650

SHUBERT THEATRE
225 W. 44th St.—just west of Broadway

```
Ass'd Val. ............$1,400,000
Built ........................1912
Seats ......................1,400
```

One of the many houses owned, controlled or managed by the Shuberts whose commanding position in the theatrical world has never wavered in over twenty years.

IRVING BERLIN'S MUSIC BOX
239 W. 45th St.—just west of Broadway

```
Cost ....................$1,000,000
Built ........................1921
Seats ......................1,005
```

"Wise chaps" shook their heads and predicted that this house would never pay. But Irving Berlin just smiled. The first production alone made a profit of close to $400,000!

GUILD THEATRE
253 W. 52nd St.—near Broadway

```
Est. Val. ................$850,000
Built ........................1925
Seats ........................934
```

Where the Theatre Guild sponsors plays of *merit* with the idea of artistic production rather than the consideration of box office receipts.

PALACE THEATRE
1564 Broadway. Between 46th & 47th Sts.

```
Ass'd Val. ............$1,800 000
Built ........................1913
Seats ......................1,800
```

From its opening night the "Palace" has played to full houses, as the cream of the entire vaudeville profession comprise the weekly bill.

ETHEL BARRYMORE THEATRE
243 W. 47th St. Just off of B'dway
```
Ass'd Val. ............$700,000
Built ........................1928
Seats ......................1,090
```
One of the most popular and best patronized theaters in the Great White Way district.

ALBEE THEATRE
7 DeKalb Ave., Brooklyn
```
Cost ................$5,000 000
Built ........................1925
Seats ......................2,000
```
At the time of completion, reputed to be the most magnificent theater in the world. Rare paintings, costly tapestries and every luxury.

Chanin's Beautiful
BILTMORE THEATRE
261 W. 47th St.
Ass'd Val. $505,000
One of the *class* theatres of the Great White Way District

Interior view of the new $4,500,000
EARL CARROLL THEATRE
S. W. Cor. 50th St. at 7th Ave.

HOME OF EARL CARROLL'S VANITIES

Over 3,000 can be seated —thus enabling popular prices.

SOME OF THE NEW INNOVATIONS

Auditorium enclosed with metal doors, preventing late arrivals from disturbing the audience.
Disappearing orchestra.
Also all parts of stage may be raised or lowered.
"Spectators' Box"— back of stage.
"Official Box" for royalty or notable guests.

```
Built 1931
Archt.......Geo. Keister
Bldr., M. Shapiro & Son
Mgr...Norman S. Carroll
```

ROXY THEATRE
N. E. Cor. 50th St. & Seventh Ave.—
A few steps east of Broadway.

THE MOST MAGNIFICENT MOTION PICTURE HOUSE IN ANY CITY, OR ANY COUNTRY, ANYWHERE

Assessed Value......................$4,700,000
Built.........1927   Seats........4,000

Not only the most gorgeous "Movie" House in the world, but presenting the most elaborate spectacles and extravaganza produced on any stage. An orchestra of over 100 expert musicians, close to a thousand performers, and a fortune spent in costuming and scenery every week! In addition to these indescribably beautiful and collossal performances, classics of the screen are included in the daily program. The immense house seats 4,000 and yet the sign "Standing Room Only" is so often displayed that patrons have learned the wisdom of going early.

PARAMOUNT THEATRE

Broadway from 43rd to 44th Streets.

Ass'd Val....$15,100,000
Built.............1927
Seats............4,000

New York home of Paramount Pictures. Gorgeous foyer and exquisitely beautiful interior theatre. Like one of the sumptuous palaces described in old Arabian Nights tales. Wonderful entertainment staged in connection with the motion pictures shown.

CAPITOL THEATRE

1645 Bdwy.
S. W. Cor.
51st Street.

Grand Stairway

Ass'd Val.
$3,450,000

Built
1920

Seats
5,400

At time built the CAPITOL was the greatest moving picture house in the country,

Showing Immense Seating Capacity

The greatest moving picture theatre in the country at the time it was opened and still setting a pace which makes newer "movie" palaces work overtime to equal the stupendous spectacles and delightful entertainment that has made the CAPITOL so popular with the pleasure loving public. A symphony orchestra of close to 100 musical artists, trained ballets, and first run pictures.

Average weekly attendance over 100,000.

NEW YORK and CRITERION

Extending full block on Broadway from 44th to 45th Streets.

Ass'd Val...........$5,300,000

Designed and built by Oscar Hammerstein. In the nineties this was one of the nation's grandest theatre buildings.

THE STRAND
1579 Broadway—N. W. Cor. 47th Street.

Ass'd Val.............$4,000,000
Completed.................1914
Seats.....................3,200

The Strand was the first deluxe moving picture palace of New York.

From its opening night, this beautiful "movie" house has been famous for its great orchestra—every member of which is an individual artist.

New York's first picture house to offer extravanganza and feature bills. The house is now controlled by Warner Bros.

THE RIVOLI
1620 Broadway—Between 49th & 50th Streets.

Ass'd Val......................$1,900,000
Completed...........................1917
Seats..............................2,206

One of the highest class strictly motion picture houses in all America, where an air of quiet elegance and refinement attract the high type "movie" clientele of the city. Every feature picture shown is linked with a faithful portrayal of atmosphere analogeous with the theme or story of the picture itself.

THE RIALTO
N. E. Cor. 42nd St. & 7th Ave.—Opposite Times Sq. Bldg.

Ass'd Val..................$3,225,000
Completed.....................1899
Seats.........................2,020

Occupies the site of the famous old "Hammerstein Roof Garden." Over 25,000,000 people have patronized the Rialto. "Roxy" was the "Rialto's" first manager. The first symphonic orchestra was a Rialto innovation. Practically every screen star and theatrical head liner has appeared in person at the Rialto, which continues to play to packed houses.

One of the many "Loew" theatres in New York.

LOEW'S 175th STREET THEATRE
175th Street and Broadway.

Built 1930, and seating 3,441, Loew's 175th Street Theatre is a sample of some of the magnificent million dollar motion picture theatres scattered all over New York.

NEW YORKER
(Formerly the famous "GALLO THEATRE") 254 W. 54th St. between Broadway & 8th Ave.

Ass'd Val......$1,220,000
Seats..............1,290

The theatre is one of the most beautiful in the city.

Also the home of the
WIVEL RESTAURANT

The great rendezvous of New York's higher type Scandinavian.

The WIVEL Cooks Food
DELICIOUSLY!

NEW FOX ACADEMY
126 E. 14th St. near 3rd Ave.

Ass'd Val. over....$1,210,000
Completed............1927
Seats................2,500

THE BIG "FOX" THEATRE OF NEW YORK

One of the million dollar movie palaces outside the Great White Way section.

The Famous Old
WINTER GARDEN
1646 Broadway—Cor. 50th St.
Now controlled by Warner Bros. as a moving picture palace.

Ass'd Val....$2,650,000
Built............1911
Seats............1,573

For over a quarter of a century, one of New York's most famous homes of extravaganza and "million dollar" productions until taken over by Warner Bros. It was at the Winter Garden that Al Jolson, the Dolly Sisters, Marilyn Miller and many other stage stars won their way to fame.

One of the Radio Keith Orpheum houses opened in 1930 on the site of the famous old Columbia Burlesque House. Built as nearly perfect for sound production as modern skill makes possible.

MAYFAIR THEATRE
N. E. Cor. 7th Ave. & 47th Street.

Ass'd Val....$1,900,000
Rebuilt............1930
Seats............2,300

TWO OF THE FIVE DELUXE NEW YORK THEATRES CONTROLLED BY THE WELL-KNOWN WARNER BROTHERS IN NEW YORK

Warner Bros. have proven themselves wizards in the motion picture world. This enterprising trio were first in the field with *Talking* Pictures and in less than ten years have risen from comparative obscurity to a supreme position in the great industry. They have not only won international renown as producers but as operators of strictly high class theatres all over the country. In New York Warner Bros. control:

THE STRAND
THE WINTER GARDEN
THE BEACON
THE HOLLYWOOD THEATRE
WARNER BROS. THEATRE

WARNER BROS. THEATRE
1664 Broadway.

Ass'd Val....$1,010,000
Rebuilt............1927
Seats............1,200

HOLLYWOOD THEATRE
1641 Broadway— Cor. 51st St.

Ass'd Val....$3,250,000
Built............1930
Seats............1,210

FOUR FAMOUS HALLS OF NEW YORK

CARNEGIE HALL
154 W. 57th St.— S. E. Cor. 7th Ave.
Ass'd Val...$3,000,000
Built............1891
Seats............2,800

STEINWAY HALL
109 W. 54th St.
Near 7th Ave.
Ass'd Val.....$2,875,000
Built..............1924
Art. Warren & Wetmore

AEOLIAN HALL
N. E. Cor. 5th Ave. & 54th St.
Ass'd Val...$2,850,000
Built..............1926
Art. Warren & Wetmore

TOWN HALL
123 W. 43rd St.— East of Broadway.
Ass'd Val......$1,075,000
Built..1922 Seats..1500
Art.. McKim, Mead & White

THE NEWSPAPERS OF NEW YORK

Over 5,000,000 New York newspapers are printed daily, sales amounting to almost $100,000—ten million pennies!

One New York newspaper has a circulation of 1,400,000 daily!

New Yorkers are great patronizers of the daily press.

Thousands take two and three morning papers, then buy "evening" papers all through the day keeping in touch with market reports, baseball scores and other special activities.

The New York Press is the greatest disseminator of news in the world and there is a constant contest on the part of the publishers for circulation.

All the big Press Associations of the country have their headquarters in New York, and the big Syndicating Companies are all New York institutions or have New York headquarters.

Papers are printed in nearly fifteen different tongues in New York—a number of them being dailies.

Practically every known field of activity is covered by New York papers and periodicals—financial, religion, sporting, legal, theatrical, and almost every trade known. Nearly 300 Trade Papers alone are published in New York.

Over $200,000,000 is invested in New York's publishing plants.

NEW YORK TIMES "ANNEX"
229 West 43rd St. Just west of Broadway
Founded 1851

The New York TIMES has become world-famous as a result of its policy in printing "All the News that's Fit to Print." In politics the TIMES is an independent morning paper. Circulation, over 475,000 daily and over 775,000 Sunday.

The TIMES caters to New York's very best element of readers and is recognized as America's greatest newspaper. It is read in nearly all the better class homes of this eastern country, as well as all over the world, and is more frequently quoted abroad than any other newspaper in America —see picture of Mr. Ochs, the publisher on page 206.

Ass'd Val	$3,050,000
221 ft. high	20 Floors
Completed	1912-1924-1931
Owners	N. Y. Times Co.
Arch	Ludlow & Peabody and firm of Ely Jacques Kahn
Bldrs	Geo. A. Fuller Co.

NEW YORK AMERICAN AND EVENING JOURNAL BUILDING
210 South St.—facing East River

All the Hearst papers are independent in politics, and dominate circulation in almost every city where published. Hearst papers employ tens of thousands. Hearst papers circulate over 5,500,000 Sundays and over 5,400,000 daily.

Hearst papers are published in 18 cities: New York, Boston, Chicago, San Francisco, Los Angeles, Pittsburgh, Detroit, Milwaukee, Atlanta, Seattle, Albany, San Antonio, Rochester, Baltimore, Oakland, Washington, Syracuse and Omaha.

Mr. Hearst also publishes many nationally known magazines including the COSMOPOLITAN.

Ass'd Val	$1,800,000
6 Floors	
Space	244,800 sq. ft.
Built	1927
Owner, N.Y. Eve. Journ. Inc.	
Archt	Chas. E. Birge
Bldr	Turner Const Co.

NEW YORK HERALD TRIBUNE BUILDING
230 W. 41st St.—Just west of 7th Ave.
Through block to 40th St.

Building assessed at $2,600,000
HERALD founded 1839
TRIBUNE founded 1841
Papers merged 1924
Circulation HERALD TRIBUNE Sunday 440,000

A morning "paper"   Daily   300,000
Politics—Republican

For many years James Gordon Bennett's HERALD and Whitelaw Reid's TRIBUNE were two of the outstanding dailies in all newspaperdom, and the consolidation of these two famous sheets under the masterful leadership of Mr. Ogden Reid has placed the HERALD-TRIBUNE among the leading newspapers of the world.

NEW YORK SUN BUILDING
280 Broadway—From Chambers to Reade Sts.

Ass'd Val. $3,250,000
SUN founded 1833
Circulation 304,000
an evening paper
Politics—Independent

The Sun, was started in 1833 at 222 William Street under the editorship and ownership of Benj. H. Day. After various transfers it was purchased in 1916 by the late Frank A. Munsey. After Mr. Munsey's death it was purchased by William T. Dewart who under plan of mutualization has made it one of the great papers of the country. The Sun Building was originally known as the Stewart Building having been built by that great merchant in 1845. In 1928 it was purchased by Mr. Dewart as a permanent home for the Sun and renamed the Sun Building. It occupies a site overlooking City Hall and its surrounding park and is one of the landmarks of lower New York.

NEW YORK WORLD-TELEGRAM BLDG.
Barclay and Wests Streets

World founded 1861
Telegram founded 1867
Papers merged Feb. 1931
Circulation 350,000
Politics Independent
An evening paper

The Scripps-Howard Co. secured control of the TELEGRAM in 1927 and the WORLD in 1931. The *Telegram* was built up from a wavering financial uncertainty into one of the soundest institutions in New York's newspaper field, and with the acquisition of the WORLD in February 1931, the WORLD-TELEGRAM is already a powerful factor in moulding public opinion—commanding the attention and respect of all who read it.

NEW DOWN-TOWN PLANT OF WORLD-TELEGRAM
Barclay and West Streets

Ass'd Val. $1,500,000

WORLD BLDG.
53 Park Row at Brooklyn Bridge
Val. $3,000,000
357 ft. high
Built 1888

The WORLD printed its last issue in February, 1931. Started in 1861 by Joseph Pulitzer it forged to the front as one of the outstanding democratic sheets of the country, but due to various causes after the death of its founder, the paper failed to pay in recent years, and was taken over by the Scripps-Howard interests. The price paid was something around $5,000,000.

NEW YORK EVENING POST BUILDING

75 West St. thru Block to Washington St.

Paper founded 1801
Circulation 100,833
An evening paper
Politics ....Ind.-Republican

Mr. Cyrus H. K. Curtis, present owner of the *Evening Post* (also owner of Philadelphia's great *Saturday Evening Post*) has built up this sheet into the favorite evening paper of a constantly increasing clientele of New York's better class who consider the *Evening Post* editorially sound and always reliable.

Ass'd Val. $3,500,000
229 ft. high.....20 Floors
Year Built 1926
Owner Eve. Post Rlty. Corp.
Archt. ..Horace Trumbauer
Bldr. ..Thompson-Starrett Co.

THE NEWS

220 E. 42nd St.—extending thru to 41st St.
With enormous 10 story "L," to 2nd Ave.

SEE PAGE 232 FOR DATA CONCERNING BUILDING

The *News* is New York's first "tabloid" sheet.

When Mr. Joseph Medill Patterson started this paper in New York (June, 1919), he little visioned the tremendous success his experiment of furnishing a pictorial daily in tabloid form would make. But from the very first issue, circulation increased at such a rate that all records for speedy and sustained growth have been repeatedly broken.

CIRCULATION 1,400,000 DAILY
A morning paper

Pacific & Atlantic Photo

EVENING GRAPHIC

346 Hudson St.—full block from King to Charlton St.

Mr. Bernarr MacFadden's *Graphic* is a tabloid sheet profusely illustrated and distinctive for the snappy brevity with which it covers the news of the day.

Paper founded 1924
Ass'd Val. ...$1,125,000
115 ft. high....8 Floors
Built 1927..Houses 3,000
Rent Area 210,000 sq. ft.
Owner ..Evening Graphic

The *Graphic* Building is most ideally day-lighted. 70,000 square feet of its immense floor space being devoted to the interests of the paper itself.

An evening paper.

DAILY MIRROR

235 E. 45th St.—near 3d Ave.

The Daily *Mirror* has forged to the front at such a rapid pace that notwithstanding the comparatively few years since its entry in the newspaper world it already ranks with the "big circulations" of the newspaper world.

Pictures, Brevity and Exclusive Features spell the secret of the *Mirror's* justified popularity and success. A live wire by the name

Ass'd Val. $1,400,000
245 ft. high........19 Floors
Built 1928
Owner...Daily Mirror Bldg. Corp.
Archt. ....Emery Roth
Bldr.......Taylor Const. Co.

of "Bloom" at the head of the Mirror's circulation department has also played a very important part in the great strides the paper has taken in reaching over 600,000 readers daily.

An evening paper.

74

BROOKLYN EAGLE BUILDING

Johnson & Adams Streets.

Founded 1841
Circulation 106,000
A morning paper
Politics—Independent

"With its vast power over an intelligent population like that of Brooklyn, The Eagle has achieved a unique position in journalism. *I am aware of no other newspaper that has so deeply entered into the life of its readers as The Eagle.*" This striking tribute is from the great British publisher, Lord Northcliffe, while the following expert evaluation is from Adolph S. Ochs, "The Eagle is the primer, the reader, the history, the guide, the philosopher and friend of the best family life in Brooklyn."

STAATS-HEROLD BUILDING

22 North William Street.

The New Yorker Staats-Zeitung was founded as a weekly in 1834 by Wilhelm Newmann under the title of "Der Freischuetz." A few years later the publication was acquired by Jacob Uhl, who changed the title to NEW·YORKER STAATS-ZEITUNG and published the paper daily. In 1901, the late Herman Ridder acquired the paper. His sons Bernard H., Joseph E. and Victor F. Ridder now own it. In 1920, the Staats Herold Corp. was organized for the purpose of publishing an evening edition—THE NEW YORKER HEROLD, as well as the SONNTAGSBLATT STAATS-ZEITUNG & HEROLD (Sunday edition) also the DEUTSCH-AMERICAN—(an illustrated weekly.) Politics Independent.

Circulation
NEW YORKER STAATS-ZEITUNG....	52,000
NEW YORKER HEROLD.............	38,000
SONNTAGSBLATT S-Z & HEROLD...	108,000
DEUTSCH AMERICAN..............	20,000

OTHER NEW YORK DAILIES

BROOKLYN DAILY TIMES	540 Atlantic Ave., (Brooklyn)	
BROOKLYN STANDARD UNION	325 Gold St., (Brooklyn)	
MORNING TELEGRAPH	822 8th Ave.	(Theatrical, Sporting)
WALL STREET JOURNAL	44 Broad Street	(Financial)
JOURNAL OF COMMERCE	46 Barclay Street	(Financial)
INVESTMENT NEWS	346 Hudston Street	(Financial)
NEW YORK EVENING ENQUIRER	200 Varick Street	
HOME NEWS	West 125th Street	(Local)
THE FILM DAILY	1650 Broadway	(Movie pictures)
DAILY RUNNING HORSE	157 East 32nd Street	(Sporting)
NEW YORK DAILY MARKET REPORT	313 Washington Street	
NEW YORK DAILY FRUIT REPORTER	323 Greenwich Street	
THE JEWISH DAILY FREIHEIT	50 East 13th Street	(Jewish)
JEWISH DAILY FORWARD	175 East Broadway	(Jewish)
JEWISH MORNING JOURNAL	77 Bowery	(Jewish)
THE NEW YORK JEWISH DAILY		(Jewish)
GERMAN DAILY VOLKSZEITUNG	1133 Broadway	(German)
NEW YORK VOLKSZEITUNG	47 Walker Street	(German)
CORRIERE D'AMERICA	309 Lafayette Street	(Italian)
COURRIER DES ETATS-UNIS	195 Fulton Street	(French)
IL PROGRESSO ITALO-AMERICANO	42 Elm Street	(Italian)
ITALIAN EVENING BULLETIN	42 Elm Street	(Italian)
PROGRESSO ITALO-AMERICANO	42 Elm Street	(Italian)
CHINESE JOURNAL	196 Canal Street	(Chinese)
CHINESE NATIONALIST DAILY	16 Pell Street	(Chinese)
THE GREEK DAILY ATLANTIS	203 West 25th Street	(Greek)
RUSSKY GOLOS	64 East 7th Street	(Russian)
SPANISH DAILY NEWSPAPER LA PRENSA	245 Canal Street	(Spanish)
SVIJET	216 West 18th Street	(Croation)
SZABADSAG HUNGARIAN DAILY	154 Nassau Street	(Hungarian)
UKRAINIAN DAILY NEWS	17 East 3rd Street	(Ukrainian)

There are weeklies, bi-monthlies and monthlies in New York printed in most every known tongue such as Swedish, Persian, Japanese, etc., etc.

FAMOUS STORES and SHOPS of NEW YORK

"There is nothing money can buy that cannot be bought in New York!"

New York shops are famous for the splendor of their stores, the variety of their offerings, and for the initiative, the aggressiveness and the liberality of their enterprising merchants.

Thousands of shoppers from all over America come to New York to do their buying.

It is impossible to state the accurate total of New York's retail business, but the city supports over 25,000 retail establishments, and by a careful compilation and analysis of figures a conservative estimate has been made of $5,500,000,000—over $18,000,000 each working day of the year.

"WANAMAKER'S" (John Wanamaker)

Covers two squares—On Broadway, 8th to 10th Streets, to 4th Avenue.

Appraised Val. $8,260,000
Floor space.....1,126,320 sq. ft.
Store opened 1896
Old building.......Built in 1872
New building.......Built in 1907

Wanamaker's is not only one of the old landmarks of New York but is so definitely linked with the city's history itself for the past 35 years, that it is one of the principal points of interest to visitors from all parts of the world. The name "Wanamaker" is synonymous with "best."

"ALTMAN'S" (B. Altman & Co.)

Covers entire square. Fifth Ave. to Madison Ave., 34th to 35th Streets.

Ass'd Value, $17,850,000

When Mr. B. Altman died, he left a will which well rewarded the army of faithful employees who had helped him build one of the greatest retail establishments of the age. It is doubtful if in all the history of business, any store has ever enjoyed (or at *present* enjoys) a better reputation for honorable dealing, courteous treatment or a higher class line of merchandise. "Altman's" is a store of which all New York is proud. It is a most dependable place to trade.

"MACY'S" (R. H. Macy & Co.)

Broadway—34th to 35th Sts., through to 7th Ave.

Ass'd Value, $23,000,000

"Macy's" is an actual city in itself. The high quality of the goods carried, the genuine bargains which "cash purchase" makes possible, the enormous variety from which to select, and the unusual courtesy extended by the thousands of obliging personnel, account very largely for the tremendous growth of this huge institution. From time to time Macy's has been forced to add extra space until it now ranks as the largest "strictly cash" retail store in the world, doing a business up in the millions *monthly!* At the Seventh Avenue end of their huge building they have just completed a 20-story addition—a most imposing structure.

"GIMBEL'S" (Gimbel Bros.)

Full block on Broadway—From 32nd to 33rd Streets.
"Annex" on 32nd St. connected by bridge with main building.

Ass'd Val. Main Building........$9,400,000
Ass'd Val. Annex Building...... 1,700,000

Founded in 1842 by Adam Gimbel. In 1910 the Gimbel organization, having huge stores in Milwaukee and Philadelphia, opened the present New York store, occupying an entire city block and at peak seasons Gimbels employ over 18,000 help! "You can buy anything at Gimbels," even theatre tickets, automobile licenses, cut flowers, photos, also cleaning and dyeing, shoe repairs, telegrams, beauty shop, interior decorating, yes, and banking!

Gimbel's is one of the largest retail organizations in America. Gimbel's do a business of close to $125,000,000 a year.

McCREERY'S (Jas. McCreery & Co.)
4 W. 34th St.—Entrances on both 34th St. and Fifth Avenue.

Ass'd Val.....$4,850,000

McCreery's is just across the street from the new Empire State (tallest building in the world) *on 34th St.* It is just across the street from Altman's on *Fifth Ave.*, and it is right in the *middle* of the street recognized as *Heaven* to lady shoppers who appreciate the superlative in "women's fixings" and practically everything dear to women who love pretty things. McCreery's is one of the most popular shops in New York.

"BEST'S" (Best & Co.)
N. W. Cor. Fifth Ave. & 35th St.

Ass'd Val...$4,450,000
Store opened.....1879

Best & Co. cater to those who discriminate.

As an example of how "BEST" prices and "BEST" quality appeals to those who appreciate value and high class merchandise, their annual sales exceeding $14,-000,000 is the BEST answer.

Nearly 1,500 employees are required to handle the constantly increasing patronage of this extremely progressive institution.

"FRANKLIN SIMONS"
414 Fifth Ave.—S. W. Cor. 38th St.

Ass'd Val........$2,960,000

Less than thirty years ago Mr. Franklin Simon envisioned the trend of business to Fifth Avenue and blazed the trail by establishing a "fashion shop" on his present corner (formerly the home of Jno. Jacob Astor's sister—Mrs. O. Wilson). He was the pioneer of the present great Fifth Avenue Shopping center and his steady climb to prestige and position among the "famed shops of New York" is due almost as much to his foresight and initiative as to his leadership in being first to introduce the newest and smartest styles in ladies wear generally.

THE WORLD FAMED
JEWELRY HOUSE OF

TIFFANY
S. E. Cor. Fifth Ave. & 37th Street.

Ass'd Val.........$4,400,000

See picture of Mr. Chas. Tiffany the founder, on Page 119.

77

"LORD & TAYLOR'S"
N. W. Cor. Fifth Ave. and 38th St.

Ass'd Val. $9,000,000

One of the famous dry goods and department stores of the country. Lord & Taylor's is a household name, not only in New York, but wherever refined families reside and wish to trade at a dependable shop carrying the very highest class goods obtainable, and where maximum service, maximum value, and maximum satisfaction can always be found.

The mere announcement of any special offering by Lord & Taylor generally "packs the house." No store in the world seems to have a stronger hold on the confidence of its patrons.

"OVINGTON'S"
S. E. Cor. 5th Ave. and 39th St.

Ass'd Val. $2,000,000

Known as THE GIFT SHOP OF FIFTH AVENUE

The Ovington building is not only an outstanding feature of one of the world's smartest shopping districts, but the firm of Ovington's has for 84 years been identified with all that is attractive and correct in gifts for every occasion.

Ovington's is divided into shops of china, crystal, silver, pewter, objects d'art of all sorts, lamps, furnishings, mirrors, etc. Its gift table department epitomizes the shop as a whole . . . there thousands of gifts are classified according to price. Ovington's has a price for any purse and the same high standard of attractiveness for all.

"ARNOLD CONSTABLE"
S. E. Cor. Fifth Ave. and 40th St.

Ass'd Val. $4,500,000

Many of our grandmothers bought their wedding trousseaus of Arnold Constable. This famous old institution dates back to the early day when 14th Street and Fifth Avenue was the aristocratic shopping center of the city and where the then magnificent building of Arnold Constable on 18th Street and Fifth Avenue was *the* store of the city—just as it is today *the* store of thousands of satisfied customers who cannot be induced to trade anywhere else.

"STERN BROS."
41 W. 42nd St. between 5th and 6th Aves. Extending through to 43rd St.

Ass'd Val. $10,800,000

One of New York's most popular stores. For many years "Stern's" occupied an immense frontage on 23rd Street between 5th and 6th Avenues. In 1918 they moved to their present quarters shown at right on which recently $2,000,000 has been spent in remodeling and making it one of the most beautiful "shops" in the world. Stern Bros. have always been famous for high quality merchandise at honest values.

15 New York Department Stores give employment to nearly 70,000 help during peak seasons; operate over 300 motor trucks; pay taxes on more than $130,000,000 invested in buildings and property; and do an annual business in excess of $300,000,000. There is scarcely any item known to merchandising that cannot be found on sale in these huge emporiums or, if not in stock can be furnished on short notice. Even a monkey, an elephant or a farm tractor can be supplied! This is one reason why America comes to New York to shop.

"BONWIT TELLER'S"
721 Fifth Avenue and N. E. Cor 56th St.

Ass'd.Val. $6,000,000

The growth and popularity of Bonwit-Teller is largely due to the foresight and courage of a management which recognized that the *best* is none too good for New York and have consistently offered newest styles and latest designs in "ladies things" which have won for the house the name of "Little Paris." Bonwit-Teller have for many years built a constantly increasing clientele as a result of being first in the field with the most delightful innovations in ladies' wear.

"SAKS"
Fifth Ave.—from 50th to 51st St.

Ass'd Val. $11,300,000

One of the most palatial "Shops" in the world—Where the aristocracy of New York can find the rarest and best from European, Oriental, and other world markets, as well as the best that American manufactures afford. "Saks" business however is not confined to its wealthy patronage as the same attention and courtesy is paid to the requirements and prices demanded by the masses, as to their "limousine clientele." The magnificent interior of Saks with its regal and luxurious appointments attract the better class of visitors to New York, and the ladies who go through the immense institution, insist that "Saks is one of the great sights of the City."

"BLOOMINGDALE'S"
Lexington Ave. to 3rd Ave. and East 59th to 60th St.

Ass'd Val. $7,800,000
Store opened 1872

Bloomingdale's success and progress has been almost a miracle! For years their advertising of "great bargains" did not seem to be taken seriously by New York's "Upper Crust" as "Third Avenue" savored of the tenement section.

In 1930, however, the magnificent new structure shown herewith was completed. Now all New York is patronizing the place! Bloomingdale's business in 1930 approximated $25,000,000—3,000 employees.

"ABRAHAM & STRAUS'S"
420 Fulton Street—BROOKLYN

BROOKLYN'S BIGGEST "SHOP"

All Brooklyn trades at Abraham & Straus's. The immense institution has recently added the new building shown here, to its great area and caters to every class of trade from the ultra rich to the lowliest laborer. One can buy a Paris gown or an "89c mother hubbard" at this world mart. An army of help is employed to serve the thousands of patrons who daily patronize Brooklyn's outstanding department store which does a business of well up in the millions annually.

Most of New York Department Stores make a specialty of carpets, rugs, and furniture, and for courtesies extended, we want to mention the CARPET & UPHOLSTERY REVIEW of 31 East 17th St. which is the pioneer and premier trade paper of the floor covering field. This very popular journal was founded in 1870 and has been in semi-monthly circulation for over 60 years. It's aim has been to make a "newspaper" rather than a magazine of its pages and it has a host of subscribers not identified with the carpet business in any way. We suggest that you send for a sample copy.

BOROUGH OF
THE BRONX ⤳

The Bronx is a separate and complete city in itself and although a part of New York, would, if segregated, rank as sixth city of the nation in population.

The Bronx has 4,420 acres in Parks—Pelham Bay Park being the largest in New York; the Bronx is also one of the greatest "industrial" areas of the city. Population of the Bronx is over 1,250,000 and has an exceedingly high percentage of skilled labor within its confines.

The "Grand Concourse" in the Bronx is one of New York's most interesting boulevards. Extending from NEW COURT BUILDING IN THE BRONX Mott Street to Kingsbridge Road, this wide and beautiful avenue is lined on both sides for several miles with hundreds of modern apartment buildings, homes and business houses which sprung up almost overnight upon completion of the subways "elevated extension" Close to 200,000 now reside on or adjacent to "Grand Concourse."

Every trunk line railroad entering New York (except the Penn) has a terminal in the Bronx and with 60 miles of water front, the industrial and commercial development of the community is a considerable factor in New York's teeming business activities.

The Bronx is a very important part of New York.

BOROUGH OF
QUEENS ⤳ LONG ISLAND CITY AND ENVIRONS

The Borough of Queens is another very outstanding part of New York. According to the records of the Industrial Bureau of the Queensboro Chamber of Commerce, Queens has close to 2,500 industrial plants, valued at nearly $400,000,000, employing nearly 100,000 wage earners, and producing a product of nearly half a billion dollars annually.

The "Long Island Star" the leading daily newspaper of Queens is recognized as one of the best edited, best managed and best paying newspapers in New York. Loose Wiles Company, makers of the famous "Sunshine Biscuits" have their enormous factory in Queens. In fact, many of the nations large industrial concerns operate their plants in Queens.

Queens has an area of 117 square miles, and a population of approximately 1,200,000 and is directly across East River from Mid-Manhattan.

Queens has five rapid transit extensions of the Interboro & B.M.T. Subway lines, and 71 miles of Long Island railroad tracks within its borders, thus furnishing adequate transportation facilities between Manhattan and Brooklyn.

The Queensboro Chamber of Commerce, which maintains offices on the Bridge Plaza, Long Island City, will supply information regarding the industrial, residential and commercial advantages and possibilities of that Borough. There are 64 residential and industrial communities in Queens, among which are the following: Long Island City, Elmhurst, Jackson Heights, Corona, Forest Hills, Kew Gardens, Ridgewood, Flushing, College Point, Whitestone, Bayside, Richmond Hill, Jamaica, Woodhaven, Far Rockaway, Rockaway Beach, and Rockaway Park.

BOROUGH OF
RICHMOND ⤳ STATEN ISLAND

Present population close to 160,000. Area two and a half times that of Manhattan. Presents New York's greatest opportunity for growth.

When the three new bridges to Perth Amboy, Bayonne and Elizabeth are completed, an influx of population will undoubtedly follow and materially add to the growth and prosperity of the Island. Seven ferries at present connect Staten Island with New York, Brooklyn and New Jersey.

The Baltimore and Ohio Railroad operate electric passenger lines the entire length of the Island, having direct connections with 23 other railroads.

Low water rates, combined with rail bring a large volume of coastwise business to Staten Island. 51 foreign lines operate out of the port, reaching every point of the globe. 21 "one thousand foot piers" provide a capacity of over 20,000,000 tons a year.

The Borough of Richmond has a large number of bathing beaches, amusement parks, athletic grounds, golf courses, and clubs and is an ideal home center—only half an hour or so from congested Manhattan.

The Borough is represented by the Staten Island Chamber of Commerce, Chamber of Commerce Bldg., 57 Bay Street, St. George, Staten Island. Write to them for booklet.

CIVIC BUILDINGS

OWNED BY THE CITY OF NEW YORK.
©Irving Underhill

©Irving Underhill

CITY HALL

At City Hall Park.
(See Page 190)

Appraised Value of Building and Park
$37,250,000

Marble home of New York's Mayor, President of the Board of Aldermen, and meeting rooms of the Aldermanic Board. Built 100 years ago. One of the finest examples of perfect colonial architecture in the country.

HALL OF RECORDS

Cor. Chambers & Center Sts.—Opposite City Hall Park.
Appraised at over......$8,000,000
Contains huge fireproof vaults which provide absolute safety for deeds of all Manhattan property.
Built on site of the old Hall of Records—formerly used as a debtor's jail. Many Revolutionary patriots were imprisoned there.

MUNICIPAL BUILDING

Opposite City Hall Park.
Just north of Brooklyn Bridge.

Appraised Val......$17,500,000
Floor area........600,000 sq. ft.
Excavations........130 ft. deep
Height, 584 ft.......42 Stories

Building contains the offices of the various city departments.

CRIMINAL COURTS BLDG.

Center, Elm, Franklin & White Sts.

Ass'd Val.......$2,000,000
Built in 1891 on site of old New Haven depot—connected with the Tombs by bridge—known as the "Bridge of Sighs."

Here is where Criminal Court Sessions are held, also General Sessions and Special Sessions Courts.

THE TOMBS

(CITY JAIL)

Connected by "Bridge of Sighs" with the Criminal Courts Building.

320 cells.
2 chapels.
2 dormitories.
4 hospital cells, etc.
Annex has 144 cells.

POLICE HEADQUARTERS

Center, Grand, Broome and Market Streets.
Value.......$800,000
Here are the offices of the Police Commissioner, his chief aides, and Detective Bureau. A large drill room, a play room and roof garden for lost children and 75 cells are part of the building's equipment.

HOUSE OF DETENTION
10 Greenwich Ave.—
Cor. W. 10th St.

Cost...........................$1,810,000
135 ft. high......................14 Floors
Built.................................1931

City Prison for women who misbehave, break laws or who otherwise must be "detained" for mixing up in matters which interfere with the required ethics of municipal peace and harmony.

The new House of Detention is not only modern in its every appointment, but has every convenience and comfort for the welfare of its inmates. It is one of the most ideal "jails" in all America. Plans drawn by Architects Sloan & Robertson.

GOVERNMENT AND STATE BLDGS.

© Irving Underhill

U. S. CUSTOM HOUSE

Occupies entire square—foot of Broadway. Faces Bowling Green Park.

Appraised Val. $13,000,000

Has area of 381,800 square feet of usable space. Cornerstone laid Oct. 7, 1902.

Here are the offices of Collector of Ports, Surveyor of Port, Naval Offices of Port, the Internal Revenue Dept. etc. Architecture is French Renaissance—one of the grandest buildings of the city; in fact a credit to the entire nation.

U. S. APPRAISERS STORES

201 Varick Street

Cost $7,500,000

1,000,000 sq. ft. usable space. Built 1928

U. S. FEDERAL RESERVE BANK

33 Liberty St.—Nassau and Maiden Lane

Value $14,500,000

Depository of the largest amount of money in the world. The gold and silver formerly stored in the vaults of the old Sub Treasury Bldg. are now kept here.

Built in 1928—blocks of solid granite with huge iron gratings at windows. One of the most imposing structures in the nation.

The firm of Ely Jacques Kahn drew the plans and Shroder & Koppel erected the building.

Covers entire square, enormous, massive, modern and beautiful.

U. S. SUB-TREASURY

N. E. Cor. Wall and Nassau Streets

Constructed for custom service in 1842. In 1862 it became the Sub Treasury. Has marble walls five feet thick. In the huge vaults millions of gold and silver were stored until completion of the new Federal Reserve Building.

Site of old Federal Hall where George Washington was inaugurated President.

U. S. POST OFFICE

Extends 2 blocks on 8th Ave from 31st to 33rd Streets

Appraised Val. $10,600,000

Built directly over the Pennsylvania R. R. tracks. Mail is delivered to mail cars below thru convenient chutes. The most ideal Post Office building in the country. Built 1914.

Architects—McKim, Mead & White. Builder—Geo. A. Fuller Co.

NEW YORK COUNTY COURT HOUSE

Occupying full square facing Center St., S. E. Cor. Worth St.

Cost $11,000,000

Magnificent granite structure in Italian Renaissance. Built 1927. Houses 40 Court Rooms with attendant jury rooms, council rooms, library, cafe, etc. The Justice chambers occupy most of the two top floors.

Building is hexagonal in shape with large central rotunda.

NEW YORK STATE OFFICE BUILDING

Occupies full Square faces Center St. N. E. Cor. Worth St.

This Magnificent Structure Cost $6,000,000

Completed in 1930. Has 10 floors. Usable space 300,000 sq. ft. Owned by the State of New York. In the building are the various State offices with which the general public has the most business. Motor Vehicles, Income Tax, Workmen's Compensation, Employment, etc.

PUBLIC BUILDINGS, MUSEUMS, ETC.

Ewing Galloway

NEW YORK PUBLIC LIBRARY AND BRYANT PARK

Fifth Ave. from 41st to 42nd St. extending thru to Sixth Ave. Occupying the site of the old "42nd St. Reservoir"

Valued at $15,000,000

Opened in 1911. Founded in 1895 by the consolidation of the Astor and Lenox libraries and the Tilden Trust. In 1901 the N. Y. Circulation Library joined the consolidation. The library has 43 branches throughout Greater New York. In this main building are 3,000,000 volumes and pamphlets. The Circulation Dept. alone inventories over 1,185,000 books, comprising the leading municipal collection of literature in the nation.

THE AQUARIUM

Extreme southerly point of Battery Park

Formerly known as Castle Garden Fort. Located on southwest sea wall of Battery Park. Free to the public—9 A.M. until 5 P.M. Here in large glass tanks is one of the most valuable and complete collections of over 7,000 deep sea fish and other sea specimens in the world. Average attendance over 2,000,000 yearly.

AMERICAN MUSEUM OF NATURAL HISTORY

77th St. to 81st St. from Columbus Ave. to Central Park West. 4 entire squares.

One of the great museums of the world, founded in 1869. Here will be found unrivaled collections of birds, insects, fossils, Indian relics, minerals, and countless other specimens scientifically classified and ingeniously displayed. Entire days can be spent to advantage in the huge institution. The "Hall of Gems" donated by J. Pierpont Morgan contains one of the largest and finest collections in existence.

METROPOLITAN MUSEUM OF ART

Central Park at Fifth Ave. and 82nd St.

Covers many acres and cost over $20,000,000. Unparalleled in many respects by any art museum in the world. Rich in priceless art treasures, sculpture, paintings, architectural models, etc.

A large number of old and rare paintings by the world's greatest artists will be found on exhibition. The public is admitted free on most days of the week.

ROERICH MUSEUM

N.E. Cor. Riverside Drive and 103rd St.

Ass'd Value, $2,725,000

A combination of museum, art school and a sufficient number of studio apartments to produce an income for financial support. The schools are of architecture, sculpture, painting, interior decoration, music, dancing, and the stage. There is also a public restaurant and a cozy theatre.

The building is equipped with every conceivable comfort and convenience—28 floors.

Architects—Corbett, Harrison & McMurray and Sugarman & Berger.

OTHER NEW YORK MUSEUMS

American Numismatic Sy.
See page 223
Brooklyn Arts & Sciences
See page 84
Hispania Society of America
See page 223
Jumel Mansion
See page 44
Museum of the City of N. Y.
88th St. and East River
New York Historical Society
170 Central Park West
Van Cortlandt Mansion
See page 84
Museum of Amer. Indian
See page 223
Geographical Society
See page 223

THE PARKS OF NEW YORK

A dozen pages this size would not be adequate to describe
New York's Parks. No city in the world provides its citizens with such huge acreage of park land or spends such
princely sums in equipping and beautifying them.

New York supports *194 parks, 82 play grounds,* and *24 parkways*—comprising the
astounding total of *8,703* acres in its park system. The value in dollars of the land
alone is up in the hundreds of millions!
Every *square foot* of Battery Park, City
Hall Park, Union Square and Madison
Square Parks, Bryant Park and even Central Park is worth more than a full acre
of land in the average town, and yet added
to the worth of the property itself, New
York has spent *tens of millions* in park
buildings and other improvements.

Van Cortlandt Mansion—Van Cortlandt
Park

Botanical Museum—Bronx Park

In Bronx Park there is the greatest botanical museum on the globe, also the
largest zoo. Elephants have a building
all to themselves. So have the lions,
zebras, monkeys, reptiles, birds, etc.
The rhinoceroses, hippotami, giraffes
and other rare members of the animal,
bird and reptile world occupy *huge*
structures.

Prospect Park in Brooklyn is almost as famous for its beauty and
countless attractions as Central
Park in Manhattan. Van Cortlandt Park is so immense one can
easily "get lost."

Bethesda Fountain & Sunken Gardens—Central Park

Riverside Park (pictured on page
283) extending along Riverside
Drive from 72nd Street to Grant's
Tomb at 122nd Street, has been
very materially enlarged by the
reclaiming of 84 acres of land by
filling in 4,000,000 cubic yards of
material from subway excavations, thus adding property to
New York's park lands valued at
$29,000,000!

The Mall—Central Park

It is estimated that in the good
old summer time over two million
men, women and children patronize New York parks daily—
one of the reasons why New
Yorkers are so healthy!

Brooklyn Institute Arts & Sciences—Prospect Park

OLD LAND MARKS OF NEW YORK

New York in the "gay nineties" was a very different New York from what it is today. The following pictures may bring back many cherished memories to "old timers."

RECTORS   DELMONICO'S   SHERRY'S   DREAMLAND

OLD ASTOR HOUSE   MAD. SQ. GARDEN   OLD 5TH AVE. HOTEL

OLD GRAND CENT. STATION   EMANU-EL   42nd ST. RESERVOIR

NETHERLAND & SAVOY   WALDORF ASTORIA   SIEGEL-COOPERS

On page 221 note the old Casino Theatre
On page 153 note old "No. ONE" Wall Street
And so on thru the book.

We are indebted to the Manhattan Post Card Co. for most of these pictures.

100 OUTSTANDING FIGURES IN NEW YORK'S GROWTH AND FAME

Never in the history of any nation has there ever been shown in one publication a more interesting galaxy or red-blooded *he-men* than will be found in the following pages, presenting short biographical sketches and half-tone cuts of the 100 outstanding figures who have so largely contributed in making New York what it is today—*truly*, the wonder city of the world!

Nothing *could* prevent New York from attaining its present undisputed supremacy, with 100 such men living within its confines and directing their talents and tremendous activities for the common weal. Travel the world over and you will find it difficult to find another Joseph P. Day, August Heckscher, Fred French, Vincent Astor, Irving T. Bush, Owen D. Young, and so on. In fact, we could keep right on until we had named the entire hundred.

There is a tremendous significance and a most impressive sermon in the consideration and analysis of this group of men. As you read the life sketch of each, you will observe that most of them were complete strangers to "Easy Street" in their early youth. Not one in ten had the advantage of family, wealth, or influence. Most of them experienced genuine hardship, privation or even poverty, starting life with practically nothing but ambition and determination to "get somewhere" and yet, these 100 men have proven themselves the very backbone of our wonder city. It is they who by their initiative, their daring, and their sound judgment have made *New York of today*— not only in the real estate and building sense, but in industrial, merchandising, journalistic, educational, and other channels.

Just read the little "life stories" of these men. You will find same not only extremely interesting, but most inspiring. And we consider it fitting to start our "photo album" with an excellent likeness of Joseph P. Day—the one man who seems to be generally conceded head and shoulders above all others in having contributed most to New York's phenomenal growth and greatness.

MR. JOSEPH P. DAY

Mr. Day was born in New York City, Sept. 22nd, 1873. He made his first dollar working for James Talcott the wholesale dry goods merchant—receiving the munificent sum of $1.92 per week the first year. At the age of 21, he started in business for himself, selecting the real estate field. By hardest kind of work, clever initiative, sterling honesty and grit, he soon forged to the front and built the foundation of what is now recognized as the largest real estate concern in the world. Time and again Mr. Day has broken all records for volume sales. In 1910 his sales totaled over $80,000,000. In one day (1920) he sold $26,000,000 in *one day*—the largest auction sale ever recorded. Mr. Day is practically the father of "auctioning real estate." Mr. Day never follows beaten paths. He blazes his own trails. Even today—at 58, he has more energy, pep and ambition than most of our young chaps. When "Joe Day" steps on the gas, no one ever tries to keep pace with him. Mr. Day is now one of the wealthiest men in New York. He carries $3,250,000 life insurance, is a director of many nationally institutions such as Metropolitan Life Insurance, etc. Mr. Day is one man money has not spoiled. He is intensely human, kind hearted, and no husband, father, or friend is more universally beloved by all who know him.

NEW YORKERS ALL NEW YORK KNOWS

HON. JAMES J. WALKER

As Mayor of the city of New York, Mr. Walker has both his enthusiastic admirers and his fault-finding critics. But this is to be expected by the incumbent of any mayor's chair, in any large city. However, New York has had but few mayors who have functioned as satisfactorily as has the buoyant and popular "Jimmy." When Mr. Walker assumed the responsibilities of · Burgomaster of the big town, he faced many man-sized problems, and a lot of situations which were certain to produce criticism, no matter which way he moved, or what decisions he made. Place *yourself* in the Mayor's seat, and what would *you* do! Mr. Walker has kept his word to maintain a five cent fare, and under his administration, the widow's pension, relief from housing congestion and other measures have been passed. Don't blame him entirely for the "Speak-easies"—read page 24, then blame *yourself*. Mr. Walker was born in New York City, June 19, 1881. After studying law at the New York Law School, he was admitted to the Bar in 1912. He was elected State Senator and been "busy" ever since. Mr. Walker has a keen mind, is an eloquent speaker, and there is no disputing the fact that he is one of the most popular mayors New York has ever known.

MR. GROVER A. WHALEN

Grover Whalen probably knows more important personages than any other one man in all New York. As "City Greeter," Police Commissioner, and from long connection with the great Wanamaker Store, Mr. Whalen has come more or less in contact with every member of Royalty or person of importance that has visited New York in years. Mr. Whalen is strictly a self-made man. Born in lower East Side June 22, 1882, with no advantages of either wealth or influence, he worked his way up thru sheer grit and not only won for himself an excellent education, but acquired a polish and poise that stamps him as the real gentleman he is. Mr. Whalen is one of the head executives of Wanamakers, and an officer or director of many large corporations. His dynamic force, his very affable personality and his sound principles, ready wit and ever-willingness to extend a helping hand to any worthy cause has endeared him to all New York.

MR. JOHN H. FINLEY

Kaiden-Keystone Studios

Mr. John Houston Finley is called upon in New York whenever a man "ready for any emergency" is required. If Aviators, Royalty, or others whom the city wishes to honor, are given ovations, receptions, or are tendered civic courtesies, Mr. John Houston ·Finley can always be relied upon to do the right thing, say the right thing, and create the right impression. Mr. Finley excels in everything he undertakes—either as an editor of a magazine, or newspaper, as a public speaker, lecturer, or "glad-hand" exponent. Few men in all New York are more beloved, more highly respected, or more able to function in any commission assigned. Mr. Finley has functioned as Editor of *Harper's Magazine*, Editor of the *New York Times*, Trustee of the Sage Foundation, former President of Knox College, staff member of both Princeton and Harvard Colleges, and is author of many books.

All groups are listed alphabetically

NATIONALLY KNOWN NEW YORKERS

MR. WILLIAM RANDOLPH HEARST

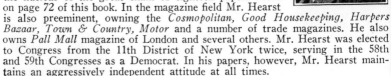

Mr. Hearst began his journalistic career shortly after graduating from Harvard College in 1885, returning to California (his native state, having been born in San Francisco in April, 1863) where he became editor and proprietor of the *San Francisco Examiner*. He built it up from an unimportant political organ into the greatest paper on the Pacific Coast. He then bought the *New York Journal*, which was barely "making a living" and changed the name to the *New York American* and then established the *Evening Journal*. These papers became the nucleus of the great chain of eighteen papers listed on page 72 of this book. In the magazine field Mr. Hearst is also preeminent, owning the *Cosmopolitan, Good Housekeeping, Harpers Bazaar, Town & Country, Motor* and a number of trade magazines. He also owns *Pall Mall* magazine of London and several others. Mr. Hearst was elected to Congress from the 11th District of New York twice, serving in the 58th and 59th Congresses as a Democrat. In his papers, however, Mr. Hearst maintains an aggressively independent attitude at all times.

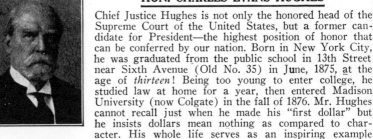

HON. CHARLES EVANS HUGHES

Chief Justice Hughes is not only the honored head of the Supreme Court of the United States, but a former candidate for President—the highest position of honor that can be conferred by our nation. Born in New York City, he was graduated from the public school in 13th Street near Sixth Avenue (Old No. 35) in June, 1875, at the age of *thirteen*! Being too young to enter college, he studied law at home for a year, then entered Madison University (now Colgate) in the fall of 1876. Mr. Hughes cannot recall just when he made his "first dollar" but he insists dollars mean nothing as compared to character. His whole life serves as an inspiring example of what genuine integrity, conscientious allegiance to duty, and earnest work can accomplish. Chief Justice Hughes is not only a credit to New York, but to the entire country.

MR. JOHN D. ROCKEFELLER

It is doubtful. if there is any better known name in all the world than that of John D. Rockefeller. Born in Richford (Tioga Co.) N. Y., July 9, 1839, he has reached the ripe old age of 92 and is "still going strong!" His family settled in Cleveland in 1853, where, after securing a high school education, he was given his first "job" at $4 per week. In 1859, with $1,000 he borrowed from his father, he started his fortune. Notwithstanding that every prominent man is more or less abused (and Mr. Rockefeller has come in for his full share), his record of kindly deeds and benefactions for the public good has endeared him to every fair minded citizen of our great country. Mr. Rockefeller has contributed OVER $500,000,000 to the welfare of his fellow man. It would require over a dozen pages to list even a part of what he has done for humanity. Long life to "John D."!

All groups are listed alphabetically

NATIONALLY KNOWN NEW YORKERS

© Pirie MacDonald

HON. ELIHU ROOT

New York has produced but few men who have had as many honors conferred upon them as have been bestowed upon Elihu Root. America itself has produced but few men who have registered as nearly 100% in capacity for such honors. Born in Clinton, N. Y., Feb. 15, 1845, Mr. Root applied himself from early youth to the mastery of whatever subject or problem he took up. As a lawyer, he became one of the outstanding leaders in the legal profession. As a diplomat and statesman, he served as Secretary of War under McKinley, as Secretary of State under Roosevelt and as Ambassador to Russia at the time of the Revolution. As a journalist, he served as editor of the New York *Sun* (1909 to 1915). In whatever capacity he served, or in whatever activity he engaged, he excelled. Mr. Root is now in his 86th year and yet his mind is as virile, his enjoyment of life as keen, and his interest in affairs as earnest as when at the age of 22, he was admitted to the New York Bar and started his practice of law. All America is proud of the Honorable Elihu Root.

HON. ALFRED E. SMITH

"Al Smith," as everybody familiarly calls him, is undoubtedly one of the most beloved men who ever entered public service. His life story is an absolute inspiration to any young man who wants to "be somebody." Of obscure yet sterling parentage, young Alfred had but few of the good things of life when a boy, but "Al" was a he-boy, just as he has proven to be a he-man, and having an excellent mind, a ready wit, and that wonderful quality of being a good "mixer," he made friends of everybody, and was always willing to help everybody. This is why Alfred E. Smith rose to the exalted position of Governor of New York State, and became candidate for President of the United States in 1928. At present he is the President of the company owning the great EMPIRE STATE building.

Blank Stoller, Inc.

MR. CHARLES M. SCHWAB

Born in Williamsburg, Pa., Feb. 18, 1862, "Charlie Schwab" needs no introduction to the American public, as few names in all our nation are better known than this genial miracle man who rose from a steel puddler to the presidency of the great U. S. Steel Co. As a young man Mr. Schwab got a job with the Edgar Thompson Works of the Carnegie Steel Company at a dollar per day! Seven years later he was chief of the engineering department. In 1892 he became superintendent of the Homestead Works. In 1896 he was elected to the Board of Managers of the Carnegie Co. When Carnegie and U. S. Steel merged in 1901, Mr. Schwab became President. Mr. Schwab is a Director in so many nationally known institutions that there is not space to list them all here, but among the number might be mentioned Bethlehem Steel, the Chase National Bank, Met. Life Ins. Co., American Surety, Loew's, Inc., Empire Trust, etc. Mr. Schwab's residence on Riverside Drive is one of the most palatial homes in all America.

All groups are listed alphabetically

OUTSTANDING EDUCATORS

Koike Studios

CHANCELLOR ELMER ELLSWORTH BROWN

Chancellor Brown has been President of New York University since July 1st, 1911. From early boyhood he has been a most consistent student. Born in Kiantone, N. Y., August 28, 1861, he graduated from the State Normal University at the age of twenty and later from the University of Michigan, with a degree of A.B. He has also received degrees of Ph.D. and LL.D. Chancellor Brown has been identified with educational and uplift work all his life. He has served as officer and director of many organizations, and has always been a power in any capacity in which he engaged. He is a Congregationalist, and a staunch Republican. He is the author of many books, a number of them being masterly written and profound in their treatment.

DR. NICHOLAS MURRAY BUTLER

Kaiden Studios

Dr. Nicholas Murray Butler is about as nearly a human dynamo as this nation of ours has ever produced. Born in Elizabeth, N. J., April 2, 1862, he was from early childhood one of the busiest youngsters in his community. As he grew older, he evidenced an insatiable penchant for knowledge. Dr. Butler has received so many degrees and honors, and is so internationally known, that we will not attempt to refer to his achievements here, other than to state that when twenty-three (1885), he was appointed on the faculty of Columbia University, and has been President of that world-famous institution since 1902. In 1920 his name was presented to the Republican National Committee as nominee for President of the United States—receiving 69 votes! Dr. Butler is a *business* man as well as an educator, writer, lecturer, etc., being a Director of the New York Life Insurance Company.

Underwood & Underwood

DR. JOHN ROBERT GREGG

Few names in all America are better known than John Gregg —founder of the Gregg System of Shorthand. This invention of his has possibly assisted more young men and women to economic independence than any other contribution to self-help in recent years. Such men as John J. Raskob, Samuel Insul, Alba B. Johnson, George B. Cortelyou frankly admit they owe a very considerable share of their success in life to the start they got thru the medium of their short-hand skill! Born in Ireland sixty-four years ago, John Robert Gregg experienced hardship up to the age of twenty-six, at which time he completed his first short-hand manual, and came to this country with just enough money to print a small edition of 500 copies. Mr. Gregg is now a millionaire whose every dollar came to him as a result of giving the world an instrument of writing that has saved millions of hours. Personally, Dr. Gregg is extremely democratic, easily approachable and wears the same size hat he wore when poor.

DR. FREDERICK B. ROBINSON—*See Page 51*

OUTSTANDING PHILANTHROPISTS

MR. AUGUST HECKSCHER

Mr. August Heckscher was born in Germany in 1848, and came to this country at about the age of nineteen, with $500—his entire worldly possessions. His first venture in business was in the Reading coal fields. Borrowing some money in Germany, he made a small fortune, but later lost it. Recovering, he repaid in full. His life has been replete with strenuous activities, both in mining and real estate. Mr. Heckscher has amassed a fortune, and is spending a very considerable share of it in philanthropic work, having established the "Heckscher Foundation for Children," given enormous sums for playgrounds, camps and parks, etc., and Mr. Heckscher has also done big things in helping develop New York—having erected the magnificent "Heckscher Building" at 57th St., the "Heckscher Apartments" at 277 Park Ave. and other splendid structures. Mr. Heckscher, like most men who have become *big*, is extremely modest, very retiring, and dislikes publicity, but the writer succeeeded in securing a personal interview and found him the personification of kindness, chivalry, and generosity. His one purpose in life seems to be to want to help others.

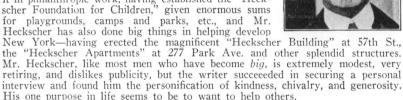

MR. JOHN D. ROCKEFELLER, JR.

Seldom do "rich men's sons" distinguish themselves and retain the spotlight held by their fathers, but "John D.," Jr., has proven a marked exception. Born in Cleveland, Ohio, Jan. 29th, 1874, he has has devoted the greater part of his life to philanthropic activities—not only following out many started by his father, but inaugurating extensive ones of his own. After several years of intensive study of tenement conditions, he personally financed the erection of many modern multiple family buildings which he rented to the working classes at modest figures. In 1924 he gave and endowed "INTERNATIONAL HOUSE" for the furtherance of international friendships. John D. Rockefeller, Jr., has endeared himself to all humanity by his generous benefactions toward the welfare of mankind in general. At present, he is investing $250,000,000 in "Rockefeller City." (See page 249.)

MR. FELIX WARBURG

The great fatherland of Germany has contributed many wonderful men to America, and Hamburg, Germany, sent us Felix Warburg. Mr. Warburg was born in Hamburg, January 14, 1871. From his early youth he has been interested in finance. He was engaged in the banking business in Frankfort just before he came to this country to accept an opening with Kuhn, Loeb & Co., of which firm he is one of its chief heads and directors. Mr. Warburg has devoted a very considerable share of his life and fortune to the welfare of his fellow men. He is Chairman of the Board of the "Federation for Support of Jewish Philanthropies," and his personal benefactions to both Jewish and non-sectarian charities totals a sum which no one knows but himself. Mr. Warburg belongs to the class who do not believe in allowing "the right hand to know what the left hand is doing"! Mr. Warburg is a great lover of the beautiful, a great reader, and a "good Republican"!

OUTSTANDING FINANCIERS

Muray Studios

MR. OTTO H. KAHN

Mr. Otto H. Kahn was born in Mannheim, Germany, Feb. 21, 1867. His father had previously come to America and been naturalized as an American citizen, but falling in love with a young German girl, he could secure her parents' consent to marriage only on condition that he return to Germany. Therefore Otto Kahn was born in Germany, notwithstanding he had an American father. The young man devoted his early youth to the study of banking and music and made marked progress in both. In August, 1893, Mr. Kahn came to America. His rise here was rapid. On Jan. 1, 1897, he entered the firm of Kuhn, Loeb & Co. as a partner, and later became E. H. Harriman's most intimate associate. Mr. Kahn's constructive mentality and keen comprehension of finance and "big business" soon identified him among the most powerful factors in Wall St. He became an authority on practical economics and international affairs, and was much in demand as a public speaker. Today, the name of Otto H. Kahn is one of the biggest in the nation—not only in finance and big business, but as a supporter of the best in both music and art.

MR. CHARLES E. MITCHELL

Nicholas Murray

Mr. Charles Edwin Mitchell is head of the vast financial organization grouped around the National City Bank of New York. Born Oct. 6, 1877, at Chelsea, Mass., he graduated from Amherst College in 1899. His first business connection was with the Western Electric Co. in Chicago, where he progressed rapidly until he became assistant to the president. In 1906 he entered the field of finance, and later was induced to accept the vice-presidency of the National City Co. In 1921 he was elected president of the great National City Bank, and on April 2, 1929, appointed Chairman. Mr. Mitchell is also president and director of many nationally known institutions. He is a modest man, and yet possessed of the force, magnetism, and ability which make him a natural leader.

Underwood & Underwood

MR. J. PIERPONT MORGAN

Mr. J. Pierpont Morgan was born in Irvington, N. Y., Sept. 7, 1867. In all the financial universe there is no better-known name than that of J. Pierpont Morgan—both father and grandfather having been powers in financial circles before him. The present J. Pierpont Morgan (who bears the same name as his father) has not merely carried on the great institution developed by his predecessor, but enjoys the distinction of having achieved an even more commanding position in the banking fraternity, and not only holds the respect, but the confidence of financiers the world over. Mr. Morgan is an enthusiastic patron of the arts, a generous contributor to philanthropies, and ever ready to lend his influence to a worthy cause.

All groups are listed alphabetically

OUTSTANDING FINANCIERS (*Continued*)

MR. SEWARD PROSSER

Mr. Prosser was born in Buffalo, N. Y., May 1, 1871. He did not have the advantages of a collegiate education, having to go to work as soon as he had graduated from public schools. He began his business career with the Equitable Life Assurance Society. In 1907 he became Vice-President of the Astor Trust Co. In 1912 he was appointed President of the Liberty National Bank, and in 1914 became President of the world known BANKERS TRUST CO. Mr. Prosser is one of New York's most highly considered bankers, and is a Director or Trustee in many of New York's largest and nationally known institutions.

MR. CHARLES H. SABIN

Mr. Sabin started life in the flour business, securing his first job with Mr. Henry Russell, a flour merchant of Williamstown, Mass., where Mr. Sabin first saw the light of day Aug. 24, 1868. But Destiny evidently had slated Mr. Sabin for the financial world, for in 1889 he was offered a position with an Albany bank, and was soon promoted. His rise was steadily upward and in 1907 he became President of the National Copper Bank of New York City. In 1910 he became Vice-President of the great Guaranty Trust Co. Five years later he was appointed President, and in October 1921 became Chairman of the Board.

MR. JAMES A. SPEYER

Mr. Speyer was born in New York in 1861. He comes of a Frankfort-on-Main family that has been prominent since the seventeenth century. After receiving his business education in Frankfort, Paris, and London, Mr. Speyer returned to New York in 1885, and is now senior partner in the world-famous banking house of "SPEYER & CO." The members of the Speyer family have long been known for their broad spirit of philanthropy, and for their well directed efforts towards aiding their fellowmen. James Speyer has followed his family traditions, and devotes a great deal of his time to educational and philanthropic work.

MR. ALBERT H. WIGGIN

Mr. Albert H. Wiggin (born in Medfield, Mass., Feb. 2, 1868) belongs to the class of self-made men of whom there are so many in the great "Wonder City." Graduating from high school at seventeen, he secured a position in a Boston bank, and by the time he was 23, had become a bank examiner. Before he was thirty (1897) he was appointed Vice-President of the Eliot National Bank of Boston, coming to New York shortly afterwards where his rise was rapid. In 1904 Mr. Wiggin became Vice-President and director of the Chase National Bank, being appointed its President in 1911. In 1930 he was appointed Chairman of the Governing Board. The Chase National Bank, of which he is the head, is recognized as the most powerful financial institution in all Christendom.

All groups are listed alphabetically

OUTSTANDING INDUSTRIALISTS

Kaiden Keystone

MR. IRVING T. BUSH

Few men have manifested more initiative than Irving T. Bush—founder and general-in-chief of BUSH TERMINAL. Doubleday, Doran & Co. have recently published the life story of Mr. Bush, entitled "WORKING WITH THE WORLD" which is one of the most interesting and inspiring stories of "big business" ever chronicled. Inheriting a little fortune from his father, Mr. Bush had a "dream." He had always been interested in the sea, in ships, in wharves, and the great world beyond. His father had an oil refining plant on the South Brooklyn waterfront, which after his death was absorbed by the Standard Oil Co. Unfinished bulkheads filled the young man with a desire to build something. Even then he envisioned the present Bush Terminal—now one of the most stupendous factors in New York's industrial development, but the building of which was fraught with opposition, obstacles and hardships such as few men have ever experienced. But with marvelous courage, indomitable perseverance and almost superhuman effort, Mr. Bush succeeded, as results prove.

MR. WALTER P. CHRYSLER

Blank & Stoller

If Walter P. Chrysler (born Wamego, Kans., 1877) had done nothing else in life than build his palatial Chrysler Building at the corner of 42nd and Lexington Avenue, he would be famous. But Mr. Chrysler has built another monument to his name in his great Chrysler automobile of which hundreds of thousands have given such complete satisfaction to owners. Altho Mr. Chrysler's motor factory is located in Detroit, New York is his home, and New York will likely always be his home as Mr. Chrysler is a big man and would not be content in any city other than the biggest. Everything Mr. Chrysler does is done in a big way. When he built his Chrysler building it was the *biggest* (in height) in the world. His automobile factories rank with the biggest in the world, and his car is enthusiastically acclaimed by those who own Chryslers as the biggest value in motor cars! Mr. Chrysler is a young man, dynamic, and possessed of more genuine friends than he has windows in his huge skyscraper!

Underwood & Underwood

MR. GEORGE B. CORTELYOU

Mr. Cortelyou first came into national prominence as secretary to President McKinley in 1900. Upon the assassination of McKinley, he continued as Secretary to President Roosevelt. In 1903 Mr. Cortelyou was appointed Secretary of the newly created Department of Commerce and Labor; appointed Postmaster General in 1905; and Secretary of the Treasury in 1909, all three appointments in the Roosevelt Cabinet. At the close of that administration, Mr. Cortelyou returned to New York City (having been born in New York July 26, 1862) and accepted the Presidency of the Consolidated Gas Company of New York, whose commodious home is shown on page 199 of this volume. Mr. Cortelyou has continued up to the present in that capacity, as well as serving as Director in many of New York's other large corporations. He is a member of many New York Clubs, and one of the city's most outstanding and highly respected citizens.

All groups are listed alphabetically

OUTSTANDING INDUSTRIALISTS (Continued)

MR. PHILIP A. S. FRANKLIN

Mrs. W. Burden Stage

Mr. Franklin began his business career as a cowboy out in "wild and wooly" Wyoming! Altho born in New York City, he headed west as a young man. But Wyoming was a long way from salt water, and so he came back home where destiny had decreed he was needed in the shipping business. Today Mr. Franklin is at the head of the International Mercantile Marine—one of the largest steamship organizations in the world (see page 168 for illustration of the I. M. M. building at No. "One Broadway.") P. A. S. Franklin is not only a big name in steamship circles, but a most highly esteemed one in business, club, and financial arenas.

Kaiden Keystone

MR. WALTER S. GIFFORD

The world's largest enterprise is recognized as the "American Telephone & Telegraph Co." Walter S. Gifford was appointed President of this great institution in 1925, at the age of *forty*! Born in Salem, Mass., he was graduated at Harvard when but nineteen, and secured his first job as clerk with the Western Electric Co. In 1908 he was called to the A. T. & T. Co. During the World War, President Wilson selected him as the Director of the Council of National Defense. After the war, Mr. Gifford returned to the A. T. & T. Co. and was elected Vice-Pres. in 1920. In January, 1925, he became President. Under Mr. Gifford's guidance, the immense institution today has resources in excess of FIVE BILLIONS!

MR. LEONARD FRESNEL LOREE

© Blank & Stoller

Mr. Loree commenced his railroad career at the early age of nineteen, as an assistant in the engineering corps of the Pennsylvania System in 1877. Two years later, he became Superintendent of the Cleveland & Pittsburgh Division, and General Manager in 1896. On June 1, 1901, he was appointed President of the great Baltimore & Ohio System. On April 10, 1907, he accepted the Presidency of the Delaware and Hudson Lines. Mr. Loree is President of 34 other affiliated companies, and yet he always seems to find time to mix with his vast army of admirers and warm friends. Mr. Loree is unquestionably one of the most popular officials in all railway-dom.

MR. OWEN D. YOUNG

Young in name, Young in looks, and Young in age for the great success, the fame, and the great ability he has manifested! Owen D. Young is yet in his fifties! But his name is known and respected the world over. Mr. Young has *done* things. All Europe knows of his "plan" in the solution of one of the greatest of World War problems. Mr. Young was born in Van Hornesville, N. Y., Oct. 2, 1874. After receiving his degree of A.B. at St. Lawrence University and his LL.B. at Boston Law School he started the career that has made him an international character. In 1922 he was appointed Chairman of the Board of the great General Electric Co. Altho Mr. Young retains his home up state, most of his time is spent in New York.

All groups are listed alphabetically

OUTSTANDING MERCHANTS

MR. BERNARD F. GIMBEL

Bernard F. Gimbel, "merchant prince" and sportsman, was born in Vincennes, Indiana, in 1885—son of the late Isaac Gimbel, and grandson of Adam Gimbel, who founded the great Gimbel organization. After graduating from the University of Pennsylvania in 1907, Mr. Gimbel began his business career with the Philadelphia store of the Company, working in every branch of the business and qualifying himself for the presidency, which he assumed in 1927. During the time he has been president, the annual sales volume of the seven stores operated by Gimbel Brothers, Inc., in New York, Philadelphia, Chicago, Pittsburgh and Milwaukee, three of which are Saks stores, two in New York and one in Chicago, has reached $125,000,000, and in peak seasons, has employed 18,000 people! Mr. Gimbel instills confidence in all those about him. He has an uncanny memory, is keen and most considerate of others. As an organizer, and as an executive he has manifested the most marked ability, and has earned his reputation as being one of New York's most capable captains of industry. Mr. Gimbel is an enthusiast on all outdoor sports and firmly believes that to do his best, one must be physically fit.

MR. PHILIP LeBOUTILLIER

"BEST'S," one of Fifth Avenue's most famous and popular shops for women and children, owes its great prestige and success largely to Philip LeBoutillier, who after serving in various capacities with Sibley, Lindsey & Carr (Rochester), Jordan Marsh (Boston), John Wanamaker (New York), etc., joined "Best & Co." in 1913. In 1917 he was appointed General Manager. In 1924 he was made Vice President, and in 1927 became President. Mr. LeBoutillier is recognized as one of the most able merchandisers in all New York. His comprehensive vision and initiative, added to his aggressive personality have made him a power in department store circles. Best & Co. seem to be first in the field with what "goes" with women, and the steady growth and popularity of the house is common comment.

MR. JAMES CASH PENNEY

When Mr. Penney's folks named him James "CASH," they evidently knew their business, as the young man from early boyhood manifested his ability to "get the money!" Few of America's wealthy men are more *entitled* to "cash" and the good things cash can buy, than James Cash Penney. Mr. Penney was born in Hamilton, Mo., Sept. 15, 1875. He is founder and Chairman of the Board of the great chain of stores operated by the J. C. Penney Corp., numbering nearly 1,000 in forty-six states! Mr. Penney is using his wealth for the betterment of his fellowman. He is one of the most approachable, kindest

hearted, and most philanthropic men in our whole nation. He is sincere in his religion. Until recently he was President of the Christian Herald. He is a member of the Executive Committee of the Christian Endeavor organization and a liberal contributor to any worthy causes which mean the good of humanity, such as his recent establishment of the Memorial Community for Retired Religious Workers at Penney Farms, Fla. Mr. Penney is a prohibitionist. He is a member of many clubs, a wonderful "mixer" and a *man among men*. If our country had more "JAMES CASH PENNEYS" among its wealthy citizens, this would be a much better old world to live in!

All groups are listed alphabetically

OUTSTANDING MERCHANTS (*Continued*)

MR. SAMUEL REYBURN

Few men in New York have achieved such commanding respect and popularity in the mercantile field as has Samuel Reyburn, former President of the great house of Lord & Taylor. Mr. Reyburn resigned his position with this famous old firm in April (1931) to become President of the Associated Dry Goods Corporation with head offices in New York. Under Mr. Reyburn's regime as President of Lord & Taylor, his achievements were well-nigh miraculous. Altho the firm was established over 100 years ago (1826) and grew to be one of the most outstanding mercantile institutions in the country, various causes contributed to a situation which demanded a master mind to solve. Samuel Reyburn accepted the responsibility and in ten years wiped out a deficit of over $10,000,000 and brought the business to a handsome paying basis. The Lord & Taylor firm is one of eight department stores controlled by the Associated Dry Goods Corp.—the present company of which Mr. Reyburn is the head. Mr. Reyburn is a Director of the I. R. T. Co., the Federal Reserve Bank, and a member of many of New York's most important clubs. He is one of the city's real *assets*.

MR. FRANKLIN SIMON

Blank & Stoller

Altho Mr. Simon is past fifty, he is one of the youngest men in New York. In fact he is about the youngest person ever referred to as "father" of an important movement, for it was *he* who first visioned the great possibilities of Fifth Avenue as the coming shopping center of the city. He opened up Fifth Avenue's first great fashion shop in 1902. The big department stores paid little attention to "fashion," and the prices of private dress makers were more or less prohibitive. Mr. Simon conceived the idea of offering something "in between." He trained New York's first "fashion executives"; he organized the first Paris fashion office; and he created the famous "Bramley fashions"—the only American mode that has ever been recognized in Paris, and enjoys an international reputation. Mr. Simon is not only a "live wire," but every inch a *gentleman*.

MR. JESSE ISIDOR STRAUS

Mr. Jesse Isidor Straus is the son of the highly respected and much revered Isidor Straus (lately deceased) who endeared himself to all humanity by his devotion to various philanthropies for the good of mankind. Jesse Isidor Straus was born in New York City, June 25, 1872, and being educated in New York schools was graduated from Harvard in 1893. His first position in business was with the Hanover National Bank as a clerk. Later he became an executive in the Abraham & Straus Department Store in Brooklyn, from which institution he joined "Macy's"—becoming President of the company in 1919. Mr. Straus has proven himself not only a masterful executive, but one of New York's most respected citizens. "Macy's" under his regime has been the talk of the entire department store world.

OUTSTANDING ATTORNEYS AND JURISTS

Mishkin

MR. GEORGE GORDON BATTLE

In selecting the names of our outstanding attorneys and judges, thirty representative New Yorkers were consulted. *Every one of them* voted Mr. Battle as one of the brainiest, most ethical, and best versed in law. Mr. Battle was born in North Carolina, Oct. 26, 1868, and after graduating from the State University, came to New York in 1890, where he studied law at Columbia—which university recommended him to the N. Y. District Attorney. From then on, his rise was consistent with his remarkable attainments, his masterful intellect, and keen knowledge of human nature. Mr. Battle is a thorough gentleman, has a winning personality, and a sterling integrity that has never been questioned. GEORGE GORDON BATTLE is a big name in New York's legal circles.

HON. FREDERICK E. CRANE

M. Beverle

Judge Crane was born in Brooklyn, N. Y., March 2, 1869. He received his LL.B. at Columbia University in 1889, and his LL.D. in 1893. He was appointed Judge (Kings County) in 1901, and Justice of the Supreme Court New York (2nd District) 1906. In 1920 he was transferred to Court of Appeals. He is highly esteemed for his logical reasoning, and fair decisions. He has a record for strictest integrity, and has made a wonderful name for himself as a result of his impartial and unprejudiced opinions. Judge Crane has always been an enthusiast on tennis, swimming and outdoor sports. He is also no "duffer" at golf!

Pach Bros.

MR. JOHN W. DAVIS

John W. Davis is not only one of New York's leading attorneys, but also one of New York's soundest business men. He is a Director of the Mutual Life Ins. Co., the National Bank of Commerce, the U. S. Rubber Co. Born in Clarksburg, W. Va., he was educated at Washington and Lee University, receiving his degree of A.B. in 1892 and his LL.B. in 1895. He was admitted to the Bar in 1915, elected to Congress in 1911, appointed Ambassador to Great Britain in 1918 (serving until 1921) and was the Democratic candidate for President of the United States in 1924. Mr. Davis is yet in his fifties (born in April, 1873) and has lived a most eventful life to date—also a most useful one.

HON. VICTOR JAMES DOWLING

Edward F. Foley

Judge Dowling was born in New York City, July 20, 1866. He studied law at New York University, receiving first prize in his graduating examinations. Becoming interested in politics, he served as a Member of the Assembly in 1894, and as State Senator from 1900 to 1904. In 1904 he was elected a Justice of the Supreme Court of the State, which position he faithfully held for 27 years, serving as a member of the Appelate Division from 1910, and as Presiding Justice from 1927. In 1931 he tendered his resignation to the deep regret of every member of the New York Bar, and the entire community as well.

All groups are listed alphabetically

98

OUTSTANDING ATTORNEYS AND JURISTS—*Continued*

HON. LEARNED HAND

New York has many brilliant attorneys, many of whom have won national prominence for their keen knowledge of the law and their masterful ability to convince juries. And Judge Learned Hand has for many years ranked with the leading legal headliners of the country. Born in Albany, N. Y., he was educated at Harvard and Columbia, receiving his A.B. degree in 1893, and his LL.D. at Harvard Law School in 1896. Admitted to the Bar in 1897, he devoted the two years following to his legal practice But his great ability soon manifested itself and he was appointed Judge in the United States District Court—Southern Division of N. Y., in 1909. Julge Hand is a great walker and traveler, and is a great believer in the "big out-doors." Clubs—the University, Harvard, and Century.

HON. NATHAN L. MILLER

Solon, N. Y., boasts of having presented Nathan L. Miller to the world, at which place he was born Oct. 10, 1868. Educated in the normal school, Mr. Miller was admitted to the New York Bar in 1893. Proving himself one of the most brilliant attorneys in the city, he soon became prominent in politics, and was appoined Justice of the Supreme Court in 1903. In 1921 he was elected Governor of New York State on the Republican ticket, serving two years. He resigned public office, however, to resume his law practice, and is recognized as one of New York's most outstanding legal lights. Mr. Miller is a quiet man, but has a dynamic force which, plus his brilliant mind and keen knowledge of law, *wins cases!*

HON. SAMUEL SEABURY

Judge Seabury is a "native son"—having been born in New York, where, after studying law, he was admitted to the Bar and made such a name for himself, he was elected Justice of the City Court. In 1907, he became Justice of the Supreme Court (New York), First District, and in 1914 elected Associate Judge of the Court of Appeals. He resigned public office, however, in 1916 to resume private practice. That same year he was induced to run for Governor as a candidate on the Democratic ticket. Judge Seabury has come into national prominence of late as a result of his forceful aggressiveness in connection with his investigation of City Hall and Tammany officials.

HON. GEORGE WOODWARD WICKERSHAM

Mr. Wickersham has again come into national prominence recently as a result of his strenuous activities as Chairman of President Hoover's Law Enforcement Commission. Mr. Wickersham has lived a most eventful career. Born in Pittsburgh, Sept. 19, 1858, he was educated by private tutors, later securing his degree of LL. B. at University of Pennsylvania, and his LL.D. at Harvard. He came to New York in 1882, and soon became prominent in politics. He served as Attorney General of the U.S. (1909-1913) under the Taft administration, and has occupied many offices of prominence in his loyalty to civic and charitable welfare.

99

OUTSTANDING JOURNALISTS

MR. PAUL BLOCK

Paul Block, President and Publisher of the Brooklyn STANDARD UNION and nine other big newspaper plants in Newark, Pittsburgh, Toledo, Duluth, Milwaukee, Los Angeles, etc., was most indifferent to being classed among the 100 outstanding men of New York, as he insists that he belongs to the *masses*. But those who *know* Mr. Block, and are conversant with his achievements, will confirm the judgment of our Committee who voted him as one of "New York's *outstanding* 100!" Mr. Block's $100,000 bequest to Yale, his generalship in raising over $5,000,000 for the support of Jewish Philanthropic Societies and his many activities in helping the poor, etc., has endeared him to all humanity.

MR. ARTHUR BRISBANE

It is doubtful if *any one* living today has written as many *"words"* that have been read, pondered, and appreciated as has Mr. Arthur Brisbane. For over forty years he has been engaged in journalism, starting to work for the *Sun* when but nineteen. Several years later, he became its editor. Afterwards, he managed the *World*. Then came his connection with Mr. Hearst, and the syndication of his writings for 200 newspapers. Not only in journalism, but in every activity to which Mr. Brisbane has applied himself, he is successful. As a boxer, he knocked down Charlie Mitchell, the famous English prize fighter. As a business man, he has made a fortune in real estate. He built Ritz Tower.

MR. CYRUS H. K. CURTIS

Mr. Curtis was born in Portland, Me., June 18, 1850, and started in the publishing business at the age of 22 in Boston, establishing the *Peoples Ledger*. He moved to Philadelphia four years later, and year by year acquired various publications. It was in 1883 that he secured the *Ladies' Home Journal*. In 1890 he established the now famous Curtis Publishing Co.—securing the *Saturday Evening Post* in 1897. In addition to purchasing and starting other papers, he bought the *New York Evening Post* (founded in 1801—130 years ago) which for many years was so ably edited by William Cullen Bryant. Mr. Curtis spends only part of his time in New York, having two other beautiful homes in Wyncote, Pa., and Camden, Maine. His hobbies are music, yachting, and literature.

MR. WILLIAM T. DEWART

Portrait by Salisbury

Here is one of the best pictures ever taken of Mr. William T. Dewart, Publisher of the *Sun*—one of New York's oldest and most popular dailies—founded 98 years ago! Mr. Dewart was born in Fenelon Falls, Ontario, January 29, 1875. He came to this country in 1881. The *Sun* has had many brilliant editors in its long career, but even the famous Charles A. Dana did not approach the financial success which Mr. Dewart is making with the paper. Mr. Dewart is still in his early fifties, but has manifested a journalistic ability that stamps him as a genius. He has brought the old *Sun* up to a standard that ranks it with the truly great newssheets of the world. Mr. Dewart is President of the Frank A. Munsey Co.

and interested in many other business enterprises. He is a Republican in politics, and a member of many clubs.

OUTSTANDING JOURNALISTS (Continued)

MR. FRANK E. GANNETT

Pioneering spirit brought Frank E. Gannett's ancestors to America in 1638. A century and a half later Frank E. Gannett pioneered journalism in Central New York. To-day, in his early fifties, he is the guiding force of the *Brooklyn Eagle*, the *Hartford Times* and 15 other news-papers in the East, including the leading dailies in Albany, Rochester, Utica, Elmira, N. Y., and Plainfield, N. J.

Attempting new things in journalism, he succeeded in divorcing newspapers from political control. Under Mr. Gannett's ownership the *Eagle* has built a new home and increased its circulation more than 30 per cent. Newspaper work paid Mr. Gannett's expenses through Cornell University, of which he is now a trustee. He became a newspaper owner in 1906 by buying a half interest in the *Elmira Gazette*. He has been presi-dent of the Publishers Association, the Press Association and the Associated Dailies of New York State.

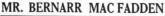
Nicholas Murray

MR. ROY W. HOWARD

Here is the picture of Roy W. Howard, editor and president of the *World-Telegram*. In 1927 Mr. Howard purchased the *old Telegram* and in four years' time transformed it from a cheap and unprofitable sporting sheet into one of the most outstanding and popular dailies in this eastern country.

In February (1931) Mr. Howard purchased the famous old *New York World* (see page 73). Incidentally, Mr. Howard is Chairman of the Board of the 25 Scripps-Howard newspapers of which the combined *World-Telegram* is one. Mr. Howard is still in his forties (having been born at Gano, Ohio, Jan. 1, 1883). In his early youth he played a cornet in a newsboys' band. He admits he made a great con-tribution to music when he sidetracked the cornet for a reporters job on the Indianapolis *Star*. At the early age of 28 he became President of the United Press—which now serves 45 foreign nations in 10 languages. His record during the World War was spectacular. Mr. Howard hates golf, bridge and champagne, but loves poker, shooting, and real beer.

MR. BERNARR MAC FADDEN

Bernarr MacFadden is one of New York's most dynamic, most successful and most interesting citizens. Born in Mill Springs, Mo., Aug. 16, 1868, his early life was spent on a farm as chore boy. Later he moved to St. Louis where he found a job as clerk in a shoe store. But Bernarr MacFadden was not destined to be either a farm hand or a shoe clerk.

From his early teens, he was obsessed with the importance of "physical culture." For nearly forty years he has been emphasizing, advocating, and preaching the gospel of health, proper exercise, etc. Mr. MacFadden is the author of many books on the subject, and is known as the "Father of Physical Culture." He founded the *Physical Culture Magazine* in 1898, and thus became a *publisher*. Today, Mr. MacFadden is one of the largest "publishers" in America. In addition to publishing TEN nationally circulated magazines, he publishes the *New York Graphic* (see page 74).

MR. ADOLPH S. OCHS

Mr. Ochs was born in 'Cincinnati, March 12, 1858. He began his business career at eleven years of age delivering news-papers. At the age of seventeen, he accepted a job with the *Courier Journal* at Louisville, Ky. Two years later he be-came identified with the *Chattanooga Daily Dispatch*. The paper failed, however, and Mr. Ochs was appointed receiver.

Succeeding in liquidating his debts, he then arranged a consolidation with the *Chattanooga Times* (in which he secured control—and still owns) and built this up to one of the best and most successful papers in the south. In 1896 Mr. Ochs secured control of the *New York Times* (established in 1851) which had become involved in financial difficulties, but which he succeeded in building up to its present commanding position as the *leading newspaper of the world*.

All groups are listed alphabetically

OUTSTANDING DIVINES

© D. E. Kane

DR. S. PARKES CADMAN

Born in Shropshire, England, in December, 1864, (graduating from London University) Dr. Cadman came to America in 1890 with scarcely a penny and owing $500! As a boy, he walked six miles daily to his work in a coal mine. His wages were so meager that they taught him the side of life which served as the basis for the career to which he has devoted his energies (advising unfortunates, relieving distress, and helping to solve problems confronting the masses). Dr. Cadman is not only an outstanding New Yorker, but a national character, *known and beloved by the entire nation.* For thirty years he has served as minister of the famous Congregational Church of Brooklyn. If a list of his honorary positions and fruitful activities were chronicled, several pages would be required. Dr. S. Parkes Cadman is a *HE*-MAN in every meaning of the term. After showing the writer thru his immense church auditorium (seating over 2,000) he said "Now come in the office, let's have a little *smoke* and a *drink*—of Croton water!"

REV. HARRY EMERSON FOSDICK

D. Jay Culver

Few Divines are as liberal, as charitable in their views, or as *big* in their broad comprehension of life, religion and of human nature as the Rev. Harry Emerson Fosdick. And this is why Dr. Fosdick is so nationally known, so universally respected, and so keenly beloved. Born in Buffalo, May 24, 1878, he came to New York in 1901 as a student in Union Theological Seminary and Columbia University, and his first activities were in connection with a Mission in the Bowery. From then on, he has devoted his life to the ministry and welfare work. Dr. Fosdick has written a dozen books, several of which are exceedingly popular. Four years ago, he was called to Riverside Church (see page 53) of which he is now the head. Dr. Fosdick is recognized as one of the most brilliant speakers in the American pulpit.

G. Felicit Romo

HIS EMINENCE, PATRICK CARDINAL HAYES

Born in New York City, Cardinal Patrick Hayes has become one of the city's most outstanding men. Sterling character, brilliant achievement, and that rare something that commands both love and respect of all, have won for this great man so many honors, pages would be required to cite them. Even as a young man of 21, he obtained the degree of A.B. and at 25 obtained Priesthood (St. Joseph's Seminary at Troy, N. Y., 1892). In 1904 (Rome, Italy) he became a Doctor of Divinity, and in 1907 was appointed Prelate to the Pope. He became Archbishop of New York in 1919, and was created a Cardinal at Rome March 24, 1924. Cardinal Hayes is intensely human, and has a personality that commands the love and esteem of Protestant and Jew, as well as Catholic.

All groups are listed alphabetically

102

OUTSTANDING DIVINES (*continued*)

BISHOP OF NEW YORK
REV. WILLIAM T. MANNING

Bishop Wm. T. Manning was born in England in 1866, coming to America with his parents in his boyhood. He was educated at the University of the South (Sewanee, Tenn.) and later received honorary degrees from nearly a dozen important colleges. He has served as Rector of Protestant Episcopal Parishes in California, Tennessee, Ohio, Pennsylvania, and also of Trinity Church (New York). Bishop Manning has been one of the chief factors in the construction of the Cathedral of St. John the Divine, which when completed will be one of the largest and most magnificent church edifices in the world. The corner stone of this great cathedral was laid in 1892, and $13,000,000 has already been raised—largely due to the efforts of Bishop Manning—whose life has been spent in the service of others, and who, both as a man and a church dignitary has proven himself one of New York's greatest citizens.

REV. CHRISTIAN F. REISNER

It would require almost half this book to enumerate the activities and schedule the achievements of Dr. Christian F. Reisner—outstanding clergyman, advertising genius, and business man, all combined in one! Dr. Reisner was one of thirteen children, and was born in Atchison, Kansas, June 3, 1872. From the day he graduated from college he has been one of the busiest "preachers" America has ever produced. Called to Grace Methodist Church (New York) his first move was to raise $70,000, and liquidate debts of nineteen years standing. Today he is building BROADWAY TEMPLE (see page 54) costing over $6,000,000, guiding the campaign

which raised $3,500,000 in subscriptions within a few months. Altho Dr. Reisner is simplicity itself, he is dynamic in manner, and has organized and instituted more original ideas and innovations in church life, than any other "parson" of our era. He is a powerful writer, a brilliant lecturer, and a convincing interpreter of the gospel. He has received nearly 10,000 members into the churches he has served. The West lost one of its chief power plants when Dr. Reisner moved to New York!

DR. STEPHEN S. WISE

Dr. Stephen S. Wise is a descendant of a long line of rabbis who have been active in Jewish life in the German speaking lands of Europe. He was brought to this country as an infant in 1875, receiving his early education in the public schools, and later graduating from Columbia in 1892. Dr. Wise has lived a busy life. He is not only one of the founders of the original Zionist movement, and of the American Jewish Congress, but himself founded the first Zionist organization of America—the great Free Synagogue of New York. He has ever been active in religious, civic, and educational work, and is the author of many volumes of importance in the religious and literary field. Few men in all New York are more universally admired and respected for unselfish devotion to the welfare of others than this talented and very earnest worker in humanity's cause.

All groups are listed alphabetically

OUTSTANDING HOTEL OPERATORS

MR. LUCIUS M. BOOMER

There are few names in the hotel world as big as that of Lucius M. Boomer. Born in Poughkeepsie, N. Y., Aug. 22, 1878, he was educated at the University of Chicago, and secured his first hotel job with the Flagler Hotel System in 1897. From the very start, his initiative his close application to any task he undertook, and his well balanced judgment and fearless courage, soon forced him to the attention of the "big fellows" in the hotel arena. At the early age of 25, he became manager of the famous Royal Muskoka—Muskoka Lakes, Canada. From then on his advancement was rapid—Plaza Hotel (N. Y.), Taft Hotel (New Haven), McAlpin Hotel, etc. Then came his connection with Senator Dupont in the purchase of the great Waldorf Astoria. Today, Mr. Boomer's hotel interests include Louis Sherry's, The Sherry-Netherland, The Savarin chain of restaurants, and the new Waldorf-Astoria—the greatest hotel in existence. Mr. Boomer is one of the busiest men living, and yet he is always approachable, very democratic, and a prince of good fellows.

MR. JOHN McENTEE BOWMAN

Underwood & Underwood

Mr. Bowman is one of the most outstanding examples of a "self-made" man in all New York. Born in Toronto, Canada, July 20, 1875, he struggled through a common school education, then headed for New York at the age of seventeen. He had no friends, but finally secured a job at the old Holland House. Just allow John Bowman an "entering wedge," and *he* will do the rest. His original ideas, far-sightedness, and good business head soon attracted attention. In due time he became assistant manager. Today, Mr. Bowman is President of the Biltmore Hotels Corp. which not only controls the sumptuous Biltmore and Commodore Hotels of New York, but *eleven other* magnificent and palatial Biltmore Hotels in eleven leading cities of the country.

Passed to the Great Beyond—Oct. 28, 1931

GENERAL JAMES LESLIE KINCAID

©Geo. Maillard Kesslere

General James Leslie Kincaid started life as a lawyer, being admitted to the New York bar in 1909. He was born at Syracuse, N. Y., Nov. 28, 1884. Becoming interested in hotel life he forged his way into prominence and became Vice-President of the United Hotels Co. of America in 1921. In 1924 he became President of the great American Hotels Corporation. He is also President of the magnificent Lexington Hotel at 48th and Lexington Ave., and a number of other large hotel organizations.

General Kincaid is very active in aviation and not only a Director of American Airports Corporation, Colonial Western Airways, Inc., and Colonial Air Transport, but an officer or director in many other industrial organizations.

His career in the army has been a brilliant one and many decorations have been conferred upon him.

General Kincaid is a Republican, Methodist, Mason, and belongs to many prominent clubs, including the Metropolitan Club, Army and Navy Club, etc. He is a *he* man all the way through and numbers his friends in four figures.

OUTSTANDING HOTEL OPERATORS *(Continued)*

MR. DAVID HURST KNOTT

In whatever field Mr. Knott concentrates his attention, he has a habit of "making good." As a politician, he made good as early as 1913 in the New York State Assembly. From 1918 to 1922, he made good as Sheriff of New York County. As a business man, he is making good as Trustee or Director in a number of New York's most important banks. In the hotel world, he is considered a *genius,* having made good as the head of a group of hotels known as the "Knott Chain," a number of which are illustrated in this book. Mr. Knott enjoys the esteem of both guests and employees—the *sure* test of having made good. He has also made good as a father, being the proud possessor of four most interesting young Knotts!

MR. FREDERICK A. MUSCHENHEIM

Born in Braunfels, Prussia, February 27, 1871. Mr. Muschenheim came to America to see what this country had to offer him. He liked it so well he became an American citizen and today his name is the biggest in hoteldom in the entire nation. In his earlier days Mr. Muschenheim was an engineer and by the time he was thirty, became factory superintendent of the Western Electric. Shortly afterwards he started his hotel career and has been connected with the hotel Astor ever since 1903—almost 30 years. Mr. Muschenheim is President and Treasurer of Hotel Astor, President of the Hotel Association of New York, and connected with many organizations— among which, he is trustee of the Franklin Savings Bank and Stevens Institute of Technology. Mr. Muschenheim is a forceful man and has countless friends.

MR. GEORGE W. SWEENEY

Born in New York City, June 23, 1863, Mr. George W. Sweeney had nothing but a common school education. At the age of thirteen, he was forced to go to work. His first job was washing dishes in a downtown restaurant. But Mr. Sweeney washed dishes *well.* In fact, Mr. Sweeney has been doing things well ever since. Men of the Sweeney type cannot be kept at washing dishes very long, and young George found himself even at a youthful age filling the position of manager in a big Rochester hotel. By 1901 he was a real factor in hotel circles and, returning to New York, purchased the old Victoria Hotel on Fifth Avenue, just above Madison Square. Today, Mr. Sweeney is Vice-President of the Bowman-Biltmore Hotels Corp. and Managing Director of the magnificent Commodore. Mr. Sweeney's vast popularity is evidenced by the fact that he has served as President of the American Hotel Association, the New York Hotel Association, The Hotel Men's Mutual Benefit Association, etc. When you're at the Biltmore, meet him—you'll like him.

OUTSTANDING REAL ESTATE BROKERS

MR. MORTON R. CROSS

Mr. Morton R. Cross is President of the great real estate firm of Cross & Brown—which he founded in 1909. Born in Wakefield, R. I., he came to New York in 1903 and soon became an aggressive factor in real estate circles. When "Cross & Brown" started business their force consisted of a few over half a dozen workers. Today over 200 are kept busy. Mr. Cross has always been a firm believer in the idea that absolute integrity and frankness are the foundation stones of surest success, and he has so thoroughly inculcated this policy into his organization, that it is conceded that few houses in his line have a higher type clientele. Mr. Cross is a man of dynamic energy and one who lives up to his word—no matter what the cost.

MR. WARREN CRUIKSHANK

Mr. Warren Cruikshank has been engaged in the real estate business since 1877. The firm was established in 1794 by his grandfather, who came to America from Scotland—where he was born. The real estate house of Cruikshank has been continued by the family for 137 years, during which time they have handled the business of some of the oldest families of New York. Mr. Cruikshank has always been enthusiastic about fishing, hunting and outdoor life and, as a result, has enjoyed excellent health. He is a Director of the Irving Trust Company, Fulton Trust Company of New York, Almy Realty Corporation and other banking and business institutions. His judgment is sound, his integrity unquestioned and his standing in the community the highest.

Underwood & Underwood

MR. DOUGLAS L. ELLIMAN

Mr. Elliman began his business career as clerk in a bank at $5 per week. Today he is the President and head of Douglas L. Elliman & Co. —one of the most outstanding real estate firms in the city. His concern is largely responsible for the vast development of "Mid-town New York," having been most active in the organization and development of the magnificent Roosevelt Hotel, the Lexington, Pierre, Park Lane, and other palatial hotels and apartment buildings. His firm is also largely responsible for many of the big town's largest office and commercial structures. It would require several pages to list the Elliman operations in the purchase of land, promotion of huge building projects, and their extensive renting and managing activities, but the sum involves scores of millions! Mr. Elliman is the type of man who can look one squarely in the eye and not only win confidence, but hold it. He is an officer or director in many business institutions and clubs, an ardent golfer, an enthusiastic yachtsman, and a real man. Altho one of the busiest individuals in all the city, he always seems to be able to find time to lend his assistance to any worthy cause or enterprise.

Blank & Stoller Inc.

MR. LAWRENCE B. ELLIMAN

Mr. Lawrence B. Elliman is president of the great real estate firm of Pease & Elliman. He was born in Flushing, N. Y., September 11th, 1876—one of the "centennial boys"! When the writer first met Mr. Elliman, his handshake was all that was needed to evidence the cause of his great success in business. The man is so saturated with good nature, magnetic personality, and general responsiveness, that you can just feel he is "with you" before you start telling him what is on your mind. . . . Mr. Elliman's parents were of English descent, who came to this country in 1635—one of his great-grandfathers being one of the original patentees of what is now the town of Flushing. Mr. Elliman was graduated at Flushing Institute and Berkley School, New York City. He entered business when quite young with his father at the age of eighteen, but had a leaning for real estate, and formed the firm of Pease & Elliman three years later (1897) which was incorporated in 1901. . . . There is scarcely a citizen of New York who does not know of Pease & Elliman as for over thirty years they have been recognized as a house of not only sterling integrity, but one of aggressive and painstaking care of the customers' interests. Some years ago Mr. Elliman purchased the Pease holdings in the firm. . . . Mr. Elliman is a member of so many clubs, and a director or officer in so many large institutions, there is not room here to cite them all, but his firm is responsible to a very large extent for the development of Park Avenue to its present supremacy as one of the finest residence thoroughfares in all the world. They are also responsible for the erection of some of Fifth Avenue's most palatial apartment buildings. . . . It is not only a pleasure and an honor to know Mr. Elliman, but Greater New York owes him a genuine debt of gratitude for what he and his firm have done towards its higher type development.

All groups are listed alphabetically
106

OUTSTANDING REAL ESTATE BROKERS—*(Continued)*

MR. PETER GRIMM

Altho still in his early forties (born in New York City Jan. 12, 1886), Peter Grimm is becoming a big name in Real Estate circles. Mr. Grimm worked his way thru college, graduating from Columbia in 1911. He immediately entered the business of real estate as a leasing broker, and soon worked his way to prominence, and became President of the Building Managers and Owners Assn. in 1925. In 1927 he became President of the Real Estate Board, which position he has held ever since. Mr. Grimm is president of Wm. A. White & Sons, agents for the Radio City development and for the United States Government in assembling the block Barclay, Vesey, Church Streets and West Broadway, where the new general Post Office will be located. He is also chairman of the Mayor's Committee on Taxation and Provisional Chairman of the Citizens' Budget Committee.

MR. ALFRED E. MARLING

Mr. Alfred E. Marling is not only President of the famous old real estate brokerage firm of Horace S. Ely Co., but Trustee of the Mutual Life Ins. Co., Fulton Trust Co., Title Guarantee & Trust Co., and a Director in many other nationally known corporations of New York. Mr. Marling was born in Toronto, Canada. Oct. 5, 1858, but came to New York many years ago and has grown up with the city. He is a man of quiet dignity, but of dynamic force, and has brought the house of Ely up to one of the most outstanding real estate brokerage firms in all New York. He is an enthusiastic member of New York's great Chamber of Commerce, and also a member of many of the city's most important clubs, among which are the Union League, Metropolitan, Union, etc.

MR. CHARLES F. NOYES

Mr. Charles F. Noyes is known in the real estate world as the "MANAGER OF A THOUSAND BUILDINGS". The firm of Charles F. Noyes Co., Inc., have so far outdistanced all competitors in the real estate brokerage line they are now recognized as the world's largest operators. Mr. Noyes is also the head of the C. F. Noyes National Realty Corp. which supports offices in both New York and Chicago. The Chas. F. Noyes Co., Inc., have a "tenant roll" of approximately 10,000, employ over 2,000 help, and have one of the most highly standardized organizations for efficiency in the entire real estate world. Each tenant is given the same personal attention, and each building managed by the Noyes Co. is given the same individual service as if he were the only "customer" on the Noyes records.

MR. ROBERT P. DOWLING

BING & BING

MR. WILLIAM H. WHEELOCK

Three other big names in New York's Real Estate World

OUTSTANDING ADVERTISING SPECIALISTS

MR. BRUCE BARTON

Bruce Barton, son of the late Rev. William E. Barton, D.D., distinguished clergyman and biographer of Abraham Lincoln. He was born in Robbins, Tennessee, and subsequently lived with his parents in Ohio, Massachusetts and Illinois. Graduated from Amherst in 1907, and, after engaging in various publishing enterprises, entered the advertisine business on January 1, 1919, as president of Barton, Dursting & Osborn, Inc. Ten years later this agency was consolidated with George Batten Co., and Mr. Barton became chairman of the board of Batten, Barton, Durstine & Osborn, Inc. He is widely known as a writer of books and magazine articles.

MR. WILLIAM H. RANKIN

Mr. Rankin was born in New Albany, Ind. February 18, 1878. He was educated at the New Albany High School and Spencerian Business College of Louisville, Ky.

William H. Ranklin is a forceful man, an optimist, and always cheerful. He is a thinker and thinks along sound lines. He is a doer and does what he undertakes in a dynamic way. He is unquestionably one of the best informed advertising men in all America and the position the Wm. H. Rankin Co. holds in the advertising field today, is due to his great vision, initiative and forceful way of *getting results*. Ever since his early activities in a newspaper office Mr. Rankin has been identified with big men and big doings. His patriotic service during the World War won him international appreciation. Mr. Rankin is a member of many clubs and his hobbies are advertising, golf, baseball and books.

MR. STANLEY RESOR

Mr. Resor has been president of J. Walter Thompson Co., the well-known advertising house since 1917. Born in Cincinnati, April 30, 1879, Mr. Resor graduated from Yale with the degree of B.A. in 1901, and ever since embarking in the business world he has been more or less actively engaged in the advertising business.

After serving with Proctor & Collier of Cincinnati for a number of years, he went with the J. Walter Thompson Co., and in 1912 was appointed vice-president and general manager becoming president in 1917. Under his regime this institution has become one of the leading advertising institutions in the country. Mr. Resor has been very active in hospital work and is a board member of several of the large hospitals in the city. He is a member of many clubs and one of New York's most respected citizens.

MR. FRANK J. REYNOLDS

Mr. Frank J. Reynolds is not only a self made man but one who did a *good job* in "making" himself. (Born in New York in 1890) he became identified with the advertising house of Albert Frank & Co. in 1909 as filing clerk at the munificent stipend of $2.00 a week. But whatever Mr. Reynolds attempts, he does well. He did his filing so *well* that he was assigned other tasks. He did *them* well also. His advancement was continuous. Although not yet forty-two years of age he is today president of the institution. Mr. Reynolds has a genial and snappy way about him that folks like and the advertising concern of Albert Frank & Co. largely owes its great success to his popularity and executive ability.

OUTSTANDING REAL ESTATE INVESTORS

MR. VINCENT ASTOR

Inheriting one of the largest fortunes of the age, Mr. Vincent Astor, from his early youth, has manifested the keenest regard for things worth while, and an earnest interest in business. Born in New York City, Nov. 15, 1891—the only son of the late John Jacob, and Ava Willing Astor. Graduating from Harvard in 1912, he immediately became active in learning "business." When the world war broke out, he enlisted as a Lieutenant in the U. S. Navy and had active duty in European waters. Mr. Astor has invested millions in palatial apartment buildings in the Carl Schurz Park area.

MR. IRWIN S. CHANIN

When a young man starts life with only a few dollars and becomes a multi-millionaire in his thirties, and makes every dollar of it by legitimate investment and hard work, he is quite qualified to rank among New York's "100 wonder men." Irwin S. Chanin was born in Brooklyn on October 29, 1892. After his graduation as an engineer from Cooper Union and World War service in 1919, he undertook his first building venture —a one-family frame house in Bensonhurst, Long Island. Today he has to his credit six "legitimate" New York theatres, the Roxy Theatre, largest in the world, the 30-story Hotel Lincoln, 56-story Chanin Building, 30-story Majestic Apartments and 30-story Century Apartments, all, with the exception of the Roxy, built and owned by the Chanin Co.

MR. FRED F. FRENCH

Mr. Fred F. French comes from a family who have done things. His mother was a niece of President Fillmore. Born in New York City Oct. 14, 1883, he worked his way to Mexico after graduating from Princeton. There he spent a year among cow boys. Returning to New York in 1905 he became interested in building. In 1910 he organized the Fred F. French Co., drawing $15 per week as president. His working force was one small boy. His first building job was an apartment house in the Bronx which he built on borrowed money, but he made it pay. In 1921 he devised the "Fred F. French Plan" and offered to share his profits with the public. Tudor City and many other beautiful structures are the result.

MR. HENRY MANDEL

Henry Mandel exemplifies what hard work and courage can accomplish. At sixteen he was a bookkeeper for a plumber. At twenty he was in business for himself, and succeeded in building his first structure on Broadway and 96th St. Today he is head of the Henry Mandel Companies—one of New York's largest realty operators. The achievement which brought him his reputation for daring was the Pershing Square Building in the Grand Central zone. It has earned large dividends from the beginning. Later, he built "One Park Ave." building. His crowning achievement however is "London Terrace"—a $25,000,000 project (see page 269). Mr. Mandel is only forty-five years of age.

All groups are listed alphabetically

OUTSTANDING BUILDING CONTRACTORS

MR. LOU R. CRANDALL

Three years ago (at the age of thirty-three) Lou R. Crandall, born on a farm near Sylvania, Ohio, came to the "wonder city" to become President of one of the world's largest building contracting concerns—the George A. Fuller Co., founded in Chicago in 1890. Today, at thirty-six, Mr. Crandall is still the youngest executive in this field of big business. After finishing college, he worked his way up from a graduate engineer to his present position. Mr. Crandall can be found at his desk on a top floor of his own new Fuller building, which in 1930 succeeded the famous old "Flatiron Building" as New York headquarters of the company—subsidiary of the famous property-holding U. S. Realty & Improvement Corp.

MR. LOUIS J. HOROWITZ

Fate itself is impotent to prevent certain men from forging to the front. Such a man is Louis J. Horowitz, Chairman of the Board of Directors of the Thompson-Starrett Co., Inc., builders of the Woolworth, Equitable Office, Equitable Trust, Municipal building and the majestic Waldorf-Astoria. Mr. Horowitz was born in Chenstochowa, Poland, Jan. 1, 1875, coming to America in 1891, and making his first American dollar working as a cash boy for the famous old clothing house of Brill Bros. In 1898 he connected with the Thompson Starrett Co. and by 1903 had demonstrated such ability that he was appointed President of that organization which office he held continuously until made Chairman of the Board.

MR. FRED T. LEY

In his nearly sixty years of active life, Mr. Fred T. Ley has been consistently accomplishing things. He was born in Springfield, Mass., April 22, 1872. After a high school education, he became interested in "building," and at the age of 21, founded the firm of Fred T. Ley, Inc. His company has erected many of New York's outstanding structures, among which might be mentioned the famous Chrysler, the Fisk, the Westinghouse, and others too numerous to list. Mr. Ley is an enthusiastic club man. He is President of Fisk Building Corp., Kingston Consolidated Railway, etc.

MR. MILLARD SHRODER

When a man becomes one of the owners of a great business in his early thirties, and constructs tens of millions of dollars worth of buildings before attaining the age of forty, there is something more than "luck" in such accomplishment! At the age of seventeen, Mr. Shroder secured a job with Bing & Bing, the real estate operators, with whom he remained for seven years until 1916. In the World War young Shroder became a civilian employee of the Ordnance Department. In 1919, he started his partnership with Mr. Arthur D. Koppel, under the name of Shroder & Koppel. These two young men have constructed many of the most pretentious skyscrapers in New York, in cost aggregating over $100,000,000.

All groups are listed alphabetically

COL. W. A. STARRETT

Colonel Starrett is Vice President of Starrett Brothers and Eken, Inc., builders of the wonderful EMPIRE STATE and BANK OF MANHATTAN buildings (two of the tallest structures in the world). In this book are pictured other magnificent structures erected by his firm. Colonel Starrett was born June 14, 1877, at Lawrence, Kansas. On leaving college he became interested in building, and was one of the original founders of the Thompson-Starrett Company. At the outbreak of the World War he was called into service as Major of Engineers, and assigned to duty as Chairman of Emergency Construction Section of the War Industries Board, charged with establishing the Army's war construction program and in complete charge of all Army construction work for war purposes in this country. At the close of the war he joined the George A. Fuller Company as a Vice President. In 1922, he and his brother, Paul Starrett, and Andrew J. Eken, founded Starrett Brothers, Inc. (now Starrett Brothers and Eken, Inc.). In June, 1931, the University of Michigan conferred upon Colonel Starrett the honorary degree of Doctor of Engineering. Colonel Starrett is a facile writer (Atlantic Monthly, Scientific American, Scribner's, Saturday Evening Post, etc.), is a member of many clubs, a good "mixer" and has a most magnetic personality. Few men have more sincere friends.

MR. JOHN REYNARD TODD

Mr. Todd was born October 27, 1867, at Johnstown, Wis. He graduated from Princeton (A.B.) 1889, (A.M.) 1893. Studied law and was admitted to the bar in Tennessee. He formed a partnership with Henry C. Irons under the firm name of Irons & Todd. Formed originally to practice law, the firm almost immediately entered construction and engineering work in New York City. Mr. Todd became President of Todd, Robertson, Todd, Engineering Corporation in 1920. These two concerns have done much building work in New York City. At the present time Todd, Robertson, Todd Engineering Corp. and Todd & Brown (of which Webster B. Todd is President) have in hand the rebuilding of Williamsburg, Va., and the entire handling of the $250,000,000 Rockefeller City in New York.

MR. HENRY C. TURNER

Mr. Turner is a builder. And he is a *good* builder. Graduating from Swarthmore College in 1893, he became greatly interested in the growth of what was then a new industry—reinforced concrete. Devoting his energies to its development, he organized the Turner Construction Co., and from a modest beginning of $40,000 business the first year, the company has had a steady and substantial growth. Today, the Turner Construction Co. ranks among the largest institutions of its kind in the country, having constructed over 1400 buildings, costing in excess of $350,000,000! Mr. Turner's reputation for integrity and absolute dependability, are largely responsible for the fact that for 29 years a steady and increasing number of business men have been turning over their construction work to this very able firm.

OUTSTANDING ARCHITECTS

MR. HARVEY WILEY CORBETT

Mr. Corbett ranks with the outstanding architects of the world! Here are a few of his degrees and titles: B.S., A.D.G., M.Arch., F.A.I.A., F.R.I.B.A., Litt.D., LLD., and N.A. He is Chairman of the Commission entrusted with the architectural construction of Chicago's great World's Fair of 1933, evidence in itself of his high standing. Mr. Corbett is a disciple of the "old school" at heart, but his versatile talents have enabled him to combine modernistic tendencies in his designs in such a manner as to command respect of advocates of both curves and straight lines! Mr. Corbett was born in San Francisco in 1873.

MR. ELY JACQUES KAHN

Ely Jacques Kahn is individual. He thinks for himself, and has the courage to back up any stand he takes. Born June 1, 1884, Mr. Kahn is still in his forties, and yet he is today recognized as not only one of the outstanding architects of the city, but of the entire country. His father was a manufacturer and wanted young Ely to learn the business, but architecture called more strongly, and today Ely Jacques Kahn is one of the leading exponents of what is known as the "modern School." As Vice President of the Architectural League, he has had much to do with the handling of practical ends of his profession.

MR. WILLIAM M. KENDALL

Known as the "Grand old Gentleman" in the architectural world, Mr. Kendall is rather along in years (having been born in 1856) but the "old" in reference to him, is more in the nature of endearment than age. Mr. Kendall is yet one of the "young men" in so far as zest for further achievement is concerned. Mr. Kendall is emphatically a rabid adherent of the "old school" in architecture and thus his soubriquet "Old Hat"! He is serving his fiftieth year as a member of the great architectural firm of McKim, Mead & White, and is credited with having been the master mind that has made this famous organization so highly considered.

MR. GOODHUE LIVINGSTON

Mr. Goodhue Livingston is not only a native New Yorker, but about as nearly a "100% American citizen" as can be found in our country—his first ancestor having come to these shores from Scotland in 1673! Mr. Livingston's great grandfather inaugurated George Washington as first President of the United States. Born in New York City in 1867, Mr. Livingston graduated from Columbia College with highest honors, and entered the architectural profession after securing a diploma from the School of Architecture. He is the surviving member of the outstanding firm of Trowbridge & Livingston which has drawn plans for so many of New York's most imposing and beautiful buildings (Equitable Trust, Stock Exchange Addition, etc.).

All groups are listed alphabetically

OUTSTANDING ARCHITECTS—*Continued*

MR. SIMON I. SCHWARTZ

Mr. Schwartz was born in New York City, May 6, 1876. From earliest boyhood he had a zest for drawing, but wherever he applied for a "job" he was asked to *pay* for the first year's training. But he finally secured an opening with Henry Anderson at $2 per week and applied himself so diligently that his rise was rapid. Today his firm, "Schwartz & Gross," are one of the leading architectural firms in the city. You will find pictures of some of the mammoth buildings for which they have drawn plans all through this volume.

MR. JOHN SLOAN

John Sloan was born in N. Y. City, March 6, 1884, and started in business for himself at the age of 21 (1905). Two years later, he left for the Philippine Islands as Architect and Supt. of Construction for the War Department. When the World War broke out, he was commissioned as Captain in the 72nd Division Army Air Service. In 1924 the present partnership of Sloan & Robertson was organized and the success of the firm is attested by many magnificent buildings scattered over New York, among which are the gigantic Graybar building, the Chanin, Maritime Exchange, "29 Broadway," House of Detention and other magnificent skyscrapers.

NEW YORK ARCHITECTS

New York is recognized as the home of the greatest architects in the world and there are fully *twenty* who are *outstanding*. We show pictures of six who have drawn plans for so many of the great buildings illustrated in this book. For instance, the firm of Ely Jacques Kahn drew plans for over 25 magnificent buildings herein. Below are a dozen of the number shown:

		Page			Page
$10,000,000	120 Wall St. Building...	160	$6,000,000	111 John Street Building.	182
8,350,000	2 Park Ave. Building....	207	5,500,000	1441 Broadway Building..	223
8,000,000	1400 Broadway Building..	220	5,500,000	Holland Plaza Building..	197
8,300,000	Squibb Building	257	5,000,000	1410 Broadway Building..	221
6,000,000	1450 Broadway Building..	229	5,000,000	Borden Building	244
6,000,000	30 E. 42nd St. Building..	234	5,000,000	261 Fifth Ave. Building..	208

New York owes its world-famed skyline, its massive beauty and safety itself to its masterful architects and building contractors who, thru long years of experience, have forged to the front as undisputed kings in their profession. In the following list are some of the outstanding firms who have drawn plans for buildings shown herein:—

Geo. & Edwd. Blum, 415 Lexington Ave.
Boak & Paris, Inc., 10 E. 40th St.
Wm. Lawrence Bottomley, 60 E. 42nd St.
Rosario Candela, 578 Madison
J. E. R. Carpenter, 598 Madison
Robert M. Carrere, 38 E. 57th
Clinton & Russell, 17 John St.
Corbett, Harrison & McM., 130 W. 42nd
Cross & Cross, 385 Madison
Delano & Aldrich, 370 Lexington Ave.
Cass, Gilbert, 244 Madison Ave.
Raymond Hood, Godley & F., 40 W. 40th
John Mead Howells, 154 E. 46th
Firm of Ely Jacques Kahn, 2 Park Ave.
Ludlow & Peabody, 101 Park Ave.
McKim, Mead & White, 101 Park Ave.
Yasuo Matsui, 101 Park Ave.
Firm Kenneth M. Murchison, 101 Park Ave.

H. I. Oser, 1140 Broadway
John Russell Pope, 542 Fifth Ave.
Van F. Pruitt, 342 Madison
Geo. P. Post & Sons, 101 Park Ave.
Emery Roth, 1440 Broadway
Schultze & Weaver, 347 Fifth Ave.
Schwartz & Gross, 347 Fifth Ave.
H. Craig Severance, 36 W. 44th
Shampan & Shampan, Brooklyn
Shreve, Lamb & Harmon, 11 E. 44th
Sloan & Robertson, 420 Lexington Ave.
Starrett & Van Vleck, 393 7th Ave.
Trowbridge & Livingston, 527 Fifth Ave.
Wm. Van Alen, 405 Lexington Ave.
Voorhees, Gmelin & Walker, 101 Park Ave.
D. Everett Ware.
Warren & Wetmore, 16. E. 47th
York & Sawyer, 100 E. 42nd
And many others.

All groups are listed alphabetically

OUTSTANDING STAGE FAVORITES

Randall Studio

MR. DEWOLF HOPPER

Here is a most excellent likeness of Mr. DeWolf Hopper—one of New York's most entertaining, most famous, and most beloved young men. It is doubtful if any theatre-goer in all the country does not know him, as he is one of the city's most promising young actors. Although Mr. Hopper has been pleasing people and making them laugh for forty years, he is just as young today as when he first stepped before the footlights. Some folks refuse to recognize such a thing as a calendar, and Mr. Hopper always refers to years as "just a few weeks ago"! He has played to more successes, and given more genuine theatrical enjoyment than possibly any one man who ever played in musical comedy. He made "Wang" a classic. Come on everybody, give the young man a good hand!

MISS BILLIE BURKE

Hal Phyfe

The stage has had but few actresses as magnetic, as popular, and as beautiful, as "Billie Burke." Miss Burke has always had a rare personal charm, and a most unusual talent. Altho born in Washington, D. C., she made her first stage appearance in London, England. Upon returning to America, she made her debut as leading woman with John Drew in "MY WIFE." She made an instantaneous hit and established herself at once as one of America's foremost actresses. Recently she has been starring in "THE TRUTH GAME". Off the stage, Miss Burke is MRS. FLORENZ ZIEGFELD.

Offner Photo

MISS ETHEL BARRYMORE
Dramatic Star

HERE ARE ONLY A FEW OF NEW YORK'S SCORES OF GREAT STAGE FAVORITES

Miss Maude Adams	Mr. John Barrymore
Miss Mary Boland	Mr. Sidney Blackmer
Miss Fannie Brice	Mr. Donald Brian
Mrs. Patrick Campbell	Mr. Eddie Cantor
Miss Ina Claire	Mr. Otto Cruger
Miss Katherine Cornell	Mr. Frank Craven
Miss Dorothy Gish	Mr. Lew Fields
Miss Char'l Greenwood	Mr. Ernest Glendining
Miss Mitzi Hajos	Mr. Henry Hull
Miss Crystal Herne	Mr. Al Jolson
Miss Madge Kennedy	Mr. Bert Lytell
Miss Marilyn Miller	Mr. A. E. Matthews
Miss Nazimova	Mr. Frank Morgan
Miss Anne Pennington	Mr. Rollo Peters
Miss Julia Sanderson	Mr. Otis Skinner
Miss Vivian Segal	Mr. Fred Stone
Miss Leonore Ulrich	Mr. Ernest Truex
Miss Lynn Fontaine	Mr. & Mrs. C. Coburn

Pach Bros.

MISS IRENE BORDONI
Musical Comedy Star

Pach Bros.

MR. ALFRED LUNT
A Matinee Idol

Pach Bros.

MR. WILLIAM GILLETTE
As Sherlock Holmes

Pach Bros.

MR. GEORGE ARLISS
Famous as "Disraeli"

MR. ED. WYNN
As "Simple Simon"

OUTSTANDING FIGURES IN MUSIC AND ART

MR. WALTER JOHANNES DAMROSCH

A most interesting autobiography is "My Musical Life," written by Mr. Walter Damrosch. Mr. Damrosch was born in Breslau, Silesia, Jan. 30, 1862, coming to America with his parents at the age of nine. He studied music from early childhood, and succeeded his father as conductor of the New York Symphony Society in 1885. He also became conductor of the New York Oratorio Society and of German Opera at the Metropolitan Opera House. Mr. Damrosch has composed many meritorious operettas and other music. He is a gentleman, a man of strictest integrity, and one of New York's highest type citizens.

MR. GEORGE GERSHWIN

Altho just 33 years of age (Mr. Gershwin was born Sept. 26, 1898) this young man has already won a world-wide reputation as one of America's leading composers. Mr. Gershwin's versatility stamps him as one of the great musical geniuses of the age. He was the first composer to write "jazz" for the concert hall. On the other hand he is the composer of "Concerto in F" and other remarkable numbers featured by Walter Damrosch as conductor of both the New York and Philharmonic Symphony orchestras. Mr. Gershwin has written 35 musical comedies such as "Lady Be Good," "Girl Crazy," etc. He is recognized as one of America's most talented composers.

MR. IRVING BERLIN

Irving Berlin is one of New York's most interesting characters. He has earned his way thru his marvelous ability to write songs which induce the whole world to want to hear or sing them. Born in the lower East Side on May 11, 1888, he experienced genuine poverty in his early days, but smiling thru it all, he sang his way to recognition, and without knowing either notes or the first rudiments of music. His music may not be "classic" but it *sells*, and Mr. Berlin's fortune is estimated in seven figures. Mr. Berlin had but two years education in the public schools, but has educated himself. Success has not spoiled Irving Berlin—he is just as democratic in his wealth as he was in his poverty.

MR. J. PHILLIP SCHMAND

Those who have seen portraits painted by J. Phillip Schmand are firm in their conviction that no artist could surpass his ability at portraying perfect likeness. Mr. Schmand was born at Germania, Pa., Feb. 24, 1871. He began to study art at an early age and was a pupil of several of the most masterful portrait painters of his day. From the beginning Mr. Schmand evidenced unusual skill. His portraits of Blackstone, Pitt, Mansfield, and John Marshall which grace the walls of the New York Lawyers Club, are said to be among the highest type portrait paintings in the city. His portrait of John R. Patterson, owned by the National Cash Register Co., is a masterpiece, as is also his late portrait of Judge Gary.

OUTSTANDING THEATRICAL PRODUCERS

MR. DANIEL FROHMAN

The name Frohman is as well known in the theatrical world, as the name of Barnum in circus life. The Frohman Brothers have presented to the theatre-going public more world-famous stars than any other producers in America's theatrical history. As will be recalled, Mr. Charles Frohman lost his life in the sinking of the *Lusitania*, but Mr. Daniel Frohman—one of America's grand old men of the theatre—is still preserved to us and at present is concerned chiefly in his activities for the "Actor's Fund of America." Mr. Daniel Frohman's first job was with Horace Greeley as office boy on the New York Tribune.

MR. GEORGE M. COHAN

Few names are better known the world over than that of George M. Cohan—born July 4, 1878 at Providence, R. I. As a dancer, actor, playwright, composer and producer, his millions of admirers and his wealth itself, tell the story. "Mr. George M. Cohan won the World War," stated a member of the British Parliament one evening at a banquet. He then went on to explain that the morale of the combined allied troops was such, that everything looked hopeless. Suddenly Mr. Cohan's stirring little ditty, "Over There," struck Europe with the cheerful message that "The Yanks are coming," and overnight, an entirely new spirit was manifested and the boys held the ground until the Yanks did come!

MR. LEE SHUBERT

Mr. Lee Shubert and his two brothers (Sam. S. and Jacob J.) came to New York from Syracuse when very young men. They had little money, but they had some great ideas about the "booking and managing business." Upon arriving, however, they learned that independent producers were out of luck—a powerful syndicate had secured control of nearly all the theatres in the country. They had cabled Sarah Bernhardt and succeeded in booking her at $1800 a day for 200 performances! When she arrived, however, there were no theatres available. They induced her to "show" in a *tent*. "Sarah" liked their courage and did her best for them. The boys made a "barrel of money." Crowds of 15,000 turned out nightly.

MR. FLORENZ ZIEGFELD

Altho Mr. Florenz Ziegfeld has never known want, he has labored like a galley-slave all his life. Born in Chicago of a distinguished father who founded the Chicago College of Music, young Ziegfeld was brilliantly educated, but from early youth he had ambitions to become a showman. In 1907 he produced his first "Ziegfeld Follies." As a judge of feminine beauty, Mr. Ziegfeld has won an international reputation. Among his many great successes are "Sally," "Rio Rita," "Show Boat," "Whoopee," etc. Mr. Ziegfeld spares no expense as he insists he must have proper settings in "glorifying" the American Girl! Mr. Ziegfeld's charming wife is well known to theatre goers as "Billie Burke."

OUTSTANDING MOTION PICTURE PRODUCERS

MR. ADOLPH ZUKOR

Mr. Zukor conceived and then built the magnificent Paramount Theatre at 43rd and Broadway. But this is only *one* of Mr. Zukor's achievements. It was his genius which is largely responsible for bringing films from penny arcades and nickelodions to the present day high type photo plays. It was he who in 1912, "took a plunge" and presented to the public Sara Bernhardt in "Queen Elizabeth." It was he who offered the unheard-of salary of $50,000 a year to D. W. Griffith, and it was he who brought Mary Pickford into the limelight. Mr. Zukor came to America from his native town in Hungary with very little more than good health and a willingness to work. Today he is one of the kings in moving picturedom. He is a quiet man, unostentatious, and quite simple in his tastes, but he is revered by all who know him for his generosity and charity.

WARNER BROTHERS

Major Albert Warner (left)
H. M. Warner (center)
Jack L. Warner (right)

The development of the Warner enterprises and the great success of this trio has astounded the amusement world. Their entry into the moving picture field as proprietors of the little "Bijou" picture house at New Castle in 1903 started their career—which has landed them in the front row of the great moving picture producers of the present day.

Harry the eldest, Albert, and Jack the youngest of a large family, experienced poverty and hardship in their youths, but by sheer grit, made good. They gave the vitaphone synchronization its first trial. From that time to this, their success has been meteoric. Note pages 70 and 71 and observe pictures of four of the palatial theatres among the many that they control.

MR. CARL LAEMMLE

The entire moving picture world knows "Carl Laemmle," President of Universal Pictures, which organization he founded in 1912. Mr. Laemmle came to America from Laupheim, Germany, at the age of 17 with only $50 in all the world. Came along with him four other adventurous youths with even less money. Today, all four of these men are wealthy. Mr. Laemmle entered the "movie" field at Chicago in 1906. Due to his keen foresight and aggressive efforts, he forged to the front rapidly and became a power in the industry. The "Universal lot" at Hollywood is one of the great points of interest in glorious California. Mr. Laemmle has a genial personality, is a wonderful "mixer," and is genuinely beloved by those who know him.

In Memoriam 4 GREAT NEW YORKERS WHO PASSED TO THEIR REWARD DURING 1931

GEO. W. BAKER   DAVID BELASCO   COL. M. FRIEDSAM   L. W. FLAUNLACHER

OUTSTANDING NEW YORKERS WHO HAVE PASSED TO THE GREAT BEYOND
Selected from New York's Chamber of Commerce Membership Roll

JOHN JACOB ASTOR
Born 1763. Died 1848. The founder of the Astor fortune. Came to New York and engaged in fur trade—invested largely in real estate and would never sell land once purchased.

WILLIAM B. ASTOR
Born 1792. Died 1875. Father of William Waldorf Astor. Made fortune in real estate and was interested in many New York enterprises.

CORNELIUS VANDERBILT
Born 1794. Died 1877. Began his career as a ferryman and became largest steamboat owner in America. Later he devoted his energies to railroads.

WM. H. VANDERBILT
Born 1821. Died 1885. Son of Cornelius and largely responsible for the building up of the great New York Central Railroad.

SAMUEL F. B. MORSE
Born 1791. Died 1872. In 1844 he sent the first telegraphic message with the Morse code and was also one of the projectors of first Atlantic cable.

PETER COOPER
Born 1781. Died 1883. Inventor, merchant and philanthropist engaged in machinery, coach making, grocery and glue trade. Founded and endowed Cooper Union.

CYRUS W. FIELD
Born 1819. Died 1892. Began life as a clerk in store of A. T. Stewart. Went in business for himself at age of 21. Founder of first Atlantic cable and promoted elevated railway system.

WM. CULLEN BRYANT
Born 1794. Died 1878. Poet and editor in chief of N. Y. Evening Post. The first to suggest and advocate our present great Central Park.

CARL SCHURZ
Born 1829. Died 1906. Minister to Spain under Lincoln and also served in the Civil War. Very influential with German-Americans, and won fame for his advocacy of sound currency.

ANDREW CARNEGIE
Born 1835. Died 1919. Began career as a telegraph operator, served in Civil War, then became interested in steel business which finally developed into the U. S. Steel Corporation.

THEO. A. HAVEMEYER
Born 1838. Died 1897. Developed his father's small sugar refinery into one of the great industries of the country and the largest sugar refinery in the world.

JACOB LORILLARD
Born 1774. Died 1838. Tanner, currier and dealer in hides. Also one of the founders of the great Lorillard Tobacco industry.

COLLIS P. HUNTINGTON
Born 1821. Died 1900. Founder of the great Southern Pacific Railroad.

JAMES J. HILL
Born 1838. Died 1916. Known as the "Empire Builder." Founded the Great Northern Railroad.

J. PIERPONT MORGAN
Born 1837. Died 1919. Founded J. P. Morgan & Co., the great banking house and called the "statesman of the Financial World."

118

OUTSTANDING NEW YORKERS WHO HAVE PASSED TO THE GREAT BEYOND
Selected from New York's Chamber of Commerce Membership Roll

JOSEPH SELIGMAN
Born 1819. Died 1880. Founder and head of the great banking house of J. & W. Seligman; Chairman of New York's first Rapid Transit Commission.

JACOB H. SCHIFF
Born 1847. Died 1920. Banker and philanthropist. Former head of the famous banking house of Kuhn Loeb & Co. Strong supporter of education and culture.

GEORGE PEABODY
Born 1795. Died 1867. Founder of the house of George Peabody & Company, brokers, who gave large sums to education and philanthropies.

LEVI P. MORTON
Born 1824. Died 1920. Merchant, banker and broker. Represented New York in U. S. Congress. Minister to France. Vice-President of U. S. and Governor of N. Y.

SETH LOW
Born 1850. Died 1916. Merchant, Mayor of Brooklyn (1882-85) Mayor of New York (1902-04), President of Columbia University and philanthropist.

JOHN WANAMAKER
Born 1838. Died 1922. One of the world's greatest merchants. Started life as errand boy at $1.25 per week. Entering business for himself in 1861.

HORACE B. CLAFLIN
Born 1811. Died 1885. Head of the world-famous drygoods store of H. B. Claflin & Co. A man of dynamic personality and great business ability.

A. T. STEWART
Born 1803. Died 1876. Founder of the great A. T. Stewart Dry Goods House and known as the foremost retailer of his day. Store succeeded by John Wanamaker.

ISADOR STRAUS
Born 1845. Died 1912. Came to New York at close of Civil War and later joined the firm of R. H. Macy & Co.(1888). Made a fortune and was known for his philanthropies.

GEORGE A. HEARN
Born 1835. Died 1912. Founder of the dry goods house of James A. Hearn & Son. Mr. Hearn amassed a great fortune, was a patron of art and one of New York's public spirited citizens.

JAMES M. CONSTABLE
Born 1811. Died 1900. Worked up from a clerk in the store of Aaron Arnold and became a partner. Name later changed to Arnold-Constable Company—one of America's great stores.

JAMES TALCOTT
Born 1835. Died 1916. Entered business for himself in 1854 selling and financing products of cotton and woollen mills. Joseph P. Day secured his first job with Mr. Talcott at $1.92 a week.

JOHN SLOANE
Born 1834. Died 1905. Son of the founder of W. & J. Sloane, dealers in carpets, rugs, etc. Director in many banks and other institutions. Belonged to New York's aristocracy.

CHARLES L. TIFFANY
Born 1812. Died 1902. Founder of the great jewelry house of 'Tiffany's' one of the best known business institutions in the world. Above portrait by William M. Chase.

FRANK W. WOOLWORTH
Born 1852. Died 1919. The man who made millions out of 5 & 10 cent sales and who built the famous Woolworth Building. Woolworth stores are found in all big cities.

119

50 GIANT HOTELS OF NEW YORK

SEE PAGES 121 TO 147

It is estimated that over 300,000 strangers visit New York daily—a number equal to the entire population of such well known cities as Atlanta, Ga., Birmingham, Ala., Omaha, Nebr., Denver, Colo., San Antonio, Texas, Akron, Ohio, etc., etc.

This vast army spends, at *hotels alone*, close to $1,000,000 every twenty-four hours.

In addition to this daily income divided among the hostelries of New York nearly every hotel in the city has a more or less extensive clientele of permanent guests who make their regular homes at these institutions and rent rooms or suites by the year.

There are nearly 300 high class apartment hotels in New York at which comparatively few transients stop, unless they are in the city for an extended stay or have friends who are living in the building and wish to be in close touch with them.

However, practically all of these apartment hotels reserve a number of rooms or suites for out-of-town guests and strive to induce their patronage—those who desire a home atmosphere and the quiet which location away from the noisy streets of general traffic affords.

Downtown hotels, however, secure the bulk of the "big trade" due to proximity to business, the theatres and the teeming activity of New York life. Within a radius of half a mile or so from 42nd street and the "roaring forties," are located the most palatial, most stupendous, and most famous hotels in the world.

Prices at New York hotels range from most any price one wants to pay, up to three figures. A clean, cosy room with bath, can be had in a high-class modern New York hotel as low as $2.00 a day, or one can pay "a small fortune" a day if one wants genuine luxury.

Pictured below are two of the oldest and best known hotels of earlier days, both of them still going strong—notwithstanding that our grandfathers and grandmothers used to patronize them. The high ceilings, wide corridors and spacious rooms speak of fifty years ago. The atmosphere of by-gone days is still preserved in spite of modern improvements and up-to-date management. The same high class clientele, and New York's aristocracy, still continue to support these two famous old French institutions which have never deviated from their policy of serving "the best meals in New York." Newer and grander hotels have been built but the old Brevoort and its twin, the old Lafayette, hold their own with the best of them.

These two hotels are managed by the owner — Mr. Raymond Orteig who won international fame by paying the prize he offered of $25,000 for the first successful flight across the Atlantic to Col. Chas. Lindbergh.

THE BREVOORT
5th Ave. and 8th St.
Ass'd Val. $865,000

HOTEL LAFAYETTE
University Plaza and 9th St.
Ass'd Val. $405,000

HOTEL GOVERNOR CLINTON

S. E. Cor. 31st St. & 7th Ave.

This magnificent hotel is named after Governor George Clinton who for eighteen years served as Governor of New York and who was twice Vice President of the United States.

The Governor Clinton was opened August 19, 1929, with a magnificent banquet tendered to Gov. Franklin Roosevelt. Among the guests present were Ex-Governor "Al" Smith, Mayor Walker and many other notables—proving to be one of the most important and delightful functions in New York's social history.

Ass'd Val.	$10,000,000
378 feet high	32 Floors
1,200 rooms	Built 1929

Every room is an "outside" one with bath, servidor, running ice water, French phone, bed lamps, full length mirror, and radio.
Rates......$3.00 per day and up
Arch.....Murga, Troys and Ogden
Bldrs.......Thompson Starrett Co.

In keeping with the high character of the great man whose name it bears, the Governor Clinton Hotel is everything that money and experienced hotel men can make it in the way of luxurious appointments, ideal service and conscientious consideration for the comfort and enjoyment of guests.

Situated at the very threshold of New York's great shopping center, theatres and clubs, with handy transit facilities (connected by underground passage with the Pennsylvania Terminal, also with the Interboro Subway—just one station below Times Square) the location of Hotel Governor Clinton is dominant.

A most exquisite lobby, absolutely unique in its original arrangement, with rich furnishings and draped fabrics, impart an atmosphere of refined elegance, and the unusually moderate tariff charged for rooms, and in the cafes, has made the Governor Clinton most popular.

THE HOTEL GOVERNOR CLINTON IS ONE OF THE MOST DELIGHTFUL HOTELS IN NEW YORK

In giving number of floors to building, we include Basement and Penthouse floors.

VANDERBILT HOTEL
Park Ave.—From 33rd to 34th Streets

ONE OF THE FAMOUS HOTELS OF THE WORLD

Said to be the only building ever constructed **WITHOUT ONE POUND OF COMBUSTIBLE** material in its entire make up!

600 Rooms exposed to direct sunlight.
3 minutes from Grand Central Terminal.
3 minutes from Pennsylvania Terminal.

Patronized by the royalty of Europe, the elite of America and the best people everywhere, who appreciate refinement, luxury and an atmosphere of general charm.

The Vanderbilt kitchen is known from San Francisco to Rome for its excellent cuisine. Guests are permitted to visit them. No home kitchen is more immaculate.

The enchanting lobby of the Vanderbilt suggests the Riviera, and its comfortable lounge is luxuriant—the "garden restaurant" directly to the left is one of the most delightful places to dine in all New York. For nearly 20 years the Vanderbilt has been one of the supreme hotels of the city.

Ass'd Val.	$3,205,000
260 ft. high	20 Floors
Sun lighted rooms	600
Completed	1912
Owners	Vand. Hotel Corp.
Archts	Warren & Wetmore

McALPIN HOTEL
Broadway—From 33rd to 34th Streets.
$2,000,000 recently spent in making it *new* all over.

HERE ARE A FEW REASONS WHY THE McALPIN IS SO POPULAR

WONDERFUL LOCATION
Faces full block on Broadway; across the Street from Gimbels, Saks and Macy's—three of New York's largest department stores. Less than a block from Altman's and McCreery's; only a block from Fifth Ave., the World's most famous shopping district. Only a few doors removed from the world's tallest office building (the Empire State) and only three minutes from Times Square and the Great White Way.

MAGNIFICENT BUILDING
Lobby, mezzanine, corridors, cafes, ball rooms, roof garden; every part of the institution is gorgeous.

UNSURPASSABLE CUISINE
No more delicious meals served anywhere.

COURTEOUS SERVICE
Guaranteed.

Ass'd Val.	$11,400,000	
322 ft. high	27 Floors	**1440 Rooms**
Completed in	1913	$2.50 per
1,444 Rooms	$2.50 and up	day and up
Owners	Greely Sq. Hotel Co.	
Archts	F. M. Andrews	
Bldrs., Thompson Starrett Co.		

122

HOTEL PENNSYLVANIA
7th Avenue—32nd to 33rd Streets

ONE OF THE TWELVE LARGEST HOTELS IN THE WORLD
Every luxury, every delight that can please, are the reasons why the Pennsylvania is so popular.

Nearly $20,000,000 invested—

One of the great "Statler" hotels. . . . Directly across the street from the Pennsylvania Terminal (connected by underground passage). . . . 2,200 guest rooms —each with private bath. . . . Radio in every room, circulating ice water, servidor and many other special features. . . . Enough machinery in 4th subfloor to operate an enormous factory. . . . Air is washed, purified and sanitized. . . . A dozen restaurants, grills and places to eat. . . . Grand Ball Room, Convention Hall, Roof Garden, well stocked Library for guests, etc.

Plans for this hotel were drawn by one of the most outstanding architectural firms in the city, McKim, Mead & White.

Ass'd Val	nearly $20,000,000
310 feet high	30 Floors
Ground plot—almost a square block	
ROOMS	2,200
Owner	Hotel Statler Co., Inc.
Arch	McKim, Mead & White
Bldr	Geo. A. Fuller Co.

NEW YORKER HOTEL

Full Block on Eighth Avenue—from 34th to 35th Streets

Cost nearly $20,000,000—43 Stories

NEW YORK IS PROUD OF ITS MANY GIGANTIC HOTELS, BUT IS ESPECIALLY PROUD OF THE "NEW YORKER."

Notwithstanding its immensity, each guest is assured personal and individual consideration.

To sense the massiveness of the "New Yorker," its gorgeous beauty, its sumptuous grandeur, and numberless points of appeal, a personal visit is necessary. But Mr. Ralph Hitz, the Hotel's dynamic managing director, has already made the place famous in millions of homes through the nation-wide radio hook-up, four nights a week, from the New Yorker's "Terrace Restaurant" where one of New York's greatest syncopated orchestras plays daily.

Note the following data:

Building is 525 feet high.

One of the most magnificent hotel lobbies in the world.

In Manhattan Restaurant, one of the luxurious eating places of the hotel, the walls are built of Persian walnut inlaid with solid bronze—the windows facing 34th St. being of hand-carved glass.

Ten private dining salons, five restaurants and grills, and two ballrooms provide for food and social functions.

35 master cooks are employed in the kitchens which are as clean as a model private home kitchen.

23 elevators, with a speed of 800 feet a minute, transfer the 10,000 daily visitors and guests to the various floors.

There is "made-to-order" weather throughout the huge structure.

An army of bell boys are drilled and as well dressed and "snappy" looking as West Pointers.

Every bedroom has a radio loud speaker with a choice of four programs—loud speakers in building require 25 miles of wiring.

There are 100 suites consisting of a parlor and one or two bedrooms; some of them have private roof gardens—many of them have terraces.

The "New Yorker's" barber shop is one of the largest in the world—42 chairs and 20 manicurists.

In the laundry is machinery costing half a million dollars and requiring 150 employees—over 350,000 pieces washed daily.

78 feet below the sidewalk is the largest private power plant in America.

92 telephone girls are employed on the huge switchboards on the 41st floor.

The New Yorker is a city within itself.

Built, 1930.

Owner, New Yorker Hotel Corp.

Builder, Mack Kanner.

Architect, Sugarman & Berger.

Rates, $3.50 per day and up.

124

HOTEL COMMODORE

42nd St. & Lexington Ave.—covering almost a full square.

FAMOUS FOR ITS MANY EXCLUSIVE FEATURES

Famous for its unique and artistic "Stairway Entrance," its Spanish-Patio Lobby—indescribably beautiful, its popular "afternoon tea" Lounge, its delightful Restaurants and Grills, its famous "Tavern Club" and its refined clientele, its many important functions, its magnificent Banquet and Ball Room—said to be the largest in the United States, seating over 3,500 and in which many of the most important functions in the country are held. Famous for its many "Big Nights" (see below) and its good times.

A BIG NIGHT AT THE COMMODORE

An entire book could be written about "Big Nights at the Commodore"—but reference herewith will be made to only one—the one entered on the log book as "Circus Night."

The occasion was a big dinner in which John Ringling, the big circus king, and many other notables figured.

The enormous ballroom was rigged up in genuine circus style with a big sawdust ring, pink lemonade, peanuts, ballyhoo men, sheiks, freaks, elephants to ride, monkeys, lions, tigers, horses and even "snakes." Bareback riders, cowboys, trapeze performers, tightrope walkers and clowns, all did their stunts and a circus band furnished the music. It was surely a "Big Night."

But as stated the Commodore is famous for its Big Nights.

Ass'd Val.	$17,000,000
317 feet high	28 Floors
GUEST ROOMS	1,956
Year Built	1919
Owners	New York Cent. R. R. Co.
Arch.	Warren & Wetmore
Bldrs.	Geo. W. Fuller Co.

ASTOR HOTEL

Broadway—from 44th to 45th Street

NEW YORK'S GREAT CONVENTION CENTER AND ONE OF THE FAMOUS HOTELS OF THE WORLD

For 27 years, the Astor has been one of the livest spots in all New York. Millions have passed thru its entrances on Broadway, 44th St. and 45th St. It has been the scene of more conventions, more banquets, more big social functions and more good times than any other hotel in the city.

The Astor's location is in the very heart of New York's Rialto, within a few steps of the city's leading theatres and in the very center of Manhattan's most active business district. The Astor Roof and the Astor's Cafes are the best patronized in all New York.

DIXIE HOTEL

251 W. 42nd St.—just west of Broadway

The "Dixie" has won a reputation for true southern hospitality. Right in the center of New York's business activities during the day, and within the glow of Broadway's Great White Way at night.

```
Ass'd Val...$2,400,000
267 ft. high..25 Floors
650 GUEST ROOMS
Completed ......1930
Owner...Jerrold Hold.
Corp.
Arch......Emery Roth
Bldr......Harper Org.
Rates....$3.00 and up
```

PICCADILLY HOTEL

227 W. 45th St.—just west of Broadway

```
Ass'd Val...$3,750,000
280 ft. high..26 Floors
Completed ......1928
Owner .....Paramount
Hotel Corp.
Arch.....Geo. & Edw.
Blum
Bldr., Paramount Hotel
Corp.
Rates....$3.00 and up
```

Less than two minutes from the bright lights of Broadway, yet far enough away to escape the noise and din of its strenuous business and night life. Furnished in magnificent good taste with a cuisine which insures a return visit.

HOTEL ROOSEVELT

Covers entire square—45th to 46th Streets —Madison to Vanderbilt Avenues.

THE SUPREME ACHIEVEMENT IN HOTEL POPULARITY

Refined, luxurious and with a typical metropolitan home atmosphere. Also genuine hospitality and sincere desire to please. The "Teddy Bear Cave," the Hendryck Hudson Room, Library, Gymnasium, and a dozen other features which have added to its popularity, explains why the Roosevelt is becoming *more and more* popular.

```
Cost .........$12,000,000
253 feet high....24 Floors
1,100 GUEST ROOMS
Completed ..........1924
Owner......N. Y. United
Hotels Co.
Arch. Geo. M. Post & Son
Bldr....Thompson Starrett
Co.
Rates........$5.00 and up
```

126

BILTMORE HOTEL

Occupies entire square from 43rd to 44th—bet. Madison Ave. & Vanderbilt Ave.

ROYALTY AND "SMALL TOWN FOLKS" ARE EQUALLY WELCOME AT THE BILTMORE— ONE OF THE NATION'S GRANDEST HOTELS.

Every comfort, every convenience and every luxury known to modern achievement in hotel construction and perfect service can be found at the Biltmore. From the internationally celebrated summer dining room atop the immense building known as "The Cascades" down to the popular grill in the basement, an atmosphere of elegance, refinement and good taste pervades the entire establishment. The late Sir Arthur Conan Doyle, Sir Thomas Lipton, Ex-President Calvin Coolidge and other notables of both Europe and America select the Biltmore as "home" while in New York because of its freedom from all ostentation, yet at the same time retaining every phase of sumptuous home life.

The New York Biltmore is only one of *twelve* magnificent Biltmore Hotels operated over the country by the Bowman Biltmore Hotels Corp. of which John McE. Bowman is President.

Ass'd Val....	$14,000,000
321 ft. high....	30 Floors
Usable Floor Space..	830 sq. ft.
No. of rooms......	1,000
Built	1914
Owner....N. Y. Central R. R. Co.	
Arch. Warren & Wetmore	
Bldr..Geo. A. Fuller Co.	
Rates......	$6.00 and up

BILTMORE HOTELS

The Biltmore
New York City

Providence Biltmore
Providence, R. I.

Belleview Biltmore
Bellaire, Fla.

Miami Biltmore
Coral Gables, Fla.

Atlanta Biltmore
Atlanta, Ga.

Los Angeles Biltmore
Los Angeles, Cal.

Santa Barbara Biltmore
Santa Barbara, Cal.

Flintridge Biltmore
Pasadena, Calif.

Arizona Biltmore
Phoenix, Ariz.

Dupont Biltmore
Wilmington, Del.

Dayton Biltmore
Dayton, Ohio

Sevilla Biltmore
Havana, Cuba

"LINCOLN HOTEL"

Full block on Eighth Avenue—
From 44th to 45th Streets.
Just one block west of Broadway.

CATERS TO THE BETTER ELEMENT OF THE MASSES

WHETHER BELONGING TO THE MERCHANT CLASS OR TO THE ARISTOCRACY OF WEALTH OR BIRTH.

Gorgeous is the only term that fitly conveys any idea of the unique, and truly beautiful lobby, mezzanine, corridors and entrances of the huge palatial structure.

It is not only the largest and most magnificent of the many beautiful hotels in the Times Square district but its open kitchen grill (known as the "Tavern") and its basement cafeteria, provide delicious food at honest-value prices.

MANY OF AMERICA'S MOST PROMINENT BUSINES MEN AND MANY OF THE COUNTRY'S WEALTHIEST FAMILIES STOP AT THE LINCOLN WHEN IN NEW YORK BECAUSE OF ITS MANY POINTS OF APPEAL.

Ass'd Val............	$5,300,000
327 ft. high...........	30 Floors
Guest Rooms.............	1,400
Completed.................	1928
Owner......United Cigar Stores	
	Realty Co.
Archt........Schwartz & Gross	
Builder......Chanin Const. Co.	
Rates.....$3.00 per day and Up	

CONTINUED FROM PAGE 94

MR. JAMES AUGUSTINE FARRELL

"James Augustine" is a *whole lot of name* to bestow on one little chap upon being launched into this great big world of ours. Yet James Augustine Farrell has proven himself capable of living up to the dignity and prestige of his "august" appellation! Born Feb. 15, 1863 at New Haven, Conn., the young man demonstrated an excellent business head at an early age. From the day he started his career, he had a liking for foundries, and secured a job in one. He soon became noticed in steel circles, and became most successful. In 1911 he was appointed President of the United States Steel Corporation, in which capacity he has served now for over twenty years. Mr. Farrel is a staunch supporter of every agency for good. He is a member of many of New York's most exclusive Clubs.

128

THE WALDORF-ASTORIA

COVERS ENTIRE SQUARE—Park Ave., 49th St., Lexington Ave. and 50th St.

TALLEST AND MOST BEAUTIFUL HOTEL IN ALL THE WORLD

47 STORIES
625 FEET HIGH
COST NEARLY $40,000,000

Nothing has ever approached the magnitude, daring, ingenuity, and achievement in hotel construction that is exemplified in the new Waldorf-Astoria just completed.

Words convey but a faint impression of the stupendity, the grandeur, and the magnificence of this wonder hotel.

Neither time, effort, nor expense has been spared, not only to build a house that would be in keeping with the old Waldorf-Astoria traditions, but to provide for making it the premier hotel of the world 50 years to come!

Note a few of these provisions—

Radio in every room.

Wired for television.

Private driveway through the center of the building—90 feet wide by 200 feet long.

An air-conditioning plant that insures ideal weather within, no matter how hot or cold without.

Private railroad siding *underneath the hotel* where guests fortunate enough to own private cars when leaving Palm Beach, Chicago, Bar Harbor, etc., can have their cars routed direct to the Waldorf.

In the Twin Towers are 500 rooms divided into various sized apartments with open fireplaces, large boudoirs and baths as luxurious as any Fifth Avenue home. Many of New York's most aristocratic families will make the hotel their permanent residence.

The main ball room—four stories high, with three tiers of boxes, is one of the most regal in all the world.

"Peacock Alley" is alive again, but this time trebled in dimensions and indescribably elegant in its quiet richness.

Mr. Morris Bagby will resume his December and January "Musical Mornings" which for over 25 years have been such a charming feature of the old Waldorf.

OH, YES—"OSCAR" IS ON HAND, TOO.

THE MARGUERY

270 Park Ave.—From 47th to 48th.

A King's Palace is no more sumptuous or more beautiful than the Marguery.

When Dr. Charles Paterno erected this hotel he spared neither effort or expense in his endeavors to make it the last word in refined elegance.

The famous Marguery restaurant is patronized by the elite of the city. The cuisine is excellent, the service faultless, and the surroundings luxurious.

RITZ-CARLTON HOTEL

Covers entire square.
From 46th to 47th Sts. bet. Madison & Vanderbilt Ave.

A HOTEL OF DISTINCTION—
FAMOUS FOR ITS DISTINGUISHED GUESTS

Where Royalty and American Wealth make their home while visiting New York.

Unusual facilities for entertaining. Here the daughters of New York's most prominent families are presented to society. Here are notable weddings, dinners and dances. Exclusive, Refined, Dignified, and Luxurious.

Cost	$9,835,000
Height	212 ft.
Floors	18
Guest Rooms	375
Built	1910
Owner	Robert W. Goelet
Arch	Warren & Wetmore
Bldr.	M. Reed & Sons.
Rates	$8 and up

There are few dining places or hotels in the world that compare with the Marguery.

Est. Val	$7,500,000
12 stories and 3 sub-basements	137 apartments
Year built	1918
Ownr	Dr. Chas. V. Paterno
Archt.	Warren & Wetmore
Bldr.	Paterno Const Co
Agent	DOUGLAS L. ELLIMAN & CO.

HOTEL PARAMOUNT

235 W. 46th St.—Just a few steps west of Bway.

YOU LIKE IT AT THE PARAMOUNT.

The Paramount caters especially to those who love life, enjoy good times, like to meet fine people and who like to mix in a little pleasure in business when coming to New York.

Twin Art Studios

Cost
$4,600,000
Height
252 ft.
Floors...22
700 Guest
Rooms
Built..1928
Owner, 235
W. 46th
Corp.
Arch. Thos.
W. Lamb
Rates
$3.00 & up

DON'T FAIL TO VISIT THE FAMOUS PARAMOUNT GRILL

EDISON HOTEL

228 W. 47th St.—Just west of Broadway.

One of New York's newest and most beautiful hotels. An outstanding feature is its regal ball room of 8,000 square feet, being a reproduction of one of the famous halls in the French Riviera the gorgeous domed ceiling of which beggars description.

Ass'd Val.,
$1,600,000
Height
287 ft.
26 Floors
1000 Guest
Rooms
Built..1931
Owner
Milnag
Realty Co.
Arch.
Herbert J.
Knapp
Rates $2.50
per day &
up

130

HOTEL LEXINGTON

513 Lexington Ave., S. E. Cor. 48th St.

"The Hotel With a Heart"

Whoever *visits* the Lexington, and those making a permanent home there, seems to be unanimous in enthusiastic praise of the generally delightful atmosphere of this sumptuous hostelry.

They term it "The Hotel With a Heart" as everybody connected with the place from Bell Boy to President seems to have been drilled in the art of courtesy and a desire to please.

Location is ideal. Building gorgeous and furnishings in excellent taste. Prices moderate.

```
Ass'd Val. ...............$7,000,000
336 ft. high...............30 Floors
801 Guest Rooms
Owner........Lexington Hotel Corp.
Architect........Schu'tze & Weaver
Builder...........Turner Const. Co.
Agent.....Douglas L. Elliman & Co.
Rates.................$3.50 and Up
```

Photo by Wurts Bros.

BARCLAY HOTEL

111 E. 48th St. Full block on Lexington Ave. to 49th St.

The regal Barclay caters only to the most refined, offering luxury of seclusiveness in a section of the city where New York is smartest, gayest and busiest—where there is the comforting preassurance of the prestige of one's fellow guests.

```
Ass'd Val........$6,000,000
157 ft. high.......14 Floors
850 Guest Rooms
Completed ............1927
Owners..Barclay Park Corp.
Architects....Cross & Cross
Builders, Todd, Robertson &
                        Todd
Rates.........$6.00 and Up
```

HOTEL SHELTON

S. E. Cor. 49th St. & Lexington Ave.

Has one of the most magnificent and costly swimming pools in the country—free to guests . . . Has a most delightful roof garden with playing fountains, growing shrubs, and "cosy nooks" . . . Four different lounges in the building where guests may read, rest, chat or enjoy a rubber of bridge. Also game rooms. If you enjoy backgammon, you will find plenty of players among other Sheltonates . . . The Shelton is more like a big home or club than a hotel . . . No hotel in New York offers a greater variety of appeals to those who appreciate genuine home life, than the popular Shelton.

ALL READY FOR A PLUNGE IN THE MAGNIFICENT SHELTON POOL

```
Ass'd Val........$5,300,000
412 ft. high.......34 Floors
1,200 guest rooms
Built ...................1924
Owners. Shelton Hotel Corp.
Arch......Arthur L. Harmon
Rates.........$2.50 and Up
```

MONTCLAIR HOTEL

545 Lextington Ave.—N. E. Cor. 49th St.

WHERE SERVICE, COURTESY AND EFFORTS TO PLEASE ARE THE CHIEF CONSIDERATIONS OF THE MANAGEMENT.

"Give me a force of courteous and obliging employees, and I can bring back every guest who ever registers at our hotels" is the principle on which President S. Gregory Taylor operates the "Montclair," the "Buckingham," the "St. Moritz," the "Dixie," and others.

Ass'd Val	$4,150,000
200 ft. high	18 Floors
Guest Rooms	900
Completed	1928
Owners, Telecons Hldg. Corp.	
Archt.	Emery Roth
Bldrs., Harper Organization	
Rates	$3.00 and Up

Photo by Criterion Photocraft Co.

BEVERLY HOTEL

N. E. Cor. 50th St. & Lexington Ave.

A QUALITY HOTEL CATERING TO QUALITY PEOPLE

The Beverly is a strictly high class institution offering an especial appeal to those who want a permanent home amidst luxurious surroundings and a superior type of fellow-residents. An atomsphere of gentility is apparent the moment one enters the palatial lobby with its magnificent architectural beauty and gorgeous furnishings. The intimacy and coziness of the Beverly contrasts strongly with the modern tendency of the day to garish splendor and large lobby area.

With its many sunny outdoor terraces, the Beverly offers a view, fresh air and sunshine one ordinarily gets from a mountain top. The rooms are ideally arranged for entertainment purposes, including refrigerator, servicing pantries, etc. Strangers from out of the city are always welcome.

Ass'd Val	$2,025,000
350 ft. high	32 Floors
Guest Rooms	350
Completed	1927
Owner. . Lex. Concord Corp.	
Rates	$6.00 and Up
Archt.	Emery Roth
Builder. . Lex. Concord Corp.	
Agent	DOUGLAS L. ELLIMAN & CO.

HOTEL NEW WESTON

34 E. 50th St.—S. W. Cor. Madison Ave.
Extends thru to 318 E. 49th St.

ANOTHER OF THE EXCEEDINGLY POPULAR KNOTT HOTELS. BUILT ON SITE FORMERLY OCCUPIED BY COLUMBIA COLLEGE

Mr. Knott says "Urban New York built the New Weston—the New York element who knows New York and knows what it wants and precisely where it

Ass'd Val	$3,300,000
258 ft. high	23 Floors
Guest Rooms	700
Completed	1930
Owners	New Weston Hotel Corp.
Archts.	Robert W. Lyons
Bldrs., GeeKie Naughton Inc.	
Rates	$5.00 and Up

wants to live—near amusements, parks, clubs, shops, etc., and yet a quiet night's sleep." The New Weston meets these very requirements. Write for folder.

HOTEL PARK CENTRAL

7th Avenue—Full block from 55th to 56th Sts.

WHERE ONE CAN LIVE LIKE A KING

OR

Where One Can Live Sumptuously on a Modest Income.

The picture at right conveys but a slight conception of either the immensity or the regal splendor of the magnificent Park Central Hotel with its 40 floors (including basements). Luxuriously appointed arrangements—l o b - bies, cafes, dining rooms, club rooms, rest rooms, g u e s t rooms, terraces, banquet hall, roof garden, library, gymnasium, swimming pool, and a dozen other features, all contribute to the Park Central's popularity.

Ass'd Val. $10,800 000
350 feet high......38 Floors
1,600 Guest Rooms
Completed 1927
Arch..Groneberg & Leuchtag
Bldr........Lanzner & Baer
Rates....$4.00 per day up.

HOTEL DORSET

30 W. 54th St. Just west of Fifth Ave.

AN APARTMENT HOTEL

FOLKS WHO EVER STOP ONE NIGHT AT THE DORSET, ALWAYS WANT TO STAY INDEFINITELY

The building is beautiful, the furnishings luxurious and the atmosphere of the whole institution refined. The Dorset caters to permanent residents and yet always welcomes the stranger.

Ass'd Val. $3,050,000
236 feet high......21 Floors
393 Guest Rooms
Completed 1927
Owner...Dorwood Realty Co.
Architect ....Emery Roth
Builder........Bing & Bing
Rates..........$8.00 and up

133

Photo by Howard Cox

Photo by Howard Cox

HOTEL TAFT

formerly the "MANGER"

771 Seventh Ave.—50th to 51st Sts.

A STRICTLY HIGH CLASS
HOTEL AT LOWEST CON-
SISTENT PRICES

*Stupendous in size
Beautiful and attractive lobby
Absolutely modern
Light and airy rooms
And "always busy"!*

Ass'd Val	$10,000,000
222 ft. high	21 Floors
2,000 rooms	
Completed	1927
Architect	H. Craig Severance
Bldr	Bing & Bing
Rates	$2.50 to $5.00

The Taft is especially popular with commercial travelers, buyers and business men who run in to New York on business errands where they can generally find old friends who, like themselves, invariably "stop at the Taft"— which is right in the heart of commercial New York. Only a block distant from the Great White Way at night—Broadway's theatrical and amusement district. "Roxy's" is right on the corner.

VICTORIA HOTEL

781 Seventh Ave.—Cor 51st St.

STOP AT THE VICTORIA JUST ONCE AND AFTERWARDS YOU'LL BE A GUEST OF THE VICTORIA EVERY TRIP YOU COME TO NEW YORK.

Majestic, luxurious and every inch of it modern . . . A magnificent yet cosy lobby . . . Radio in every room and free library . . . Circulating ice water . . . Sunshine and breeze swept golf course on the roof . . . Only a block from Roxy's . . . Only a block from Broadway's theatres . . . Only a block from the Great White Way . . . In the thick of everything . . . And the most comfortable beds and best food in town, at least that's what Mr. Moulton says.

Ass'd Val	$3,400,000
270 feet high	25 Floors
1000 Guest Rooms	
Completed	1928
Owner	Victoria Operating Co.
Arch	Schwartz & Gross
Rates	$3.00 and up

134

HOTEL RITZ TOWER

465 Park Ave., N. E. Cor.
57th St.

Hotel Ritz Tower is "just a bit of Paris" fitted into the American setting of magnificent Park Avenue.

Of course, English is spoken if desired, but those who wish to try out their "Parlez-vous Francais" will find an excellent opportunity to do so with genuine native Frenchmen who most obligingly accommodate any guest wishing to "brush up" his or her French.

F. F. Foley

MR. EDWARD CLINTON FOGG

Continued from Page 105

Born in Deering, Maine, June 28, 1870, Mr. Fogg made his first dollar in a canning factory, and secured his first *hotel* job as a "bell hop" at the age of 21. His genial personality, obliging manner, and his marked ability soon won him recognition, and coming to New York in 1899, his rise was rapid. In 1913 he was appointed manager of the famous Copley Plaza Hotel at Boston, serving until 1921, when he was called to manage the Plaza at New York. In 1924 he took charge of the Roosevelt, becoming Vice-President of the company. Mr. Fogg is one of the most capable and popular hotel men in the entire field.

WARWICK HOTEL

65 W. 54th St. N. W. Cor. Sixth Ave

AN APARTMENT HOTEL CATERING ALSO TO OUT-OF-TOWN CITY GUESTS

The Warwick is a most imposing structure towering 36 stories in a neighborhood both residential and commercial. Some of New York's finest homes are in close proximity and yet the busy shops of Fifth Avenue are only a block distant.

Ass'd Val.	$5,000,000
370 feet high	36 Floors
512 GUEST ROOMS	7 Elevators
Ground area	12,000 sq. ft.
Completed	1926
Owner	W. A. R. Realty Co.
Arch	Geo. B. Post Co.
Bldr	Dwight P. Robinson Co.
Rates	$6.00 and up

The Warwick was designed for discriminating people accustomed to superior living, who wish to live close to business and prefer apartment house life to the cares and responsibilities of keeping up a home. Warwick suites have large closets, completely equipped pantry, automatic refrigeration, and the rooms themselves are spacious, light, and ideal in their appointments. Everything about the Warwick is in keeping with the refinement and good taste of its beautiful decorations and furnishings.

HOTEL ST. REGIS

S. E. Cor. Fifth Ave. & 55th St.

THE HOME FOR OVER 20 YEARS OF MANY OF NEW YORK'S MOST ARISTOCRATIC FAMILIES

The St. Regis is the scene of many famous social functions where Royalty has been entertained.

Within the past year a new addition has been added to the famous St. Regis as large as the main building itself, which has recently been altered and modernized, thus making the aristocratic old St. Regis one of the newest and most imposing of New York's magnificent hotels. John Jacob Astor built the original St. Regis, which at the time of completion was the grandest and most luxurious hotel in the world —the furniture was especially made in Paris. The new "Seaglade" and Roof Garden restaurants are certainly superb, as is also the main "Oakroom" dining hall.

Ass'd Val.	$6,500,000
255 feet high	22 Floors
650 GUEST ROOMS	
Completed 1905 and 1929	
Owner Durham Realty Co.	
Arch	Sloan & Robertson
Bldr	Leddy & Moore

DELMONICO HOTEL

502 Park Ave. N.W. Cor. 58th St.

Consistent with the name it bears, the "Delmonico" is living up to the high standard set by the man who for over thirty years catered to New York's ultra aristocracy, and who established a reputation for concoction of foods that made him internationally famous.

The Delmonico today, under the able direction of its president, Mr. John F. Sanderson, has taken its place as one of the outstanding hotels in this city of a thousand hostelries, and ranks with the very foremost of them.

The hotel is designed especially for those who wish suites of several rooms with the idea of remaining as permanent guests. Quarters are also available for those who visit the city for short stays and the same courteous attention is extended strangers as to those who are regular residents.

Ass'd Val.	$7,000,000
380 feet high..500 Rooms..32 Floors	
Completed	1928
Owner	Benjamin Winter, Inc.
Arch.	Goldner & Goldner
Rates	$8.00 and up

APARTMENT HOTELS IN THE CITY OF NEW YORK

New York is a city of hotels unexcelled by those of any other city in the world. Although New York conducts no systematic campaign of "booster" publicity, yet such is the extent of its business and its cosmopolitan life that there are always tens of thousands of strangers in the city. There are 150 modern hotels which cater almost exclusively to the traveling public, and provide 62,000 rooms for guests. In addition, there are many others which cater largely to permanent guests, such as the Delmonico and similar "Apartment Hotels"—But out-of-the-city visitors who wish to get away from the noise and strenuosity of the busy streets, are always welcome.

FOUR MAGNIFICENT PARK AVENUE HOTELS

In all four of which an atmosphere of culture and refinement appeals strongly to those accustomed to living well and can afford the luxurious yet unostentatious surroundings such as the Ambassador, Park Lane, Drake and Mayfair House afford. Each of these palatial hotels caters especially to permanent guests who want a city home in an ideal location.

Photo by Standard Flashlight

"HOTEL AMBASSADOR"
Cor. Park Ave. and 51st St.

The "Ambassador"—one of the most aristocratic hotels in New York—is located in the very heart of Park Avenue's most palatial apartment house center. The furnishings are copies of the highest class craftsmanship known to the decorative world.

NAMES FROM AMBASSADOR'S REGISTERS

Queen Marie of Roumania; Prince Nicholas of Roumania; Prince Christopher of Greece; Prince Hohenloe; Prince Bismark; Lord & Lady Mountbatten; Andrew W. Mellon; Mrs. Wm. Vanderbilt; Mary Pickford; John Barrymore; Mme. Galli-Curci.

The Ambassador is the last word in refined elegance.

Ass'd Val.	$9,000,000
270 feet high	23 Floors
500 GUEST ROOMS	
Completed	1921
Owner, Ambassador Hotel	
Arch...Warren & Wetmore	
Bldrs., Thompson Starrett	
Rates	$6.00 and up

THE PARK LANE
299 Park Ave. from 48th to 49th Sts.

Est. Val.	$5,000,000
170 feet high	14 Floors
600 GUEST ROOMS	
Built	1924
Owner, Fullerton S. Weaver	
Arch., Schultze & Weaver	
Bldr., Geo. A. Fuller Co.	
Rates	$7.00 and up

THE DRAKE
440 Park Ave., N. W. Cor. Fifth Ave.

Cost	$5,500,000
230 feet high	21 Floors
189 suites of 2 and 3 rooms	
Built	1927
Owner	Bing & Bing
Architect	Emery Roth
Builder	Bing & Bing
Agent	Bing & Bing

MAYFAIR HOUSE
610 Park Ave., S. E. Cor. 65th

Ass'd Val.	$3,150,000
190 feet high	17 Floors
400 GUEST ROOMS	
Built	1925
Owner, 60 E. 65th St. Corp.	
Arch...J. E. R. Carpenter	
Bldr., D. P. Robinson Co.	
Rates	$7.00 and up

THE
BARBIZON-PLAZA

N. W. Cor. 6th Ave. & 58th St.

This imposing and beautiful building is the forerunner of a *new* epoch, and the centennial of an *old* one,—inspired by the Barbizon Painters who a century ago developed a new conception of an old art.

The Barbizon Plaza is New York's first residential hotel catering to artists, whether men or women, and whether engaged in the ART of BUSINESS, or the BUSINESS of ART,—piano, palette, pen or commercial.

The Barbizon has proximity to art galleries, music halls, libraries, clubs, cafes and recreation. Among its appeals are: Atmosphere . . . Intimacy . . . Sun-tan Glass enclosed Roof . . . Deck tennis courts . . . Library . . . Art gallery . . . Salon de Musique . . . Sound-proof studios . . . Studio for sculpture and painting . . . Business Men's Art Club . . . And many other features appealing to artists, musicians, singers, writers, reporters, students and to business people interested in any form of art, even though it be commercial.

Ass'd Val........$10,000,000
437 ft. high........43 Floors
Rooms................1,500
Completed............1930
Owner. . Park 6th Ave. Corp.
Archt..Ogden & Murgatroyd
Builder....Chas. G. Duffy
Rates....$3.00 Day and up

BUCKINGHAM HOTEL

101 W. 57th Street—N. W. Cor. Sixth Avenue.

THIS IS ANOTHER "S. GREGORY TAYLOR HOTEL"

The Buckingham is one of New York's most popular residential hotels, being formerly located at Fifth Avenue and 56th Street.

This modern and wonderfully located building houses many of New York's finest families. Out-of-town guests will find a "hominess" about the place that is truly delightful.

And like all "S. Gregory Hotels" the rates are low in comparison with the genuine value given.

Ass'd Val........$1,900,000
200 ft. high........18 Floors
Elevators................3
Guest Rooms............312
Ground Plot....7,500 sq. ft.
Built................1925
Owrs.57th St. & 6th Av. Cor.
Arct..Emery Roth & N. Korn
Builder. Harper organization
Rates.........$5.00 and up

HOTEL PLAZA

Facing Fifth Avenue—
full block from 58th to 59th Sts.

FOR 23 YEARS ONE OF
NEW YORK'S SMARTEST AND
MOST FAMOUS HOTELS

Ass'd Val.	$13,700,000
290 feet high	20 Floors
1098 GUEST ROOMS	
12 Elevators	
Ground area approx. 57,000 sq. ft.	
Built 1907; Addition 1921	
Owner	Plaza Operating Co.
Architect	Warren & Wetmore
(H. J. Hardenbergh—Architect for original building)	
Builder	Geo. A. Fuller Co.
Rates	$7.00 and up

The rendezvous of wealth.
The home of notables.
The stopping place of royalty.

Travel the world over and it will be difficult to find a grander location, a more imposing building, or more sumptuous hotel in every meaning of the term as applied to hoteldom. For 25 years the stately Plaza has ranked with the supreme hotels of America and bids fair to hold its same commanding position for another 25 years and more. Long reign the Plaza!

MAYFLOWER HOTEL

N. W. Cor. 61st St. and Central Park West

The Mayflower has nearly 500 windows. Directly overlooks beautiful Central Park.

The Mayflower is only a block from New York's famous Columbus Circle, only half a block from Broadway, only 3 minutes by subway to Times Square, the theatres and the "Great White Way," and less than 5 minutes by 59th St. trolley from Fifth Avenue and the great shopping district.

And yet at night, one can sleep in quiet, away from all noise and din, hear the crickets of Central Park during the night hours, and the chirping of birds at sun up!

But best of all, there is a most homey atmosphere at the Mayflower, seldom found in metropolitan hotel's. Mr. John H. Spaulding, the genial General Manager, is the personification of affability, courtesy and good fellowship, and has been able to transfuse his hospitable friendliness as a sort of leaven among the many delightful families who make his ideal hotel their permanent home.

A Hotel That Home-Lovers Love

Ass'd Val.	$6,000,000
200 feet high	18 Floors
600 GUEST ROOMS	
Completed	1926
Owner	Nausau Holding Corp.
Architect	Emery Roth
Builders	Jos. Gilbert
Rates	$5.00 and up

HOTEL ST. MORITZ

56 Central Park South (59th St.) S. W. Corner 6th Ave.
Another model hotel under "S. Gregory Taylor" management.

OVERLOOKING CENTRAL PARK—A SERIES OF TERRACES, LIKE A PICTURESQUE CLIFF, AMIDST TOWERING TREES TO THE NORTH AND OTHER SOARING SKYSCRAPERS TO THE SOUTH.

"Hotel St. Moritz" was designed as a cosmopolitan home combining Continental hospitality with American comforts and service—where both Continental and American can meet and enjoy that delightful charm resulting from European polish and American culture.

Rumpelmayer, the world famed Parisian caterer, delights diners in the Tea Room, Grill and Roof Garden—where the great St. Moritz orchestra entertains with both classic and syncopated music as preferred.

A spacious lobby, luxuriously furnished, provides a charming rendezvous for meeting of friends and social intercourse.

The various guest rooms, suites —especially the pent house suites, with cooling park breezes and sumptuous furnishings, impress all who see them with the painstaking care exercised by the management.

Both rooms and suites may be rented unfurnished by those wishing to use their own belongings.

The St. Moritz is built on the site of the old New York Athletic Club and has *close to 400* windows on Central Park South directly facing the Park—in addition to *over 300* more windows on 6th Ave.—partly view the park.

Est. Cost	$6,000,000
395 feet high	36 Floors
1,000 Rooms	6 Elevators
Year Built	1930
Owner	S. G. Taylor
Arch.	E. Ross
Bldr.	Harper Org.

ESSEX HOUSE

160 Central Park South (59th St.), between
6th & 7th Avenues

Essex house towers 464 feet high,
has 43 floors and cost close to

$10,000,000

Its upper floors have one of the most
commanding views of any buildings in
the city. For three miles to the north
Central Park offers an unbroken vista
—unequalled anywhere else in the city.

The Essex was originally named the
Seville, by the promoter and builder,
A. E. Lefcourt. But before completed
it passed out of his hands and was renamed the Essex.

Few apartment buildings in the
world are more ideally located or more
lavishly appointed.

HAMPSHIRE HOUSE

150 Central Park South (59th St.), between
6th & 7th Avenues

Suites range from 14 rooms to 1.
Its appointments represent the very
last word in everything that spells
luxury, convenience and efficiency.

The laying of the corner stone was
the occasion of much preparation and
considerable ceremony. The huge
building contains what was accepted
as the best books, best selection of
music, best example of sculpture, art
and design for 1931!

Hampshire House really offers a
"new era in living" in luxurious arrangement and equipment of suites,
ideal location, proximity to theatres
(and yet is away from the bustle and
noise of business).

Sutton, Blagden & Lynch, Inc., Agts.

SHERRY-NETHERLAND HOTEL

S. E. Cor. Fifth Ave. at 59th
Facing Central Park and
Central Park Plaza.

"MORE THAN A PLACE TO LIVE— A NEW WAY OF LIVING"

No hotel in any city can offer more varied attraction for ideal home life— either permanent or temporary. Overlooking Central Park Plaza and Central Park itself with its grand shade trees, artistic statues, and artificial lakes, there is no more entrancing vista in all New York.

The Sherry-Netherland is under "Boomer" management—the same as the great "Waldorf Astoria," "Sherry's" on Park Ave., the Savarin Restaurants, etc.

Ass'd Val. $6,650,000
573 feet high......40 Floors
525 GUEST ROOMS
Completed 1927
Owner, 59th St. & Fif.h Corp.
Arch., Schultze Weaver and
firm of Ely Jacques K hn
Bldrs., Schroeder & Koppel

MR. LOUIS SHERRY
Famed caterer to New
York's aristocracy

"SHERRY'S" ON PARK AVENUE

300 Park Ave.—50th to 51st St.
Note picture of this $6,000,000 palace on page 277.

Although Louis Sherry has passed to the Great Beyond. LOUIS SHERRY, INC., still continues to carry on— perpetuating the memory of one of New York's most outstanding characters. The life story of Mr. Sherry is so linked with the history of New York's social aristocracy (revealing inside information in connection with the spectacular entertainment of earlier days) that for a number of years the attention of the entire social world was focused on the city's famous "old 400."

Continued on next page

SAVOY-PLAZA HOTEL Full block on Fifth Ave., 58th to 59th St.

MAGNIFICENT REGAL

Although a favorite with New Yorkers, the patronage of the Savoy-Plaza Hotel is cosmopolitan. Its roster of guests is checkered with the names of internationally known notables and distinguished personages from all parts of the world.

Its traditions of many years' standing have been faithfully observed and its record of s e r v i c e and achievement has never been sullied by any interruption of strict and continued observance of duty.

With a location unsurpassed in the entire hotel world, and with a panoramic view of the city second to none in all New Y o r k, the Savoy-Plaza offers an ideal home life which appeals to both New Yorkers and out of town visitors.

Val. $17,800,000
419 feet high........37 Floors
855 GUEST ROOMS
Completed 1927
Owner ......Savoy-Plaza Corp.
Arch...McKim, Mead & White
Bldr.....George A. Fuller Co.

Continued from page 143

Just the simple name "SHERRY'S" conjures to the mind memories of lavish dinners, magnificent balls, and elaborate social affairs, the grandeur of which caused international comment. Mr. Sherry opened his first candy shop and restaurant in 1881. It was small and unpretentious, but he knew his business; he sold good candy and served good meals. He soon commanded attention. He was alive to opportunity and knew how to make and hold friends like Herman Oelrichs, J. Pierpont Morgan, Wm. C. Whitney and a hundred other men who have proven powers in New York's social, financial and business world. Mr. Sherry not only succeeded in earning fame, but also a fortune and LOUIS SHERRY, INC., is not only living up to the traditions established by the man whose name the Company bears, but continues to serve the flower of New York's wealth and elite.

Strangers who visit New York will find at 300 Park Avenue the best that highly trained chefs can serve, amidst sumptuous and refined surroundings not surpassed in the palaces of Europe.

HOTEL PIERRE

S. E. Cor. 61st St.
and Fifth Avenue

BEAUTIFUL
GORGEOUS
DISTINCTIVE

Built on the site of the famous old home of Commodore Gerry.

Stately, imposing, and located in a setting absolutely ideal for a hotel of its ultra high type. the "Pierre" towers 503 feet on Fifth Ave., overlooking Central Park at 61st Street, a monument of beauty and one of the most majestic structures in all New York.

The Pierre caters to only those of refined tastes who can afford the best in the way of hotel luxury.

This is another magnificent property for which New York is largely indebted to Douglas L. Elliman Company, who purchased the land and engineered the proposition thru to success.

COST OF LIVING IN NEW YORK

One can spend more or spend less for living in the City of New York than in any other modern city in the world. Apartments may be rented from a few dollars to several thousand dollars per month. Food costs vary also. The National Industrial Board, 247 Park Avenue, made a report upon the cost of living in the Metropolitan District. This survey showed that Brooklyn was the cheapest place to live. It was found that an industrial worker with a wife and one child could maintain a fair American standard of living in Brooklyn for a weekly cost of $25.94, as against $26.63 in Queens, $26.79 in the Bronx, $26.83 in Manhattan, $27.51 in Richmond. The weekly expenses of an office worker with the same sized family would be $29.10 in Brooklyn, $29.04 in the Bronx, $30.10 in Manhattan, $30.24 in Queens, $31.31 in Richmond.

ROOM AND BOARD.—The daily newspapers contain hundreds of advertisements of those desiring roomers and boarders. The following associations also will be of assistance: Association to Promote Proper Housing for Girls, Inc., 108 E. 30th St.; League of Catholic Women, 371 Lexington Ave.; Room Registry for Jewish Girls and Women, 2875 Broadway; Young Men's Christian Ass'n, 347 Madison Ave.; Young Women's Christian Ass'n, 129 E. 52nd St.

ANSONIA HOTEL

175 W. 73rd—
Full Block on Broadway to 74th St.

ONE OF THE MOST FAMOUS OF NEW YORK'S OLDER PALACES

Now under the same management as the Biltmore and Commodore. Another Jno McE. Bowman hotel. And, as might be expected of any hotel the "Bowman" interests take over, the magnificent old Ansonia has been thoroughly renovated, remodeled and refurnished, and once more restored to its rightful position among the "Class" hostelries of the City.

The Ansonia was originally owned and operated by the famous Stokes, one of old New York's most spectacular characters.

Ass'd Val.	.... $4,900,000
Height	.... 200 ft.
Floors	 18
Built	 1902
Bldr.	.. Onward Cons. Co.

HOTEL OLIVER CROMWELL

12 W. 72nd St.—Just a few steps west of Central Park.

Sumptuously furnished and ideally located in one of New York's most desirable home sections—only a stone's throw from Central Park, and about three minutes walk from Broadway, this magnificent hotel has a strong appeal to those who appreciate the most their money can secure in the matter of living quarters.

Cost	.... $2,500,000
Height	.... 350 ft.
1000	.... Guest Rooms
Completed	 1927
Owner	.... Sun Holding Corp.
Arch.	.... Emery Roth
Agt.	.... H. R. H. Management Corp.
Bldr.	.... H. R. H. Construction Co.
Rates	

BEACON HOTEL

2130 Broadway—
S. W. Cor. 75th St. thru block to Amsterdam Ave.

The Beacon caters especially to New Yorkers who favor the atmosphere of the upper Broadway section with its many social activities, beautiful restaurants, and many high grade moving picture palaces.

Built by Chanin Realty Co. from plans drawn by W. W. Ahlschlager. The beautiful "Chanin Theatre" controlled by Warner Bros. is in this building and is one of upper Broadway's most magnificent moving picture houses.

Cost	.... $7,000,000
Height	.... 300 feet
Floors	 25
505 Rooms	.... 311 Suites
Built	 1928

ALDEN HOTEL

225 Central Park West—
Covering full block from 82nd to 83rd St.

Facing the most beautiful section of Central Park's 3-mile frontage on Central Park West.

Ass'd Val.	..$2,000,000
232 ft. high..19 Floors	
Archt.	.. Emery Roth
Bldr.	... Bing & Bing

146

HOTEL CARLYLE

Cor. Madison Ave. & 76th St.

NEWEST AND MOST STATELY APARTMENT HOTEL IN ALL UPPER NEW YORK

Equipped with gymnasium, kindergarten, playroom (sand-box, see-saw, etc.) roof-garden, 40 delightful terraces and many other special features or innovations.

In any other city than New York, this stupendous and gorgeous hotel would attract state wide attention, and yet New York is so vast and has seen the erection of so many ernormous and palatial skyscrapers in all parts of the huge city, scarcely any one outside its immediate neighborhood even heard of the "Carlyle" prior to the announcement of its opening, during the past year.

The Carlyle houses a small city—extending a full block on Madison Avenue from 76th to 77th Streets.

Ass'd Val	$3,200,000
426 ft. high	38 Floors
600 Guest Rooms	
Completed	1930
Owner	Calvin Morris Corp.
Arch	Bien & Prince
Bldr	Calvin Morris Corp.

Agent
DOUGLAS L. ELLIMAN & CO.

PARK ROYAL HOTEL

23 W. 73rd St.
Only a half block west of Central Park.

From the gorgeous lobby with its beautiful art fountain to the various terraces atop, this ideal apartment home and hotel is "the last word". Grand dining room and excellent meals.

Ass'd Val	$2,650,000
16 Floors	510 Rooms
Built	1926
Owner	P. Krassner
Architect	Geo. F. Pelham
Bldr	Aaron Lapedus

OTHER BIG AND WELL KNOWN HOTELS

FIFTH AVE. HOTEL
N. W. Cor. 5th Ave.
and 9th Street.

Ass'd Val...$3,070,000
233 ft. high..18 Floors
Rooms............630
Built............1926
Where everything
that can be desired in a
hotel is in evidence.

GEO. WASHINGTON
23 Lexington Ave. at
23rd Street.

Cost......$2,200,000
200 ft. high..18 Floors
622 Rooms.5 Elevators
Built............1930
A delightful permanent or transient home
for *women* exclusively.

HOTEL PRINCE GEO.
14 E. 28th St. Bet.
6th & Madison Aves.

Ass'd Val...$2,650,000
13 Floors.1000 Rooms
Rates....$2.50 and up
Built............1919
Every traveler knows
the Prince George.
There's a reason!

HOTEL MARTINIQUE
N. E. Cor. Broadway
and 32nd Street.

Cost......$5,000,000
17 Floors..600 Rooms
Rates...$1.50 and up
Built............1911
One of New York's
truly magnificent
hotels.

HOTEL IMPERIAL
S. E. Cor. Broadway
& 32nd Street.

Cost......$4,000,000
17 Floors...555 Rooms
Rates....$2.00 and up
Built............1891
For Forty years the
Imperial has increased
in popularity each year!

HOTEL WHITE
N. E. Cor. Lexington
Ave. & 37th St.

Ass'd Val...$2,500,000
17 Floors...407 Rooms
Rates....$5.00 and up
Built............1925
An ideal hotel home
away from noise and
business but just around
the corner from it.

HOTEL TIMES SQ.
N. E. Cor. 43rd &
8th Avenue.

Cost......$1,500,000
16 Floors..1000 Rooms
Rates....$1.75 and up
Built............1924
Originally the "Claman"—a hotel for bachelors—*now* open to all.

CLARIDGE HOTEL
160 W. 44th St.—
Cor. Broadway.

Ass'd Val...$3,550,000
19 Floors...700 Rooms
Rates....$2.50 and up
Built............1911
This is the magnificent hotel the famous
George Rector built.

WINTHROP HOTEL
N. E. Cor. Lexington
Ave. & 47th St.

Cost......$2,000,000
18 Floors.190 ft. high
Rates....$4.00 and up
Built............1927
All Suites have pantries
200 Rooms or Suites.
An ideal "home hotel."
Transients like it too.

HOTEL BRISTOL
129 W. 48th St.—
East of Broadway.

Ass'd Val...$1,130,000
15 Floors...410 Rooms
Built............1918
Rates....$2.00 and up
FAMOUS 50c and
$1.00 Table d'hote. Attractive & cosy rooms.

HOTEL BELVEDERE
319 W. 48th St.—
Near 8th Ave.

Ass'd Val...$1,500,000
20 Floors...450 Rooms
Rates....$3.00 and up
Year Built.......1926
One of the most
beautiful and modern
hotels of New York.

HOTEL PLYMOUTH
143 W. 49th St.

Ass'd Val...$1,275,000
18 Floors...400 Rooms
Built............1929
Rates....$2.50 and up
Every room has a
Radio. One of the best
cabarets in N. Y.

THE BERKSHIRE
21 E. 52nd St. &
Madison Ave.

Ass'd Val...$2,750,000
21 Floors...350 Rooms
Built...........1926
Caters especially to
those who appreciate
the best.

HOTEL WEYLIN
54th St.—
Cor. Madison Ave.

Val. over...$2,500,000
16 Floors...400 Rooms
Rates...$4.00 and up
Rebuilt.........1926
Headquarters for the
royalty of Europe and
the elite of America.

GOTHAM HOTEL
S. W. Cor. 5th Ave.
& 55th St.

Ass'd Val...$5,000,000
252 ft. high...22 Floors
Rates....$4.00 and up
420 Rooms...Blt. 1901
The home of New
York's aristocracy for
over twenty-five years.

LOMBARDY HOTEL
111 E. 56th St. Bet.
Lexington & Park Av.

Ass'd Val...$2,900,000
22 Floors...350 Rooms
Bldr....Henry Mandel
Built...........1927
Magnificently fur-
nished. Just east of
Park Avenue.

ALAMAC HOTEL
S. E. Cor. 71st St.
and Broadway.

Ass'd Val...$4,000,000
21 Floors...600 Rooms
Rates....$2.50 and up
Built...........1925
Where there is action
and something doing.
Visit the roof!

**HOTEL ROBERT
FULTON**
228 W. 71st St.—
Near Broadway.

Ass'd Val...$1,000,000
14 Floors...300 Rooms
Built...........1917
Owr.Gresham Rty.Co.
Archt...Emery Roth
An absolutely homey
atmosphere—the acme
of refinement.

**HOTEL
WELLINGTON**
871 7th Ave.
N. E. Cor.
55th Street.

Assessed Value...
....$1,370,000
Height....329 ft.
Floors.........28
Rooms.......750
Built........1930

**ONE OF
THE GREAT
KNOTT
CHAIN OF
HOTELS**

A Word
of
Explanation

Some of the
hotels pictured
on this and preceding pages, really class
among the GIANT HOTELS of New
York, but we were delayed in securing
photographs and data when compiling the
hotel pages—thus these smaller cuts.

There are over a hundred other "million
dollar" hotels in the city, but our space is
limited, and we will therefore include these
in our new book entitled "THE HOTELS
OF NEW YORK"—which we believe will
be recognized as the greatest hotel publication ever printed.

THE WESTOVER
253 W. 72nd St.—
Near West End Ave.

A'd Vl.over $2,000,000
25 Floors...432 Rooms
Arct.Schwartz & Gross
Built...........1928
One of the most popu-
lar hotels in all the
"West End" district.

OLCOTT HOTEL
27 W. 72nd St.—
Near Central Park.

Est. Cost...$4,500,000
17 Floors...498 Rooms
Year Built......1925
Mgr...Alfred A. Drew
Sumptuously equip-
ped and only a stone's
throw from Central Pk.

ST. GEORGE HOTEL, BROOKLYN

51 Clark St.—Covers entire square—Clark, Henry, Pineapple and Hicks Sts.

APPRAISED VALUATION
$18,000,000
2632 GUEST ROOMS

Height.......tower section 400 ft.
Floors...........tower section 33
Original hotel of 30 rooms built
on part of present plot in 1885.
Last addition (tower section) built
in 1930.
Architect (Tower Section).......Emery Roth
Builder (Tower Section).......Bing & Bing
Rates...............$2.50 and Up
Owners..............Bing & Bing

THE LARGEST HOTEL IN EASTERN AMERICA

Only 4 minutes from Wall Street—Subway right in Building.
Many New Yorkers make their permanent home here.
Luxurious, up to date and the social mecca of all Brooklyn.
Largest and most magnificent swimming pool in the world. Cost $1,264,000.
Enormous Banquet Hall—Seats 2,500 and accommodates 3,000 dancers.

HERE ARE SOME FIGURES ILLUSTRATING THE IMMENSITY OF THE ST. GEORGE

Largest private incinerator in the world—capacity 26 tons daily.
73 ventilating fans—circulating 8,000,000 cubic feet per minute.
Over 6,000 windows.
7½ miles of corridors and 21 elevators.
Over 66,000 electric bulbs.
20,000 chairs, 61,000 sheets, 560,000 pillow cases and 655,000 pieces of table
linen. The silverware alone of the St. George cost over $450,000.
THE ST. GEORGE IS A GOOD SIZED CITY IN ITSELF. IT CAN SEAT AND SERVE FOOD
IN ITS CAFES AND EATING PLACES TO 10,000 AT ONE TIME.

Out-of-city guests, who have business in the lower part of the City will find
the St. George both convenient and delightful.

LEVERICH TOWERS (Brooklyn) — Clark and Willow and Pineapple Streets

"JUST ACROSS THE RIVER FROM WALL STREET"

A deluxe apartment hotel in the aristocratic social district of Brooklyn Heights, surrounded by historical and
social traditions, jealously guarded by each succeeding
generation.

Located on the very shore of
East River with cooling breezes
in summer, unsurpassed view and
with every comfort in keeping
with magnificent appointment and
gorgeous furnishings, living at
Leverich Towers approaches the
actual *ideal*. Out-of-town guests
are always welcome.

Underwood & Underwood

Ass'd Val. $2,800,000
Height 183 ft......18 Floor
Ground Plot...15,000 sq. ft.
585 Guest Rooms
6 Elevators
Year Built 1927
Owner..Amer. Bond & Mort.
Co.
Arch...Starrett & Van Vleck
Bldr....Brookhold Cons. Co.
Rates.........$3.00 and Up

150

THE SKYSCRAPERS OF NEW YORK

NEW YORK'S 100 HIGHEST BUILDINGS

As the average **10** story building is seldom as high as 150 feet high, the following list will give some conception of why New York's sky line is so famous. See Index for picture, location, etc.

Buildings marked * are not yet completed.

		Height				Height
1	Empire State	1,248 ft.	51	Paramount		455 ft.
2	Chrysler	1,046 ft.	52	Lefcourt Colonial		454 ft.
3	Cities Service	950 ft.	53	444 Madison		453 ft.
4	Bank of Manhattan Trust	927 ft.	54	Squibb		451 ft.
5	Woolworth	792 ft.	55	19 Rector		450 ft.
6	City Bank Farmers Trust	760 ft.	32	Hotel New Yorker		525 ft.
7	Broadway Temple*	705 ft.	57	Commerce		443 ft.
8	500 Fifth Ave	701 ft.	58	21 West		442 ft.
9	Metropolitan Life	700 ft.	59	Equitable Society		440 lt.
10	Radio City Main Bldg.*	700 ft.	60	63 Wall		440 ft.
11	Chanin	680 ft.	61	Empire Trust		438 ft.
12	Lincoln	673 ft.	62	Barbizon Plaza		437 ft.
13	Waldorf Astoria	672 ft.	63	1400 Broadway		436 ft.
14	Irving Trust	654 ft.	64	535 Fifth Ave		432 ft.
15	R. C. A	642 ft.	65	120 Wall St		430 ft.
16	10 East 40th St	632 ft.	66	52 Wall		430 ft.
17	New York Life	617 ft.	67	116 John		430 ft.
18	Singer Tower	612 ft.	68	Bush Terminal		430 ft.
19	Ritz Tower	592 ft.	69	Hotel Carlyle		426 ft.
20	Municipal Bldg	584 ft.	70	Adams Express		424 ft.
21	Sherry Netherland	573 ft.	71	Bricken Textile		421 ft.
22	New York Central	566 ft.	72	Savoy Plaza		419 ft.
23	Continental Bank*	564 ft.	73	50 Broadway		418 ft.
24	Nelson Tower	560 ft.	74	Whitehall		416 ft.
25	Navarre Mercantile Bldg	555 ft.	75	American Express Bldg		415 ft.
26	120 Broadway	542 ft.	76	N. Y. Tel., 24 Walker		414 ft.
27	Bankers Trust	540 ft.	77	Hotel Shelton		412 ft.
28	Equitable Trust	540 ft.	78	Bricken Casino		408 ft.
29	Transportation	540 ft.	79	530 7th Ave		405 ft.
30	Park Central Hotel	540 ft.	80	Century Apartments		405 ft.
31	Downtown Athletic Club	534 ft.	81	International Combustion		404 ft.
32	Continental Office Bldg	524 ft.	82	501 Madison		403 ft.
33	Bank of N. Y. & Trust Co	513 ft.	83	Beresford Apartments		402 ft.
34	Williamsburg Savings Bank	512 ft.	84	San Remo Towers		401 ft.
35	22 East 40th	508 ft.	85	Sinclair Oil Co		400 ft.
36	Standard Oil	505 ft.	86	N. Y. Cornell Hospital		400 ft.
37	Hotel Pierre	503 ft.	87	Western Union Tel		400 ft.
38	140 West	498 ft.	88	Graybar		400 ft.
39	Chase National Bank	496 ft.	89	St. George Hotel		400 ft.
40	Fuller Bldg	491 ft.	90	270 Broadway		397 ft.
41	Lefcourt National	490 ft.	91	Hotel St. Moritz		395 ft.
42	McGraw Hill	488 ft.	92	Munson		390 ft.
43	Hotel & Institute Mart	482 ft.	93	Majestic Apartments		390 ft.
44	Hampshire House	480 ft.	94	15 Park Row		387 ft.
45	Benenson	480 ft.	95	Eldorado Apartments		364 ft.
46	News	476 ft.	96	Maritime Exchange		385 ft.
47	N. Y. Times	476 ft.	97	Hotel Delmonico		380 ft.
48	Essex Apartment Bldg	464 ft.	98	Hotel Governor Clinton		378 ft.
49	International Tel. & Tel	456 ft.	99	60 John		378 ft.
50	Fred F. French Bldg	456 ft.	100	Woodstock Towers		376 ft.

Copyrighted photo by Orren R. Louden.

Courtesy of Walter Trumbull

SKY LINE AT CENTRAL PARK

1932

Half a dozen years ago there was not a building higher than 20 stories skirting the entire park in this section.

WATCH NEW YORK GROW!

WALL STREET

Extends from Trinity Church at Broadway to East River.
About a quarter of a mile long.

Wall Street derived its name from a massive stockade, built as a protection from Indians, after a massacre in which 120 lives were lost. This stockade extended all the way across the lower part of the island from East River to the Hudson.

Just why the western end of the little alley did not retain the name of "Wall" is another story, but the five short blocks from East River to Trinity (on Broadway)—famous as Wall Street, is without exaggeration the best known quarter of a mile the world over.

Here is located the old historical "Subtreasury" built on the site where George Washington took his oath of office as President of the United States.

Here is located the New York Stock Exchange, the banking house of J. P. Morgan & Co., and (either directly on Wall Street itself, or within practically a stone's throw) a number of the largest banks in existence anywhere.

Observe the pictures on following pages of the Irving Trust Bank, the Bank of Manhattan, the Bank of New York & Trust Co., the Chase National Bank, the Equitable Trust Co., and numerous other skyscrapers costing fabulous sums—well up in the millions, all located on Wall Street, or a stone's throw away.

WALL STREET IN CIVIL WAR DAYS

From a photo owned by David M. Morrison, of the Warburton Trust Co. Showing from 36 to 54 Wall. Only one of these buildings was standing 25 years ago today—the old Bank of New York. See page 25 for their magnificent new structure.

Wall Street is the financial center of the globe.

Millions and even billions are here the transactions of a day!

Fortunes are made and lost in twenty-four hours when there is any unusual activity in the stock market.

History has written countless names of those who have risen from poverty to affluence, or been reduced from great wealth to penury as a result of having been on the right or wrong side of Wall Street!

In the crash, that in October, 1929, started securities down the toboggan ten to even thirty and forty points in a few hours, *billions* of losses were sustained by those who were so unfortunate as not to have foreseen what was coming.

All the wealth of other nations and financial centers combined could not have faced such conditions as Wall Street experienced during this period, without general bankruptcy and panic, and yet—"Wall Street" absorbed the shocks as rapidly as the ticker clicked the appalling figures, and the Wall Street bankers who have made Wall Street what it is, met the exigencies of the situation, and averted what would have undoubtedly been the most serious panic in all history.

Many may curse and execrate Wall Street, but the fact remains that Wall Street is the bulwark of our entire national financial strength.

WALL STREET BUILDINGS IN 1932—Every one of these have entrances on Wall

IRVING TRUST CO'S. BUILDING

Also known as "ONE WALL STREET."
No. 1 Wall St.—S. E. Cor. Broadway. Frontages on Broadway, Wall and New Streets.

ONE OF THE MOST VALUABLE CORNERS
IN ALL THE WORLD

This palatial new IRVING TRUST CO'S. building towers so high above the soaring spire of old Trinity Church just across the street, that it almost dwarfs that famous old steeple—which in days gone by inspired the awe of all New York on account of its extreme height!

"ONE WALL STREET" is but one of nearly fifty new skyscraper buildings erected in lower Manhattan recently, many of which are whole cities in themselves, housing from 5,000 to even 15,000 and 20,000 workers! Although this sumptuous structure was not completed until early in 1931, the many advantages it offers in light, air, location, transportation, and every modern convenience, practically insure full tenancy in record time.

Ass'd Val.	$22,100.000
654 feet high	52 Floors
Rent area	500,000 sq. ft.
Housing capacity	5,000
Building completed	1931
Owner	Irving Trust Co.
Architect	Voorhees, Gmelin & Walker
Builder	Marc Eidlitz & Son
Agent	CRUIKSHANK CO.

The Irving Trust Company *banking quarters,* located on the lower floors, are equalled by but few other financial institutions in all America, in point of quiet elegance. They are superb.

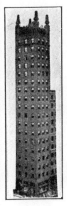

THIS FAMOUS
BUILDING
TORN DOWN!

In order to construct the new "IRVING TRUST," the 18-story building shown at the left was demolished. This old "ONE WALL" building was less than 30 feet wide on Broadway, and not even 40 feet long on Wall Street, and yet—this small ground floor space and basement rented for $100 per day! In 1910, this corner was reputed to be the most valuable parcel of real estate in the entire world.

Ass'd Val. $23,500.000
340 feet high ......26 Floors
Area ....175,000 sq. ft.
Housing capacity 2,500
Completed (corner bldg.), 1922
Owner, New York Stock Exch.
Arch., Trowbridge & Livingston

NEW YORK STOCK EXCHANGE

11 Wall St.—S. W. Cor. Broad St.

Entrance also at 18 Broad St.

Prior to the Revolutionary War, securities were practically unknown in America, but our first Congress in 1790 authorized an issue of $80,000,-000 in bonds. The sale of these securities developed under an old tree which stood where the building at 68 Wall Street now stands. The present New York Stock Exchange traces its origin to a group who met daily under that old tree to trade. The present membership is 1,375.

HOUSE OF J. P. MORGAN & CO.

23 Wall Street—S. E. Cor. Broad

BUILT OF WHITE MARBLE

The J. P. Morgan Bank is one of the most famous financial institutions in all the universe.

Ass'd Val. $7,000,000
90 feet high ....7 Floors
Completed 1915
Arch., Trowbridge & Livingston
Bldr. .....Marc. Eidlitz & Son

Photo by Louis H. Dreyer

BANK OF AMERICA

44 Wall Street—N. W. Cor. Willam

Ass'd Val. $7,500,000
329 feet high ....29 Floors
Rent area ....190,000 sq. ft.
Housing capacity 2,200
Completed 1926
Owner ....44 Wall St. Corp.
Arch., Trowbridge & Livingston
Bldr. ....C. T. Wills, Inc.
Agt., Brown Wheelock H. V. Co.

Front and side views of building

NATIONAL CITY CO.'S BUILDING

Better known as "52 WALL"—52 Wall Street, just east of William

Ass'd Val. $5,400,000
430 feet high....35 Floors
Rent area ..218,000 sq. ft.
Housing capacity ..2,500
Ground area 12,214 sq. ft.
11 Elevators
Owner ..National City Co.
Arch., McKim, Mead & White
Bldr., Geo. A. Fuller & Co.
Completed 1928
Agent ....On premises

NATIONAL CITY BANK BUILDING

55 Wall Street—
William to Hanover Streets

Ass'd Val. $8,800,000
114 feet high ..11 Floors
Rent area ..181,000 sq. ft.
Housing capacity ...2,100
Owner, National City Bank
Ground Area, 30,576 sq. ft.
12 Elevators
Arch., McKim, Mead & White
Bldr. ..Fuller Const. Co.
Agent ......Nat. City Co.

BANKERS TRUST BUILDING

16 Wall St.—N. E. Cor. Nassau St. Opposite New York Stock Exchange

ONE OF THE FIRST OUTSTANDING
SKYSCRAPERS OF LOWER MANHATTAN

For nearly twenty years, the Bankers Trust Company's building has been one of the dominating towers of lower New York's famous skyline. Among the nearly fifty colossal new structures recently erected in this neighborhood, this stately building continues as one of the most outstanding. And its new addition (now in course of construction) will keep the "Bankers Trust" building in a dominating position.

Few, except those versed in Wall Street property, realize the enormous value of land in this great financial section. Even twenty years ago, $820 a *square foot* was paid for the plot on which the Bankers Trust now stands—which at that time (1910) was the highest price ever paid for "dirt."

Directly north of the Bankers Trust building, and shown in picture, was the old Hanover Bank building. This 23 story palace has recently been demolished, and the Bankers Trust Company are now erecting a magnificent new "L" addition—the building to the west having also been razed.

The Bankers Trust Company is one of the oldest and most powerful financial institutions in all New York, and many nationally known names are included among its officers and directors.

President......S. Sloan Colt
Chairman....Seward Prosser

Statement, July, 1931

Deposits,
$604,225,290.90
Cap. Sur. Undivided **Prof.**,
$112,792,422.23
Resources,
$840,555,062.29

Ass'd Val.	$10,650,000
540 feet high	41 Floors
Housing capacity	1,500
Ground area approx.	4,900 sq. ft.
Elevators	16
Completed	1912
Owner	Bankers Trust Company
Architect	Trowbridge & Livingston
Agents	Brown Wheelock Harris
Builders	Marc Eidlitz & Son

"60 WALL STREET"

Showing front and rear
towers
Just East of William St.

Ass'd Val.	$3,100,000
346 ft. high	27 Floors
Ground Area	15,000 sq. ft.
Rent Area	160,000 sq. ft.
Housing	2,000
8 Elevators	
Year Built	1905
Owner	60 Wall St. Corp.
Arch	Clinton & Russell
Bldr	Chas. T. Wills
Agent	Owners

ATLANTIC BLDG.

49 Wall St.—S. W. Cor.
William

HOME OF THE ATLANTIC
MUTUAL INSURANCE CO.

Ass'd Val.	$4,000,000
236 ft. high	21 Floors
Year Built	1901
Owner	Atlantic Mut. Ins. Co.
Bldr., Thompson & Starrett Co.	
Agent	Brown Wheelock H. V. Co.

SEAMENS BANK

74 Wall N. W. Cor. Pearl

Ass'd Val. $3,600,000

Only 15 floors, but one
of the most beautiful buildings in all the Wall Street
section.

Chartered in 1829 this
substantial old institution
celebrated its 100th anniversary year before last.

MUNSON BLDG.

67 Wall, S. W. Cor. Pearl
160 feet on Beaver

FLAT-IRON SHAPED

One of Wall Street's most
imposing structures

Ass'd Val.	$4,300,000
390 ft. high	26 Floors
Ground Area	11,817 sq. ft.
Rent Area	240,000 sq. ft.
House Capacity	2,700
10 Elevators	
Year Built	1921
Owner	Munson Bld. Co.
Arch	K. M. Murchison
Bldr	Geo. A. Fuller Co.
Agent	Owner

"99 WALL STREET"

A block from East River

Built on ground that in
earlier days was a tiny island connected with Wall
Street by a small bridge.

Cost	$2,200,000
300 ft. high	29 Floors
Rent Area	70,000 sq. ft.
Housing Capacity	800
Year Built	1931
Owner	99 Wall St. Corp.
Arch	Schwartz & Gross
Bldr	Shroder & Koppel
Agent, Brown Wheelock H. V. Co.	

POSTAL BLDG.

20 Broad St.
A few steps south of Wall

This famous old building,
adjoining the New York
Stock Exchange, has been
purchased by that famous
organization and is now
owned by the "Exchange."
The "Postal" was one of
the famous skyscrapers of
the world when erected and
it is still one of the imposing and beautiful buildings
of the Wall Street section
—extending thru the block
to New Street.

20 Broad is an address
that has carried prestige for
nearly thirty years.

BANK OF MANHATTAN TRUST BUILDING

Also known as "40 Wall."
40 Wall St.—Between Nassau and William Streets.

FOURTH TALLEST OFFICE BUILDING IN THE WORLD

ONLY EXCEEDED BY THE "EMPIRE STATE" (See page 211)
THE "CHRYSLER" BUILDING (See page 233)
AND "CITIES SERVICE" BUILDING (See page 179)

Second Oldest Bank in the United States—founded in 1799 by Alexander Hamilton and associates.

Ass'd Val.	$25,550,000
927 feet high	70 Floors
Rent area	845,000 sq. ft.
Housing capacity	10,000
Elevators	41
Completed	1930
Owner	40 Wall St. Corp.
Arch	H. Craig Severance, and Yasuo Matsui, associate.
Builder	Starrett Bros. & Eken

ONE OF THE GREATEST SIGHTS IN THE CITY

This marvelous example of architectural and building skill is not only a credit to New York, but to all *America*.

No building ever constructed more t h o r o u g h l y typifies the American spirit of hustle than does this extraordinary structure —built in less than one year.

Two years was the estimated time required to erect this prodigious building, covering a plot of 33,600 sq. feet and towering over 70 stories skyward. But the architects, "Craig Severance, Inc.," and associates made up fifty different sets of blue prints. The building organization of Starrett Bros. & Eken Inc. rushed the work thru, breaking all time records in construction work. Within eleven months from the day the wrecking of the 15-story building formerly occupying the site was begun, the herculean job was completed and tenants were moving in.

Words are inadequate to convey even a faint conception of the splendor or the wonder of this magnificent building.

BANK OF NEW YORK AND TRUST BUILDING

48 Wall St.—N. E. Cor. William St.

OLDEST BANK IN NEW YORK

The Bank of New York & Trust Company occupies the site which it purchased in 1797. The bank was founded in 1784, the group of backers being headed by Alexander Hamilton, who became the first Secretary of the Treasury. The first loan to the United States Government was negotiated with this bank.

The Banking rooms possess a quiet elegance and are among the most beautiful in the country. The mural decorations portray the progress of the institution along with important epochs of national history. The stately old Colonial clock which stood in the hallway of the old bank building in 1797 continues to point the hour to employees and visitors at the famous old institution.

Deposits $108,071,183.63
Capital & Surplus......$20,254,896.58
Resources $137,596,578.21

The Bank of New York & Trust Company is proud of its beautiful home and of its fine traditions, and enjoys a select clientele.

Completed in 1928	
Assessed Valuation $7,400,000	
513 feet high...........32 Floors..........210,758 sq. ft.	
9 Public Elevators and 4 Private	
Owner......................Bank of New York & Trust Co.	
Architect..................................Ben . W. Morris	
Agents....................................H S. Ely & Co.	
Builder...........................Marc Eidlitz & Son, Inc.	
Ground floor area............................11,613 sq. ft.	

"63 WALL STREET" BUILDING

S. E. Cor. William. Covers half square—Wall, William and Beaver Sts.

ONE OF THE GRANDEST BUILDINGS IN NEW YORK

From the unique and bizarre entrance and lobby, to the very top floor, there is evidence of the superior craftsmanship of the architects—Delano & Aldrich, in association with the very talented Yasuo Matsui. No building in all New York has been more masterly conceived.

Ass'd Val. ...$7,500,000
440 feet high..37 Floors
Rent Area 315,000 sq. ft.
Housing 4,000
Built 1927
Owner, Wall-Hanover Co.
Architect ......Delano &
Aldrich & Yasuo Matsui
Builder ...Starrett Bros.
Agent, Brown, Wheelock

"63 Wall" is the home of a hundred nationally known institutions and business concerns, among whom may be mentioned the internationally famous houses of:

Brown Bros.-Harriman
Clark Childs & Co.
Bond & Goodwin
Brown Wheelock Harris & Co.

Directly across the street from the great National City Bank, and only a stone's throw from a dozen of New York's most gigantic banking institutions, the New York Stock Exchange, the New York Cotton Exchange and right in the very heart of Wall Street's most strenuous activities, "63 Wall" is one of the most desirable locations in the financial district, and the magnificent building itself is quite in keeping with the prestige of its location.

"120 WALL ST."

Covering over half a square, with frontages on Wall, South and Pine Streets.

ANOTHER ENORMOUS BUILDING THAT HOUSES AN ENTIRE CITY

Only four blocks from N. Y. Stock Exchange. 100% daylight. River breezes. 12-foot ceilings. Every comfort and convenience.

"120 Wall" Building stands on the site of Murray's old wharf at which General George Washington landed April 23, 1789, on the occasion of his visit to New York to take his oath of office as first President of the United States. He was welcomed by Governor Clinton amidst the booming of cannon and the enthusiastic plaudits of grateful people.

From Pearl Street east, "Wall" gradually widens from its narrow "alley" width, ending at South Street (on the N.E. corner of which is "120 Wall") where the short thoroughfare is at its widest— 125 feet.

Cost	$10,000,000
430 feet high	36 Floors
Rent Area	467,000 sq. ft.
Housing	6,000
Completed	1930
Owner	Greemal Holding Corp.
Architect	Firm of Ely Jacques Kahn
Bldr.	Greemal Holding Corp.
Agent, Chas. F. Noyes Co., Inc.	

NEW YORK BANK CLEARINGS
AND THE GREAT VOLUME OF BUSINESS TRANSACTED IN NEW YORK

During 1929 the total bank clearings of the United States were $727,848,371,330, of which $477,242,282,161, or over 65 per cent., were in the City of New York.

In New York will be found the great exchanges of the world, notably the Stock, the Cotton and the Produce. Merely those securities in which members of the New York Stock Exchange are authorized to deal represent a value well above $110,591,000,000 as of January 1, 1930.

The nation's wealth is estimated for 1928 by the National Industrial Conference Board at $360,100,000,000, it is apparent that a large percentage of it, represented in corporate securities, is traded in upon the New York Stock Exchange. As the estimated wealth of the State of New York is over $42,000,000,000, considerably less than the value of stocks and bonds on the New York Stock Exchange, it is obvious that the entire country must be represented on this Board. In fact, around 1,307 different stock issues are listed. Of this number comparatively few are New York corporations.

EQUITABLE TRUST BUILDING

15 Broad St.—N. E. Cor. Exchange Place with entrances at 51 Ex. Place and 37 Wall St.

ONE OF THE 20 LARGEST OFFICE BUILDINGS IN THE WORLD

This great structure with its Wall Street "L", is not only one of the most impressive of lower Broadway's huge business buildings, but is one of the most symmetrical and beautiful. The interior is superb—rich, but not garish, luxurious without evidence of either ostentation or poor taste.

The architects, Trowbridge & Livingston (who also drew plans for the Bankers Trust Co., New York Stock Exchange, Bank of America, J. P. Morgan Bank and other famous Wall Street buildings) are responsible for this great architectural achievement.

The Equitable Trust Co. is one of the units of the Chase National Bank organization—the largest and most powerful banking institution in the world.

Ass'd Val. 15 Broad $17,250,00
540 feet high........43 Floors
Rent Area......750,000 sq. ft.
Housing Capacity 10,000
Year Built 1928
Owners......Chase Natl. Bank
Architects.......Trowbridge & Livingston
Bldrs., Thompson Starrett Co.
Agent.....Douglas Cruikshank

THESE TWO FAMOUS OLD SKYSCRAPERS ADJOIN THE EQUITABLE TRUST BUILDING (shown above)—AND NOW BELONG TO THE CHASE NATIONAL BANK ORGANIZATION

39 WALL STREET

37 WALL—The building at left was originally known as "THE TRUST CO. OF AMERICA BUILDING" and was owned by the Lands Purchase Co.

Ass'd Val. ...$3,900,000
317 feet high..24 Floors
Housing Capacity..1,000
Year Built 1907
Owner, Chase Nat. Bank
Arch. ....Francis H. Kimball
Bldr., Geo. A. Fuller Co.

The WALL ST. EXCHANGE building at right was formerly owned by the State Bank of New York—now a part of the Chase National Bank.

Ass'd Val. ...$3,500,000
337 feet high..26 Floors
Rent Area, 129,240 sq. ft.
Housing Capacity ..1,600
Year Built 1903
Owner, Chase Natl. Bank
Arch., Clinton & Russell
Bldr., Geo. A. Fuller Co.

43 EXCHANGE PLACE

BROAD EXCHANGE BUILDING

S. E. Cor. Broad St. & Exchange Place

Better known as

25 BROAD

A mammoth building which for many years has housed, and still houses a host of America's most famous corporations.

Directly in front of 25 Broad was operated (in the open air) the New York Curb Market, which institution now occupies its own magnificent building at 78 Trinity Place. See Page 172.

The picture gives but a faint conception of the immensity of this enormous building.

Ass'd Val.	$6,800,000
279 ft. high	20 Floors
Ground Area	28,000 sq. ft.
Rent Area	340,000 sq. ft.
Houses	4,000
18 Elevators	Year Built 1901
Owner	Broad Exch. Co.
Archt.	Clinton & Russel
Bldr.	Geo. A. Fuller Co.
Agent	Abex Realty Co.

60 BROAD ST. BUILDING

Between Beaver & Ex. Pl.

Ass'd Val.	$2,000,000
170 ft. high	23 Floors
Ground Area	3,000 sq ft.
Rent Area	72,000 sq. ft.
Houses	1,000
3 Elevators	
Year Built	1927
Owner	Radio Real Est. Corp.
Archt.	Firm-Ely Jacq Kahn
Bldr.	Harper Organ
Agent	Wm. A. White & Sons

27 WILLIAM ST. BUILDING

S. W. Cor. Ex. Place (40 Exchange Pl.)

Ass'd Val.	$3,900,000
265 ft. high	20 Floors
Rent Area	190,000 sq. ft.
Houses	2200
Year Built	1898
Owner	Wm. St. Ex Place Corp.
Agent	Chas. F. Noyes & Co.

CORN EXCHANGE BANK BUILDING

21 William St.
N. W. Cor. Beaver St.

Home of one of New York's soundest Banks. Resources over $300,000,000.

Ass'd Val.	$2,875,000
262 ft. high	20 Floors
Rent Area	112,500 sq. ft.
Houses	1700
Year Built	1903
Owner	Corn Ex. Bank Trust Co.
Archt.	Robinson & Potter
Bldr.	John Downey
Agent	Geo. R. Read & Co.

CONTINENTAL BANK BUILDING

30 Broad—thru to New St.

New home of the Continental Bank & Trust Co. now located in the Broad St. Exchange Building at 25 Broad St., pictured above.

Work is already progressing on this giant skyscraper which, including its basement floors, will add another 50 story office palace to Lower Broadway's great group of heaven-piercing structures.

Notwithstanding the many towering buildings of New York's wonderful financial center, and the fact that business conditions have not yet entirely recovered from our two years' "depression," here's another $16,000,000 goliath which is stated to be ready for occupancy in the Spring of 1932!

AND THUS NEW YORK GROWS

Est. Cost	$16,000,000
564 ft. high	50 Floors
Rent Area	300,000 sq. ft.
Year Built	1932
Owner	30 Broad Corp.
Archt.	Morris & O'Connor
Bldr.	Thompson Starrett Co.
Agent	Cruikshank & Co.

INTERNATIONAL
TEL^{EPHONE} and TEL^{EGRAPH}
BUILDING

67 Broad St.—S. E. Cor. Beaver St.

This superb building towers among the skyscrapers of lower New York, as one of the most outstanding examples of architectural and structural skill.

Its interior is in keeping with the beauty of the building itself and the dignity and standing of the distinguished organization it houses.

This is the home of the INTERNATIONAL TELEPHONE AND TELEGRAPH CORP. a n d associated companies, whose activities cover forty-four countries in all parts of the world.

It is the center for the world-wide communication network of the international system comprising the

"POSTAL TELEGRAPH COMPANY"
(furnishing telegraphic service to 70,000 points in the United States and Canada)

"ALL AMERICAN CABLES"
(providing service to the whole of Central and South America)

"COMMERCIAL CABLES"
(providing service to European countries and connecting with Japan, Asia, Africa, etc.)
AND
"MACKAY RADIO"
(radio service to ships at sea in both oceans, as well as the whole of the United States, etc.)

Ass'd Val.	$9,400,000
456 ft. high	38 Floors
Floor Area	456,000 sq. ft.
Houses	5200
Completed	1930
Owner	Int. Tel. & Tel. Co.
Arch'tect	Louis S. Weeks
Builder	A. E. Lefcourt Co.

ASSESSED VALUATIONS IN NEW YORK

ASSESSED VALUATIONS.—Some conception of the magnitude of the City is given by the record of assessed valuation of property subject to taxes. This valuation in 1930, according to the Department of Taxes and Assessments, was $18,583,987,402, an increase of $1,138,157,467 over 1929. This amount is over 4 per cent. of the wealth of the United States, which has been estimated at $320,863,862,000. It is also over 25 per cent. of the aggregated assessed valuations of all the cities of 30,000 inhabitants and upwards in the United States and is greater than Philadelphia, Chicago, Detroit, Cleveland, St. Louis and Boston combined.

The assessment announced in February, 1930, for real estate was $17,248,324,717, an increase over 1929 of $1,025,881,247. Personal property was assessed at $380,-439,130, an increase of $68,524,005.

The assessments, as announced by the Authorities of the City of New York in February, 1929, totalled $16,222,345,970 for real estate alone. This was an increase of $1,223,321,000 over the preceding year. New dwellings exempt from taxation until 1931 are assessed at $916,384,320.

MARITIME EXCHANGE BUILDING

Also known as "80 Broad"

80 Broad St.
Between Beaver & Stone Streets.

An enormous structure of 36 floors towering 385 feet above the pavement and furnishing office space for over 3,500 workers.

By the "set in" treatment of windows, "80 Broad" is one of the best day-lighted buildings in the entire financial section and the very accommodating managers, Hanford & Henderson, are also making the building one of the most popular.

Every detail of the huge structure is modern thruout and spells efficiency, convenience and comfort.

Broad Street is rapidly becoming a continued succession of tower skyscrapers.

```
Est. Cost ....................$3,000,000
385 ft. high....................38 Floors
Rent Area................308,900 sq. ft.
Housing ...........................3500
Year Built ........................1931
Owner................Marex Realty Co.
Architects...........Sloan & Robertson
Builders.............Adelson Const. Co.
Agent............Hanford & Henderson
```

90 BROAD ST. BLDG.

Between Bridge & Stone Sts.

ANOTHER TOWER THAT HAS REPLACED OLD LANDMARKS

Foundations have been laid for *fifty* stories, and plans for the additional floors have already been drawn. As soon as renting conditions justify, these extra floors will be added.

```
Est. Cost ........$2,300,000
276 ft. high........24 Floors
Rent Area....273,000 sq. ft.
Houses ..............2,500
Year Built ...........1931
Ownr. Stone-Webster Bld. Cp.
Architects....Cross & Cross
Builder .....A. L. Hartridge
Agent ....Brown, Wheelock,
Harris & Co.
```

7 HANOVER BUILDING

Also 76 Beaver
S. E. Corner

A distinctive building with all the points of appeal which modern constructed buildings offer. "7 Hanover" places emphatic stress on its attractive rooms and reasonable rentals.

```
Cost .....$1,700,000
292 ft. high 28 Floors
Houses ........1,000
Rent Area.....78,000 sq. ft.
Year Built ............1931
Owner..Charason Realty Co.
Archt.....Chester B. Storm
Bldr......Fred T. Ley Co.
Agent......Leonard J. Beck
```

One of the famous corners of olden days

CITY BANK FARMERS TRUST BUILDING

22 William St.

Covers Entire Square—Exchange Place, William, Beaver & Hanover Streets.

> ## ALMOST AS HIGH
> ## AS THE WOOLWORTH

ONE OF THE UNITS OF THE NATIONAL CITY BANK

One of the sights of New York.

Everything in connection with this monumental building expresses beauty, completeness and grandeur.

Every floor is provided with refrigerated and ozonited water.

All radiators are recessed within walls, thus permitting every foot of floor space to be used.

Windows are plate glass.

Three way under-floor ducts provide any desired outlet for telephones, lighting fixtures, or buzzers.

Thirty-one latest type elevators—8 of which operate at highest speed permitted by law.

Every part and every detail of this colossal structure is right up to the minute.

The building throughout is the very last word in all that spells DELUXE.

No one visiting New York should fail to visit the "City Bank Farmers Trust" edifice—this magnificent and beautiful pile of marble, stone, and masonry is one of the sights of the city.

```
          A $12,000,000 Palace
760 feet high..54 Stories..57 Floors
Ground Area.........24,188 sq. ft.
Rent Area...........533,000 sq. ft.
Housing Capacity ............6,500
Elevators ......................30
Year Built ...................1931
Archt. ...............Cross & Cross
Builder...Geo. A. Ful'er Const. Co.
Agent.........Natl. City Realty Co.
```

BROADWAY

No street in all the world is better known than Broadway, unless it be Wall Street or Fifth Avenue. Commencing at Bowling Green and extending northwesterly for over 20 miles, this famous thoroughfare is lined on either side with continuous buildings (from "One Broadway" to 240th St.), ranging in size from one-story "taxpayers" up to the stately "Woolworth" with its 58 stories.

The actual value of the land (and thousands of buildings facing on Broadway) totals up in the *billions*, and yet this world renowned lane is only one of almost countless *others* comprising the streets of New York representing other billions of value which old Peter Minuet—bought from the Indians for $24 worth of bright colored beads! Today there is not a square foot of this over 22,000-acre-purchase that could be bought for anywhere near that amount—and yet this very profitable little real estate deal was consummated only about 300 years ago.

Courtesy Int. Mercantile Marine

WHERE BROADWAY BEGINS— AT BOWLING GREEN

The cut above shows New York's aristocracy out for a "fashion parade" on Easter Sunday in 1835. The building on the corner (S. W. Cor. Broadway and Whitehall, now known as "One Broadway"— (see page 168) was the mansion of the wealthy Archibald Kennedy of those days. The three buildings to the north were the Watts home, Livingston home and Stevens home, in the order named. The large building on the right of Bowling Green was the Adelphi Hotel, one of the largest structures in the country at that period—on the site of which the Standard Oil building now stands. Turn to page 168 and 172 and note the magnificent Washington Building, Bowling Green Buiding and Cunard Building now built on the sites of these four old mansions.

BROADWAY TODAY

BROADWAY, as a street, is famous in prose, poetry and song.

BROADWAY, in the Wall Street district, has experienced all the thrills and tragedies of frenzied finance.

BROADWAY, at 14th St., has had its P. T. Barnum, its first vaudeville, its Academy of Music and Tammany Hall—only a stone's throw away.

BROADWAY, at 23rd St., has had its "Old Chelsea" to the west, its Madison Square Garden (where Stanford White was murdered); its Hoffman House, great Fifth Ave. Hotel and its world discussed "Flat Iron" building.

BROADWAY, at 34th (Herald Square), has had its James Gordon Bennett, its Weber & Field's, its red light section to the west, and its Waldorf Astoria to the east.

BROADWAY, at 42nd St. and the Great White Way neighborhood, has had its Grand Opera, its Rector, Martin, Shanley and Churchill, its "Tin Pan Alley," its palatial bars, and gay night life. Also *its* headaches, heartaches and tragedies.

In fact, BROADWAY, can furnish material for more *history*, more reflection, and more retrospection than any other street in the world! And, Broadway is still going strong.

STANDARD OIL BUILDING

Equally well known as 26 BROADWAY.
Across Beaver Street from the Produce Exchange—circling the north-easterly corner about where Broadway commences.

Built on the site of the old Adelphi Hotel—which a hundred years ago was one of the big buildings of the times and the scene of many a big function attended by the old colonial aristocracy—note outline of the "Adelphi" with tower (to the right of Bowling Green) in picture on opposite page.

A BUILDING WITH A HISTORY

A BUILDING OF DISTINCTION

A BUILDING KNOWN THE WORLD OVER

As one steps into the imposing and very dignified entrance of the Standard Oil Building, one can almost *feel* the presence of John D. Rockefeller (founder of the Standard Oil Co.) whose life-like stone bust looks down from its circular niche in the wall, and seems to say "Welcome."

The plain and simple treatment of the gray stone walls of both lobby and corridor are so in keeping with the quiet reserve which Mr. Rockefeller himself so manifests, that many who visit the building for the first time declare there is no other structure in all the city where the impress of the personality of the founder of a business is so marked.

Many of the great firms of the nation have their offices here.

Ass'd Val.	........$13,250,000
505 ft. high	..........31 Floors
Rent Area	......505,000 sq. ft.
Ground Area	....40,000 sq. ft.
Houses	6,000
24 Elevators	
Rebuilt	1925
Owner..Standard Oil of N. Y.	
Archts.....Carrere & Hastings and Shreve & Lamb	
Builders........Chas. T. Wills	
Agent ....Owner operated	

NEW YORK COTTON EXCHANGE

60 Beaver Street—
S. E. Cor. William St.

Ass'd Val...$4,300,000
316 ft. high. .27 Floors
Floor Ar.165,000 sq. ft.
Housing capacity.2,000
Built...............1923
Ownr..N. Y. Cot. Exc.
Archt....Donn Barber
Bdr.Geo. W. Fuller Co.

One of the great indus-
trial and commercial insti-
tucions of the U. S. First
attempt to organize was in
1868. In 1870 the Ex-
change adopted by-laws
and rented quarters at 142
Pearl St. In 1872 they
moved to India House. In
1885, they built their first
building (8 stories) on the
sight of their present palace
shown herewith. The N.Y.
Cotton Exchange is largely
responsible for the great growth of the cotton industry in the U. S. Membership limited to 450. Present valuation of membership—$19,000.

NEW YORK PRODUCE EXCHANGE

No. 2 Broadway

Chartered in 1862, and has had a continual
existence for nearly 70 years.

Building has largest trading floor of any Exchange in the U. S. with facilities for trading in
securities, pro-
visions, grain and
various other
products. No
other organization
offers facilities for
a greater variety
of dealings.

Ass'd Val.....$7,800,000
200 ft. high....11 Floors
Rent Area.200,000 sq. ft.
Housing..........2,300
Completed........1884
Owr.N. Y. Produce Exc.
Arct..Geo. B. Post & Co.

WASHINGTON BUILDING

One Broadway—Where Broadway Begins.

NOT A SKYSCRAPER—
BUT ONE OF THE MOST MAGNIFICENT
BUILDINGS IN NEW YORK.

Home of the International Mercantile Marine—one of the
greatest aggregation of steamship companies in the world (White
Star, White Star Dominion, Red Star, Atlantic Transport
and Leland Lines, etc.).

Ass'd Val.....$4,100,000
178 ft. high....15 Floors
Rent. Ar..134,6000 sq. ft.
Housing..........2,000
Built............1921
Owr.."1 Bdwy. Corp."
Arct...W. B. Chambers
Agent...........Owners

This regal building with its marble
floors and magnificent booking office
(160 feet long — two stories high),
stands on the site made famous in
Revolutionary days as Gen. Geo.
Washington's headquarters during his
defense of New York. It was erected
in 1921 for the various activities of
the International Mercantile Marine.

BOWLING GREEN OFFICES

No. 11 Broadway—Overlooking Bowling Green Park
Extending through block to Greenwich Street.

Just a few feet from the Bowling Green Building is where
Peter Minuet handed over his famous $24 worth of "junk" to
the Indians for the purchase of Manhattan Island. And a short
distance to the south is where the first Dutch Colonial Fort
was built.

The Bowling Green Offices (although erected over 30 years ago)
rank today with even the present palaces of business, as the
owners figured far in advance of their time and have spared neither
effort nor expense in their zeal to con-
tinue "11 Broadway" as one of the
outstanding highest type buildings of
the city. Its spacious lobby, high
ceilings, wonderful ventilation system
and new improvements from time to
time hold the very desirable clientele
which have for so many years enjoyed
their tenancy in this palatial home—
recognized as headquarters for con-
cerns interested in the Steamship Business and affiliated interests,
Lawyers, Financial and Industrial corporations.

Ass'd Val.....$5,900,000
350 ft. high....24 Floors
Rent Area.300,000 sq. ft.
Housing..........5,000
Built............1897
Ownr..Bdway Rlty. Co.
Arct.W. G. Audsley Co.&
            Ludlow Peabody
Builder....M. P. Smith
Agent..........Owners

WHITEHALL BUILDING

17 Battery Place—N. E. Cor. West St. extending to Washington St.

ONE OF THE MAGNIFICENT SKYSCRAPERS WHICH FOR YEARS HAS MADE NEW YORK'S SKYLINE FAMOUS

To appreciate the magnitude of the Whitehall Building, one must *see* it, go *thru* it, and then *walk around* it. Built over 20 years ago, it continues to be one of the most up-to-date office homes in the city, and keeps right up to date with those of strictly modern construction.

VALUE—OVER $10,000,000

416 ft. high......32 Stories.....29 Elevators	
Rentable Space................545,615 sq. ft.	
Ground Area ....55,000 sq. ft.	
Old section built in 1903....New section 1910	
Architects.................Clinton & Russell	
Builders...............George A. Fuller Co.	
Owner........U. S. Realty Improvement Co.	

Many people think that as soon as one of the grand new modern buildings is completed, tenants in old buildings give up their old quarters (as leases expire) and move to the new.

This need not be the case *IF* the management of the old building is *awake*. In buildings like the Whitehall, Bowling Green Offices, "170 Broadway," etc., etc., modern improvements are installed and new wrinkles adopted as rapidly as proven practical or profitable.

Furthermore, relations between landlord and tenants become intimate, and the personal equation is a sufficient hold—not to mention the firm belief among many business men that "a move" is worse than a fire.

THE WHITEHALL BUILDING HAS NOT ONLY RETAINED MOST OF ITS TENANTS FOR YEARS, BUT IS GENERALLY SUCCESSFUL IN QUICKLY REPLACING VACANCIES.

Some of the Whitehall Building's prominent tenants:

Gulf Refining Co.
Corn Products Co.
Tide Water Oil Co.
United States Weather Bureau
United States Internal Revenue Dept.
Barber Steamship Line
Quaker Oats Co.
Bon Ami Company
Penn Coal & Coke
Knickerbocker Fuel Co.

21 WEST ST. BUILDING

One block north of Battery Park

AN ARCHITECTURAL TRIUMPH OF BRICK AND TERRA COTTA

This very attractive structure commands a view of New York Bay and Hudson River, second to no other building in the city. It has unobstructed daylight, fresh air, "Hudson breezes," and proximity to the Hudson Docks, just across beautiful wide West Street. These features make offices in "21 West" especially desirable for those interested in shipping, transportation or maritime activities. It also appeals to those engaged in the Produce Business (the produce markets being close by), likewise those interested in big commercial or financial operations who prefer a less congested district than the Wall Street or Broadway section—only about three minutes' walk East.

```
Ass'd Val.  ...... $2,200,000
442 ft. high........31 Floors
12 Elevators
Rent Area....250,000 sq. ft.
Housing  ..............4,000
Completed  ............1931
Owners....21 West St. Corp.
Arch...Starrett & Van Vleck
Builders, Rhinestein Cons.Co.
Agent..Wm. A. White & Son
```

FIGURES SHOWING THE GROWTH OF NEW YORK—

1725	8,000
1750	12,000
1775	23,000
1800	79,000
1830	242,000
1850	696,000
1880	1,912,000
1900	3,437,000
1910	4,785,000
1920	5,643,440
1930	6,930,446
1932	7,250,000*

No city in the history of man has ever equalled such phenomenal growth as the accompanying tabulation presents.

New York is not only the center of population, but the center of wealth, culture, art, music, business, and practically every activity known to life

As a place to live, New York offers more appeal than any other city in the universe (See Page 7 "HOME LIFE IN NEW YORK"). Its climate, its harbors, its surrounding scenic beauty and its many other physical advantages all contribute to the cause of its general supremacy.

[* Estimated.]

19 RECTOR BUILDING

S. E. Cor. Washington St.
Between Broadway and Hudson River

A comparatively few years ago the corner of Rector and Washington Streets was more or less off the beaten paths of those engaged in big business. *Rector Street* enjoyed some prominence due to three or four big buildings, such as the Empire Building (Cor. Rector and Broadway), "2 Rector," "70 West," etc., but *Washington Street* was largely lined with old and unimportant buildings occupied by small concerns. The whole neighborhood had little in common with the gigantic business operations being carried on in nearby territory.

BUT TODAY —

"19 Rector" is only one of a *number* of mammoth skyscrapers that are rapidly replacing the old shacks west of Broadway and emphasizing the vastness of New York's ever-increasing growth.

"19 Rector," like New York's other towering new skyscrapers, is modern throughout. Information concerning its many special features may be learned by addressing Chas. F. Noyes and Co.

Est. Cost	$2,500,000
450 ft. high	38 Floors
Rent Area	315,000
Housing	3,600
Completed	1930
Owner	Gening Realty Co.
Architect	L. A. Goldstone
Builder	Gresham Realty Co.
Agent	Chas. F. Noyes & Co.
225 Broadway	

WEST ST. BUILDING

90 West St.—Cedar to Albany Sts.

Architecturally, "90 West" is considered one of the most beautiful and artistic office buildings ever erected.

Overlooking the stately Hudson and directly across the street from the docks and wharves at which great ocean vessels anchor, this first big skyscraper of West Street has had an especial appeal to not only those interested in shipping and allied interests, but to those who appreciate view, daylight, air, and more "quiet" than congested centers offer.

Mr. Cass Gilbert who drew the plans for "90 West" and who a few years later designed the stately Woolworth Building ranks with the leading architects of the world.

Est. Cost	$4,000,000
324 ft. high	24 Floors
Rent Area	234,000 sq. ft.
Housing	2700
Built	1907
Owner	West St. Improv. Co.
Architect	Cass Gilbert
Builder	Jno. Pierre Co.
Agent	Chas. A. Noyes & Co.

"ELECTRIC BOND & SHARE" BUILDING

Better known as "TWO RECTOR ST."
Cor. Rector St. & Trinity Place.

ONE OF THE BEST KNOWN ADDRESSES IN ALL NEW YORK

Ass'd Val...$5,100,000
350 ft. high..26 Floors
Grd. Area,11,205 sq.ft.
Rent Ar.271,000 sq.ft.
Houses..........3,000
Elevators..........10
Year Built.......1906
Owr.2 Rector St. Crp.
Arct.Clinton & Russell
Builder.....Thompson
          Starrett Co.
Agent....On Premises

TRINITY COURT BUILDING

74 Trinity Place

"T" extension to Greenwich Street.

Adjoins N. Y. Curb Exchange and overlooks Trinity Churchyard.

Racketeers, "l o a n sharks" and all undesirable tenants barred. The mere address "74 Trinity" serves as a basis for confidence.

Ass'd Val..$3,100,000
312 ft. high..25 Floors
Gd. Area.7,500 sq.ft.
Rent Ar.135,000 sq.ft.
Houses..........1,500
Year Built......1927
Elevators..........5
Owr.Burda Hldg. Corp
Arc't.....H. I. Oser
Bldr.Magoba Con. Co.
Agent......Hanford &
          Henderson, Inc.

NEW YORK CURB EXCHANGE

86 Trinity Place—Thru block to Church St.

The history of the New York Curb Exchange reads like an Aladdin Lamp Story. Its Director of Publicity (Mr. Chas. T. Murphy) is very generous. We suggest addressing a letter to Mr. Murphy (enclosing 6c for postage) and requesting a copy of the splendidly illustrated and very interesting 60 page book issued by the exchange, entitled, "NEW YORK CURB EXCHANGE."

Ass'd Val.$2,300,000
218 ft. high.15 Floors
Completed.....1930
Owr.N. Y. Curb Exc.
Art.Starret & Van Vl.
Bdr....Thompson &
          Starret Co.

CUNARD BUILDING

25 Broadway—Extends through block to Greenwich St.

ONE OF THE MAGNIFICENT BUILDINGS OF THE WORLD

A $15,000,000 PALACE

No business building *anywhere* can surpass the regal grandeur of this superb building, with its magnificent mural and mosaic decorations.

The Cunard Steamship Co. occupies the entire first four floors—the remaining stories being rented to an exceptionally high class tenancy.

This entire neighborhood is rich in Revolutionary history, also as being the home of many great men.

Cox Stephens (inventor of the screw propellor) and Robert Fulton (father of the steamboat) both lived in these precincts.

Ass'd Val....$13,250,000
350 ft. high....25 Floors
Grd. Area.48,400 sq. ft.
Rent Area.660,000 sq. ft.
Houses...........9,000
Elevators..........36
Year Built........1921
Ownr..25 Bwdy. Corp.
Archt..Benj. W. Morris
Bldr...Todd Robertson
          & Todd

29 BROADWAY

Est. Cost.$4,000,000
375 ft. high.30 Floors
Rt. Ar.,180,000 sq.ft.
Houses........2,100
Year Built....1931
Owr.Abe N. Adelson
Art.Sloan & Robert'n
Bdr.Adelson Cn. Co.
Agt.C.F.Noyes&Co.

42 BROADWAY

Ass'd Val..$6,000,000
243 ft. high.22 Floors
Rt. Ar.253,100 sq.ft.
Houses........2,900
Year Built.....1903
Owr..42 Bdwy. Co.
Art. H. Ives Cobb
Bdr.Geo. A. FullerCo
Agent...On Premises

The story is absorbing, ably written and valuably informative. It tells of the evolution of the Exchange from a small beginning (*when* operations were carried on in the open street between two "curbs") to the institution of national prominence it holds today.

FRED F. FRENCH BROADWAY BLDG.

39 Broadway—Just a few paces north of Bowling Green

FORMERLY KNOWN AS THE HARRIMAN BUILDING

The French Co. have leased the "air rights" above the six story structure to the south (note picture) which insures permanent daylight and ventilation to the 20 story "L" extension in the rear, for all time.

OLD "RIP" LOST A GOOD BET

Land in any part of lower Broadway has been steadily increasing in value every year.

In the old days, country folk used to drive to town to attend the annual May Festival held at Bowling Green—tethering their horses on the grassy slope where the Fred F. French building now stands.

For *less* than the taxable *value* of 39 Broadway today, *both sides* of this famous old thoroughfare could have been purchased for *over half a mile,* in those days!

What a snap for old Rip Van Winkle, if before he took his long snooze, he had tied up a few parcels, and then postponed his awakening until 1931!

Ass'd Val.	.......$7,300,000
456 ft. high	.......38 Floors
Rent Area	....326,500 sq. ft.
Houses	4,000
Year Built	1928
Owner	....39 Broadway Corp.
Archt.	........Cross & Cross
Bldr.	......Fuller Cons. Co.
Agent	...Fred F. French Co.

AREA OF THE CITY OF NEW YORK

New York, the oldest incorporated city of the 248 largest cities of the country, covered 191,360 land acres in the 1925 Federal Census. This is the largest area of any city in the United States, excepting the 262,896 acres of Los Angeles, and compares with 125,430 acres in Chicago and 81,920 acres in Philadelphia.

From the Battery northward to the city line there is a distance of 15½ miles. From the Battery southeast to Coney Island there is a distance, in a direct line, of about 10 miles. The distance to the extreme eastern limit of Queens Borough is about 17 miles. It is about 19 miles from the Battery south to the lower end of Staten Island. Although very irregular in shape, the city is, in extreme dimensions, about 35 miles long by 17 wide.

Borough Areas	Sq. Miles	Acres
Area Borough of Queens	121.11	77,516
Area Borough of Manhattan	21.9	14,056
Area Borough of Brooklyn	80.95	51,807
Area Borough of Bronx	38.87	21,680
Area Borough of Richmond	57.2	36,600
Area Greater New York	320.03	201,659

50 BROADWAY BUILDING Also 41 New Street

A few steps south of Wall Street—Extends thru to New Street

ONLY 300 FEET FROM THE NEW YORK STOCK EXCHANGE
"RIGHT IN THE THICK" OF WALL STREET'S COLOSSAL BANKS

Has entrance on New Street, thus enabling brokers and clearing house runners to make quick contacts in emergencies.

EXTREMELY DESIRABLE FOR STOCK EXCHANGE AND IN-VESTMENT HOUSES, LAW FIRMS, STEAMSHIP LINES, ETC.

The genial George A. Frimpter (renting and managing agent) has his offices right in the building.

Ass'd Val.	$6,000,000
418 ft. high	37 Floors
Rent Area	250,000 sq. ft.
Housing	2,800
Owners	Lower Broadway Prop's Inc.
Arch.	H. Craig Severance
Builders	Chas. L. Fraser
Agent	Geo. A. Frimpter

On the site of where 50 Broadway now stands, stood the famous old TOWER BUILDING—New York's first "dangerous" skyscraper! It was over twelve stories high and until the "gigantic" steel skyscraper of 17 stories was built by the Home Life Insurance Company in 1894 at 256 Broadway (see picture of this "sky-soaring" structure on page 188) it commanded the awe and wonderment of the entire populace—many of whom were fearful lest it would topple over!

Pictured below is one of the most important as well as one of the most beautiful buildings in the city—the New York Clearing House, conservator of sound banking. Here is where the *billions* involved in New York's enormous financial transactions are cleared.

NEW YORK CLEARING HOUSE

77 Cedar St.

Organized 1853
Building Erected 1896
Architect,
    R. W. Gibson
Builder,
  Marc Eidletz & Son

ADAMS EXPRESS BUILDING

Better known as "61 BROADWAY"—N. W. Cor. "Tin Pot Alley"
Extends thru to Trinity Place

HOME OF THE WORLD FAMOUS
NORTH GERMAN LLOYD

There have been few buildings added to lower Manhattan's famous skyline that have so dominated the view from ocean vessels entering New York Bay as "61 Broadway". Not only is the height of the structure commanding, but the great white glazed southern exposure, extending thru to Trinity Place, is even more conspicuous than many of Broadway's and Wall Street's mightiest towers.

THE ADAMS EXPRESS COMPANY is now one of the units of the great RAILWAY EXPRESS AGENCY, successors to the American Railway Express Company, which was the outcome of a consolidation in 1918 of the big individually operated express companies of the country at that time, including the Adams Express, American Express, U. S. Express, Wells Fargo and others.

The RAILWAY EXPRESS AGENCY is owned by a combination of Railways. It is not a government-owned property which so many erroneously believe. The headquarters of the organization are at 230 Park Avenue.

Ass'd V^l.	$11,300,000
424 ft. high	33 Floors
Rent area	455,000 sq. ft.
Housing	5,500
Built	1914
Owner	Bdway Ex. Corp.
Architect	Frances H. Kimball
Agent	Chas. F. Noyes Co.

The Adams Express Co. started with a wheelbarrow. Here is a picture of Mr. Alvin Adams himself (Founder of the Company) making a delivery in the old days.

AMER. EXPRESS BUILDING

Also known as
"65 BROADWAY"
Near Rector

Ass'd Val., $5,500,000
297 ft. high, 23 Floors
Rent Area ... 162,000
sq. ft.
Houses 2,000
Year Built 1917
Owner, Amer. Ex. Co.
Builder, .. Caldwell &
Wingate
Agent .. On Premises

70 BROADWAY

Near Wall St.
Former home of the
great Manhattan Life
Ins. Co. — NOW
owned and occupied
by the CENTRAL
HANOVER NA-
TIONAL BANK.

When built, this
was one of the tallest
buildings in the world
—361 feet. It com-
manded the attention
of all America.

EMPIRE BLDG.

Better known as
71 BROADWAY
S. W. Cor. Rector St.
One of the old
regal skyscrapers that
keeps right up-to-date.

Ass'd Val., $5,300,000
320 ft. high, 25 Floors
Gnd. Area 14,000 sq. ft.
Rent Area 190,000 sq. ft.
Houses 2.200
Year Built 1898
10 Elevators
Owner 71 Bdway Corp.
Archt., Kimball & T.
Bldr. .. Marc Eidlitz

"31 NASSAU" BUILDING

Northwest Corner
Nassau and Cedar Sts.

Ass'd Val. $3,500,000

Formerly known as
the National Bank of
Commerce Building—
now the property of
the Guaranty Trust
Co. — second largest
banking organization
in the world.

AMERICAN SURETY BUILDING

Also known as
"100 BROADWAY"

100 Broadway—Cor. Pine St.

The history and growth
of the great American
Surety Company reads
like a fairy tale. Organ-
ized in 1884 with a capital
of only $500,000, it has
developed into one of the
outstanding surety institutions of the nation. Even
before the close of the
World War, their prem-
iums in one year totaled
nearly $7,000,000!

If you will write to the
Amer. Surety Co. and request the story of their great
institution (including a *most interesting* account of their
reconstructed new build-
ing shown here) you will
receive a beautiful deluxe
brochure which contains
very valuable historical
information and is *magnificently* illustrated. Anyone sending for it will be
amply repaid.

Ass'd Val. $8,100,000
338 feet high........26 Floors
Floor area......230,000 sq. ft.
Housing capacity 2,700
Reconstructed 1921
Owner....American Surety Co.
Arch. ...Hermann Lee Meade
Bldr. ..Cauldwell Wingate Co.
Agent......Horace S. Ely Co.

TRINITY BUILDING
111 Broadway

U. S. REALTY BUILDING
115 Broadway

Ass'd Val. $16,000,000
Year Built, 1905 .... 29 Elevators
308 ft. high .... 23 Floors
Ground { TRINITY—18,936 sq ft.
Area   { U. S. REALTY—16,592 sq. ft
Rent Area .... 552,000 sq. ft.
Owner..Trinity Building Corp.—a sub-
sidiary of U. S. Realty & Imp. Co
Archt. .... Francis H. Kimb ''
Bldr. .... Geo. A. Fuller Co.

120 BROADWAY—EQUITABLE BUILDING

Covers entire Square—Broadway, Cedar, Nassau and Pine

City building laws now demand "set back" construction so as to allow more light and air in the canyons formed by high buildings. Note that the Equitable is over 40 stories *straight up*— built before this law went into effect.

A CITY IN ITSELF
HOUSING 16,000 SOULS

When the great fire on the bitterly cold winter morning of 1913 gutted the old Equitable Life Assurance Society building at 120 Broadway, the Directors of the Company decided to build the largest office building in the world on their famous and valuable site. The picture below illustrates the structure erected.

Photo by Murray Kendall Keyes

THE MOST VALUABLE OFFICE BUILDING IN THE WORLD— UP UNTIL 1931

Only the "Empire State" and Waldorf Astoria surpass it.

ASSESSED AT
$31,750,000

In 1931, the Empire State Building was completed at a cost of over $55,000,000, thus taking the prestige held so many years by the Equitable as being the costliest office building ever constructed.

The general offices of the Equitable Life Assurance Society are now located in their magnificent new home at 393 Seventh Avenue—S. E. Cor. of 32nd St. (see page 208). A branch office, however, is still maintained at 120 Broadway.

Assessed Value ..	$31,750,000
542 ft. high	44 Floors
Rent Area ..	1,250,000 sq. ft.
Housing	16,000
Completed	1915
Owner	Equitable Office Building Co.
Architect ...	E. R. Graham
Builder ..	Thompson Starrett
Agent	Owners

CHASE NATIONAL BANK BUILDING

20 Pine, N. E. Cor. Nassau—Extends thru
block to Cedar—Entrance at 60 Cedar

Assessed at $10,900,000
496 Feet High
38 Floors
Built 1928

HEADQUARTERS OF THE CHASE NATIONAL BANK, LARGEST BANKING ORGANIZATION IN THE WORLD

Entrance to Bank is No. 18 Pine.
Entrances to building proper—
20 Pine and 60 Cedar.

Nothing in the building line could be more modern than the "Chase National," and yet there is no indication of the futuristic in its style—such as curveless angles, squared unsightliness and ugly contours, which characterize modernistic tendencies, so increasingly fashionable in building construction these days.

The picture shows the Sub-Treasury building in the foreground (on Wall St.), the CHASE NATIONAL fronting on Pine Street, a block to the rear; the tall tower-like building immediately back of the Pine Street exposure is the Cedar Street extension with entrance at 60 Cedar.

The building is so colossal, and has such an acreage of floor space that eight to ten thousand workers can easily be accommodated.

Although assessed at only $10,900,000, the Chase National Building is fully as imposing as a number of other New York structures costing $15,000,000 and over.

Continued from page 51

PETER COOPER UNION Junction of 3rd and 4th Aves. at head of the Bowery.

Assessed evaluation $560,000

Over 200,000 men and women have received free education at this famous institution founded by Peter Cooper in 1859 for advancement of science and art.

INTERNATIONAL HOUSE
500 Riverside Drive—near Grant's Tomb
Ass'd Val. $1,200,000
1700 members—500 live in house

Home for the improvement of the intellectual, physical and social welfare of foreign students, without discrimination as to race, color, creed or sex.

CITIES SERVICE BUILDING

Covers Almost an Entire Square—Pine, Pearl and Cedar Sts.

THIRD HIGHEST BUSINESS BUILDING IN THE WORLD

ANOTHER HENRY L. DOHERTY ACHIEVEMENT

A $15,000,000 investment by a man who, when a boy, sold newspapers on the street to make his living!

Ass'd Val.	$15,000,000
950 feet high	67 Floors
Rent area ...	680,000 sq. ft.
Housing capacity	7,500
Ground area ..	32,000 sq. ft.
Completed	1931
Owner ..	Pine St. Realty Co.
Arch. ...	Clinton & Russell, Holton & George
Bldrs. ...	Jas. Stewart & Co.
Renting agent	Owners

The new "Cities Service Building," now in course of construction, is slated to be finished by October, 1931, and will not only be the third tallest office building ever erected, but one of the most beautiful architecturally. It is absolutely the very last word in modern construction.

Note the Following Innovations

Escalators on the first seven floors.

The first building in New York to have "double-deck" elevators ("two-story" cars), taking on and discharging passengers on two floors at once. There are 8 of these—24 elevators all told.

Aluminum window frames which make the weight of the windows so light that it is a pleasure to open or shut them.

New style of roof architecture which is almost sensational in its "different-ness."

A dozen other new and novel features including equipment for heating the building with hot water.

THE HIGHEST BUILDING OF ALL THE SKYSCRAPERS IN WALL STREET AND LOWER BROADWAY

SINCLAIR OIL BUILDING
55 Liberty St., N. W. Cor. Nassau.

Unique Gothic architecture with walls of polished white terracotta, and roof of green copper combine to make "Sinclair Oil" one of the most imposing buildings in the Wall St. section. The vestibule is superb with its vaulted ceiling, tapering from beautiful mural paintings—"Spring and Youth" on one side, "Autumn, Age and Achievement," on the other.

The Sinclair Oil Building stands on the plot on which stood the old home of the poet, William Cullen Bryant, and the tallest building in the world on so small an area of ground.

```
Ass'd Val.....$2,100,000
400 ft. high....33 Floors
Rent area 115,000 sq. ft.
Housing capacity...1,500
Completed........1910
Owner, Sinclair Bldg. Co.
Arch...Henry Ives Cobb
Bldr.C.L.Gray Cons.Co.
Agt.Lee ThompsonSmith
```

"30 PINE"
Between Nassau and William St.

New home of Goldman Sachs Co.

```
Ass'd Val.....$2,600,000
225 ft. high....22 Floors
Rent area. 120,000 sq. ft.
Housing capacity...1,500
Completed........1931
Owner. . Goldman Sachs.
Arch.......A. F. Gilbert
Bldr.. Thompson Starrett
Agt.Wm.A. White & Son
```

"ONE CEDAR"
Full block in Pearl St. through to Maiden Lane.

Built near the old home of Aaron Burr.

```
Ass'd Val.....$2,400,000
300 ft. high....26 Floors
Rent area. 175,000 sq. ft.
Housing capacity...2,100
Completed........1930
Owner. . One Cedar Corp.
Arch...Clinton & Russell
Bldr...Shroder & Koppel
Agt. Horace S. Ely & Co.
```

80 MAIDEN LANE

also known as

27 CEDAR

Extends all the way thru block between William and Pearl Sts.

CONTINENTAL FIRE INSURANCE CO'S BLDG.

For many years, "80 Maiden Lane" has enjoyed the distinction of being one of the most popular of the high type buildings in New York's great insurance center. Its spacious lobby, fifty feet wide, extends the full length of the structure from Maiden Lane to Cedar Street.

Hot and cold water, free light and heat, day and night elevator service, free vacuum and janitor service, and a most accommodating management keep "80 MaidenLane" 100% rented year after year.

```
Ass'd Val.....$4,225,000
230 ft. high....28 Floors
Rent area. 354,000 sq. ft.
Housing capacity...4,200
Completed........1912
Owner, Fire Co. Bldg. C.
Arch. D. H. BurnhamCo.
Bldr. Thompson Starrett
```

"MUTUAL LIFE BUILDING"
Nassau, Liberty, Cedar and William Sts.

Thirty years ago, this was the largest and most costly office building in America. It covers practically an entire square. The Mutual Life Insurance Co. is one of the most outstanding insurance organizations in the world and the new building they are planning will likely be the talk of the nation *again!*

HUDSON TERMINAL TWIN BUILDINGS

30 Church and 50 Church Street

NOT A MERE BUILDING—AN ACTUAL CITY!

Covers almost two square blocks, with bridges over Dey Street connecting the two huge structures at the 3rd and 17th stories. Fronts *two* blocks on *Church St.* with nearly full block frontages, on *Fulton, Dey* and *Cortlandt* Streets.

ONE OF THE LARGEST OFFICE BUILDINGS IN THE WORLD

ALSO ONE OF THE MOST UP-TO-DATE AND ONE OF THE BEST MANAGED— WHERE TENANTS SWEAR BY THE "HUDSON," AND RETAIN THEIR QUARTERS YEAR AFTER YEAR

Few office buildings anywhere possess such varied and unusual transportation facilities. Five major trunk lines are at its doors, or actually within the building itself (7th Ave. Interboro, B. M. T. Subway, Hudson Tunnels, 9th Ave. Elevated, and 6th Ave. Elevated). The Municipal Subway will also have an entrance in the building when completed.

The immense sub-basements and arcades constitute a veritable city, with their varied shops, stores, counters, and sales places, vending most everything desired from fruits, foods and candy, to wearing apparel, hardware, and household items.

Many of America's largest industrial corporations "office" here and the largest post-office sub-station in the city (employing 1,200) is right in the building.

Ass'd Val. $14,000,000
275 ft. high ...... 26 Floors
Rent Area .. 1,100,000 sq. ft.
39 Elevators
Housing 12,500
Completed 1908
Owner .... Hudson & Manhattan R. R. Co.
Architects, Clinton & Russell
Builders, Fuller Construction Co.
Agents .... Owners

TYLER BUILDING

17 John Street
Near Broadway

Ass'd Val., ... $1,650,000
18 Floors
97,000 sq. ft.
Arch., Laurence Peck
Bldr., Starrett Bros.
Agt., Wm. A. White
& Son

"80 JOHN ST." BUILDING

80 John, 23 Gold and
27 Platt Streets

Ass'd Val. $2,475,000
306 ft. high .... 27 Floors
Rent area .. 220,000 sq. ft.
Housing capacity ... 2,500
Built 1926
Owner .. 80 John St. Corp.
Arch. .. Ely Jacques Kahn
Bldr., John-Gold St. Corp.
Agt., Horace S. Ely & Co.

"110 WILLIAM ST." BUILDING

N. E. Cor. John Street

Ass'd Val .. $2,775,000
262 feet high, 22 Floors
Rent area, 188,000 sq. ft.
8 Elevators
Housing capacity .. 2,200
Completed 1920
Ownr., 110 Wm. St. Corp.
Arch., Frank H. Quimby
Bldr. Wm. Kennedy Co.
Agt.....C. B. VanValen
Ground Plot 11,685 sq. ft.

"90 JOHN ST." BUILDING

Fronting on Gold
from John to Platt

Cost cf building without land ..$2,500,000
326 ft. high 30 Floors
Rent 250,000 sq. ft.
Housing 2,800
Completed 1931
Own Pent'bo Rlty Corp
Arch. ....Springstem
Bldr., Pent'bo Rlty.
Agt., Brown Wheelock

Each of these four magnificent buildings should have been shown with as large a cut as the two below—an error, too late for correction, is responsible.

Cost $4,500,000
430 feet high, 38 Floors
Rent area, 300,000 sq. ft.
Housing capacity, 3,500
Completed 1931
Ownr., Platt Holding Cor.
Arch., Louis Abramson
Bldr., Shroder & Koppel
Agt., Chas. F. Noyes & Co.

"111 JOHN ST."

Extending full block
from Cliff St. to
Pearl St.

"111 JOHN" is
both a giant and an
"aristocrat" among
the mammoth office
buildings catering to
insurance interests.

HEADQUARTERS OF
Hanover Fire Insurance Company, Indemnity Insurance Co. of No. Amer., Importer & Exporters Ins. Co., Standard Accident Ins. Company, Southern Surety Co.

AND MANY OTHERS

Cost $6,000,000
334 feet high, 25 Floors
Rent area, 293,000 sq. ft.
Housing 4,000
Ownr, 111 John St. Corp.
Arch., Ely Jacques Kahn
Bldr. .. Starrett Bros.-
Eken
Agent .. Thoens-Fl'ncher
Ground Plot,
over 16,000 sq. ft.

Twelve elevators (with a speed
of 800 to 900 ft. a minute) insure quick transportation and the
architect's ingenious layout provides every one of the 35 upper
floors with direct natural daylight.

"116 JOHN ST."

Fronting on Pearl Street
from John to Platt Sts.

Gen. News Photo Service

"60 JOHN ST." and "150 WILLIAM ST."

S. W. Cor. William St.—Extending along "John" almost to Nassau St.

PALATIAL NEW BUILDING OF THE
NEW AMSTERDAM CASUALTY CO.

THE PRIDE OF NEW YORK'S GREAT INSURANCE CENTER

Few people realize the immense volume of insurance written annually in New York's busy insurance center—aggregating *thousands of millions*, and furnishing employment to a vast army of workers. "60 John" is the home of *many* of these big companies.

"60 John" has been the address of the New Amsterdam Casualty Co. for some time and their beautiful twenty story building which forms the right half of structure shown in picture, has been notable among the many big buildings in this section ever since it was completed.

Property was recently acquired by the Company all the way through to William St. and in the summer of 1930, work was started on the new tower addition. "60 John" (as the combined buildings are known) is now ready for occupancy, and offers that office accommodation in modern construction and latest efficient equipment which the most discriminating desire.

Chas. B. Van Valen, Inc. the renting agents, deem it both a pleasure and a privilege to "show their wares" and cordially invite inspection of this towering and sumptuous new addition to John Street's display of new structures.

Estimated Cost....	$10,000,000
378 ft. high..........	31 Floors
Rent Area......	320,000 sq. ft.
Housing...............	3700
Completed..............	1931
Owner.	New Ams. Casualty Co.
Architect....	Clinton & Russel,
	Holten & George
Builder..	James Stewart & Co.
Agent....	Chas. B. Van Valen

SINGER TOWER

149 Broadway—S. W. Cor. Dey St.

FROM 1908 TO 1913

AMERICA'S MOST FAMOUS BUILDING

The Singer Building was the tallest office building in the world at time of completion, and for five years (up to the time the Woolworth was erected) was the "pride of America."

Thousands of travelers came to New York especially to see this modern "Tower of Babel," gladly paying fifty cents to ride to the "observation balcony" atop, to view the city and surrounding vista from the highest business structure ever erected by man.

"SUICIDE PINNACLE"

The observation balcony seemed to have a strong appeal to those who were soured on life.

50c was much cheaper than the price of a "gun" and the stunt of jumping into space became more or less popular, with the result that the owners of the building suddenly dispensed with this source of revenue and closed the balcony permanently.

But the "Old Singer" continues to hold its place as one of the grandest buildings in the city, and has retained most of its high type tenancy through all these years. The address "149 Broadway" lends prestige to those who office at the stately old "Singer."

Ass'd Val.	$8,500,000
612 ft. high	47 Floors
Rent Area	312,440 sq. ft.
Housing	3,700
Completed	1908
Owner	Singer Mfg. Co.
Architect	Ernest Flagg
Agent	A. J. Bleeker

BENENSON BLDG

Better known as "165 BROADWAY"
S. W. Cor. Cortland St.
—Extends through block to Church St.

Less than a hundred years ago, what is
now "165 Broadway" could have been
purchased for what an automobile costs
today.—Note picture at right.

SITE OF THE BENENSON BUILDING
IN 1846

Even modern skyscrapers of the present do not surpass in elegance and dignity this magnificent building, the lobby of which is finished in solid marble, 30 to 50 feet wide and 40 feet high, extends entire length of the building, a full block.

The grandeur of the "BENENSON" is not confined to its lower floor however—even the woodwork throughout the enormous structure is genuine mahogany.

The small building on the corner was purchased years ago to insure permanent light and air. Few buildings in all the country compare with the beautiful "BENENSON."

Ass'd Val.	$10,400,000
Height	480 feet
Number of floors	34
Rentable Area	559,000 sq. ft.
Housing Capacity	7,800
Year Built	1908
Architect, Francis H. Kimball	
Builder	Heddon Const. Co.
Agent	Wm. F. Howard

Continued from page 105

MR. ALBERT KELLER Mr. Keller was born in Baden-Baden, Germany, in 1879, the son of a hotel man. Following a college education, he began his career as a cook in accordance with the European system of thorough training. By sheer merit he worked his way to the head of the Ritz-Carlton chain of hotels—known as the smartest group of hotels in the world. Mr. Keller has made a record for himself as one of the brainiest and most capable men in all hoteldom. Sincerity, strict integrity, and dependability are the outstanding qualities that have so endeared him to his public, friends and business associates. In 1910, he was "tried out" as manager of the famous "Ritz-Carlton of New York." In 1912, he became General Manager. In 1925, he was made Managing Director of all the Ritz-Carlton hotels this side of the Atlantic. And in 1927, he was made President of the Ritz-Carlton Corporation. Mr. Keller is a most polished gentleman, an art collector, and a man of the world, having many and very influential friends all over Europe. He has been decorated many times.

WESTERN UNION TELEGRAPH CO.'S
REGAL NEW HOME
60 Hudson St.

Covers entire square—Hudson, Thomas, Worth & West Broadway

VALUE $13,500,000
LARGEST TELEGRAPH STRUCTURE IN THE WORLD

Has a wire system reaching to every corner of the map.

Every invention and device for efficiency, comfort, and convenience,—luxurious executive offices, cafeteria (meals at cost for the 6,000 employees), training school completely equipped, workshops for boys, private auditorium (seating 1,000), rest rooms, reading rooms, etc., and other departments for the general welfare of employees.

The Western Union Telegraph Co. was organized in 1856, at Rochester, N. Y. In 1866, the company moved its headquarters to New York—145 Broadway.

Cost	$13,500,000
400 ft. high	25 Floors
Floor Space	1,000,000 sq. ft.
Employees over	6,000
Year Built	1930
Owner	West. Union Tel. Co.
Arcts.,	Voorhees Gmelin & Walker
Builder	Marc Eidlitz & Son

AMERICAN TEL. & TEL. BLDG.
American Telephone & Telegraph Company
195 Broadway—S. W. Corner

ANOTHER OF THE HUGE BUILDINGS OF BROADWAY

32 FLOORS 27 above side walk
5 below street level

Only one of the many buildings completely or partially occupied by the great Bell Telephone System. NOTE PAGES 193, 194 and 195.

Assessed Valuation $18,200,000

365 ft. high	32 Floors
Ground Area	40,960 sq. ft.
Floor Space	645,900 sq. ft.
Houses	8,000
Elevators	34
Built in three sections	1913, 1916, 1922
Owner	195 Broadway Corp.
Archt	Wm. Wells Bosworth
Builder	Marc Eidlitz & Son

WESTINGHOUSE BLDG
150 Bdwy., N. E. Cor. Liberty St.

Ass'd Val	$5,000,000
271 ft. high	25 Floors
Rentables	246,000 sq. ft.
Housing	2,800
Completed	1924
Owner	Ley Realty Co.
Archt	Starrett & Van V.
Bldr	Fred T. Ley Co.
Agent	Owners

"170 BROADWAY" BLDG
S. E. Cor. Maiden Lane

Ass'd Val	$3,000,000
254 ft. high	19 Floors
Rentable	112,000 sq. ft.
Houses	1,300
Year Built	1902
Owner	Bdway Bldg. Co.
Archt	Clinton & Russell
Bldr	Geo. A. Fuller Co.
Agent	On Premises

TRANSPORTATION BUILDING
225 Broadway. S. W. Cor. Barclay St.

BUSINESS HOME OF CHAS. A. NOYES & CO. REPUTED TO BE LARGEST REAL ESTATE BROKERS IN AMERICA.

Every little detail which can add to the comfort, convenience and satisfaction of tenants seems to be part of the Chas. F. Noyes Co. policy. As the Transportation Building is the home of this enterprising organization—which manages, or acts as renting agents for A THOUSAND BUILDINGS, it can easily be imagined that "225 Broadway" is not neglected!

Among the novel innovations here might be mentioned the corps of snappy looking young girls, who operate the self-stopping elevators, uniformed in attractive brown military costume with s a u c y little "doughgirl" cap.

Ass'd Val	$7,000,000
540 ft. high	45 Floors
Rentables	350,000 sq. ft.
Housing	4,000
Built	1928
Owner, Bdwy Barclay Corp.	
Archt	York & Sawyer
Bldr	Bricken Const. Co.
Agt	Chas. F. Noyes Co.

"HOME LIFE INSURANCE" BLDG.

256 Broadway—Between Warren & Murray Streets.

> ### THE HIGHEST BUILDING ON EARTH AT THE TIME OF COMPLETION IN 1894

Faces 55 feet on Broadway. Depth 107 feet.

When the "Home Life" was built, it was so *high* it created a scare! Tenants in near-by buildings moved to a "safer neighborhood!"

When in December 1898, the Rogers Peet building (next door north) was wrecked by fire, the interior of the "Home Life" was destroyed, but the steel walls were not harmed. A severe wind was blowing at the time and newspapers admitted that had it not been for the Home Life's steel building, all lower New York would have burned.

Ass'd Val.........	$1,500,000
287 ft. high.........	16 Floors
Rent area.....	56,456 sq. ft.
Ground area.....	5,885 sq. ft.
Elevators.................	4
Completed..............	1894
Owner....	Home Life Ins. Co.
Archt......	N. LeBrun & Son
Builder.......	John Downey
Agent..........	On Premises

The "Home Life Ins. Co." was founded in 1860. It has an unbroken record of faithful and honorable dealing for over 71 years. The company has outstanding insurance in force of over $400,000,000 and cash assets of $75,000,-000. It is a strictly mutual company.

"270 BROADWAY" BLDG.

S. W. Cor. Chambers St.

The picture at right, shows Broadway entrance. Picture at left, shows frontage on Chambers Street.

LOWER BROADWAY'S GREAT "DAYLIGHT BUILDING" is said to have more windows per rentable area than any other big building in the city.

Ass'd Val......	$4,000,000
397 ft. high.....	30 Floors
Rent area...	320,000 sq. ft.
Housing............	3,700
Completed..........	1930
Owner....	270 Bway Corp.
Archt..	E. H. Faile & Co.
Builder....	Starrett Bros.
Agent........	On Premises

AVIATION IN NEW YORK—Continued from Page 29.

Mr. Robert A. Smith

Aviators keep records of the number of hours they fly. 3,000 hours means an average of *over eight hours a day* for a *full year*, and yet Robert A. Smith, Manager of the Air-view Dept. of Fairchild Aerial Surveys Inc. (note his picture at left) has been "up in the air" far in excess of 3,000 hours! He has flown over eight different countries, approximating 300,000 miles! His nearest escape of "going all the way to Heaven" was when he was lost in the Everglades of Florida—being rescued by George Haldeman who later flew the Atlantic. All through this volume will be found air-views taken by Mr. Smith himself. It was he who took the famous picture of "The Woolworth through the Clouds" shown herewith. Mr. Smith is a Fellow of the Royal Photographic Society, and Associate of the Royal Aeronautical Society—both of Great Britain.

Fairchild Aerial Surveys, Inc.

WOOLWORTH BUILDING

233 Broadway—Full block on Broadway from Park Place to Barclay St.

(1913 to 1930)

FOR A PERIOD OF 18 YEARS THE WOOLWORTH HELD THE DISTINCTION OF BEING THE HIGHEST BUSINESS BUILDING IN THE WORLD.

Note Higher Buildings (built recently) on Page 151.

Note Higher Buildings (built recently) on Page 151.

Photo by J. C. Mangan

Notwithstanding the larger, higher and more costly skyscrapers erected in recent years the Woolworth is still one of the most commanding buildings in all America.

When, on the night of April 24th, 1913, President Woodrow Wilson pressed a tiny button in the White House, and 80,000 brilliant lights instantly flashed throughout the-just-completed Woolworth Building the greatest achievement of the architectural and building world was heralded to the public.

It was a memorable night! A banquet was served on the 27th floor to a host of statesmen, captains of industry, financiers, merchants, and prominent figures in American life. All paid homage to the man who started life with only a few dollars but who, as a result of his idea of starting 10c stores, had erected this gigantic edifice without borrowing a dollar. Mr. Woolworth personally financed this famous building.

Ass'd Val.	$11,250,000
792 ft. high	60 Floors
Rent Area	550,000 sq. ft.
Housing	10,000
Completed	1913
Owner	Woolworth Company
Architect	Cass Gilbert
Builder, Thompson Starrett Co.	
Agent	Edward J. Hogan

CITY HALL PARK and PARK ROW
Broadway, Chambers, Park Row

The above picture presents view of the new City Hall Park when proposed improvements shall have been made.

No. 4 in the drawing shows new approach to Brooklyn Bridge.

No. 11 shows site where the old Federal Building (Post Office) now stands. When the old structure is finally demolished, this will make "Civic Center" almost a complete triangle—Broadway on the East, Chambers Street on the North and Park Row completing the triangle.

The old City Hall Building (No. 1) the towering Municipal Building (No. 3) the Hall of Records (No. 10) and Brooklyn Bridge (No. 4) constitute the city owned property of the district. Most of the other structures are the former homes of New York's famous old daily papers.

Park Row for nearly forty years was the newspaper publishing center of New York. Note the old WORLD building (No. 5) the old TRIBUNE building (No. 6) the old SUN building (No. 7) and the old TIMES building (No. 8). Practically all the other papers were printed in the immediate neighborhood also. Today they are scattered all over Manhattan—note pages 72 to 75 showing their present homes and addresses.

No. 9 in the picture is the famous old Potter Building, No. 2 is the Emigrant Industrial Savings Bank, No. 13 Brooklyn Bridge, No. 12 Manhattan Bridge, No. 14 Williamsburg Bridge.

OLD "TRIBUNE" and "SUN" BLDGS.
Also "41 PARK ROW" BUILDING
At Park Row—Corner of Nassau & Spruce Streets.

The large building with "spire" at left of picture, is the old *Tribune* building erected originally in 1873 but rebuilt in 1895 as a skyscraper 290 feet high. 24 floors. Now assessed at $3,250,000.

Almost as imposing, is the old *Sun* Building directly across the street—present assessed valuation $3,000,000.

The Building in right hand foreground is famous 41 Park Row—old home of the New York Times.

The picture at extreme right of page is the old

ST. PAUL BUILDING
At 220 Broadway—where Park Row commenses.

Assessed at $1,750,000   24 stories high

"15 PARK ROW" BLDG.

Only a few steps from Broadway—facing City Hall Park.

COMPLETELY REMODELED AND MODERNIZED THROUGHOUT

This famous old skyscraper (built in 1898) has been one of New York's commanding office buildings ever since the date of completion. Constructed before the city ordinances required "set back" style of architecture, it towers 32 stories in the air and at time of construction was the world's tallest office building.

"15 PARK ROW" IS NOW UNDER NEW OWNERSHIP AND NEW MANAGEMENT

A MOST POPULAR BUILDING FOR LEGAL FIRMS. Just around the corner from the New York County Lawyers Association Building, across the street from City Hall, and only a short walk from the County Court House and civic center development.

Approximately a quarter million dollars has recently been expended in alterations, improvements, and installation of latest modern equipment. As soon as the old Post Office building has been demolished and the enlarged City Hall Park has been perfected, 15 Park Row will have one of the most attractive outlooks in all New York.

Ass'd Val	$3,300,000
387 ft. high	32 Floors
Rent Area	210,000 sq. ft.
Housing	4,000
Completed	1898
Owner	W. I. M. Corp.
Architect	H. H. Robertson
Builder	August Belmont
Agent	Chas. F. Noyes & Co. Inc.

"INTERNATIONAL NEWS PHOTOS INC."

235 E. 45th St. Bet. 2nd & 3rd Avenues.

MR. PETER C. STONE

One of the most interesting establishments in New York is the "International News Photos Inc."—a Wm. Randolph Hearst enterprise, with offices all over the world from Seattle to Shanghai and from Boston to Rome.

This company supplies photos of every thing and every happening from a Russian prison in Siberia to the Hon. Al Smith eating a hog dog at Coney Island.

The beautiful picture of New York's Great White Way at night (see page 37), is a sample of the great work done by Arthur Sasse—one of the artists on the International's force.

We show herewith an excellent likeness of Mr. "Pete" Stone—the general Sales Manager who, though yet in his thirties, is in entire charge of the Sales Dept. "Pete" made his first dollar washing windows, but securing a job as errand boy with the Hearst organization he worked his way up as reporter, photographer, salesman and editor, until he became Sales Head of the immense business of "International News Photos Inc." Mr. Stone is a most approachable man with a pronounced personality and a lot of *IT*, and one of the most popular chaps in his entire field.

COURT SQUARE BUILDING

2 Lafayette St.—Covers almost an entire square.
Frontages on Lafayette, Reade, Elm and Duane Streets.

A MAGNIFICENT BUILDING MOST ABLY MANAGED BY ONE OF NEW YORK'S LIVELIEST AND MOST COURTEOUS RENTING AGENTS.— MR. LORING M. HEWEN.

This huge and beautiful building faces on four streets, tapering to its principle entrance (2 Lafayette St.) at Foley Sq., with its unobstructed view of New York's towering Municipal building and the $11,000,000 County Court House, State Build-

Ass'd Val....	$3,000,000
302 ft. high....	25 Floors
Rent Area.	300,000 sq. ft.
Housing..........	3,500
Completed........	1927
Ownr.	CourtSq.Bld.Corp
Art.Firm	Ely. Jacq Kahn
Builder.....	Harper Org.
Agt.	Lor'g M Hewen Co Inc

ing and Plaza, affording unusually abundant light and air. During excavating work for the "Court Square" building (erected on the site of Aaron Burr's old well) a number of old coins used in colonial days and numerous other very valuable relics were unearthed. Mr. Hewen is always pleased to exhibit these to those interested.

"ROYAL INSURANCE CO." BUILDING

150 William St. extending through to Gold St. between Fulton and Ann.

THIS ENORMOUS AND BEAUTIFUL STRUCTURE COVERS AN ENTIRE SQUARE

Home of the Royal Insurance Co. Ltd., the Liverpool & London & Globe Ins. Co., Ltd., and affiliated Companies. The extensive new addition — (extending through to Gold St.) just recently completed, now makes the Royal Building one of the largest and most imposing insurance structures in all America. Altho but 20 stories high, the building covers an immense plot, and has a housing capacity of over 5,000 workers. This gorgeous building stands on the site of

Assessed Value about......	$5,000,000
280 ft. high....	20 Floors
Rent area,	430,000 sq. ft.
Housing..........	5,000
Elevators...........	18
Completed........	1927
Owner,	150 Wm. St. Corp
Archt..	Starrett & Van V.
Bldr.,	Marc Eidlitz & Son

the old "North Dutch Church" built in 1769 shortly before the Revolutionary War. This church figured most prominently in the strenuous activities of those days, and was right in the thick of the Battle of Golden Hills following the cutting down of Liberty Pole.

EAST RIVER SAVINGS BANK

Bway N. E. Cor. Chambers

Est. Val.......	$4,000,000
252 ft. high.....	20 Floors
Rent Area..	82,500 sq. ft.
Housing.............	950
Completed.........	1910
Owner, East River Sav. Bk.	
Archt..	Clinton & Russell
Builder.	Geo. W. Fuller Co.
Agent.............	Owners

EMIGRANT INDUSTRIAL SAVINGS BANK

51 Chambers St.—
Opposite City Hall.

Cost...........	$4,500,000
250 ft. high.....	18 Floors
Rent Area.	176,000 sq. ft.
Housing.............	2,100
Completed.........	1913
Owner. Emigrant Sav. Bk.	
Arch. Raymond F. Admiral	
Builder, C. T. Wells & Co.	
Agent..	Thomas J. O'Reilly

PARK MURRAY BLDG.

11 Park Place—Extends through to Broadway

Ass'd Val......	$2,375,000
240 ft. high.....	20 Floors
Rent Area.	170,000 sq. ft.
Housing............	2,000
Completed.........	1927
Owner. Park Murray Corp.	
Art.Firm Ely Jacq. Kahn	
Bldr.	Caoudwell W. & Co.
Agt. Eng. Supervision Co.	

140 WEST STREET

NEW YORK TELEPHONE CO.'S LOWER BROADWAY BUILDING

Covers entire square—West, Barclay, Washington and Vesey Streets.

LARGEST AND MOST COSTLY TELEPHONE BUILDING IN THE WORLD

Sometime between 1787 and 1800, work was started on levelling the hilly ground that lay between Broadway and the Hudson River and filling in the west shore—which at that time was *east* of Washington Street.

What was then the actual *riverbed* of the Hudson is now the site on which the sumptuous New York Telephone Building pictured herewith now stands.

Superlatives would be inadequate to convey any correct visualization of the richness and grandeur of this superb building —both within and without. It is a modern *palace*.

In 1878, Alexander Graham Bell made in effect the following prophecy: "Some day, cables of telephone wire will make it possible to communicate by branch wires, with private dwellings, country homes and places of business, by uniting them thru the main cable with a central office, where the wire could be connected as desired, thus establishing direct communication between two points in a city. I also firmly believe that some day, wires will unite the head offices of telephone companies in different cities and communication by word of mouth be had between distant localities".

MR. BELL HAD VISION

Today New York people talk with California friends as distinctly as with those right in the next block. The present generation wonders how the old folks ever got a l o n g WITHOUT THE TELEPHONE in the old days.

Ass'd Val.	$12,750,000
498 feet high	34 Floors
Ground Plot	54,696 sq. ft.
Rent Area	851,390 sq. ft.
House Capacity	10,000
Elevators	27
Year Built	1926
Owner	N. Y. Telephone Co.
Arch.	McKenzie, Voorhees & Gmelin
Bldr.	Marc Eidlitz & Son

TELEPHONE CITY

GROUP OF BUILDINGS—*OWNED, LEASED* OR *OCCUPIED IN PART BY*

THE NEW YORK TELEPHONE COMPANY

The New York Telephone Co. *owns* 212 buildings in New York and *leases* 340 others!—552 in all!

The New York Telephone Co. owns 13,821,739 miles of wire, and maintains 496 central offices. Over 12,000,000 telephone messages are averaged daily.

On January 1, 1931, there were 2,925,648 telephones in use in New York of which 2,648,957 were owned and operated by the New York Telephone Co.

The New York Telephone Co. is the largest of the 25 companies which, associated with the American Telephone & Telegraph Co., comprise the great Bell System. 10,893,509 square feet of floor space is required for operations.

The assets of the New York Telephone Co. on January 1, 1931, were in excess of $816,490,000!

The New York Telephone Co. operates under a license from the Parent Company. More than 60,000 workers are employed by the New York Telephone Co.

NEW YORK TELEPHONE LABORATORIES

210 West 18th Street—near 7th Avenue

In this enormous structure the experimenting, inventive and testing work of the great Bell Telephone System is carried on.

Building is higher than many 30 story skyscrapers, floors being from 14 to 18 feet.

Ass'd Val.	$2,400,000
327 feet high	
20 Floors	8 Elevators
Floor Area	228,000 sq. ft.
Ground Plot	23,266 sq. ft.
Built	1930
Owner	New York Tel. Co.
Arch. Voorhees, Gmelin & Walker	
Bldr.	Tidewater Bld. Corp.

NEW YORK TELEPHONE CO.
Long Island Headquarters
101 Willoughby St. Cor.
Bridge St., Brooklyn.

388 ft. high..........30 Floors
Completed 1931
Ground Area....25,517 sq. ft.
13 Elevators
Arch. Voorhees, Gmelin & Walker
Bldrs. Cauldwell, Wingate Co.

194

NEW YORK TELEPHONE CO.'S "24 WALKER ST." BUILDING

24 Walker St.—a short block west of Broadway, just below Canal St. Covers entire square.

THE PICTURE BELOW SHOWS THE VERY MUCH ENLARGED "24 WALKER ST." BUILDING OF THE NEW YORK TEL. CO. 412,000 ADDITIONAL SQUARE FEET IS BEING ADDED TO THE 400,000 SQUARE FEET OF THE FORMER BUILDING, THUS GIVING THE ENORMOUS TOTAL OF 812,000 SQUARE FEET OF USABLE SPACE IN THIS GIGANTIC NEW STRUCTURE.

Seymour Hill

```
Ass'd Val.  ....$12,680,000
414 feet high....26 Floors
Ground Plot 45,945 sq. ft.
Floor Area..812,000 sq. ft.
Housing  Capacity...10,000
Elevators ..............16
Year Built....1918 & 1932
Owner.....N. Y. Tel. Co.
Arch...McKenzie, Voorhees
              & Gmelin
Bldrs. D. C. Weeks & Sons
```

A BUSY PLACE

This colossal building will be utilized for the various activities of the N. Y. Telephone Company, also by the "Long Lines Department" of the *American* Telephone & Telegraph Company. —for the expansion of its long distance central office equipment.

The long-distance telephone central-office housed in this "24 Walker St." building is the largest and most extensive in America. It consists of 1,520 switchboard and test board positions, 8,300 trunk lines to Central offices in Greater New York, 2,800 long distance lines to other cities, as well as Transatlantic radio-telephone switchboard for communication with Europe, Australia, South America and steamships enroute.

"401 BROADWAY"
N. W. Cor. Walker St.—
A few steps from Canal St.

A BUILDING THAT IS LEAVENING AN ENTIRE NEIGHBORHOOD

"401 Broadway" is the outstanding structure in about the only section of the busy business region of New York that has not responded to modern development (in the "new building" sense) in BROADWAY from Read Street to Union Square.

401 Broadway is not only pioneering this development but rehabilitating its neighborhood. It is serving as an incentive and an inspiration to property owners both north and south of Canal Street.

401 Broadway is a strictly modern building with an exceptionally well laid out arrangement of space and offices. It is proving a good investment for its owners. They had the foresight to visualize the demand that an up-to-date building in the Canal Street section would stimulate.

Est. Cost	$3,500,000
335 ft. high	31 Floors
Rent Area	210,000 sq. ft.
Housing	2400
Completed	1930
Owners	Realty Cons. Corp.
Architects	Jardin Hill & Murdock
Builders	Realty Cons. Corp.
Agents	Owners

HOW NEW YORK'S "CITY PAPAS" SPEND THE CITY'S MONEY

A compilation indicating the way the City of New York spends its money, as provided for in the Budget of 1928, is as follows: Preventive, $58,009,303; Civil Justice, $11,277,850; Unfortunates and Dependents, $30,145,371; Public Health, $46,082,487; Fire Protection, $23,594,784; Education and Recreation, $105,890,096; Commerce and Transportation, $39,654,354; Overhead, $28,216,714; Public Markets, $668,149; Total $343,539,108. Interest on debt, $76,124,110; Redemption and Amortization, $74,360,793; State Taxes, $14,126,847; Deficiencies in Taxes, $3,990,000; Classon Avenue Sewer, $387,973; Grand Total $512,528,831.

In 1929 the city spent $538,928,697.

In 1930 the city spent, $620,000,000.

Budget for 1931, Estimated over $700,000,000—more than required by the United States Government to run the nation a comparatively few years ago.

HOLLAND PLAZA DISTRICT

HOLLAND TUNNEL

Cost $48,400,000

Entrance at Canal and Varick Sts.
Outlet at 12th St. Via Jersey City.

Holland Tunnel was opened to the public Nov. 10, 1927. It was named in honor of Clifford M. Holland, First Chief Engineer, who assumed his office July 1, 1919. Ground was first broken October 12, 1920. Cost of tunnel, $48,400,000, divided evenly by the States of New York and New Jersey. Tunnel consists of two separate roadways—one for each line of traffic. 1,900 motor cars per hour is the estimated daily patronage. Total length of Tunnel—9,250 feet, nearly two miles. Width of roadways—20 feet. Headroom—13 feet, 6 inches. Estimated yearly traffic—15,000,000 vehicles. From Nov. 10, 1927, to April 1, 1931, 35,000,000 vehicles passed through the tunnel. Traffic in 1931 is 7% heavier, thus far, than in 1930.

TOLLS

Motorcycle	$ .25
Automobile, 7 passengers or less	.50
Motor Bus, 29 passengers or less	1.00
Motor Bus, 30 passengers or more	1.50
Trucks, 2 tons or less	.50
Trucks, 2 to 5 tons	.75
Trucks, 5 to 10 tons	1.00
Trucks, exceeding 10 tons	2.00

No bicycles, push-carts or horse-drawn vehicles permitted in the tunnel.

HOLLAND PLAZA BUILDING

N. W. Cor. Varick and Canal Sts.

Ass'd Val.	$5,500,000
212 feet high	18 Floors
Rent area	900,000 sq. ft.
Completed	1930
Owner	York Investing Co.
Arch.	Firm of Ely Jacques Kahn
Bldr.	Shroder & Koppel
Agts.	Brown Wheelock H. V. Co.

GRAYBAR-VARICK

180 Varick Street—Extending from Charlton to King Streets.

Ass'd Val.	$1,780,000
220 ft. high	18 Floors
Ground Plot	20,000 sq. ft.
Rent Area	325,000 sq. ft.
Elevators	7
Year Built	1930
Owner	Varick Holding Corp.
Arch.	Victor Mayper
Bldr.	Varick Holding Corp.
Agent	Brown Wheelock H. V. Co.

UNION SQUARE DISTRICT

Bounded on the south by 14th St. and on the north by 17th, between Broadway and 4th Ave. Laid out as a park in 1832.

Union Square some years ago, was what New York's Great White Way is today. It was the amusement center of the city. Keith introduced vaudeville to New York in Union Square; Barnum's Museum was located in Union Square; The Academy of Music was on the N. E. Cor. of 14th St. & Irving Place—just a short block east of Union Square, and old Tammany Hall was just next door to the Academy. Today, Union Square is devoted to business, although East 14th St. has become quite a center for movie houses, vaudeville, dance halls, and penny arcades. The Communists of New York make their headquarters at Union Square also.

Since the above picture was taken, the beautiful park in the center of the square is undergoing a great change. Due to excavations for subways, all the big shade trees were removed, grassy lawns and winding paths demolished, and the park generally wrecked. A stone wall of some 30 inches high has now been built around the entire area—broken only at intervals for entrances. This immense plot has been filled in with rich loam and when completed with new trees planted, new sod installed, winding pathways restored, and statues reset, Union Square will be even more inviting, and attractive than ever.

Union Square was originally a sand hill. Had it not been for the sand, Irving Place & Lexington Ave. would likely be part of Broadway today!

"853 BROADWAY" BLDG.

S. W. Cor. 14th St.
Faces Union Square

Ass'd Val.	$1,300,000
235 ft. high	21 Floors
Rent Area	68,600 sq. ft.
Housing	750
Completed	1928
Arch.	Emery Roth
Bldr.	G. Richardson Davis Co.

EVERETT BLDG.

45 Union Square
N. W. Cor. 16th St. & 4th Ave.

Cost	$2,500,000
252 ft. high	18 Floors
Rent Area	195,000 sq. ft.
Housing	2300
Completed	1909
Owner	Everett Investing Co.
Arch.	Starrett & Van Vleck
Bldr.	Geo. A. Fuller Co.
Agent	H. Van R. Forest

GUARDIAN LIFE BLDG.

50 Union Square
N. E. Cor. 17th St. & 4th Ave.

Cost	$2,163,000
280 ft. high	22 Floors
Rent Area	125,000 sq. ft.
Housing	1600
Completed	1911
Owner	Guardian Life Ins. Co.
Arch.	D'Oench & Yost
Bldr.	C. T. Wills & Co.
Manager	H. J. Smith

CONSOLIDATED GAS BUILDING

4 Irving Place—from 14th to 15th Streets—one block from Broadway.

MAGNIFICENT HOME OF THE
CONSOLIDATED GAS CO. OF NEW YORK
AND THE
NEW YORK EDISON CO.

Extending full block on Irving Place and extending approximately 300 feet on 15th and 320 feet on 14th Street.

Built on the site formerly occupied by the famous old Academy of Music, the equally famous old Tammany Hall, and first home of the Lotus Club.

The Consolidated Gas Co. Building is one of the most beautiful and magnificent structures in the United States. Thousands of electric bulbs gorgeously illuminate the building at night and the lantern at the top of the tower is a cast bronze structure approximately 35 feet in height, containing five beacons.

The Chimes in the clock tower are Westminster Chimes and the bells are the second largest in size in this country.

The building contains approximately one million square feet of available floor space and is occupied by about seven thousand employees of the Consolidated Gas Company and its affiliated gas and electric companies.

Ass'd Val. $15,000,000
216 feet high........26 Floors
Ground area......60,000 sq. ft.
33 Elevators
Year built.................1913
Owner............Cons. Gas Co.
Arch..........H. J. Hardenberg
Bldr...Geo. A. Fuller Const. Co.

PORT OF NEW YORK AUTHORITY and UNION INLAND TERMINAL

> Covering entire area between 15th and 16th Sts. and 8th and 9th Aves.

The Port of New York Authority was created, developed and financed by the States of New York and New Jersey for the unification of interests in shipping, trucking and the general transportation of freight involved in the enormous commerce of the Port of New York.

ONE OF THE MOST STUPENDOUS ACHIEVEMENTS OF THE AGE

Constantly moving by rail and water through the Port of New York is a vast trade whose ever increasing volume is gradually saturating every facility for commerce now available, and stagnation of commerce at the very gateway to America is being avoided by the new methods and facilities provided by the "Port of New York Authority."

The plan adopted for the handling and distribution of freight is intended to benefit shippers and receivers of goods, the public, and eventually the carriers themselves.

The simplicity of the plan (which is merely an adaptation of modern methods of terminal trucking) and the economies resulting therefrom are so evident that the interests of shipper, merchant and general public are *assured*.

For years, a consignee, upon receiving notice of the arrival of freight at railroad stations or docks had to have his truck call at the freight station and pick up his goods. Where the consignee receives freight from more than one station his task of collection is multiplied just that many times and his cost of trucking mounts proportionately. Goods from two or more stations make separate trips necessary to widely scattered stations with partially loaded trucks.

Manufacturers and merchants feel the effect of this costly and clumsy method of freight distribution, and the public at large is immediately concerned because of the high handling cost resulting from present methods, and because of the heavy vehicular traffic which clogs the streets while trucks are shipping about among the pier stations to pick up and deliver freight.

Under the Inland Terminal Plan, freight cars, inbound, will be stopped, as at present, at the rail terminals. Freight will then be taken from cars and loaded into motorized equipment, for movement via ferries or tunnels to the Inland Terminal which has been designated by the shipper. There the freight will be sorted and classified for delivery to consignees. The carriers' trucks, when they have completed deliveries, will call at the shipping berths for their return loads.

The consignee, upon receiving notice of the arrival of his goods at a specific terminal, will call and receive his freight (assembled from all of the railroads in one spot on the freight platform) in one pickup irrespective of whether his consignment was handled by one or more of the eleven railroads serving the Metropolitan Area. In the same manner shippers in Manhattan may deliver freight to all railroads by merely making one delivery at the terminal located nearest their respective place of business.

The new Inland Terminal Building (No. 1) shown above is the first of three enormous freight centers projected. It is one of the very largest buildings in the world, 15 stories high with floors ranging from 88,000 to 165,000 square feet. Ground area 206 ft. by 800 ft. The ground floor facing 8th Ave. is given over to stores, etc. The basement and balance of ground floor devoted to the handling of freight shipments. The upper floors are equipped for tenancy for office, display rooms or manufacturing.

"NEW YORK EDISON CO.'S POWER STATION"

At 14th Street and East River

A Quarter Mile in Length . . . . COST $100,000,000.

The New York Edison Company serves Manhattan, Bronx, Brooklyn, Queens, Etc.

Largest electric utility company in the world.

Total investment approximately $900,000,000.

Employs over 36,000 workers.

Served nearly 4,000,000,000 (*four billion*) kilowatt hours in 1930.

Its Hell Gate station has a capacity of 810,000 horse power—making the largest steam plant in America.   Installation of additional turbo generators at its Brooklyn plant (to be made the coming year) will give the Brooklyn plant over 1,000,000 horse power—surpassing the Hell Gate station.

It is estimated that by 1940, the New York Edison system will be prepared to carry a maximum load of 3,500,000 kilowatts and have an annual station output of *over eleven billion* kilowatt hours per annum!

The total length of distribution and transmission lines in Manhattan is over *50,000 miles*—no overhead wires or cables, but all buried!

Est. Cost. $3,000,000
210 ft. high. . .18 Floors
Rent Area. 650,000 sq. ft.
Houses. 7300
Completed. 1931

STANDARD STATISTICS BUILDING

345 Hudson St. From King to Charlton Sts.

The new home of the Standard Statistics Co.—recently completed.

An enormous building w i t h every efficiency convenience which modern construction provides.

Accommodates over 7500 workers and faces a full block on Hudson St.

COUNTY TRUST BUILDING

N. E. Cor. 14th St. & 8th Ave.

The new home of the reliable old County Trust Co.'s Bank—modern, imposing, and original in design.

Even as far south as 14th Street, big building construction is extending 8th Avenues miraculous skyline and this new addition to this now famous thoroughfare adds prestige to the 14th Street section.

Ass'd Val. . . . .
$1,450,000
275 ft. high. . . . .
22 Floors
Rent Area. . . . .
140,000 sq. ft.
Houses. . . . 1,600
Completed. .1931

MADISON SQUARE

Madison Square is bounded by 23rd Street on the south, 26th Street on the north, Madison Avenue on the east, and the junction of Fifth Avenue and Broadway on the west.

Great shade trees, cooling fountains, roomy park benches and both men's and women's comfort stations all contribute to a most inviting haven for those who wish to relax from the strenuous activities of business, shopping, etc., and enjoy the rest this very popular park offers. From early morning until late at night there is always more or less of a "full house" patronizing the park benches—the seating capacity of which is not far from 600.

FULLER BLDG.

23rd St. at junction of Fifth Ave. & Broadway.

FIRST 22-STORY STEEL SKYSCRAPER IN AMERICA—
THE FAMOUS FLAT IRON BUILDING

Ass'd Val....	$2,000,000
285 ft. high....	22 Floors
Rent Area, 115,000 sq. ft.	
Houses...........	1,300
Year Built........	1903
Elevators.........	6
Owr.U.S. Rty. & Imp Co.	
Act.D. H. Burnham & Co	
Bldr. Geo. A. Fuller Co.	
Agent......	On premises

FIFTH AVENUE BLDG.

Also known as "200 FIFTH AV."
200 Fifth Ave.—N. W. Cor.
23rd Street at Madison Square.

This very popular building stands on the site of the famous old "Fifth Avenue Hotel" which for so many years was recognized as the fashionable and political center of the city.

Ass'd Val..........	$7,635,000
200 ft. high..........	15 Floors
Rent Area.....	520,000 sq. ft.
Houses................	6,000
Year Built............	1909
Owner..Fifth Ave. Bldg. Co.	
Archt....Manyiche & Franke	
Builder.....	Hedden Cons. Co.
Agent..........	On premises

MASONIC BLDG.

71 W. 23rd Street—
N. E. Cor. 6th Ave.

The various chapters of masonry occupy all of this immense and beautiful building as lodge rooms and executive offices except five floors. The building owns its own heating and lighting plant and operates seven speed elevators.

Ass'd Val......	$1,950,000
256 ft. high......	21 Floors
Year Built..........	1912
Archt......	H. P. Knowles
Builder.Geo. A. Fuller Co.	
Agent..Chas. F. Noyes Co.	

METROPOLITAN LIFE BUILDING

Also known as "ONE MADISON AVENUE"
FACES MADISON SQUARE—Covers entire block—23rd St., Madison Ave., 24th St. & 4th Ave.

Picture shows

METROPOLITAN TOWER
and the
METROPOLITAN ANNEX
directly across the
street—at right

The METROPOLITAN LIFE INSURANCE CO. (founded in 1868) is the largest insurance organization in the world and the "METROPOLITAN LIFE" BUILDING one of the most enormous office structures in existence.

The main building (12 stories high) covers 83,937 sq. ft. of ground area and houses close to 12,000 workers. The huge structure is occupied by the Metropolitan's clerical force.

Ass'd Val	$13,750,000
700 ft. high	52 Floors
Usable Area	1,085,000 sq. ft.
Houses	12,000
Year Built 1893	Tower 1909
Owner	Met. Life Ins. Co.
Archt	N. LeBrun & Son
Builder	Hedden Cons. Co. & Fuller Cons. Co.

Plot 23rd to 24th St	83,937 sq. ft.
Plot 24th to 25 St	83,937 sq. ft.
TOTAL GROUND AREA	167,875 sq. ft.
TOTAL FLOOR SPACE OF ALL BUILDINGS	1,085,000 sq. ft.
	—About 25 ACRES

THE ANNEX AND ALL THE OTHER 15, 20 AND EVEN 22 STORY BUILDINGS IN THE ENTIRE SQUARE FROM 24TH TO 25TH STREETS ARE BEING RAZED TO MAKE PLACE FOR THE GIGANTIC NEW BUILDING DESCRIBED BELOW.

First unit of the NEW METROPOLITAN ANNEX

This "unit" will cover the entire half square from 24th to 25th Sts. on 4th Ave. The second unit will cover the remaining half square facing on Madison Avenue.

WHEN THE ENTIRE STRUCTURE IS COMPLETED, IT WILL NOT ONLY BE ONE OF THE HIGHEST OF THE WORLD'S BUILDINGS BUT ONE OF THE LARGEST AS WELL AS MOST MAGNIFICENT.

Some idea of the hugeness of this building, is suggested by the fact that 2,500 men are required for the construction of the first unit pictured at left, which will take sixteen months to complete. This section is to be only 32 stories in height but the Madison Avenue unit will be one of the highest in the world—if not the highest!

D. Everett Waid & Harvey Wiley Corbett..........Architects
Starrett Brothers & Eken...............Building Contractors

203

HERE ARE SIX OF FULLY FIFTY BUILDINGS IN THE MADISON-SQUARE DISTRICT RANGING FROM 18 TO 25 FLOORS

AMERICAN WOOLEN BLDG

221 Fourth Avenue—
N. E. Cor. 18th St.

Ass'd Val	$2,000,000
300 ft. high	21 Floors
Rent Area	190,000 sq. ft.
Housing	2,200
Completed	1910
Owner	Pocona Co.
Arch., R. H. Robertson & Son
Agt. Carstein & Linnekin, Inc.
Builder	Iron & Todd

This is the home of the American Woolen Co., one of the largest textile organizations in the world.

"11 EAST 26th" thru to 27th ST.
Bet. Broadway & Fifth Ave.

Ass'd Val	$1,300,000
267 ft. high	22 Floors
Elevators	8
Rent Area	200,000 sq. ft.
Housing	2,300
Plot	12,000 sq. ft.
Completed	1913
Ownr., 11 E. 26th St. Corp., Inc.
Arch	Rouse & Goldstone
Bldr	Jas. Gilbert, Inc.
Agent	Owners

Overlooks Madison Square between Broadway and Fifth Ave. There are only *six exposed* columns on all floors above the store. 100% sprinkler system and has smoke proof tower.

THE CROISIC BUILDING

220 Fifth Avenue—
N. W. Cor. 26th Street.

Ass'd Val	$1,350,000
302 ft. high	22 Floors
Rent Area	110,000 sq. ft.
Housing	1,300
Completed	1912
Owner	220 Fifth Ave. Corp.
Archt	Fredrick C. Brown
Builder	Chas. E. Peckwith
Agents	Spear & Co.

One of the most exquisite buildings architecturally in all New York. The interior faithfully characterizes the old medieval period when knighthood was in flower.

AMERICAN BOOK BLDG.

88 Lexington Avenue—
N. W. Cor. 26th Street.

Ass'd Val	$1,300,000
235 ft. high	18 Floors
Rent Area	150,000 sq. ft.
Housing	1,800
Completed	1927
Owner	American Book Co.
Archt. Necorsulmar & Lehlback
Builder	Leddy & Moore
Agent	Dwight, Voorhees & Perry Co., Inc.

A truly beautiful building, modern throughout, and although in the thick of one of New York's busiest sections, is a block a way from congestion and noise of traffic.

VICTORIA BUILDING
1150 Broadway—Cor. 27th St.
Extends through to Fifth Ave.

Ass'd Val	$3,100,000
285 ft. high	20 Floors
Rent Area	170,000 sq. ft.
Housing	2,000
Completed	
Owner	Vidor Realty Corp.
Arch	Schwartz & Gross
Builder	?
Agent	Bing & Bing

Glistening white in the sunlight, the VICTORIA is one of the imposing Broadway buildings just above Madison Square. A spacious arcade connects Broadway with Fifth Avenue.

GREEN CENTRAL BLDG.
4th Ave.—N. E. Cor. 29th St.

Cost	$1,000,000
262 ft. high	22 Floors
Rent Area	104,000 sq. ft.
Housing	1,300
Completed	1928
Owner	V. Green & Co. Inc.
Arch	Shampan & Shampan
Bldrs	V. Green & Co. Inc.
Agt	Realty Supervision Co.

One of the outstanding modern buildings in Fourth Avenue where the "most for the money" is the slogan in which the renting agents make good.

"NEW YORK LIFE" BUILDING

Covers entire square—Madison Avenue to Fourth Avenue & 26th to 27th Streets.

CONCEDED TO BE ONE OF THE MOST BEAUTIFUL BUSINESS BUILDINGS EVER CONSTRUCTED

Every visitor to the City should see this magnificent building and take advantage of the New York Life Insurance Company's hospitable invitation to furnish attendants to show guests through it.

BUILT ON THE SITE OF OLD MADISON SQUARE

The above cut shows the former home of the N. Y. Life Ins. Co. at 346 Broadway, extending full block on Leonard St. to Lafayette—also the "Annex" across the street.

Cost	$25,000,000
617 ft. high	40 Floors
Elevators	38
Housing	15,000
Ground area	85,000 sq. ft.
Completed	1928
Owner	N. Y. Life Ins. Co.
Archt	Cass Gilbert
Builder	Starrett Bros.
Agent, Albert B. Ashforth Co.	

Altho simplicity, dignity and unostentation has been the motif in planning and building the structure, everything about it commands admiration and wonderment.

Among the many modern utilities are included a great mechanical ventilating system, an elaborate vacuum cleaning system, the largest installation of soundproofing treatment, and the largest pneumatic tube system.

Limited space forbids description here of either this wonder building or the gigantic organization owning it. But, write to the N. Y. Life Ins. Co. and ask for their 16 page folder entitled "THE HOME OFFICE." It will be well worth your 2c stamp.

The New York Life Insurance Company occupies all or part of the first 15 floors. The balance of the space may be rented by high type firms who wish a business home unsurpassed for beauty, comfort and efficiency.

"305 SEVENTH AVENUE" BUILDING
Cor. 29th Street

Ass'd Val......$1,150,000
252 ft. high.....22 Floors
Rent Area..170,00 sq. ft.
Housing capacity....2,000
Completed..........1921
Owner.Unterberg Rlty Co.
Archt....Schwartz & Gross
Bldr. G. Richards Davis Co.
Agent.....Williams & Co.

COMMERCIAL EXCHANGE
307 Seventh Ave. and 156 W.
28th Street

Cost..........$1,850,000
285 ft. high......25 Floors
Rent Area..193,000 sq. ft.
Housing capacity....2,300
Completed..........1927
Owner...Realty Cons. Co.
Arch.Shampan & Shampan
Builder..Realty Cons. Co.
Agent.............Owners

KHEEL TOWER BUILDING
315 Seventh Avenue, S. E.
Cor. 28th St. (150 W. 28th)

Cost..........$1,000,000
278 ft. high......25 Floors
Rent Area..140,000 sq. ft.
Housing capacity....1,800
Completed..........1927
Owner......Aaron Kheel
Archt....Wm. I. Hohauser
Builder.....Samuel Kheel
Agent........On premises

Ass'd Val......$1,530,000
340 ft. high......27 Floors
Rent Area..180,000 sq. ft.
Housing capacity....2,100
Completed..........1929
Owner.Clemens Realty Co.
Archt....John H. Knubel
Bldr....G. Richards Davis
Agt. & Man.....H. Plumb

One of the best managed buildings in the entire garment section also one of the best rented.—The answer is Mr. H. Plumb.

"345 SEVENTH AVE." BLDG.
30th Street.

Built on land owned a little over 100 years ago by an Indian who sold it for a small fraction of what the taxes are today.

Ass'd Val.....$2,200,000
320 ft. high.....29 Floors
Rent Area..210,000 sq. ft.
Houses............2,500
Year Built.........1926
Owner......Fifth Ave. &
26th St. Corp.
Archt..Geo. Fred Pelham
Builder..H. & S. Sokolski

"245 FIFTH AVENUE"
S. W. Cor. 28th St.

Ass'd Val......$2,000,000
252 ft. high......22 Floors
Rent Area..255,000 sq. ft.
Ground Area.12,500 sq. ft.
Completed..1924 and 1928
Owner..Maxal Realty Co.
Archt.........Firm of Ely
Jacques Kahn and
Schwartz & Gross
Bldr...G. Richard Davis &
S. S. Roth
Bus. Mgr......F. Phelan

TWIN BLDGS.
Both owned by the Maxal Realty Co.

Another palatial loft building which spelled death to old time sweat shops.

GROSS BUILDINGS
330 Seventh Ave., at 29th St.

Ass'd Val......$3,050,000
252 ft. high......22 Floors
Rent Area..420,000 sq. ft.
Housing capacity....5,000
Ground Area.20,000 sq. ft.
Built..............1920
Elevators............12
Owner..Regent Const. Co.
Archt...Schwartz & Gross
Agent..Regent Const. Co.

"SEVENTH AVENUE" BLDG.
333 Seventh Ave., at 29th St.

"TWO PARK AVENUE" BUILDING

No. 2 Park Avenue—Extends full block from 32nd to 33rd Streets—*205 ft. deep.*

ANOTHER $10,000,000 PALACE OF BUSINESS

Ass'd Val	$8,350,000
350 ft. high	30 Floors
Rent Area	800,000 sq. ft.
Housing	9,300
Completed	1927
Owner	2 Park Ave. Corp.
Art. Firm of	Ely Jacq. Kahn
Builder	Shroder & Koppel
Agents	Cross & Brown

25 high speed elevators.

Interior freight unloading platforms and trucking driveway.

Magnificently appointed display and show rooms.

Sprinklered throughout.

Low insurance rates.

Subway station in building.

Only four minutes from Grand Central.

Splendid light and air.

One of the largest yet most courteous and obliging real estate brokerage houses in the city act as managers and renting agents of "TWO PARK AVE." See, or write Cross & Brown, 280 Madison Avenue.

"ONE PARK AVE." BUILDING

N. E. Cor. 32nd St.

Ass'd Val. $6,350,000

Built on the site of the old 4th Ave. Street Car Barns—an eyesore to the entire community until Henry Mandel erected his beautiful "ONE PARK AVE." building which has turned out to be one of the best paying properties in the city.

TEXTILE BLDG. 295 Fifth Avenue—From 30th St. to 31st Street.
As'd Val. $6,500,000
Devoted to carpet and textile trades.

NEW YORK FURNITURE EXCHANGE

206 Lexington Ave. 32nd St.—Through to 33rd Street.

Assessed Value $3,450,000

Home of New York's perpetual "Furniture Exhibition" where complete sample lines of the outstanding furniture manufacturers of the country are on display — 500 to 600 exhibitors.

EQUITABLE SOCIETY BUILDING 393 7th Ave.

Occupies entire block on 7th Ave. from 31st to 32nd Sts.

When the Equitable Life Assurance Society occupied 120 Broadway, they operated their business in the *most costly* building in the world at that time.

When they built their present imposing structure on 7th Avenue, in 1925, they moved their general headquarters to one of the most strikingly *beautiful* buildings in the world. It is valued at $16,000,000 and actually assessed at $14,500,000.

The "Equitable Life" continues to maintain downtown offices at the old address— 120 Broadway.

Ass'd Val....	$14,500,000
340 ft. high....	26 Floors
Rent Area, 740,000 sq. ft.	
Housing capacity..	8,500
Completed........	1925
Owners........	Equitable Society of U. S.
Arc. Starrett & Van Vleck	
Builder......	Thompson Starrett Co.

---

261 FIFTH AVENUE
S. E. Cor. 29th St.

Magnificent home of the Broadway National Bank & Trust Company, whose beautiful banking rooms occupy the ground floor.

Ass'd Val....	$5,000,000
332 ft. high....	28 Floors
Rent Area. 308,000 sq. ft.	
Housing capacity..	3,500
Completed........	1928
Owners....	5th Ave. & 29th St. Corp.
Archt....	Firm of ELY JACQUES KAHN
Bldr. Starrett Bros. Eken	
Agt. .Thoens-Flaunlacher	

152 MADISON AVENUE
N. W. Cor. 32nd St.

Cost....	Over a Million
260 ft. high....	26 Floors
Rent Area. 70,000 sq. ft.	
Housing capacity....	800
Completed........	1929
Owners....	152 Madison Ave. Corp.
Archt...	Henry I. Oser
Bldr. H. M. Wertzner Inc.	
Agents. .Cross & Brown	

Another Million-Dollar building on "Wonder Madison Avenue."

Madison Avenue is giving Fifth Avenue and Broadway close competition "Skyscraper Row!"

SEARS-ROEBUCK BUILDING
N. E. Cor. 31st St. & 9th Ave.

New York headquarters for the general eastern offices of Sears-Roebuck. Retail store in basement and ground floor. Offices of Mr. Julius Rosenwald Chairman of the Board, are here also.

Cost........	$2,500,000
213 ft. high....	17 Floors
Floor Area 335,000 sq. ft.	
Houses...........	4,000
Elevators...........	10
Year Built........	1931
Owner......	9th Ave. & 31st Corp.
Archt...	Frank S. Parker
Builder.....	G. Richard Davis & Co.
Agent...	Cross & Brown

GREELY SQUARE BUILDING
103 W. 31st St.— N. E. Cor. Sixth Ave.

Ass'd Val....	$2,375,000
304 ft. high....	25 Floors
Rent Area, 200,000 sq. ft.	
Housing...........	2,500
Completed........	1927
Owner....	101 W. 31st St. Corp.
Archt.....	Greenberg & Lucktag
Builder. .Langer & Baer	
Agent...........	Owners

Just south of the huge statue of Horace Greeley for whom this section was named.

PENNSYLVANIA TERMINAL
31st to 33rd Streets.   From Seventh to Eighth Avenues.

**IN MONEY
EXPENDED AND
WORK INVOLVED,
THE
PENN TERMINAL
IS SECOND ONLY
TO THE
PANAMA CANAL**

NEARLY
$80,000,000!

Few of the hundreds of thousands who pass through the enormous structure daily, have even an inkling of the tremendous task Alexander Johnson Cassett undertook when he conceived this colossal project.   Mr. Cassett (President of the great Pennsylvania System) did not live however to see the full realization of his wonderful dream, although his lifesized statue stands at the head of the main stairway—an imposing monument to his great vision and courage.

There is no more absorbing story in all Business history than that of the accomplishment of the Pennsylvania Railroad Co. in the completion of this stupendous undertaking as told in a beautifully illustrated 36 page booklet issued by the Publicity Department of the Pennsylvania. It is FREE— Send for it.

Magnificent Rotundo of the huge station extending nearly two full blocks through the building from 31st to 33rd St.

The picture at top of page shows the gigantic station building—devoted entirely to the needs and comfort of the traveling public.   A dozen pages this size would be required to convey any adequate idea of the magnitude, the grandeur or the efficient accommodation of the huge building with its various sub-levels, its 21,000 feet of train platforms, 21 tracks, etc., etc.   The picture may give an impression of "squattiness" in comparison with the dozens of towering skyscrapers in the surrounding vicinity and yet its cost would pay for "nearly half a mile" of them!

There are no offices in the Penn Terminal Building except a few in the upper floors—used solely for the administration of the station business itself. It will repay you well to send for the booklet to which reference is made, above.

The picture at the right illustrates how marvelously the Pennsylvania Station stimulated building in the Pennsylvania Zone. This air view is presented by the courtesy of the new Nelson Building —which it features.

KEY TO THE PICTURE

1-2 Penn Station & R R Yard	10-Gimbel Bros.
3- U. S. Post Office	11-Hotel McAlpin
4- Hotel New Yorker	12-Printers Craft
5- Hotel Gov. Clinton	13-Penn Office Bldg.
6- Equitable Life Bldg.	14-Hoover Bldg.
7- Hotel Pennsylvania	"EMPIRE STATE"
8- Macy Dept. Store	TOWER ONLY A
9- Saks Dept. Store	BLOCK BELOW
	HOTEL McALPIN

PRINTING CRAFTS BUILDING
461 Eighth Avenue—S. W. Cor. 34th Street.

This Enormous Building Was Erected
IN NINETEEN WEEKS!

Building proper has 22 floors, 2 basements and 2 penthouse floors, making 26 floors in all, 9,200 tons of steel, 40,000 lbs. of cement and 700,000 terra cotta blocks used in construction, 28 miles of piping used. Floor capacity, 240 lbs. per foot. Heaviest machinery can be safely installed; also, ideal for offices.

```
Ass'd Val......$4,250,000
350 ft. high.....26 Floors
Rent Area..600,000 sq. ft.
Housing capacity....7,000
Completed..........1915
Arch. & Bldrs..John A. and
                Edw. Larkin
```

Largest Building in America Devoted to Printing

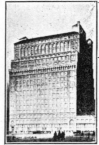

Home of J. C. Penney Department Stores of which there are 1,000

MASTER PRINTERS BLDG.
460 W. 34th Street.—

```
Cost.........$4,000,000
301 ft. high......22 Floors
Rent Area. 530,000 sq. ft.
Housing capacity....6,000
Completed..........1927
Building extends through
block to 33rd St.  Plot of
33,000 sq. ft.
```

J. C. PENNEY BUILDING
34th St.—Bet. 8th & 9th Ave.

```
Plot......46,000  sq. ft.
Ass'd Val......$4,250,000
227 ft. high.....20 Floors
Completed..........1925
Archt.. Schultze & Weaver
Builders....Starrett Bros.
Agents....Cross & Brown
```

HARDING BUILDING
370 W. 35th Street—

```
Owner does not wish
valuation to be given.
237 ft. high.....20 Floors
Rent Area..300,000 sq. ft.
Housing capacity....3,500
Archt..Storm & Rosenberg
Builders.Eisenberg & Settel
```

EVERY ONE OF THESE BUILDINGS IS A BUSINESS PALACE

EVERY ONE OF THESE BUILDINGS HOUSES THOUSANDS OF WORKERS

PENNSYLVANIA BUILDING
225 W. 34th Street—

```
Ass'd Val. over $4,000,000
274 ft. high......22 Floors
Rent Area..360,000 sq. ft.
Housing capacity....4,200
Completed..........1925
Owners.Jatison Const. Co.
Archt..Schwartz & Gross
Bldrs..Tishman Cons. Co.
```

LEFCOURT-MADISON BLDG.
20 W. 34th Street—

```
Ass'd Val......$3,575,000
241 ft. high.....21 Floors
Rent Area..290,000 sq. ft.
Housing capacity....3,200
Completed..........1926
Lefcourt Rlty. Hold. Corp.
```

180 MADISON BUILDING
S. W. Cor. 34th Street.

```
Ass'd Val......$3,000,000
297 ft. high......24 Floors
Rent Area..190,000 sq. ft.
Housing capacity....2,200
Owner......Jorose Corp.
Archt........H. I. Oser &
        Kilme & Corbett
Agent.....Cross & Brown
```

EMPIRE STATE BUILDING

350 Fifth Avenue—from 33rd to 34th Streets.

THE WORLD'S TALLEST BUILDING

TRULY—THE WONDER BUILDING OF THE WORLD.

The greatest office structure ever built by man. Words cannot describe this huge building—it must be *seen*!

Faces full block on Fifth Ave.—197 ft.
Faces 424 ft. on 33rd St.
Faces 424 ft. on 34th St.
Five entrances.
Main Fifth Ave. entrance—3 stories high.
64 latest type self-leveling elevators.
86 actual floors of offices.
2 basement and sub-basement floors.
14 floors in "mooring mast."

Counting basement and mooring-mast floors, the Empire State Building is:

102 FLOORS { 86 floors—offices, etc.
14 floors in tower.
2 sub-basement floors.

2,158,000 sq. ft. rentable area.
Housing capacity, 25,000 tenants.
Additional floating population of 40,000.
Could shelter 80,000 people.

1,250 FEET HIGH

Requires 1,250 employees to operate.
Covers a ground plot of 83,860 sq. feet.

COST $55,000,000

Architect, Shreve, Lamb & Harmon.
Builder, Starrett Bros. & Eken.

Some conception of the magnitude of this gigantic building may be had by noting the following figures giving totals of material used in its construction:—

60,000 tons of structural steel
730 tons of other types of steel
60,000 tons of stone
10,000 tons of marble
10,000,000 building brick
2,000,000 ft. of electric wiring
100 miles of piping
350,000 electric bulbs
6,000 windows

The Empire State Building caters to the highest type business organizations in the country. Only tenants of high standing (whose integrity is in keeping with the character of the building and its owners), are accepted.

HON. ALFRED E. SMITH, *Pres.*

Board of Directors

John J. Raskob   Pierre S. Dupont   Ellis P. Earl
August Heckscher Michael Friedsam* L. G. Kaufman

* Deceased.

Photo by Palmer Shannon

EIGHT ENORMOUS BUILDINGS CATERING LARGELY TO THE GARMENT INDUSTRY

"494 8th AVE." BLDG.	**HEROGEL BUILDING**	**HERALD SQUARE BUILDING**	**"36th & 37th ST. ARCADE" BUILDING**
S. W. Cor. 34th & Eighth Avenue	315 to 325 W. 36th St. —West of 8th Ave.	1350 Broadway—	520 Eighth Ave.—

	"494 8th AVE."	HEROGEL	HERALD SQUARE	"36th & 37th ST. ARCADE"
Ass'd Val	$1,130,000	$1,250,000	$3,900,000	$4,840,000
Height	250 ft. high	208 ft. high	316 ft. high	324 ft. high
Floors	24	19 floors	25 floors	27 floors
Rent Area	90,000 sq. ft.	140,000 sq. ft.	280,000 sq. ft.	400,000 sq. ft.
Housing	1,100	1,700	3,200	5,300
Built	1928	1926	1930	1926
Owner	Roher R.Es.Cor.	325 W. 36th St. Corp.	Herald Sq. Rlty. Corp.	36th & 4th Ave. Corp.
Archt.	Gronenberg & L.	Blum & Blum	Clinton & Russel	Schwartz & Gross
Builder	Paul Herring		G. Richard Davis	Frank & Frank
Agent	Rosenfeld & Herring	Geller & Durbin	On premises	A. L. Harris

HOOVER BUILDING	**LEFCOURT MARLBORO BUILDING**	**LEFCOURT EMPIRE**	**LEFCOURT STATE BUILDING**
505 Eighth Ave.— N. W. Cor. 35th St.	1351 Broadway—	989 9th Ave.— Near 36th St.	1375 Broadway—

	HOOVER	LEFCOURT MARLBORO	LEFCOURT EMPIRE	LEFCOURT STATE
Ass'd Val		$4,850,000	$890,000	$4,675,000
Height	277 ft. high	280 ft. high	236 ft. high	332 ft. high
Floors	26 floors	23 floors	21 floors	26 floors
Rent Area	237,000 sq. ft.	220,000 sq. ft.	100,000 sq. ft.	300,000 sq. ft.
Housing	2,700	2,500	1,200	3,500
Built	1930	1925	1927	1927
Archt.	Storm & Rosenberg	Geo. & Edw. Blum	Firm Ely Jacques Kahn	Firm of Ely Jacques Kahn
Bldr.	Eisenberg & Seller	Lefcourt Cons. Co.	Lefcourt Realty	Lefcourt Realty

NELSON TOWER

450 Seventh Ave.—N. W. Cor. 34th Street.
(205 West 34th Street.)

IN THE HEART OF THE "PENN ZONE," IN THE MIDST OF CLOTHING CENTER. ONLY A BLOCK FROM BROADWAY

The *latest* Seventh Ave. skyscraper.

An ideally appointed office and show-room building.

7th Ave. Subway express station in basement.

Small space, or entire floors of 15,000 square feet.

The Nelson Tower Building has a most imposing arcade lobby with expansive show windows.

Entrances on 7th Ave., 34th & 35th Sts.

Fifteen high speed Otis elevators of latest type.

Each floor has its own separate freight corridor.

A complete sprinkler system makes it possible to secure extremely low insurance rates.

The top 21 tower floors offer view, light, ventilation and comfort, second to no other building in New York. The close proximity of the "Tower" to Hotel New Yorker, the Pennsylvania, Gov. Clinton and Broadway Hotels (only a block or so distant) attracts thousands of out of town buyers, to the beautiful sun-lighted showrooms which are unquestionably the most ideal in the city.

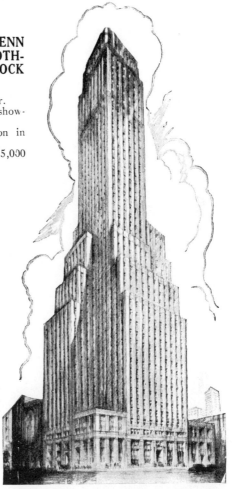

Estimated Cost	$8,000,000
560 ft. high	46 Floors
Rent Area	400,000 sq. ft.
Housing	4,500
Built	1931
Owner	450 Seventh Ave. Corp.
Archt	H. Craig Severance
Builder	Joseph E. Gilber Inc.
Agent	Michael P. Lipset & Co.

---

10 PARK AVENUE N. W. Cor. 34th Street.

See picture of completed building on page 56.

A business building, an apartment house, and a church all combined in one.

On July 1st, the picture below shows building in construction. On October 1st, it was almost ready for occupancy!

Owned by the Community Church of New York whose church home has occupied this valuable corner for many years past. Instead of including the church auditorium within the building, they have erected an annex in the rear—thus much increasing their revenue.

The ground floor is devoted to store rooms. The upper floors are for living quarters—two, three, and four room apartments.

Estimated cost of building $3,500,000. Height 320 ft. 29 Floors.

GARMENT CENTER CAPITOL
498 and 500 Seventh Ave., at 37th Street.

TWIN BUILDINGS

Cost of both Bldgs.
$13,500,000
Height:
North bldg..295 ft.
South bldg..257 ft.
Floors:
North bldg.......27
South bldg.......20
Rent..1,400,000 sq. ft.
Housing.......22,000
Owner......Garment Center Capitol, Inc.
Archt..........Mason
Builder. Mack Kanner
Agent.........Owners
Completed......1921

ONE MUST SEE THESE TWIN BUILDINGS TO GAIN ANY CONCEPTION OF THEIR IMMENSITY

They house 22,000?

SOUTH BUILDING—498 7th Ave.—S. W. Cor. 37thSt.	Annual Output of Clothing Over $200,000,000	NORTH BUILDING — 500 7th Ave.-N.W. Cor. 37th St.

This enormous project was conceived and carried through to achievement by a man who, thirty years or so ago, was a poor little Jewish boy who lived in Russia and came to America practically penniless. By sheer grit and the grasping of opportunity, he promoted and carried through to success this gigantic institution. 58 manufacturers of garments operate their business in these twin buildings, employing 22,000 workers.

519 EIGHTH AVENUE
S. W. Cor. 36th St.

Cost...............$3,500,000
303 ft. high............26 Floors
Rent Area.......240,000 sq. ft.
Housing...............2,700
Year Built..............1926
Owner...S. W. Cor. Realty Co.
Archt......Geo. & Edw. Blum
Builder...H. R. H. Cons. Co.
Agent...H. R. H. Mangmt. Co.

TWO MORE **GIGANTIC** BUILDINGS WHICH ADD PRESTIGE TO NEW YORK'S WONDERFUL MANUFACTURING DISTRICT KNOWN AS GARMENT CENTER.

HALF A MILLION WORKERS IN THE GARMENT AND ALLIED INDUSTRIES NOW LABOR IN MOST SANITARY SURROUNDINGS WITH GOOD LIGHT, GOOD AIR AND ALL MODERN CONVENIENCES.

NO MORE SWEAT SHOPS!

501 SEVENTH AVE. BLDG.
N. E. Cor. 37th Street.

Ass'd Val...............$3,825,000
257 ft. high............18 Floors
Rent Area........832,000 sq. ft.
Housing...............9,500
Year Built..............1924
Owner.......Timkin Realty Co.
Archt...Firm of E. Jacques Kahn
Builder...........Jos. E. Gilbert
Agent..........Chas. F. Noyes Co.

INTERNATIONAL COMBUSTION BUILDING

200 Madison Ave.—Extending full block on Madison Ave. from 35th to 36th Streets.

A $10,000,000 Property

ONE OF THE MOST MAGNIFICENT BUILDINGS OF THE SCORES OF NEW YORK'S REGAL BUSINESS AND RESIDENTIAL PALACES.

Marshall Field Co. of Chicago, (recognized as the largest mercantile house in the world) occupies the ground floor as their New York headquarters.

Many of the upper floors are tenanted by other large and nationally known business institutions of the highest type.

"200 Madison" is unique, in that the top and tower floors are equipped as living quarters—most regal apartments for executives and others having offices in the building, or for those who wish to live midtown.

A restful quiet is enjoyed by tenants of "200 Madison" that is most unusual in New York.

```
Ass'd Val....$7,750,000
404 ft. high....28 Floors
Rent Area, 500,000 sq. ft.
Housing..........5,500
Completed........1928
Owner....Houston Prop-
        erties Corp.
Archt.........Warren &
            Wetmore
Builder.......Dwight P.
            Robinson
Agt..Cross & Brown Co.
```

"101 WEST 37th STREET" BLDG.
N. W. Cor. 6th Avenue.

```
Ass'd Val.........$2,300,000
300 ft. high.........26 Floors
Rent Area....200,000 sq. ft.
Housing capacity.......2,300
Completed.............1926
Owner....636 Sixth Ave. Corp.
Archt....................Firm of
    ELY JACQUES KAHN
Builders...Shroder & Koppel
Agts..Shroder & Koppel Mgmt.
```

This beautiful building is not only equipped for manufacturing, but also for offices and show - rooms. Modern throughout.

AMERICAN UNION BANK BLDG.
265 W. 37th St.—N. E. Cor. 8th Ave.

The building is "Bricken Built," which is a guarantee of its high class construction and strong appeal to discriminating tenants of the clothing industry.

```
Ass'd Val.........$2,080,000
316 ft. high.........23 Floors
Completed.............1926
Owner..Bricken Properties Inc.
Archt.....Schwartz & Gross
Builder.....Bricken Cons. Co.
Agent..........S. M. Hirsch
```

215

534 EIGHTH AVE.
S. E. Cor. 37th Street

HIGH CLASS SHOW ROOM AND LOFT BUILDING FOR CLOAK AND DRESS MAKERS.

5 high speed elevators.
100% sprinkler system.
All modern conveniences, most desirably located.

"BRICKEN EIGHTH AVE." TOWER
545 Eight Avenue—
Between 37th and 38th Sts.

Ass'd Val...........$1,350,000
350 ft. high..........23 Floors
Completed...............1928
Owner.....Avrum Realty Corp.
Archt.....George & Edw. Blum
Builder.....Bricken Cons. Co.
Agent.............S. M. Hirsch

SHAMPAN BUILDING
553 Eighth Avenue—
S. W. Cor. 38th Street

Cost................$1,600,000
286 ft. high..........25 Floors
Rent Area.....158,000 sq. ft.
Housing capacity.........1,800
Completed...............1927
Owners...........Schuyler Co.
Archt.....Shampan & Shampan
Builder....Shampan & Shampan
Agent.....Sydney S. Stern, Inc.

THESE SIX ENORMOUS BUILDINGS HOUSE NEARLY 25,000 WORKERS—(Garment Center Section) CONSTITUTING A CITY IN THEMSELVES

FASHION CENTER BLDG.
525 Seventh Ave.—N. E. Cor. 38th Street (145 W. 38th St.)

Ass'd Val...........$4,300,000
301 ft. high..........22 Floors
Rent Area.....350,000 sq. ft.
Housing capacity.........4,200
Completed...............1925
Owner......Mil. Ctr. Bldg. Co.
Builder........Jos. M. Brody
Agent.............On premises

BRICKEN BROADWAY BUILDING
1385 Broadway—
S. W. Cor. 38th Street

Ass'd Val...........$4,655,000
334 ft. high..........24 Floors
Rent Area.....310,000 sq. ft.
Housing capacity.........3,600
Completed...............1926
Owner....Bricken Prop. Corp.
Archt......Schwartz & Gross
Builder....Bricken Cons. Co.
Agents.........S. M. Hirsh

LEFCOURT NORMANDY
1384 Broadway—
S. W. Cor. 38th Street

Ass'd Val...........$2,575,000
302 ft. high..........25 Floors
Rent Area.....180,000 sq. ft.
Housing.................2,100
Built...................1928
Archt......Bark & Djurup
Builder.....Lefcourt Cons. Co.

216

NAVARRE BUILDING

512 Seventh Ave.
S. W. Cor. 38th St.
(No. 200 to 210 W. 38th)

The Golden Triangle

Air view—showing how the "Navarre" dominates the Eighth Ave. sky line.

The Aladdin-like growth of New York's great clothing center has astounded the world. Between 35th and 40th on 7th Ave. and westward, there is an average density of 706 industrial firms to the square block. Six years ago it was less than 55!

The tremendous real estate development from Tudor City in East 42nd to Times Square, and then south thru the Pennsylvania zone and thence back diagonally to Tudor City, forms what is known as the "Golden Triangle" — within which is the Clothing Center.

The Navarre Building is the pride of this garment district —45 stories high, with every device for safety, comfort and conveniences that money and modern construction makes possible.

By reason of its commanding corner position, the building is made additionally cheerful by being sun and air flooded.

The Navarre is the outstanding giant of the Golden Triangle.

Value	$7,500,000
555 feet high	47 Floors
Rent area	900,000 sq. ft.
Housing	10,000
Completed	1930
Owners	Gar. Ctr. Cap., Inc.
Architects	Sugarman & Berger
Builders	Joseph Gilbert, Inc.
Agents	Owner

217

BAER BUILDING
575 Eighth Ave.—
N. W. Cor. 38th St.

LEFCOURT MANHATTAN
1412 Broadway—
N. E. Cor. 39th St.

Ass'd Val	$2,025,000
255 ft. high	23 Floors
Rent Area	220,000 sq. ft.
Houses	2,500
Year Built	1926
Owner	D. A. Schultz Inc.
Archt	Groenberg & Leuchtag
Agent	Adams & Co.

TWO BUILDINGS WHICH HAVE FEW SUPERIORS IN MAGNIFICENT APPOINTMENTS

Ass'd Val	$3,900,000
276 ft. high	22 Floors
Rent Area	275,000 sq. ft.
Houses	3,200
Year Built	1927
Archt	Geo. & Edw. Blum
Builder	Lefcourt Cons. Co.

THESE TWO LEXINGTON AVENUE BUILDINGS ARE BUT TWO SHORT BLOCKS FROM SEETHING 42nd STREET ON THE THREE CORNERS OF WHICH (ON LEXINGTON AVE.) ARE THE GIANT CHRYSLER, CHANIN, AND COMMODORE HOTEL BUILDINGS — A STONE'S THROW FROM WHICH IS THE MAMMOTH GRAYBAR BUILDING AND GRAND CENTRAL TERMINAL.

"370 LEX" and the "MOTT" not only have a most desirable location but offer all these advantages of modern construction at most attractive rentals.

370 LEXINGTON AVE. BLDG.
S. W. Cor. 41st Street

Ass'd Val	$3,800,000
322 ft. high	28 Floors
Rent Area	185,879 sq. ft.
Houses	2,200
Year Built	1930
Owner	368 Lex. Ave. Corp.
Archt	Lansiedel & Moore
Builder	Realty Managers Inc.
Agent	Cushman & Wakefield Inc.

MOTT BUILDING
369 Lexington Ave.—
Between 40th & 41st Streets.

Ass'd Val	$1,100,000
287 ft. high	26 Floors
Rent Area	66,000 sq. ft.
Houses	800
Year Built	1927
Owner	Wm. F. Chatlos
Archt	Jos. W. Northrop
Builder	Wm. F. Chatlos
Agent	Cross & Brown Co.

"530 SEVENTH AVE." BUILDING

S. W. Cor. 39th St.—Just a short block from Broadway.

A $6,000,000 GIANT—
AT THE NORTH END OF GARMENT CENTER

Both of these stupendous structures were erected by Louis Adler who has also recently built the imposing 50-story Continental Tower on Broadway at 41st St. (See page 229.) Mr. Adler has invested close to $15,000,000 in these three splendid buildings.

Ass'd Val	$4,400,000
405 ft. high	33 Floors
Rent Area	351,000 sq. ft.
Housing	4,200
Completed	1930
Owner	530 7th Ave. Corp.
Archt	Firm of Ely Jacques Kahn
Builder	Shroder & Koppel
Agent	L. Adler Realty Corp.

BUCHMAN & KAHN
ARCHITECTS

"550 SEVENTH AVENUE" BUILDING

N. W. Cor. 39th St.

This is a "sister" to the building just south (across the street) 530 7th Ave. shown on the right.

Both of these gigantic structures are Adler Buildings, representing a combined investment of close to $10,000,000.

Ass'd Val	$2,500,000
300 ft. high	25 Floors
Rent Area	200,000 sq. ft.
Housing	2,300
Completed	1924
Owner	Louis Adler Realty Co.
Archt	Firm of Ely Jacques Kahn
Builder	Shroder & Koppel
Agent	Owner

1400 BROADWAY

N. E. Cor. 38th St.—
Extends through to 39th Street.

LARGEST
DRESS BUILDING
IN THE WORLD

Headquarters for many of the leaders in the dress business whose aggregate business during 1931 will likely be:

$250,000,000

A recent survey indicates that an average of between 5,500 and 6,000 buyers visit "1400 Broadway" daily.

19 Elevators, large package chutes, entrances on 3 streets. Floors from 9,000 to 29,000 sq. ft.

Est'd Cost........	$8,000,000
436 ft. high........	40 Floors
Rent Area....	630,000 sq. ft.
Housing..............	7,500
Completed..............	1930
Owner....	Tonager Cons. Co.
Arct.Firm of Ely Jac. Kahn	
Bldr..	G. M. Weinstein & Co.
Agt....	Thoens & Flaunlacher

THE FIVE BUILDINGS BELOW are only "samples" of fully a *thousand* similar beautiful and modern new buildings that have been erected in Manhattan the past four or five years. From 15 to 18 stories yet not qualifying as skyscrapers. Many of these buildings cost upward of seven figures and would be "big structures" in any other city than New York.

SHAMPAN BLDG.
252 W. 37th St.—
West of 7th Ave.
Cost...... $1,600,000

Ass'd. $1,350,000
42 WEST 39th
Between 5th and
6th Avenues.

A'd Vl. $800,000
15 WEST 39th
West of 5th Ave.

A'd Vl. $720,000
150 WEST 28th
East of 7th Av.

Ass'd $1,000,000
55 WEST 39th
West of 5th Ave.

BRICKEN CASINO

1410 Broadway—S. E. Cor. 39th St.

BUILT ON THE SITE OF THE FAMOUS OLD CASINO THEATRE

The Old Casino

In the old days of Robson & Crane, Weber&Fields, Frank Daniels, Jimmie Powers, Della Fox, Lillian Russell, Anna Held, John Drew, Dave Warfield the Four Cohens and other great stage favorites of the gay nineties, the Casino including the famous "Casino Roof" was the "Big Noise" of New York's strenuous night life of those hilarious times.

The "Casino" was the deluxe home of musical comedy. The "Casino Roof" was supreme among music halls.

For a long time there has been a definite need in New York for a building where Department Store and Women's Specialty buyers could find under one roof, wholesalers of knit goods, negligees, hand bags, women's suits, infant wear and general accessories, and the Bricken Casino has been designed for such a center.

Est. Cost	$5,000,000
408 ft. high	38 Floors
Rent Area	270,000 sq. ft.
Houses	3,000
Year Built	1930
Owner	Bricken Cons. Co.
Archt	Firm of Ely Jacques Kahn
Builder	Bricken Cons. Co.
Agent	S. M. Hirsch & Co.

WHAT NEW YORK PAYS FOR PROTECTION

1931 Police protection...............Nearly $48,000,000
Protection from fire.............Nearly 23,000,000 (estimated)

New York spent in 1925 for its Police Department $33,307,609; and for its Fire Department, $18,303,282. The total sum spent for protection of life and property was $57,016,718, which was over 18 per cent of the entire amount thus spent by all the cities of the United States. Chicago's expenditures were $23,555,175.

The 1930 budget called for $46,661,000 for the Police Department and $20,183,432 for the Fire Department.—(Federal Census figures.)

"1440 BROADWAY BUILDING"

N. E. Cor. 40th St.— Through to 41st St.

Broadway Branch of the Bank of Manhattan Trust Co., and Broadway home of the Western Union Telegraph Co. where more business is done than in any other office in the entire chain of Western Union offices. Many large "LADIE'S WEAR" concerns have headquarters here also.

"1440 Broadway" is in the very center of New York's wonderful midtown development. Hundreds of millions have been invested in thousands of new midtown buildings.

40 skyscrapers (35 to 90 stories) and scores of other handsome b i g buildings h a v e been erected in midtown New York during the past half dozen years.

Ass'd Val	$7,300,000
293 ft. high	25 Floors
Elevators	22
Rent Area	500,000 sq. ft.
Plot	30,000 sq. ft.
Housing	7,500
Completed	1925
Owner	Broadway 40th St. Corp.
Arct., Starrett & Van Vleck	
Builder. S. S. Roth & Bros.	
Agt., Pease & Elliman, Inc.	

From the lobby on the ground floor to the "pent house" on top, there is "consideration for the tenant" manifested.

"1440 Broadway" is one of the best managed properties on the street—Pease & Elliman is the answer.

KNOX BLDG. and its neighbor "10 WEST 40th"

452 Fifth Ave.— S. W. Cor. 40th St.

Just west of Fifth Ave.

Ass'd at $1,250,000
The old Knox Building has for 34 years occupied this valuable corner as the home of the Knox hats. At the time erected it was considered one of Fifth Avenue's most beautiful business buildings. Agent, Cushman & Wakefield

"10 WEST 40th" was one of the early skyscrapers in the 42nd St. section.

265 ft. high	22 Floors
Year Built	1915
Archts	Starrett & Van Vleck
Builders	Geo. A. Fuller Co.

222

BRICKEN TEXTILE BUILDING

1441 Broadway, S. W. Cor. 40th St. Extends through to 7th Ave. (575-7th Ave.)

Built on the sight of the famous old Broadway Theatre which for nearly forty years served the public the best in amusement.

This gorgeous new Bricken Textile Building was designed to furnish to the textile trades the *best* in buildings. Neither money nor expense has been spared to make 1441 Broadway the most popular building in the textile field.

38 floors
Full block on 40th St.
Entrances at 1441 Broadway and 575 Seventh Ave.
Unobstructed light east, north, west
Floors, 5,500 to 18,500 sq. ft.
13 high speed elevators
Sprinklered
Low insurance rates
Midway between Grand Central and Pennsylvania Terminals
Center of hotel district
No better transportation facilities in the city
Building largely occupied by those in the textile trade

Estimated Cost	$5,500,000
421 ft. high	38 Floors
Rent Area	365,000 sq. ft.
Housing	4,300
Built	1929
Owners	Bricken Cons. Co.
Archt	Ely Jacques Kahn
Builders	Bricken Cons. Co.
Agents	S. M. Hirsch

(Continued from page 83)

By courtesy of the New York Sun we are permitted to show here four museums which are all within two squares of each other and which are well worth visiting.

Courtesy N. Y. Sun

GEOGRAPHICAL SOCIETY BLDG.
Broadway & 157th St.
Maps, books, drawings back to the 16th Century

MUSUEM OF THE AMERICAN INDIAN
Broadway & 155th St.
Nearly 2,000,000 exhibits

HISPANIC SOCIETY MUSEUM
156th St. & Broadway
Spanish Exhibit of 100,000 volumes
Spanish Library

NUMISMATIC MUSEUM
Broadway & 156th St.
Famous coin collection and 5000 volumes bearing on same.

"MURRAY HILL" BUILDING

Better known as "285 Madison" N. E. Cor. 40th St. and Madison Ave.

Located in the very heart of the uptown office and financial section—within a short distance of express and terminal transportation facilities.

Ass'd Val	$6,800,000
325 ft. high	27 Floors
Houses	2,700
Rent area	341,000 sq. ft.
Plot	22,000 Sq. Ft.
Completed	1925
Owner, Murray Hill Bldg. Co.
Arch	Rouse & Goldstone
Bldrs., Harby, Abrons & Melius
Agt., CROSS & BROWN CO.

AMERICAN RADIATOR BUILDING

40 W. 40th St. West of Fifth Ave. One of New York's Most Famous Buildings.

Plans drawn by one of New York's most noted architects, Mr. Raymond Hood, who was awarded the annual architectural prize in 1924 for graceful outlines and general superiority over all buildings of that year.

Ass'd Value	$1,700,000
337 ft. high	24 Floors
Rent area	76,000 sq. ft.
Housing	900
Built	1924
Owner. Titusville Bldg. Corp.
Architect	Raymond Hood
Builder Heggeman Harris Co.
Agent	Cross & Brown

"270 MADISON" BLDG.

S. W. Cor. 39th St.

Owned by Jacob Ruppert who also owns the "Yankees"—made famous by Babe Ruth.

Ass'd Val	$3,500,000
240 ft. high	22 Floors
Rent Area	192,000 sq. ft.
Housing	2200
Built	1924
Owner, J. Ruppert Realty Corp
Architect	Rouses & Goldstone
Bldr	Harby, Abrons & Melius
Agent	CROSS & BROWN

GILBERT BUILDING

205 W. 39th St.

HOME of the GREAT REAL ESTATE HOUSE OF CROSS & BROWN CO.

SCIENTIFIC AMERICAN BUILDING

24 W. 40th St. West of Fifth Ave.

Ass'd Value	$1,000,000
Height 264 ft.	19 Floors
Rent Area	60,000 sq. ft.
Housing	700
Built	1929
Owner	24 W. 40th St. Co.
Arch. Firm of Ely Jac. Kahn
Builder	I. Reis & Co.
Agent, Thoens & Flaunlacher

The home of the world-read publication SCIENTIFIC AMERICAN.

Ass'd Val	$2,200,000
202 ft. high	18 Floors
Rent Area	220,000 sq. ft.
Housing	2,500
Built	1923
Owner 205 W. 39th St. Corp.
Architect	Geo. Edw. Blum
Builder	Joseph E. Gilbert
Agent	Chas. Mortg. Co.

"22 EAST 40th" BLDG.

Also known as "277 Madison"
S. E. Cor. 40th St. and Madison Ave.

Built by the owners of the regal "International Combustion Building" at 200 Madison Ave.—(See page 215.)

RANKS WITH THE MOST ARISTOCRATIC OF ALL ARISTOCRATS CONSTITUTING THE ARISTOCRACY OF BUSINESS BUILDINGS

The following features tell the story.

Est. Cost...........$5,000,000
508 ft. high   45 Floors
Rent Area........244,000 sq. ft.
Housing...................2,800
Built......................1931
Owner, Houston Properties Corp.
Arch........Kenneth Franzhein
Builder..Dwight P. Robinson Co.
Agent.......**Cross & Brown Co.**

Sigurd Fischer

65 WEST 39th STREET BLDG.

N. E. Cor. 6th Ave.— only a block from Broadway.

Also known as "Millinery Center Building."

This huge building is in the heart of New York's great millinery center. Its beautiful bronze and marble lobby and general high class construction appeal strongly to the very best type of tenants. It has a most desirable location also.

Ass'd Val.....$2,400,000
300 ft. high....26 Floors
Rent Area.200,000 sq. ft.
Housing...........2,300
Built................1925
Owner 680 6th Ave. Corp
Arch. Firm of Ely Jac. Kahn
Bldr., Shroder & Koppel
Agent...Homer L. Pence

REAL ESTATE BOARD BLDG.

12 E. 41st St. nr. 5th Av.

Ass'd Val. $1,350,000
Built 1926

Headquarters and home of New York's great Real Estate Board of New York, Inc., with which is now merged the Building Managers and Owners Association of New York, Inc. Here is where meetings of the city's big real estate heads assemble to solve problems, enact regulations and guide the destinies of New York's big buildings and general real estate activities.

ARCHITECT'S BUILDINGS

101 Park Ave. with "L" addition with equal frontage on 41st St.

Ass'd Val. $3,250,000

This magnificent building houses a perpetual exhibition of everything modern, rich, novel and exquisite in building, equipping and furnishing a business building or home.

JOHNS-MANVILLE BLDG.

292 Madison Ave. with entrance at 21 E. 41st St.

```
Ass'd Val........$3,400,000
329 ft. high.......25 Floors
Rent Area...127,000 sq. ft.
Housing.............1,600
Built.................1924
Owner.......Jacob Ruppert
                 Realty Co.
Archt...Ludlow & Peabody
Builder.......Wm. Cranford
Agent...Cross & Brown Co.
```

FARMERS LOAN & TRUST BUILDING

245 Fifth Ave.—
S. E. Cor. 41st St.

```
Ass'd Val........$6,000,000
278 ft. high.......24 Floors
Rent Area...169,000 sq. ft.
Housing.............2,000
Built.................1926
Owner....475 5th Ave. Corp.
Archt..Starrett & Van Vleck
Builder. Rhinestein Cons. Co.
Agent..........On Premises
```

WORLD-TOWER BLDG.

40 W. 40th St. near 6th Ave.

— 30 STORIES —

ONE OF THE HIGHEST BUILDINGS IN THE WORLD, ON SO SMALL A PLOT OF GROUND.

Owned and built by Edward West Browning in 1915 and assessed at $1,700,000.

A GREAT INSTITUTION
AND THE MAN RESPONSIBLE FOR IT

Here is an excellent likeness of

HENRY TUDOR MASON
A man with a message.

Dynamic and aggressive, yet quiet, dignified, approachable. An idealist, but not a dreamer. Sound, practical, and thoroughly conversant with life. A success in whatever he undertakes.

Born in London, England, March 25th, 1882. Now a citizen of the United States.

226

10 EAST 40th BUILDING

10 East 40th Extending thru block to 39th St.
Only a few steps east of 5th Avenue

AN ARCHITECTURAL GEM

A STRUCTURE OF WHICH NEW YORK IS PROUD.

A. Tennyson Beals

Built on the highest ground of mid-town Manhattan . . . Towering above, and overlooking Fifth Ave. and Public Library . . . Thirty upper floors have daylight on all four sides . . . Entire floors (3,900 to 11,500 sq. ft.) or small offices as desired.

The disposition of many owners, architects and builders these days is to erect big buildings at the lowest possible cost consistent with safety and city building requirements. In consequence a great number of modern buildings are constructed with so little provision for the decorative, that the beauty and graceful outlines of "10 E. 40th" stand out in marked contrast.

"10 E. 40th" is just as attractive and appealing inside as it is outside. Ludlow & Peabody, the architects, are to be congratulated for having designed the plans for a building that is indeed a credit to the city.

The Henry Mandel Companies have their offices in "10 E. 40" and many New York firms nationally known call 10 E. 40 "home."

Ass'd Val.	$6,000,000
632 feet high	48 Floors
Rent Area	330,000 sq. ft.
Housing	3,800
Built	1928
Owner	10 E. 40th St. Corp.
Architect	Ludlow & Peabody
Builder	G. Richard Davis & Co.
Agent	Cross & Brown Co.

227

LEFCOURT COLONIAL BUILDING

41st St. and Madison Ave.

40 East 41st Street
295 Madison Avenue

ONE OF THE MOST BEAUTIFUL AND MOST ARTISTIC BUILDINGS IN ALL AMERICA

The LEFCOURT COLONIAL is only one of twelve magnificent Big Business Buildings the "LEFCOURT REALTY HOLDINGS", INC., have contributed to New York's growth—each of which represents millions in cost, and being the highest type business structures which money and modern methods can build.

OVER $125,000,000

is the amount the Lefcourt Company have already invested in building improvements. The LEFCOURT COLONIAL is de luxe throughout, and erected for highest type executives' offices. It has more windows per floor area than any other building of comparable size in all New York.

Cost	$5,500,000
454 feet high	45 Floors
Rent Area	265,000 sq. ft.
Housing	3,000
Year Built	1929
Architect	Chas. F. Moyer Co.

In addition to the twelve master buildings erected by the Lefcourt Company, shown in this book, they have built a score of 12- to 15-story buildings in various parts of the city—any one of which would be a credit to any community.

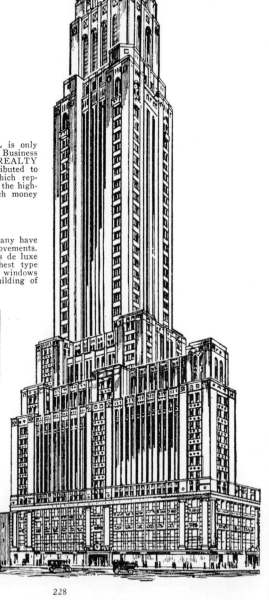

228

CONTINENTAL BUILDING
1450 Broadway, S. E. Cor. 41st Street

ANOTHER NEW BROADWAY GIANT. THE LAST WORD IN EVERYTHING THAT MEANS MODERN CONSTRUCTION, CONVENIENCE, COMFORT, SANITATION, LIGHT, VENTILATION, ETC.

The "Continental" has been built with the idea of *never having to tear it down*. The foundations have been laid to make it last *forever*, and every detail of the immense structure figured out so that it would be "good as new" fifty years hence, and in the event of any "new wrinkles" in buildings they could be immediately installed.

Everything about the huge structure from the 10 high speed, signal controlled, self leveling passenger elevators, all the way to tiled terraces with special hinged connecting doors, is the newest, latest and best. And to insure the tenants *service* that is the best, Cross & Brown were chosen to operate and manage the property, as they have won a splendid reputation for not only popularizing the buildings for which they act as managers but seem to know just where to find the right kind of tenants.

Cost	$6,000,000
524 feet high	45 Floors
Rent Area	300,000 sq. ft.
Housing	3,500
Built	1931
Owner	B'way Cont'l Corp.
Architect	Firm of Ely Jacques Kahn
Builder	Shroder & Koppel
Agent	Cross & Brown Co.

42ND STREET

The street that has astounded the world!

The street of a million daily paraders!

The street of throbbing business in day time and of unrestrained play at night—the gateway to New York's Great White Way.

25 years ago largely a residential section.

Today—a maelstrom of seething commercialism.

Ten years ago, 42nd Street gloried in its four "towering" sky-scrapers—The Times Square build-

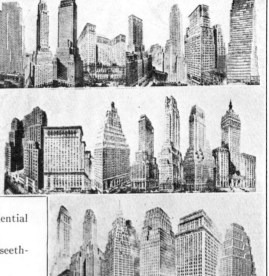

ing, Carbide and Carbon building, "501 Fifth Ave." and "50 East 42nd St." buildings. These beautiful structures were the pride of all Midtown Manhattan.

Today, over 50 *new* skyscrapers pierce the sky in this pulsating Midtown district, which tower so far above these former spires of the air that they appear like small, town buildings. 42nd Street at Broadway is reputed to be "the livest spot on earth!"

No street in the world can present such a picture! Tens of thousands of motor cars, hundreds of thousands of pedestrians and even a few horses, mill through its canyons of gigantic buildings hourly. Representatives of practically every nation of the globe, and those in every imaginable range of business from banker to newsboy, mix democratically with sightseers, pleasure seekers and the great army of the theatre district beginning at 42nd and Broadway.

25 years ago typical brown stone fronts—four and five story residential buildings lined both sides of 42nd Street.

At Fifth Avenue where the $15,-000,000 Public Library now stands, was the old Croton Reservoir (note picture on page 85) and at Broadway and Seventh Avenue the famous old Hammerstein Roof.

Yes—, 42nd Street has certainly changed!

NATIONAL CITY BANK'S MANHATTAN BLDG.

17 E. 42d at Madison Av.

Famed in days gone by as the old "Manhattan Hotel" at which so many members of European nobility made their home when visiting America. Altered in 1921 to a business building.

Ass'd Val.......$8,200,000
210 ft. high......19 Floors
Rent area...221,000 sq. ft.
Housing............2,500
Arc. McKim, Mead, White
Bldr..Geo. A. Fuller Co...

Photo by Chas. Latere Co.

GRAND CENTRAL TERMINAL

At 42nd St.—Head of Park Ave.

ONE OF THE SIGHTS OF THE WORLD!

THE GRAND CENTRAL

Largely responsible for New York's phenomenal "mid-town growth" and directly responsible for the tremendous "Grand Central Zone" development.

Nearly 100 Millions

have been spent by the great New York Central Railroad System in the twenty years they have been building and completing the colossal Grand Central Terminal and allied buildings.

AN AVERAGE OF CLOSE TO 500,000 PASS THRU THIS IMMENSE TERMINAL DAILY

None but expert engineers can form even a fair conception of the gigantic achievement in the construction of the Grand Central Terminal but from the first spade of dirt dug in excavation work to the completion of the work, hundreds of trains with their thousands of arriving and departing passengers were operated daily—right while building was actually in progress.

When the palatial New York Central Office Building at 230 Park Avenue (see page 247) was completed, an equally surprising miracle was performed—that of constructing a 34 story skyscraper on "STILTS"! This mammoth building was erected directly over a sub-area of trackage two blocks wide, and two levels *below* the street, thru which an average of 600 trains arrive or depart daily.

The Grand Central is the terminus of the New York Central and the New York, New Haven & Hartford Railways. It is the "home port" of many trains of world wide fame, such as the *20th Century Limited*, the *Lake Shore Limited, the Empire Express*.

The Grand Central Terminal covers 48 acres of land, and has two track levels below the street. 46,500,000 passengers were hauled in 1929.

Direct underground passageways lead to a number of the big buildings in the vicinity, including the Chanin, Pershing Square, Biltmore, Commodore, Roosevelt and even as far away as the Equitable Building on 45th Street at Madison Avenue.

Picture at right, shows the magnificent rotunda (ten stories high) with the bright rays of an afternoon sun flooding the enormous area.

NEWS BLDG.

220 East 42nd St.—Extends through
to 41st, with 10-story L to Second Av.
—125 feet frontage on 42nd St., 355
feet on 41st and 99 feet on Second Av.

HOME OF NEW YORK'S

DAILY NEWS

See page 74.

MOST COSTLY LOBBY IN THE WORLD

The entrance at 42nd Street leads
into a $200,000 Lobby where an im-
mense circular balcony overlooks a
spherical pit in which, revolving on a
huge angle-pivot, is an enormous
aluminum globe *of the world*, 12 feet
in diameter and weighing 4,000
pounds—constantly illuminated. The
beautiful mosaic balcony floor surrounding the globe, represents a giant
compass. The panels on the walls
constitute the most comprehensive
and instructive exhibits of meteoro-
logical and geographical charts, available to the public. Attendants and
guards explain everything.

One of the greatest points of interest in all New York to both visitor
and resident.

Cost	$10,000,000
476 ft. high	39 Floors
Rent Area	600,000 sq. ft.
Housing	6,500
Built	1930
Owner, News Syndicate Co. Inc.	
Archt	Jno. Howells & Raymond Hood
Builder	Hegeman Harris Co.
Agt., Douglas L. Elliman & Co.	

BARTHOLOMEW BUILDING

205 E. 42nd St.—Extends through block to 42nd Street.
Between 2nd and 3rd Avenues.

The Bartholomew ranks with the highest class buildings in
the city. Modern throughout. It houses many nationally
known concerns, such as the Remington-Rand Co. (who occupy
several complete floors), the Sinclair Oil Co., Union Carbide,
National Cash Register, and many others.

Ass'd Val	$5,400,000	Owners 42nd-3rd Ave. Corp.
Height 280 ft	22 Floors	Archt...Starrett & Van Vleck
Gound Plot	22,500 sq. ft.	Builder. Rheinstein Cons. Co.
Rent Area	335,000 sq. ft.	Agents.........CROSS &
Housing Capacity	4,000	BROWN CO.
Elevators	12	270 Madison Avenue
Year Built	1928	

CHRYSLER BUILDING

42nd St. to 43rd St.—Facing full block on Lexington Avenue
135 East 42nd St.   405 Lexington Ave.

AT TIME OF COMPLETION IN 1930, THE CHRYSLER WAS THE TALLEST OFFICE BUILDING IN THE WORLD

And in many other ways, it is most unique and original. Its modernistic architecture is almost sensational in its bizarre magnificence and regal splendor. The ten-story tower shines like polished silver and can be seen at a distance of over fifty miles on a clear day.

Cost of building (without land) close to $20,000,000
1,046 feet high ..77 Floors
Rent area ..850,000 sq. ft.
Housing capacity ..10,000
Year completed 1930
Owner Walter P. Chrysler Building Co.
Arch.......Wm. Van Alen
Bldr...Fred T. Ley & Co.
Agent....Brown Wheelock, Harris & Co.

THE CHRYSLER TOWER

Everyone living in New York and everyone visiting New York should see New York from the Chrysler Tower—1046 feet high!

Few appreciate the real immensity of New York and gain no true conception of its vastness unless they view the great panorama of the City from such dizzy height as that atop the Chrysler. The price is only 50 cents.

Note These Figures

20,961 tons of structural steel used in the Chrysler Building.
3,826,000 bricks.
446,000 tiles.
794,000 partition blocks.
750 miles electric wire.
10,000 electric bulbs.
35 miles of piping.
200 flights of stairs.
Nearly 5,000 windows.

Showing front and side views of the "CHRYSLER"

233

EARLY SKY SCRAPERS OF 42ND STREET

Wurts Bros.

M. P. C. Co.

CANDLER BLDG.
220 W. 42nd St. Just west of Broadway

Built from "nickels spent for the famous drink of "Asa Candler's" known as "Coca Cola."

Ass'd Val.. .$2,800,000
350 ft. high . .26 Floors
Built. 1920
Owner, Geo. G. Candler, Inc.
Arch., Shape & Brady
Bldr. . . . Cauldwell & Wingate

Photo by Byron

NEW YORK TIMES BLDG.
42nd St. & Broadway

For over 25 years one of the outstanding buildings of New York.

For over 20 years, the most famous tower of midtown New York.

Ass'd Val.. .$2,300,000
362 ft. high . .27 Floors
Completed. 1905
Owners.N.Y.Times Co.
Arch. Eidlitz & McK.
Bldrs.Geo.A.FullerCo.

BUSH TERMINAL
130 W. 42nd St.

Built on a small plot of land less than 60 feet wide. One of the world's tallest buildings on such a small lot.

Ass'd Val.. .$2,600,000
430 ft. high . .30 Floors
Area. . . .130,000 sq. ft.
Housing capacity 1,500
Built. 1918
Owner Bush Terminal
Archt. H. W. Corbett
Bldr.ThompsonStarrett
Agt. on premises

"33 WEST 42nd" BLDG.
OLD AEOLIAN HALL
Bet. 5th & 6th Aves.

For over twelve years the home of the nationally known Aeolian Co. In 1926 they built their present palatial home at Fifth Ave. and 54th St. See page 71. The entire lower floor and basement of above building is occupied by the F. W. Woolworth Co.

"50 EAST 42ND" ST. BLDG.
Cor. Madison Ave.

Conceded a "towering skyscraper" until the 53-story "Lincoln" was built half-way around it—26 stories higher! See page 119.

Ass'd Val.. .$4,350,000
27 Floors. . . . .
Rent. .104,000 sq. ft..
Completed. 1916
Owners.Nat Lloyds Co.
Bldrs. Russell B. Smith
Agts.. Cushman & W.

"501 FIFTH AVENUE" BLDG.
S. E. Cor. 42nd St.

When completed, recognized as one of the most magnificent buildings north of Wall Street, and it *STILL IS, TODAY*.

Val. $6,000,000
24 Floors. . . . .
Completed. 1917
Owners Oceanic Invst. Corp.
Arch. . Montague Flagg
Agent . . Marshall Clark

Wurts Bros.

LIGGETT BUILDING
41 E. 42nd St., N. E. Cor. Mad. Ave. Extends through to 43rd St.

One of the largest of the Liggett chain of drug stores 100% rented.
Ass'd Val. $8,825,000
313 feet high. . . . . . .23 Floors
Area. . . . . .325,000 sq. ft.
Housing capacity 4,000
Built. 1921
Owner, Louis K. Liggett Co.
Archt., Carrere-Hastings & Shreve
Bldr. . . . . . .Fred T. Ley & Co.
Agt. . . . . . . .Albert A. Ashforth

234

CHANIN BUILDING

Lexington Avenue—Full block from 41st to 42nd St.
122 E. 42nd St.   380 Lexington Ave.   125 E. 41st St.

THE FIRST OF THE GIANT SKY-SCRAPERS IN THE 42nd STREET AREA

Wurts Bros.

The exterior of the great Chanin Building is graceful and commanding,—the interior *gorgeous, u n i q u e,* original and *beautiful.*

The Chanin Bros. have startled all New York—not only with the magnitude of their operations in the building line during the past few years, but with the elegance, the superb splendor and yet perfect good taste in both design and beauty of construction.

Note these other Chanin Buildings—

Majestic Apartments
(page 281)
Century Apartments
(page 281)
Hotel Beacon
(page 146)
Biltmore Theatre
(page 68)
Lincoln Hotel
(page 128)
Also the Mansfield Theatre, Wallachs Theatre, etc.

Picture and short life sketch of Mr. Irwin Chanin —founder and head of the Chanin organizations — will be found on page 109.

Cost	$14,000,000
680 feet high	56 Floors
Ground Plot	22,000 sq. ft.
Rent Area	710,000 sq. ft.
Housing Capacity	8,000
Elevators	21
Year Built	1929
Owner	Chanin Realty Corp.
Arch.	Sloan & Robertson
Bldr.	Chanin Cons. Co.
Agent	Chanin Realty Co.

LINCOLN BULDING

60 East 42nd St.—55 E. 41st St.

Runs thru entire block with big "T" extension to Madison Ave.

ONE OF THE TEN LARGEST OFFICE BUILD-INGS IN THE WORLD. AN ARISTOCRAT AMONG N. Y. OFFICE BUILDINGS.

Cost—close to $25,000,000 . . . 54 floors . . . Nearly one million sq. ft. rentable space . . . Extends all the way thru from 42nd to 43rd . . . Also extensive wing with frontage on Madison Ave. . . . *In a location unsurpassed.*

AN ENTIRE CITY IN ONE BUILDING

The "Lincoln" houses over 12,000 workers—allowing each worker 80 square feet and more. The magnitude of this huge structure can be imagined by comparison with the "50 E. 42nd" Street building marked 5 in the picture. 50 E. 42nd at the time built, 15 years ago, was one of the tower-ing skyscrapers of the entire mid-town district.

Showing the Madison Avenue Exposure—half surrounding the "50 E. 42nd St." Bldg.

Ass'd Val.,
$20,500,000
680 ft. high.
54 floors
Rent area .. Nearly
1,000,000 sq. ft.
Housing 12,000
Completed 1930
Owner, Lincoln-42nd
St. Corp.
Arch.—
J. E. Carpenter &
Associates
Kenneth Norton
E. J. Willingte
Wm. Harmon Beers
Bldr. ... Dwight P.
Robinson & Co.,
Inc.
Agt. ...... Pease &
Elliman

KEY TO PICTURE
1—Lincoln Building
2—Old Belmont Hotel
(Demolished 1931)
3—Murray Hill Hotel
4—Vanderbilt Bldg.
5—50 East 42d
6—Union Carbide
Bldg.
7—Princeton Cornell
Club
8—Int. Natl. Combus-
tion Bldg.

This picture was taken March 4, 1930.
Showing the famous Belmont Hotel—now demolished.

500 FIFTH AVENUE BUILDING

N. W. Cor. 42nd St. and Fifth Ave.—

MIDWAY ON 42nd STREET—BETWEEN TIMES SQUARE AND GRAND CENTRAL

Traffic at this corner is said to be the most congested in the entire world. Those who "clock" crowds estimate that if all (who travel daily between Times Square and Grand Central) should drop a penny in a slot at some designated point, the sum at the end of the year would total enough to build *two* new Chrysler Buildings.—Shown on page 233.

"500 FIFTH AVE." offers every convenience that modern construction makes possible.

Ass'd Val	$8,500,000
Height	701 ft.
Number of Floors	60
Rentable Area	473,000
Housing Capacity	7,500
Year Built	1930
Owner	"500 Fifth Ave. Co."
Architect	Shreve Lamb & Harmon
Builder	C. T. Wells Co.
Agent of Bldg.	Walter J. Salmon

Continued from page 201

WHAT WOULD NEW YORK DO WITHOUT ELECTRICITY.

Electricity has changed the entire life of mankind.

It is declared that there are over 65,000 different uses for electricity.

What if electricity were to fail for 24 hours!

What would happen if elevators ceased to run, electric lights failed, street cars and subways stopped, pumping stations went dead, telephones became silent, heating and electric refrigeration plants went out of commission, etc., etc. The answer is our entire business and social life would be paralyzed.

This can never be the case in New York—the New York Edison Co., has arranged such stupendous emergency provisions that NEW YORK IS SAFE FROM SUCH A CATASTROPHE.—See Page 201.

SALMON TOWER

11 West 42nd St.
Extends thru block.
Opposite Bryant Park and
Public Library.

75 YEARS AGO!

Less than seventy-five
years ago, this section of
42nd Street was part of
the "common lands" of the
City of New York and
used as a cow pasture. The
area between 42nd and
43rd and Fifth and Sixth
Avenues was later sold by
the city at public auction
at prices as low as $200
and $300 a lot.

Since this p i c t u r e was
taken, the little 5 & 6
story buildings have been
taken down, and the 60
floor "501 FIFTH AVE."
bldg. now replaces them—
extending f r o m Salmon
Tower to the corner of
Fifth Ave.—see Page 237.

Ass'd Val.	$11,300,000
370 ft. high	32 Floors
Rent Area	567,000 sq. ft.
Housing Capacity	6,500
Year Built	1927
Owner	Walter J. Salmon
Arch.	York & Sawyer
Bldr.	Chas. T. Wills Inc.
Agent	Owner

BOWERY SAVINGS BANK BLDG.

110 E. 42nd St. near
Park Ave.

Ass'd Val.	$6,200,000
218 ft. high	20 Floors
Year Built	1923
Owner	Bowery Savings Bank
Arch.	York & Sawyer
Bldr.	Geo. A. Fuller Co.

PERSHING SQUARE BUILDING

100 E. 42nd St.
on Park Ave.

Ass'd Val.	$9,100,000
293 ft. high	27 Floors
Rent Area	444,871 sq. ft.
Housing Cap.	5,000
Year Built	1923
Owner	Persh. Sq. Bld. Corp.
Arch.	York & Sawyer—John Sloan
Bldr.	Chas. T. Wills, Inc.
Agent	Cushman & Wakefield, Inc.

McGRAW-HILL BUILDING

342 West 42nd St., Between 9th & 10th Avenues

THE BIG *GLASS* BUILDING, ONE OF THE BEST "DAY LIGHTED" STRUCTURES IN NEW YORK

Nothing could be more modern than this colossal new building of the Mc-Graw-Hill Publishing Co. Its outstanding features are the myriad glass windows and the extensive use of colored architectural terra cotta. All of the horizontal spandrels are blue-green, while the metal window frames and column casings (between the spandrels) are blue-black, presenting an artistically striking effect.

The McGraw-Hill Publishing Co. occupy the lower floors for the manufacturing and office needs of their own business. From the 16th floor up, offices are let to the public.

This is the first skyscraper erected on 42nd St. *West of Eighth Avenue.*

Only a few years ago, 42nd Street west of 9th Avenue was the gateway to New York's notorious "Hell's Kitchen" district where the most dangerous type of New York's criminals ruled the neighborhood and where life was unsafer than in the jungles of Africa—if the slightest incentive should prompt the denizens of the district to action. But under Mayor Walker's administration, Hell's Kitchen has been cleaned up and is now as safe as Fifth Avenue.

New York has a way of remedying *evils* in the same big way it does other things.

Cost	$6,500,000
488 ft. high	36 Floors
Rent area	580,000 sq. ft.
Ground area	28,000 sq. ft.
Housing	7,000
15 Elevators	
Completed	1931
Owner	342 W. 42nd St. Corp.
Arch.	Raymond Hood, Godley & Fouilhoux.
Bldr.	Starrett Bros. & Eken, Inc.
Agt.	Brown Wheelock H. & V.

NATIONAL ASSOCIATION BUILDING

25 W. 43rd St.   26 W. 44th St.
Extends through block.

Where the address *means*
something. Every applicant
for space carefully investigated.

Ass'd Val	$3,550,000
242 ft. high	23 Floors
Rent Area	251,000 sq. ft.
Housing Capacity	2,800
Year Built	1920
Ownr	Shelton Hdg. Corp.
Arct	Starrett & Van V.
Bldr	Fred T. Ley & Co.
Agent	On Premises

CRYSTAL BUILDING

801 Second Ave.—
S. W. Cor. 43rd St.

Half a block from 42nd.
Only a block from Tudor
City, only two blocks from
Grand Central Terminal,
and only three minutes
walk to the Chrysler, Chanin, Graybar, News, and
other towering skyscrapers.

KENT AUTOMATIC GARAGES

MIDTOWN BUILDING—209 E. 43rd St.—thru block to 44th St.
UPTOWN BUILDING—2 Columbus Ave. at 61st St.

ABOVE SHOWS
ARRANGE-
MENT OF CARS
ON EVERY
FLOOR.

GREATEST GARAGE BUILDINGS IN THE WORLD

EAST SIDE UNIT—209 E. 43rd—extends thru block to 44th St.
WEST SIDE UNIT—2 Columbus Ave. at 61st St.

MODERN MOTOR HOTELS

Most ideal garaging facilities ever offered motorists. Note picture
in center and see the floor layout of both buildings. High speed
double width elevators travel one floor per second. A motorist's car
is driven in a groove onto a "Kent Electric Parker" which tows
cars on and off elevators and eliminates any chance of scratching,
bumping or other damage. Makes possible the delivery of a car from
any of the 28 floors without loss of time in starting the motor.

Ass'd Val	$1,150,000
262 ft. high	23 Floors
Rent Area	115,000 sq. ft.
Housing Capacity	1,300
Year Built	1930
Owner	Crystal & Crystal
Archt	G. & E. Blum
Bldr	Crystal & Crystal
Agt	Cushman & Wakefield

**WHERE BUT IN NEW YORK, COULD SUCH INSTITUTIONS BE SUPPORTED?—JUST ANOTHER CON-
FIRMATION OF THE TRUISM THAT NEW YORK OFFERS GREATER INDUCEMENTS FOR EVERY PHASE
OF CONVENIENCE AND SATISFACTION THAN ANY CITY IN ALL THE UNIVERSE.**

PARAMOUNT BUILDING

Broadway — Full block from 43rd to 44th

Built on the site of the famous old Putnam Building

HOME OF THE FAMOUS PARAMOUNT THEATRE AND ONE OF NEW YORK'S MOST SPECTACULAR OFFICE BUILDINGS

The Paramount Building—facing Times Square, is located at not only one of New York's very busiest sections of the city in daytime, but at the very center of New York's most pulsating night life in the GREAT WHITE WAY.

"Shanleys" world-renowned cafe—dispensed hospitality for many years on the ground floor of the old Putnam Building which in 1926 was demolished to make place for this imperial structure.

The Paramount was erected by Famous Players-Lasky Corp. —producers of Paramount Pictures, as a permanent home for their organization (see page 69).

The clock in the tower is one of the largest in the world.

The "Observation tower" atop the building affords one of the most captivating views of any building in the city. Price—only 25c.

On page 117 is shown picture (including short life sketch) of Mr. Adolph Zukor, the man responsible for this magnificent building.

Ass'd Val....$15,100,000
455 ft. high....36 floors
Rent area.300,000 sq. ft.
Housing 3,500
Completed 1927
Owner ....Paramount B'way Corp.
Arch. C. W. & G. L. Rapp
Bldr., Thompson-Starrett
Agt. ....Owners

Lewis F. Nathan

COMMERCE BUILDING
153 E. 44th St., N. W. Cor. 3rd Ave.

THIRD AVENUE'S TALLEST SKYSCRAPER

Less than five years ago Third Avenue was off the map in any sense of "Big Business"—Miles of low buildings (from three to five or six stories) mostly occupied as small stores or living quarters, lined the street.

Today, there are from fifty to a hundred new modern structures of from fifteen to fifty stories within four blocks of the Commerce—a number of them between Third Avenue and East River.

AND THUS THE VASTNESS OF N. Y. GROWS VASTER.

```
Est. Cost............$3,000,000
443 ft. high..........38 Floors
Rent area........310,000 sq. ft.
Housing................3,500
Built.....................1931
Owner...Grand Cent. Const. Co.
Arch., Firm of Ely Jacques Kahn
Bldr.....Magoba Const. Co. Inc.
Arch..CROSS & BROWN CO.
```

LEFCOURT NATIONAL
521 Fifth Ave., N. E. Cor. 43rd St.

BUILT ON THE SITE FAMED AS THE HOME OF THE BEAUTIFUL OLD JEWISH SYNAGOGUE "BETH EMANUEL EL."

Notwithstanding the terrifying business depression in 1930, Fifth Avenue Property Holders had little to worry about.

In February 1931, the New York Times referred to a survey taken by John A. Daily of Cushman & Wakefield showing that in January—there were only 12 vacant store rooms in the entire length of the thoroughfare—a distance of over four miles!

John D. Rockefeller, Jr. (see page 249) is expending $250,000,000 on his Fifth Ave. Radio City.

Rentals are as high as $3,750 per front footage a year on Fifth Ave.

```
Ass'd Val............$9,750,000
490 ft. high..........40 Floors
Rent area.......260,000 sq. ft.
Housing................3,000
Completed..............1928
Arch...Shreve, Lamb & Harmon
Bldr........Lefcourt, Cons. Co.
```

GRAYBAR BUILDING

Also known as "420 Lexington Avenue" . . . Rear of building extends to Depew Place . . .
Located at 420 Lexington Avenue, head of 43rd St.

AT COMPLETION IN 1927, THE GRAYBAR WAS RECOGNIZED AS THE LARGEST OFFICE BUILDING IN THE WORLD

50 miles of freight trains would be required to move the materials used in this gigantic skyscraper (4,625 carloads) . . . Weight of materials approximately 200,000 tons . . . Over 10,000,000 bricks used in construction . . . 1,250,000 lineal feet of electric wire—over 235 miles! . . . 34 signal control elevators, with 27½ miles of cable.

The picture conveys but a faint impression of this huge structure, as it covers almost an entire square, extending back from Lexington Ave. to Depew Place—Grand Central Station.

Arrow points to the enormous *rear part* of structure

NEARLY 2,500 DIFFERENT NAMES ARE LISTED ON THE DIRECTORY BOARD IN LOBBY!

Some of these firms and institutions employ a very large number of workers. The housing capacity— 20,000.

```
Cost ......$21,000,000
400 ft. high
33 floors
34 elevators
Rent area—
1,050,000 sq. ft.
Ground area—
68,200 sq. ft.
Housing .......20,000
Completed ......1927
Owner, Eastern Offices
Arch., Sloan & Rob'son
Bldr...Todd, Robinson
& Todd Eng'n Corp.
```

Nothing in the building line could be more dignified, richer in regal splendor, or more modern in appointments. . . . Many of the nation's most prominent business firms have their headquarters in the GRAYBAR — a General Electric property.

Photo by Wurts Bros.

5 GRAND MIDTOWN BUILDINGS

CANADIAN PACIFIC BLDG.
342 Madison Avenue—
43rd to 44th Streets.

New York home of the great Canadian Pacific Railway. Fifth Church of Christ Science also has its home here.

```
Ass'd Val........$9,000,000
273 ft. high........23 Floors
Rent Area....359,525 sq. ft.
Housing Capacity......4,000
Built...................1921
Owner. Anahma Realty Corp.
Archt... Starrett & Van Vleck
Builder. .Wm. J. Taylor Co.
Agent.........Cushman &
             Wakefield, Inc.
```

BORDEN BUILDING
350 Madison Avenue—
44th to 45th Streets.

"350 Madison" is not only one of the best known addresses in the city but is another address signifying prestige.

```
Ass'd Val........$4,900,000
315 ft. high........25 Floors
Rent Area....200,000 sq. ft.
Housing Capacity......2,300
Year Built.............1921
Owner. .Borden Realty Corp.
Archt..........Firm of Ely
              Jacques Kahn
Bldr. .Cauldwell Wingate Co.
Agent.Wm. A. White & Sons
```

EQUITABLE TRUST CO.'S
UPTOWN BUILDING
347 Madison Ave.—Cor. 45th

Deluxe throughout—has a brightly lighted tiled subway passage to Grand Central Station—three blocks distant.

```
Ass'd Val........$3,950,000
257 ft. high........23 Floors
Rent Area....214,000 sq. ft.
Housing Capacity......2,400
Year Built.............1918
Owner. .347 Mad. Ave. Bld.
Archt....Warren & Wetmore
Builder, Todd Robertson Inc.
Agent....Todd & Robertson
```

VANDERBILT CONCOURSE
52 Vandervilt Ave.—40 E. 45th St.
S. W. Cor. 45th St.

```
Ass'd Val.....$2,100,000
266 ft. high....22 Floors
Rent Area.116,840 sq. ft.
Housing..........1,300
Year Built........1915
Owner........Anahma
           Realty Co.
Archt.......Carrere &
           Hastings
Builder.......Todd &
           Robertson
Agent......Cushman &
           Wakefield Inc.
```

August Heckscher, one of New York's great philanthropists, has his office on the top floor of this magnificent building.

CENTRAL ZONE BUILDING
305 E. 45th—Through to 46th St.

Between 2nd Ave. and East River, but only 3 blocks from Grand Central Terminal, the Chrysler, Chanin, etc.

```
Ass'd Val........$2,375,000
301 ft. high........26 Floors
Rent Area....180,000 sq. ft.
Ground Area..10,200 sq. ft.
Housing Capacity......2,500
Year Built.............1930
Owner...Magoba Cons. Co.
Archt.......Henry I. Oser
Builder...Magoba Cons. Co.
Agent.....Brown Wheelock
           H. V. Co.
```

244

"535 FIFTH AVE. BLDG.

N. E. Cor. 44th St.

PRINCIPAL HEADQUARTERS OF THE BANK OF THE UNITED STATES

Whose sensational failure the past year caused such general consternation in both banking and commercial circles.

Forty-fourth Street and Fifth Avenue for many years was the center of New York's gilded night life where the aristocracy of the city and wealthy out-of-towners patronized "Delmonico's" on the site of where "535 Fifth Avenue now stands.

Ass'd Val	$7,300,000
432 ft. high	38 Floors
Rent Area	240,000 sq. ft.
Housing	2,700
Completed	1926
Owner, Jacob Ruppert Realty Corp.	
Arch	H. Craig Severance
Bldr., G. Richardson Davis & Co.	
Agt	CROSS & BROWN CO.

FRED F. FRENCH FIFTH AVENUE BLDG.

551 Fifth Ave. N. E. Cor. 45th St.

Another Fred F. French building. (See pages 173, 270, 271, 276, etc.)

To those who appreciate beauty of construction, artistic decoration and masterful treatment in arrangement and equipment, this magnificent building will appeal strongly.

The Lobby is one of the most attractive in the city and the head offices of the Fred F. French Co. which occupy one of the upper floors are the very last word in refined elegance.—The Fred F. French Fifth Avenue building is one of the most popular business palaces in the entire mid-town section.

Ass'd Val	$8,600,000
428 ft. high	38 Floors
Rent Area	312,000 sq. ft.
Housing	3,500
Built	1927
Owner	"551 Fifth Ave., Inc."
Arch	French Co. & Sloan & Robertson
Bldr	Fred F. French Co.
Agt	Fred F. French Co.

GRAND CENTRAL PALACE

Full block on Lexington Ave. 46th to 47th

ONE OF THE MOST FAMOUS BUILDINGS IN ALL NEW YORK

Ass'd Val. $6,000,000
Floor 500,000 sq. ft.
Accommodates over 50,000 at one time
Built 1911

Home of most of New York's great annual industrial "shows" such as the Automobile Show, Power Show, Motor Boat Show, Chemical Show, etc. . . . In addition to big industrial expositions, there are many permanent displays. . . . On the top floor, Grantland Rice of the *Golfer Magazine* sponsors what is said to be the finest indoor golf course *anywhere*. . . ; On the tenth floor is the famous "Home Making Center" of New York, where a permanent exhibit of articles—items and matters pertaining to home life, fascinate tens of thousands of women weekly. . . . On the seventh floor, The Westinghouse Institute has a permanent exhibit, and "Clover Gardens" on the sixth floor is reputed to be the largest and most magnificent dancing hall in the country.

PARK-LEXINGTON BLD.

247 Park Ave.—46th to 47th St.
The "Park-Lex." is to the office world what Park Avenue Apartments are to home life

Ass'd Val....$5,275,000
271 ft. high....21 floors
Rentable..243,000 sq. ft.
Housing 3700
Completed 1923
Owners..Park Lex. Corp.
Arch. Warren & Wetmore
Bldrs. T. C. Desmond Co.
Agent ....Owner

POSTUM BUILDING

250 Park Ave.—from 46th to 47th Streets

The very atmosphere of this sumptuous building seems surcharged with the dignity of both the neighborhood and the high type tenancy.

General Foods Corp.
Crowell Pub. Co.
Chase Nat'l Bank
Wm. Henry Barnum & Co.
P. F. Collier & Sons
Thompson Starrett Co.
S. H. Thorp & Co.

Ass'd Val. $6,750,000
268 ft. high, 21 floors
Rentable,
.....355,000 sq. ft.
Housing 4,000
Completed 1925
Arch. Cross & Cross
Blder. Todd,
Robertson & Todd

Louis H. Dreyer

BOND BUILDING

29 W. 47th Street

Narrow and only 19 stories high but one of the most *unique* buildings in New York—in its bizarre modernistic construction reflecting great credit in the very able architects PRUITT & BROWN.

Rentable, 49,000 sq. ft.
Built 1931
Bldr., John Lowry, Inc.
Agts.,
Cushman & Wakefield

Byron Photo

"BUILDING LOAN" BUILDING

Cor. 44th and Lexington

Home of the Rail Road Cooperative Building & Loan Assn. which for 40 years has prospered —*now* the largest institution of its kind in America.

Ass'd Val....$1,550,000
Rentable, 64,215 sq. ft.
Built 1929
Arch., Ludlow Peabody
Blder.,
Geo. A. Fuller Co.
Agts.,
Cushman & Wakefield

NEW YORK CENTRAL BUILDING

230 Park Ave. Extending on 46th St. from Vanderbilt Ave. to Depew Place (in rear of Lexington Ave.) all the way thru to 45th St.

THE MOST REMARKABLE OFFICE BUILDING IN THE WORLD!

Built entirely on *"stilts"*, directly *over two tiers* of railroad tracks below!

Even the wonderful Hudson Bridge required no greater engineering skill to construct than was required to erect this huge pile of steel and masonry—directly over a hole in the ground (two to three blocks wide, and eight blocks long) sixty feet deep!

THE CONSTRUCTION OF THIS MAMMOTH BUILDING *OVER* THE GREAT CAVERN BENEATH IT IS ONE OF THE MOST REMARKABLE ENGINEERING ACHIEVEMENTS OF THE AGE.

Two driveways extend right thru the center of the building—one for uptown and the other for downtown traffic. These roads connect Park Ave. with the Elevated Concourse surrounding Grand Central Station,—extending south over the 42nd St. Viaduct into Lower Park Avenue.

The lobby, hallways, and offices of the New York Central Building are as gorgeous and magnificent as money and the latest designs of architects and skill of builders could make them.

Ass'd Val....$19,000,000
566 feet high..40 Floors
Rent Area 810,000 sq. ft.
Housing Capacity..9,000
Year Built.........1928
Owner N. Y. Cent. R. R.
Arch....Warren-Wetmore
Bldr., Jas. Stewart & Co.
Agent.......On premises

Courtesy N. Y. Central Lines

M. E. Hewitt Studio

"400 MADISON" BUILDING
47th to 48th Streets.

Located in the very midst of the most richly developed business and banking center of Upper Manhattan, (in which over a billion dollars has been recently invested.)

Ass'd Val	$3,300,000
278 ft. high	22 Floors
Rent Area	104,100 sq. ft.
Housing Capacity	1,200
Year Built	1929
Owner	G. L. Ohrstrom & Co.
Archt	H. Craig Severance
Builder	Geo. A. Fuller Co.

18 EAST 48th
Bet. 5th & Madison Aves.

Extra large windows and close together, giving an abundance of light. Small compact units of space have same conveniences as whole floors.

Ass'd Val	$1,650,000
257 ft. high	23 Floors
Year Built	1928
Ownr	Derwin Rlty. Corp.
Archt	L. A. Goldstone
Bldr	Gresham Con. Co.
Agt	Gresham Rlty. Co.

THE S. W. STRAUS BANK BUILDING
565 Fifth Avenue—N. E. Cor. 46th Street.

Regal home of the Straus Bank, famous all over the country for Straus Bonds, advertised thus:

"HAVE NEVER LOST A PENNY FOR THE INVESTOR"

Ass'd Val	$6,250,000
146 ft. high	13 Floors
Rent Area	150,000 sq. ft.
Housing Capacity	1,700
Year Built	1921
Owner	S. W. Straus Co.
Arct	Warren & Wetmore
Builder	Thompson Starrett Co.
Agent	Jno. A. Allen

NATIONAL JEWELERS BOARD OF TRADE BLDG.
22 W. 48th Street.—Just west of Fifth Avenue.

A "small building" compared with the 500 giant skyscrapers shown in this book. It has only 16 floors but this is the home of the National Jewelers Board of Trade and of interest to every jeweler in the country.

For many years the jewelery business was centered largely in Maiden Lane in lower New York. Although a number of large dealers will continue to remain in their old locations, the industry as a whole have been moving up in the "forties."

BARKIN BLDG.
64 W. 48th St.—Between 5th & 6th Avenues.

Ass'd Val	$1,200,000
210 ft. high	20 Floors
Rent Area	90,000 sq. ft.
Houses	1,200
Year Built	1926
Ownr	J. H. E. Rlty. Co.
Arct	G. & E. Blum
Agt	Byrne & Bowman

Ass'd Val	$925,000
173 ft. high	16 Floors
Rent Area	60,000 sq. ft.
Housing Capacity	900
Year Built	1925
Owner	26 W. 48th Corp.
Archt	I. Morgan & C. Glaser
Agent	Wm. B. Smith Co.

$250,000,000

THE GREATEST
BUILDING
PROJECT
IN WORLD
HISTORY

Photo by
Fairchild Aerial
Surveys, Inc.,
showing the start
in demolishing of 116
buildings on the three
double squares comprising
Radio City.

View on Sixth Avenue—
Taken from plaster model.

View from Fifth Avenue—
From architect's drawing.
By courtesy of New York TIMES.

RADIO CITY

Neither a word picture nor photograph can in any adequate way give a conception of the immensity of John D. Rockefeller, Jr.'s new "Radio City" development. When completed, Radio City can accommodate in excess of 150,000 people. . . . Although an entertainment center for motion pictures, vaudeville theatre, athletic events, and possibly grand opera, there will also be department stores, offices and many business institutions—including a bank. . . . There will be 7,000,000 square feet of space in the main buildings, which will be 68 *stories high*, and *surpass both the Empire State and Chrysler Buildings in size*—though not in height. . . . It will constitute the *greatest rental area* of any building enterprise in the world. . . . In addition to a giant structure of 68 stories, two other skyscrapers and various buildings of the group flanking them, will afford an additional usable area that brings the rentable space up to a figure that would house the entire business requirements (not including factories) of cities the size of Albany, N.Y., Richmond, Va., etc.

Work is progressing rapidly and excavations have progressed to the point that it will not be long before work in placing the steel girders will commence. Contracts involving $50,000,000 were let October 14th, 1931.

Some idea of the magnitude of this enormous undertaking may be gained by the following figures:

Buildings with an aggregate value of millions of dollars were *wrecked* to clear the ground for Radio City.

Radio City's main building will have nearly 70 elevators.

The main building will be over 700 feet in height

The National Broadcasting Co. will have 28 studios in the main building.

Buildings will have 28,000 windows, requiring quite an army of window washers to keep them clean.

Todd, Robinson & Todd Engineering Corp. are the builders.

The architects are: Corbett, Harrison & MacMurray-Raymond Hood, Godley & Fouilhoux and Reinhardt & Hofmeister Co.

William H. White & Co. are the renting agents.

Each of the three squares comprising Radio City are *double* squares, as from 5th to 6th Avenue, no street will be cut through which means that the three units of this architectural triumph will occupy six square city blocks. Every foot of this enormous area will be occupied by Radio City with one exception—and that is the northwest corner of 48th St. and 5th Ave. on which stands the Collegiate Church of St. Nicholas, whose trustees refused to consider any price for their property.

"444 MADISON" BUILDING

Extends full block on Madison from 49th to 50th Streets.

Designed as a center for one of the allied industries not yet sectionalized, this majestic building is ideally equipped for such.

A *concentration* of allied lines in *one* building or community, invariably stimulates both competition and sales, thus increasing profits. The clothing business of the city is centered in the 7th and 8th Avenues district, including Broadway from 34th to 42nd Streets. The furriers in the west "twenties", silk and textiles in the east "thirties", printing and publishing in the "forties", insurance around John St., etc. **DOUGLAS L. ELLIMAN & CO.** are agents.

Est. Cost	$3,750,000
453 ft. high	44 Floors
Rent Area	326,000 sq. ft.
Housing	3,750
Completed	1931
Owner	Paxon Realty Corp.
Arch	Kohn, Vitola & Knight
Bldr	Gresham Const. Co.
Agt. **DOUG. L. ELLIMAN & CO.**	

EMPIRE TRUST BUILDING

584 Fifth Ave., N. W. Cor. 47th St.

HOME OF ONE OF NEW YORK'S GREATEST BANKING HOUSES

Offices in this majestic building are especially desirable at this time. They are only a block removed from the great Radio Center on which Mr. John D. Rockefeller Jr. will spend $250,-000,000 and thus increase activities in this neighborhood. **CROSS & BROWN CO.** at 270 Madison Ave. are agents for the building and a letter will bring full particulars.

Ass'd Val	$5,400,000
438 ft. high	36 Floors
Rent Area	194,700 sq. ft.
Housing	2,200
Completed	1928
Owner	584 Fifth Ave. Corp.
Arch	Warren & Wetmore
Bldr	Max J. Kramer Co.
Agt	**CROSS & BROWN CO.**

R C A BUILDING
570 Lexington Ave., S. W. Cor. 51st Street

THIS IS THE NEW "RADIO CORPORATION OF AMERICA" BUILDING
ONE OF THE BEAUTIFUL NEW LEXINGTON AVE. TOWERS

This building was designed to harmonize with that of St. Bartholomew's Church adjoining. Both foyer and interior are boldly expressive of modern art at its finest. Four stone figures (each fifty feet in height) front each side of the tower—which is indisputably one of the most beautiful of the many skyscraping "spires" of the city.

Built in the midst of a *cluster* of skyscrapers. Only half a block to the south, is the 47-story Waldorf Astoria, and in the same immediate neighborhood is the Barbizon Club Tower, the Beverly, Shelton and Lexington Hotels, etc. Within half a mile or so of this R C A palace, there are 62 buildings—with an average housing capacity of from 3000 to 5000 workers (each building being a small city in itself) thus emphasizing the enormous population of which 570 Lexington Ave. is the Center.

The enterprising house of Cushman & Wakefield, Inc., are the renting and managing agents.

Est. Cost	$5,000,000
642 feet high	51 Floors
Rent Area	314,475 sq. ft.
Housing Capacity	3,500
Year Built	1931
Owner	Bartholomew Bldg. Corp.
Arch.	Cross & Cross
Bldr.	A. L. Hartridge Co.
Agent	Cushman & Wakefield, Inc.

The Radio Company of America has developed from a beginning so small that even the tales of the old Arabian Nights make us wonder what is in store for the future. Just a few years ago Radio was entirely unknown. Today it links the whole world together in an intimacy that enables New Yorkers to dance in their homes to the music of an orchestra playing in San Francisco.

What will the picture be fifty years hence? Note "NEW YORK IN 1981"
—Page 13.

COLUMBIA BROAD-CASTING BUILDING

485 Madison Avenue—
S. E. Cor. 52nd St.

The Columbia Broadcasting Company occupy five floors of *this superb building* for their own activities—(from 19th to 23rd floors) where they operate an elaborate research laboratory for the study of sound synchronization and experimental work in television. The balance of the building is rented to various industrial and professional firms.

Ass'd Val	$3,400,000
Height 320 ft	25 Floors
Rent Area	208,200 sq. ft.
Built	1930
Housing	2,500
Owner	Mad's 52nd St. Corp.
Archt	J. E. R. Carpenter
Builder	Dwight P. RobinsonCo.
Agent	J. H. Carpenter, Jr.

509 MADISON AVE.

S. W. Cor. 53rd St.

A strictly "Class" building that is not only a credit to Madison Avenue but to the entire uptown section.

Ass'd Val	$2,125,000
Floors	23
Rent Area	100,230 sq. ft.
Housing	1,200

Frederick Bradley

"5 EAST 57th" BUILDING

Just East of Fifth Ave. on 57th St.

57th St. is already famous for its many big and towering buildings but few are more beautiful in their graceful architectural lines than "5 East 57th."

Ass'd Val	$1,000,000
242 ft. high	23 Floors
Rent Area	87,000 sq. ft.
Housing	1,200
Completed	1927
Ownrs	W.A.A.Realty Co.
Archt	Emery Roth
Builders	Dwight P. Robinson & Co.

SONORA BUILDING

50 W. 57th St.—Just west of Fifth Ave.

One of the few buildings in this neighborhood permitting of light manufacturing (high class dressmaking, millinery, interior decorating, etc.), also splendidly adapted for show rooms and offices.

Alice Foote MacDougal's famous "Sevillia" Coffee Shop occupies the ground floor of this beautiful building.

Ass'd Val	$1,080,000
222 ft. high	18 Floors
Rent Area	50,000 sq. ft.
Housing	800
Completed	1927
Owner	57th St. Bldg.Co.
Builders	A. M. Eny Co.
Agent	Donald W. Brown

PROFESSIONAL BUILDING

57 West 57th St.—N. E. Cor. 6th Ave.

The dignity of this magnificent building is reflected by the high type clientele of its tenants, almost entirely professional men in the medical and dental field. Operating rooms with latest equipment and other modern appointments.

Ass'd Val	$1,500,000
212 ft. high	18 Floors
Rent Area	115,000 sq. ft.
Housing	1,500
Completed	1927
Owner	1022 6th Ave Corp
Archt	Warren & Wetmore
Builders	Dwight P. Robinson Co.
Agents	Pell & Co. See O. H. York

CURTIS-WRIGHT BUILDING

27 West 57th St.
bet. Fifth & Madison
HOME OF THE CURTIS-WRIGHT FLYING SERVICE.

Height	217 ft.
Floors	16
Area	42,000 sq. ft.
Housing	475
Completed	1923
Owners	Phipps Estate
Archt	Cross & Cross
Agent	Louis Carreau

252

"501 MADISON" BUILDING
N. E. Cor. 52nd St.

ANOTHER MADISON AVE. SKYSCRAPER

If the erection of skyscrapers continues, Madison Avenue will soon rival Fifth Avenue and Broadway. Already over fifty magnificent, towering or enormous modern structures have replaced the small office blocks or brown stone fronts of former days on this aristocratic old thoroughfare.

Est. Cost	$3,000,000
390 ft. high	34 Floors
Rent area	135,000 sq. ft.
Completed	1930
Owner	Rudo Realty Corp.
Arch	Kohn, Vitolo & Asso.
Bldr	Gresham, Con. Co.
Agt	Gresham Realty Co.

MADISON AVENUE IS BECOMING ONE OF NEW YORK'S MOST IMPORTANT AS WELL AS BEAUTIFUL STREETS

"HOTEL and INSTITUTE MART"
515 Madison Ave., N. E. Cor. 53rd St.

Permanent Exposition for equipment used in outfitting or operating hotels, cafes, schools, clubs, etc.

Fills a long felt need.

Center and *Headquarters* for *Manufacturers*, *Wholesalers* and *Retailers* of *Supplies* and *Equipment* for *Hotels*, *Cafes* and *Institutions*.

New York is at last to have a concentrated mart where buyers of equipment and supplies required by hotels and institutions can come from all over the country and transact all their business under one roof.

Estimated Cost	$4,000,000
482 ft. high	45 Floors
Rent area	260,000 sq. ft.
Housing	3,000
Completed	1931
Owner	Carpenter Madison Corp.
Arch	J. E. R. Carpenter
Bldr	Dwight P. Robinson & Co.
Agt	John H. Carpenter, Jr. Inc.

HECKSCHER BLDG.
S. W. Cor. 57th St. & 5th Ave.

PIONEER SKYSCRAPER OF UPPER FIFTH AVENUE

When Mr. Heckscher built this magnificent building, nine years ago, it was the tallest building above 42nd Street. It is yet one of the most beautiful. It was designed as a concentrated buying center for women—with attractive shops and display rooms of both retail and wholesale establishments. Cushman & Wakefield, Inc., Renting & Managing Agents.

Ass'd Val.	$7,800,000
310 ft. high	26 floors
Rent area	259,195 sq. ft.
Housing	2,800
Bldrs., Geo. Backer Const. Co.	
Owners, Anahona Realty Corp.	
Arch.	Warren & Wetmore
Completed	1922
Agts.	Cushman & Wakefield

PLAZA BUILDING
625 Madison Ave.

Ass'd Val.	$6,800,000
123 ft. high	12 floors
Area	315,000
Housing	3,300
Completed	1930
Owners Madis Realty	
Arch.	Sloan & Rob
Bldrs. Shroder & Kop	
Agts. Brown Wheelock	

LEY BUILDING
578 Madison Ave.
S. W. Cor. 57th St.

Every "new wrinkle" gained from a long and extensive experience in construction work will be found in the "Ley" Bldg.

Ass'd Val.	$2,250,000
Height	234 ft.
22 floors	4 elevators
Rent Area	107,000 sq. ft.
Ground area, 6,595 sq. ft.	
Housing	1,500
Completed	1926
Arch.	Don Barber
Bldr.	Fred T. Ley Co.

NEW YORK TRUST CO.
N. E. Cor. Fifth Ave. & 57th St.

ONE OF THE MOST REGAL BUILDINGS IN ALL THE COUNTRY

Fifteen Stories of scintillating white Georgian marble, built in the modern "set-back" vogue, classic design. This exquisite edifice is recognized by both architects and builders as one of the most "correct" buildings in all the country.

The Banking room occupies the ground floor and is sumptuous in every meaning of the term. Extending from the marble wainscoting, thirteen feet to the ceiling, are mural paintings depicting Manhattan's shipping since Hendryck Hudson first sailed up the river three hundred years ago.

231 ft. high	15 floors	Visitors, as well as those living in the city, should call and view this magnificent banking room.
Area	40,000 sq. ft.	
Housing	800	
Completed	1930	
Owners	N. Y. Trust Co.	
Arch.	Cross & Cross	
Bldrs.,	Thompson-Starrett	
Agts.	Brown Wheel, H. & V.	

FULLER BUILDING

597 Madison Ave., N. E. Cor. 57th St.

HOME OF THE GEORGE A. FULLER CONSTRUCTION COMPANY, ONE OF THE OLDEST, AS WELL AS ONE OF THE MOST SUCCESSFUL CONTRACTING AND BUILDING ORGANIZATIONS IN THE COUNTRY

The Fuller Building is most striking. Its first six stories are of black Swedish granite surmounted by 13 stories in light color with various set backs serving as a base for the 21-story tower shaft, rising in the sky to a height of 491 feet. The beautifully carved four-story Rockwood stone entrance leads into one of the most beautiful of lobbies, from which 10 elevators serve patrons.

Ass'd Val.	$5,800,000
Height	491 ft.
40 Floors	10 Elevators
Rent area	22,400 sq. ft.
Housing	2,400
Completed	1929
Owner	Geo. A. Fuller Realty Corp.
Arch.	Walker & Gillette
Bldr.	Geo. A. Fuller Corp.

Not only in New York City, but in Chicago and all parts of the country—even in Japan and other parts of the world, enormous steel structures stand as lasting monuments to the enterprise, skill and prestige of this internationally known firm of builders.

Among the hundreds of "Fuller Built" buildings erected in New York are the following outstanding or famous ones:

Flatiron Bldg.
Whitehall Bldg.
Times Square Bldg.
Trinity & U. S. Realty Bldgs.
Consolidated Gas Bldg.
Broad Exchange Bldg.
42 Broadway Bldg.
170 Broadway Bldg.
Hudson Terminal
10 West 40th St. Bldg.
Pennsylvania Station
Munson Bldg.
Fred. F. French Bldg.
Fuller Bldg.
400 Madison Ave. Bldg.
U. S. Post Office, 8th Ave.
Bowery Savings Bank
City Bank Farmers Trust
Biltmore Hotel
Commodore Hotel
Plaza Hotel
Savoy-Plaza Hotel
Pierre Hotel
Pennsylvania Hotel
AND SCORES OF OTHERS.

GENERAL MOTORS BLDG.

1775 Broadway
251 W. 57th St.
Covers entire square. From
Broadway to 8th Ave. between
57th and 58th Streets.
**IN THE HEART OF
NEW YORK'S NEW MAJOR
TRANSIT CENTER**
One of the most magnificent
buildings in America.

Ass'd Val. $9,000,000
300 ft. high.......27 Floors
Rent Area....525,000 sq. ft.
Housing Capacity 6,000
Year Built 1927
Owner...Hoffman Bldg., Inc
Archts......Shreve Lamb &
Harmon
Bldr. G. Richard Davis & Co.
Agent.....Hugo R. Hoffman

SETAY BLDG.

also known as
1776 BROADWAY
N. E. Cor. 57th St.
Many of the world's
largest corporations
have offices here.

Ass'd Val. $1,045,000
301 ft. high 25 Floors
Rent Area...117,900
Housing Cap...1,600
Year Built 1928
Owner, Setay Realty,
Inc.
Archt. G. & E. Blum
Bldr. Jos. E. Gilbert
Agent ......Owners

FISK BUILDING

250 W. 57th St.
S. W. Cor. Broadway
Extends thru block to 8th Ave.
Few buildings in New York have
a more ideal arrangement of day-
lighted offices.

Ass'd Val. $5,900,000
318 ft. high...........26 Floors
Rent Area........343,000 sq. ft.
Housing Capacity..........4,500
Year Built 1921
Owner.."1767 B'dway Co. Inc."
Archts.....Carrere & Hastings &
Shreve Lamb & Harmon
Bldr....Fred T. Ley & Co. Inc.
Agent........Cross & Brown Co.

MANUFACTURERS TRUST BUILDING

1819 Broadway at 59th St.
COLUMBUS CIRCLE

Ass'd Val. 2,150,000
270 ft. high.........25 Floors
Rent Area......137,000 sq. ft.
Housing Capacity 1,500
Year Built 1921
Owner..Gotham Nat. Bld. Inc.
Archt..Summerfield & Steckler
Bldr...,Gotham Nat. Bld. Co.
Agt Cushman & Wakefield Inc.

U. S. RUBBER CO'S BUILDING

1790 Broadway, Cor. 57th

Ass'd Val.....$2,200,000
292 ft. high....21 Floors
Rent Area 142,000 sq. ft.
Housing Capacity...1,700
Year Built 1912
Owner..U. S. Rubber Co.
Archt. Carrere & Hastings
Bldr. ....Norcross Bros.
Agt...Cross & Brown Co.

MANHATTAN LIFE BUILDING

21 E. 60th
654 Madison Ave.

Ass'd Val. ...$2,150,000
290 ft. high....25 Floors
Rent Area 160,000 sq. ft.
Housing Capacity...1,800
Year Built 1928
Owner, Jeremiah Milbank
Archt....Wm. L. Rouse
Bldr...Shroder & Koppel
Agent ..Brown Wheelock
H. V. Co.

SQUIBB BUILDING

745 Fifth Ave., S. E. Cor. 58th St.

A $10,000,000 BUSINESS PALACE OVERLOOKING CENTRAL PARK PLAZA
A SHOW BUILDING ON THE MOST FAMOUS AVENUE OF THE WORLD!

Opposite the "Plaza Fountain" and beautiful Central Park with its giant shade trees, winding paths and grassy lawns.

Ass'd Val.	$8,300,000
451 ft. high	38 Floors
Rent area	390,000 sq. ft.
Housing	4,500
Built	1930
Owner	Abenad Realty Co.
Arch.	Firm of Ely Jacques Kahn
Builders	Shroder & Koppel
Agent	Cross & Brown

A MONUMENT TO MODERN CONSTRUCTION

Faces 120 feet on Fifth Ave. and 200 feet on 58th St.

White marble and b r o n z e, blended in most artistic effect on the exterior, reflect the gorgeous interior foyer and hallways.

"The Squibb" has many tenants of national importance, and is conceded to be one of the most beautiful structures of the city. It has an unrivaled location, an address signifying prestige, and r a n k s a s O N E O F N E W YORK'S GREATEST BUILD-INGS.

Continued from page 244

ALBANO BUILDING

305 E. 45th extends thru block to 46th

One of the many new million dollar buildings erected in the "East Forties."

BROOKLYN

A New York wag claims that history is all wrong in reference to the amount Peter Minuet paid the Indians for the purchase of New York. He insists the amount was *more* than the $24.00 and history states that investigation and research proves that old Pete actually paid $24.30— the additional 30¢ being for Brooklyn!

"But even at that," he adds, "Pete made a fairly good bargain."

Brooklyn has for many years been facetiously referred to as the "dormitory" of New York. But if one will drive through the miles of Brooklyn's business and factory sections and then continue through its

BROOKLYN BOROUGH HALL

Facing Borough Hall Park at junction of Fulton and Court Sts. Built of white marble, Ionic style.
Appraised value, $8,800,000.

parks and magnificent residential avenues and note the palatial skyscrapers and regal homes of many of Brooklyn's aristocratic old families, one will wonder how referring to Brooklyn as a "dormitory" is in any way apropos.

On the contrary, Brooklyn has sustained the largest hotel in all eastern America (see page 150), one of the most powerful Savings Banks in the country, the livest Chamber of Commerce of any city east of Los Angeles, the largest docking and terminal station in America, and produces the greatest amount of manufactured products. In fact, Brooklyn furnishes the bulk of the population which makes it possible for greater New York to boast of being the largest city in the world!

Yes, the Honorable Peter Minuet proved himself the greatest trader in world history if he paid only 30¢ for Brooklyn.

Brooklyn is separated from Manhattan by the East River and connected with Manhattan by three bridges and three rapid transit tunnels.

Brooklyn has 10 trunk line railroads and, surrounded by water on three sides, enjoys important maritime advantages. Its shore front equals 201.5 miles. It has 187 piers, accommodating 700 ocean liners; 66 steamship companies operate on the water front with sailings to 200 ports of call in foreign countries. It is estimated that 55% of the freight passing through the Port of New York is handled in Brooklyn.

Brooklyn's population is estimated at considerably over 2,750,000, being unable to secure absolutely accurate statistics of recent compilation.

Brooklyn leads in importation, distribution and refining of sugar; it ranks first as a coffee importing and distributing center; it is the leading style center for women's shoes, and the annual value of shoe products exceeds all other centers. Banks, including Branches (1928): Savings, 35; National, 53; State, 50; Trust, 38; Private, 5; Savings Bank Depositors (1928), 1,203,583; Savings Bank Deposits (1928), $1,040,620,346.

Brooklyn has its own Brooklyn Chamber of Commerce, at 66 Court Street, with a membership of 6,868 (October, 1929). See opposite page.

Photo by Crossman

COPLEY PLAZA OF BROOKLYN

72 Underhill Ave.—N. E. Cor. Eastern Parkway. Cost, $1,500,000.

ST. REMO OF BROOKLYN

Near the corner of Eastern Parkway and Underhill Avenue.
Cost, $2,200,000.

The two buildings at right show the type of magnificent apartment houses being built in Brooklyn. Plans for these two buildings were drawn by one of Brooklyn's outstanding architectural firms, Shampan & Shampan.

BROOKLYN CHAMBER OF COMMERCE BLDG.

66 Court St. N. W. Cor. Livingston St. Facing Borough Hall Park, Bklyn.

VISITORS ARE ALWAYS WELCOME TO
BROOKLYN'S CHAMBER OF COMMERCE

Most cities of prominence thruout our great nation owe their position and prestige among the outstanding municipalities of the country, to the aggressive efforts of their respective Chambers of Commerce. These live organizations— comprised of up-to-date citizens of the community banded together, exploit the advantages offered by their particular city, to prospective residents, manufacturers, investors, etc., of other localities, in the hope of influencing them to locate with them and become a part of their commonwealth.

Nearly every civic center in the country sufficiently large to be classed as a city, now has a Chamber of Commerce. The more aggressively these organizations extol the virtues or attractions of their particular community, the more likely they are to grow.

The very beautiful building shown here is the home of the Brooklyn Chamber of Commerce—

ONE OF THE MOST ALERT
CIVIC ORGANIZATIONS
IN THE ENTIRE
U. S. A.—

With an annual income of $200,-000 and officered by hustlers who are firm believers in *results*, this dynamic organization has put Brooklyn very much on the map the last few years. This Chamber of Commerce has not only changed Brooklyn's Skyline, but has metamorphosed an easy-going overgrown *town* into a live up-to-date cosmopolitan *city* with residential, factory and business sections, all developing at a rate that is making the entire country sit up and take notice.

WATCH
BROOKLYN
GROW

COURT-REMSEN BUILDING—Brooklyn

26 Court St., Cor. Remsen St., Facing Borough Hall Park

No better indication of the great growth of Brooklyn can be offered than the registration figures in the last presidential election. Brooklyn's voters outstripped even Manhattan *by over 66,700!*

A leading political authority predicts that Brooklyn bids fair to acquire greater political power than *any one single community* in the nation. With its tremendous areas yet to be developed, enormous fortunes are in store for those who have the vision and enterprise to grasp the unquestioned opportunities which a returning prosperity is making possible.

THIS MODERN BUSINESS PALACE IS ONE OF BROOKLYN'S OUTSTANDING SKYSCRAPERS— FACING BOROUGH HALL SQUARE

Borough Hall Square is to Brooklyn, what Times Square is to New York—the center of both business and "bright light" activities. "26 Court" or the "Court-Remsen" building, as it is variously called, is right in the heart of the Borough Hall section. Its 30 stories emphasize Brooklyn's rapidly growing skyline.

No building in Brooklyn has a more imposing entrance and foyer. 9 high speed elevators and roomy corridors make access to offices "quick and snappy". Plenty of natural daylight, installation of modern efficiency devices and most courteous management, all combine in attracting tenants who desire space in a strictly modern class A office building.

Ass'd Val.	$3,750,000
340 feet high	30 Floors
Rent area	200,000 sq. ft.
Elevators	9
Housing	2,200
Completed	1926
Owner	Bricken Const. Co.
Arch.	Schwartz & Gross
Bldr.	Bricken Const. Co.
Agt.	A. Geo. Golden Co.

COURT-MONTAGUE BUILDING, *BROOKLYN*
16 Court St., Cor. Montague St.

Few Manhattan buildings present a more imposing or commanding front than this palatial skyscraper of Brooklyn's Borough Hall district.

Towers 28 stories above the busiest section of Brooklyn and faces Borough Hall Park where all Interboro, Rapid Transit, and Brooklyn Metropolitan Transit Subway lines center (also elevated and surface lines). There is no location in Brooklyn with such complete transportation facilities, and few buildings anywhere with more natural daylight, better ventilation or more commanding view.

Albert Rothschild

AN OUTSTANDING ARISTOCRAT AMONG BROOKLYN'S "CLASS" BUILDINGS

The "Court-Montague" is the home of many of Brooklyn's most prominent business institutions that have their headquarters in this magnificent structure. Here practically every modern convenience, and provision for comfort and efficient conduct of business was foreseen and provided.

Offices (either single or suite) range in size from a few square feet up to entire floors. All space is airy, with abundant natural daylight. Admirably arranged, "16 Court" (as the building is frequently called), is one of Brooklyn's most popular addresses.

Brooklyn is rapidly following the pace set by Manhattan in the erection of regal skyscrapers and the "Court-Montague" is a credit to all Greater New York.

Ass'd Val. $3,750,000	
425 feet high..........40 Floors	
Rentable...nearly 300,000 sq. ft.	

BUSH TERMINAL—Brooklyn

43rd Street—and contiguous territory for a number of blocks along East River

Over $50,000,000 invested in this enormous project— conceived by Irving T. Bush, exploited by Irving T. Bush, and engineered to its p r e s e n t outstanding position a m o n g w o r l d terminals by Irving T. Bush.

Photo by Brown Bros.

A MASTERFUL ACHIEVEMENT

Bush Terminal is not merely an aggregation of docks and warehouses for the handling of freight, it is a combination of everything that tends to stimulate world commerce. It might be termed a national clearing house for manufacturers and others facing the problems of overproduction, excessive costs in exportation, location of foreign markets, etc. The International Bush Service provides for distribution, financing of shipments in both transit and while carried in warehouses abroad.

Over 2,000 American producers now carry "spot stock" at Bush Terminal. Not only is Bush Terminal the geographical hub of the eastern part of the country, but its piers can accommodate 35 ships simultaneously. The Bush Service organization maintains 280 offices, and has over 900 agents among most of the nations of the world. Last year the European business alone aggregated $500,-000,000! Bush Service conveys merchandise to any point desired (Russia excepted), assumes entire responsibility for safe conduct and handling, and delivers against cash or trade acceptances at shipper's option. It will divide, assemble, repack, stamp or label, and insures prompt delivery, assuming all responsibility for error, omission or bad judgment. It arranges for insurance, attends to adjustments of any claims. With representatives in practically 1,000 foreign cities, Bush Service assists in creating and developing markets and helping locate customers.

Over 30 immense buildings with millions of feet of floor space constitute another big feature of Bush Terminal, known as the Bush manufacturing center. Nearly 400 manufacturing concerns (many of them producing millions in merchandise) have their factories here. Over 35,000 employees are on their payrolls.

BUSH TERMINAL IS ONE OF THE MOST STUPENDOUS OF UNCLE SAM'S INDUSTRIAL INSTITUTIONS

WILLIAMSBURGH SAVINGS BANK BUILDING
1 Hanson Place—at Ashland Place and Flatbush Avenue—Brooklyn

THE PRIDE OF BROOKLYN

Brooklyn is proud of both this magnificent skyscraper and of the Williamsburgh Savings Bank. By consistent adherence to sound principles and aggressive yet strictly ethical policies, this great banking institution has forged to the front as one of the most successful and substantial savings banks in the country.

The Williamsburgh Savings Bank has assets of over $220,000,000 and dates its origin back to old colonial days.

This is the fourth largest mutual savings bank in the nation, and its record of honorable dealing and helpful service reflects the greatest credit on its officers and directors. During the trying days of the Civil War, the Williamsburgh Savings Bank purchased U. S. Treasury notes in the amount of $130,000 (a considerable sum in those days when the nation's very life was at stake) and in a larger way, did its duty in the late World War.

For many years the bank's business was entirely local. Today, it has depositors in every state of the Union and in many foreign countries—even as far away as India.

The Williamsburgh Savings Bank building is a masterpiece of architecture, representing the zenith of beauty, magnificence, utility, convenience and service.
The lofty tower houses the

LARGEST 4-DIAL CLOCK IN THE WORLD

which is operated by electricity and illuminated at night with neon lights.

©SANFORD

Ass'd Val.	$6,000,000
512 feet high	42 Floors
Rent area	170,000 sq. ft.
Housing	2,000
Completed	1920
Owner	Williamsburgh Savings Bank
Arch	Halsey, McCormich & Helmer
Bldr	Wm. Kennedy Const. Co.
Agt	R. R. Dinsmore

CO-OPERATIVE APARTMENTS
OR OWNING ONE'S OWN HOME IN NEW YORK
Courtesy of Mr. Douglas L. Elliman

New York is called a city of "cliff dwellers," because the vast majority of its population lives in apartment buildings, ranging skyward up to thirty and more stories.

Although the average New Yorker would like to have "his own home," with green grass, flowers, etc., land is so extremely valuable, taxes so high and building so costly, that even those who are very wealthy prefer to *rent*.

The item of taxes alone on any desirable home site in New York amounts to considerably more than the rental charge of a fine apartment in a high class apartment building. This is the reason why the famous old "brown stone fronts" have been so rapidly disappearing, or are being turned into boarding houses, shops, etc.

Some years ago, however, an enterprising real estate operator, realizing the natural bent of humanity to own their own homes, hit upon the idea of building a "co-operative owned apartment structure" along modern and rather pretentious lines.

He organized a corporation, with a capital stock which, added to the proceeds of the permanent mortgage he took on the land and building, was sufficient to purchase the land and pay the cost of the building. In the meantime, plans and estimates having been prepared, he apportioned to the various apartments their respective values, and then invited prospective buyers to apply for shares and leases. Thus those invited to inspect the building had the opportunity of becoming actual "home-owners."

Howard Cox

40 Fifth Avenue

Of course the buyer had to agree to certain conditions pertaining to sub-letting or subsequent sale of his apartment, to provide against undesirable owner neighbors. Success of the experiment has resulted in the erection of several hundred large and beautiful co-operative owned buildings as well as many smaller ones.

The new "River House," shown on page 273, is one of the most sumptuous and desirable community of "homes" (in one building) yet attempted in the co-operative owned class of buildings. It is (including pent houses and basements) over thirty stories high cost close to $10,000,000 and covers the entire square on the banks of stately East River, from 52nd to 53rd Streets.

The apartments in this magnificent structure sell for as low as $37,000 and as high as $275,000. Apartments range from 8 to 17 rooms. A yacht landing at the river's edge enables residents to step out of a boat and be whisked immediately by fast elevator to any floor in the building. A park and landscape garden 200 feet long by 70 feet wide parallels the entire westerly facade of the building. River House is the epitome of perfection in "cliff dwelling" life in Greater New York.

We have given all these details concerning "River House" as an example of what "Co-operative owned apartment building" has become in the city. There are scores of other desirable cooperative-owned-apartments in all parts of the metropolis. New Yorkers are more and more investing in "their own homes."

HERE ARE A FEW PROMINENT NEW YORKERS WHO OWN COOPERATIVE APARTMENTS

Earl D. Babst
Mrs. August Belmont
Cornelius N. Bliss, Jr.
General Howard S. Borden
Maurice Bouvier
Irving T. Bush
Miss Alice A. DeLamar
William T. Dewart
Frederick H. Ecker
Douglas L. Elliman
Haley Fiske
Mme. Amelita Galli-Curci
Col. E. M. House
Hon. Charles Evans Hughes
Franklin L. Hutton
Gen. J. Leslie Kincaid
Ivy Lee

Col. Benjamin B. McAlpin
Sidney Z. Mitchell
Conde Nast
William Chapman Potter
George Haven Putman
Percy A. Rockefeller
John J. Raskob
Col. Jacob Ruppert
Charles H. Sabin
Gerard Swope
Mrs. W. K. Vanderbilt, 2nd
Frank D. Waterman
Wm. H. Wheelock
Albert H. Wiggin
Owen D. Young
William Ziegler, Jr.

580 Park Ave

430 E. 57

66 E. 79

1120 Fifth Ave

Four magnificent cooperative owned buildings managed by Douglas L. Elliman & Co.

WASHINGTON SQUARE
Where Fifth Avenue begins

SHOWING WASHINGTON ARCH AND ARISTOCRATIC OLD HOMES STILL REMAINING

One of the most delightful sections of old New York.

For many years, the home center of many of the city's oldest and aristocratic families.

The stately Washington Arch (from which a few paces to the north, famous Fifth Avenue begins) is one of the grandest examples of sculptural skill in America.

Showing West Side of Square and Modern Apartment buildings which have replaced the old "brown stone" and "red brick" homes.

Along the north end of the square there still remain several blocks of the "old mansions" shown in picture above.

On the west side of the square are a group of modern apartment houses, built on the site of the old "brown stone" fronted residences, which have been gradually razed to make place for the modern "cliff dwellers" (see picture at left).

To the north and east of the square are a number of imposing apartment hotels and giant apartment buildings (note the pictures below) which are not only magnificent in both architecture and appointment but which for location, ideal light and good fresh air have no superiors in the city.

Washington Square is the gateway to famous Greenwich Village, with its quaint cafes, its artistic atmosphere and gay night life.

Bordering Washington Square on the east are a number of University of New York buildings (see page 49). Immediately below is pictured the famous Judson Memorial at south side of Square.

No. ONE FIFTH AVE. APARTMENT HOTEL

Built and Owned by Fifth Ave. Corp. in 1928 — 27 floors. 475 rooms. Cost $2,500,000. A truly magnificent Fifth Avenue hotel in one of New York's most delightful resident sections.

No. ONE UNIV. PLACE APARTMENT BLDG.

at Washington Square
Ass'd Val. $1,650,000

The very last word in elegance, comfort, and luxury. One, two and three room apartments with kitchen and all modern conveniences.

JUDSON MEMORIAL

Church and hotel built by a wealthy woman as a memorial to her son lost at sea. The cross in high tower is continually illuminated.

HOLLY CHAMBERS
33 Washington Sq. W.

Another "Knott" Apartment Hotel. Cost over $1,000,000; 18 floors; built 1930. Owners, Hollywood Hotel Co. Arch., C. F. Winkleman. Builder, Geekie Naughton. Rates, $70 per month up for apartments with bath, closets, refrigerators, etc.

GREENWICH VILLAGE

Just west of Washington Square

The "Latin Quarter" of New York.

Home of artists, sculptors, writers, musicians, etc.

Here is where genius, temperament, smocks and flowing ties predominate—New York's Bohemia! Greenwich Village is famed for its unconventional modes of living and its gay night life.

COMMUNITY HOUSE
A sort of Town Hall and general community center.

Cellars, attics and even barns are utilized as studios, cafes, and clubs. A bizarre form of decoration, a unique adaptation of modern embellishment and a disposition to create "atmosphere" all combine in luring tens of thousands to Greenwich Village's "Pepper Pot," "Samovar", "Nut Club," "Pirates Den," and a hundred other popular rendezvous. Here at rough wooden tables with crude chairs fairly good meals are served.

Subdued light of tallow candles socketed in old beer bottles are used to emphasize the "atmospheric" environment and altho tea and "near beer" are supposed to be the popular stimulants which help in making merry at the various dining places of the district, it is whispered that every now and then the Volstead law is violated and that genuine "fire-water" can be located at certain oasis in the desert. Actual speak-easies are so cleverly camouflaged as to fool the cops assigned to the neighborhood—all of which seems to add to the attraction of the community as a whole and augment the crowds of visitors who visit the Village nightly.

Many famous painters, sculptors, writers and other devotees of the arts have lived in Greenwich Village, as have also many important members of the theatrical profession.

GREENWICH VILLAGE INN

The "deluxe" cafe of the district which the elite of the city (who prefer "Broadway" rather than "Greenwich Village" *atmosphere*) patronize.

THE SHENANDOAH
10 Shenandoah Square
Apartment House Hotel. One of the imposing new modern apartment buildings rapidly changing certain sections of the village.

Of late years Greenwich Village has increased its regular population by leaps and bounds as a result of the many beautiful new apartment buildings that have replaced the old rattle-trap shacks here, and are bringing in a more circumspect type of resident to the community.

New York is watching with interest the inroads of these modern buildings and wondering whether this new element will gradually crowd out the old timers and eventually usurp the place and entirely change "the atmosphere" which for so long a period has maintained.

GRAMERCY PARK

Located just east of Fourth Avenue—From 20th to 21st Streets.

For over fifty years the Gramercy Park section has been the home center of many of New York's most prominent and aristocratic old families—no neighborhood in the city can boast of more famous men.

Samuel J. Tilden, (Democratic Candidate for the U. S. Presidency in 1870), Cyrus W. Field (father of the ocean cable), Robert G. Ingersoll (noted writer and lecturer), Ex-Mayor Abram S. Hewitt, Stanford White (noted architect) James M. Gerard and other nationally known characters all had homes in Gramercy Park.

Buildings that have replaced old "Brown Stone Fronts" on north side of Gramercy Park.

Today Joseph P. Day (largest real-estate operator in the world), John R. Gregg (owner of the Gregg School of Shorthand) and other outstanding New Yorkers continue to make their homes in this beautiful and refined neighborhood.

Many years ago Samuel Ruggles, one of "Gramercy's" wealthier residents, bequeathed a plot of ground to the city comprising the full square (now Gramercy Park) provided that it should always be retained, with its trees and grassy lawns as a breathing spot for the inmates of the four blocks of buildings overlooking it. Thus those who live in the beautiful apartment structures which have replaced most of the old brown stone homes of those days enjoy a view, unobstructed sunlight and air, as ideal as if living in the country—and yet only a square removed from New York's teeming business activities.

Samuel J. Tilden's old home (15 Gramercy) is now owned by the National Arts Club; one of the highest type and most popular clubs in the city who also purchased the property in the rear and erected a 12-story extention through to 19th Street. (See page 247.)

Robert Ingersoll lived at 52 Gramercy where the magnificent new Gramercy Park Hotel now stands (see picture at left). Cyrus Field lived just acorss the street where his old home has been replaced by an apartment building and Abram S. Hewitt lived just one block north—his old mansion still standing at S. W. Cor. 22nd & Lexington opposite the Russell Sage Foundation Building.

Gramercy Park is a residential section spelling prestige, culture and the maximum in home life, comfort and convenience.

PARKSIDE HOTEL

18 Gramercy Park—South.

Ass'd Val	$875,000
193 ft. high	18 Floors
Rooms	325
Built	1927
Owr. Rosman Cn. Co.	
Agent	Murgatroyd. & Ogden
Bdr. Rosman Cn. Co.	
Restricted to Lady Residents.	

HOTEL GRAMERCY PARK

52 Gramercy Park—North

Ass'd Val	$2,400,000
191 ft. high	17 Floors
Rooms	560
Built 1924 Annex	1930
Owner. Gramercy Pk. Htl. Corp.	
Archet	Thompson & Churchill
Builder	Gresham Const. Co.
Agent	Gresham Realty Co.

CHELSEA

The district west of Sixth Avenue in the "lower twenties."

For many years "Old Chelsea"—particularly around 23rd Street from 7th to 10th Avenues, was one of the liveliest and most aristocratic sections of old New York.

Many old mansions (most of them with the standardized "brown stone front" so typical of the day) housed some of New York's grandest old families who used to entertain regally both at home and at the magnificent Chelsea Hotel—famed at that time for its spacious ball room, excellent cuisine, and gorgeous "bar."

Then there was the equally famous Grand Opera House on the north west corner of 23rd St. and 8th Avenue, with its marvelously beautiful lobby, sumptuous boxes and several balconies where the "elite" enjoyed the performances of Joseph Jefferson, Frances Wilson, Lily Langtry, Stuart Robson and other leading stars of the stage, at that time.

Lily Langtry lived at 361 West 23rd (Between 8th & 9th Avenues) which building has recently been replaced with a beautiful new modern skyscraping apartment house.

200 WEST 23d ST.
S. W. Cor. 8th Ave.

IN THE VERY
HEART OF CHELSEA

In fact, "Old Chelsea" is rapidly disappearing, and big modern apartment buildings are being constructed by the *dozen!* Note next page and observe pictures and story of "London Terrace"—Henry Mandel's recent $20,000,000 development.

Pictured below is the beautiful new Hotel Carteret, one of the most delightful hostelries in the city which has become established as a popular favorite with those who enjoy cozy and truly home like rooms, most superior food, and a hospitality such as few know how more cordially to dispense than its genial manager, Col. Frankyn D. Morgan.

Yes, "Old Chelsea" is passing—although the stately old Chelsea Hotel is still in operation and the famous old Grand Opera House continues to be thronged—as a moving picture house. But a *new* Chelsea is developing at a pace that can be visualized as one of the greatest populated residential sections of all Manhattan if there is no cessation in the ever increasing number of truly imposing apartment houses continually being erected.

HOTEL CARTERET

208 W. 23rd.
S. W. Cor.
7th Ave.

In addition to the magnificent London Terrace group of units, the Henry Mandel Companies have purchased many parcels of land all through this section and has already erected a number of truly beautiful apartment buildings at various locations on 7th Avenue as far south as 16th Street—See page 274.

Ass'd Val	$1,300,000
275 ft. high	19 Floors
Guest Rooms	350
Built	1927
Archt	Emery Roth
Bldr.II. Wertzner & Co.	
Mgr. Col. F. D. Morgan	
Rates	$3.00 and up

LONDON TERRACE

Covers entire area from 9th to 10th Ave. between 23rd and 24th Sts.

A $20,000,000 INVESTMENT

London Terrace is an example of what the vision, daring and determination of one man can accomplish—a young man yet in his forties, Henry Mandel. Just pause and contemplate the courage required to even consider such a gigantic undertaking! When the average man accumulates a "million" he is usually content to "play safe" from then on. But not Henry Mandel! It is such men as Henry Mandel who are building the New York of Today (see picture of Mr. Mandel on page 109).

London Terrace, is already a huge success. The units comprising the huge structure must be seen to give even an idea of its size, its dignity, and its desirability as a *home*. It covers a plot formerly occupied by *81 separate buildings*, housing a small city. Nearly 4,000 are living there now! In lower left hand corner, note picture showing the original plans. Instead of the big "tower" at one end and the low two story entrance at the rear, four gigantic 20 story buildings have been substituted, affording much more floor space. The picture, however, shows the beautiful interior park with its artistic graveled paths, fresh green grass, stone settees, and cooling fountain, with hardy young trees promising delightful shade as they grow larger. The fourteen imposing buildings forming the 14 units of the stupendous structure (each with penthouses) completely surround the park thus guaranteeing both exclusiveness and a pleasant social intercourse to the desirable type of tenants the Mandel Company has succeeded in attracting to this delightful home center.

Showing enclosed park

London Terrace does not appeal to those who can afford $25,000 a year rentals but to the substantial element constituting the great majority of New York's "middle class" with whom it is becoming increasingly popular. In keeping with the "London" idea which so characterizes the atmosphere of the place, fifty doormen and other attendants are outfitted in typical "Bobby" uniforms, helmets, etc. The architecture and everything about the entire institution is very English. London Terrace is one of the sights of New York which every stranger to the city should visit.

NEARLY 2,000 APARTMENTS!

Cost over	$20,000,000
Height of towers	230 ft.
Height of unit bldgs.	190 ft.
Floors towers	20
Units	14
Built	1929-31
Ownrs.	23-rd-24th St. Corp.
Archt.	Farrar & Watmough
Bldr.	H. Mandel Bldg. Corp.
Agt.	H. Mandel Mgmt. Corp.

TUDOR CITY

At the foot of
West 42nd Street
at East River

A MARVELOUS ACHIEVEMENT

A lasting monument to the
foresight, and enterprise of the
Fred F. French companies, who
have invested over

$25,000,000

in the up-building of

TUDOR CITY

AIR VIEW

Showing the
acres of ground,
which a little
over five years ago
were occupied by ram-
shackle buildings and
cheap tenement houses.

A COMPLETE CITY IN ITSELF
With its own private parks, shops, clubs, "golf course," etc.
RIGHT IN THE VERY HEART OF NEW YORK CITY

Fred F. French is a big name in New York—and rightly so.
Fred F. French conceived, planned and built Tudor City almost "over-night."
One day he had an idea—
Ideas to men like Fred French, mean action.
Today, Tudor City is the result of Fred French's idea "put in action."
Mr. French realized that thousands who "commute," would gladly be relieved of wasting *hours* each week riding on stuffy railroad trains, if they could afford to live in New York!
The commuter's, dream is now realized! He can now live in one of the most attractive and ideal home sites to be found in the entire city—only five minutes walk from Grand Central station—in the heart of everything.
Fred F. French had the courage to buy up whole squares at the east end of 42nd Street overlooking East River, and transform one of New York's slum sections into a beautiful city of modern and palatial buildings which spell comfort, convenience and all that contributes to happy home life in New York.

HOTEL TUDOR

Ass'd Val.....$2,250,000
Floors................22
Rates......$2.50 and up

On next page are shown eight of the nearly dozen "units" constituting the various buildings comprising Tudor City. But one must *see* the *parks* (*genuine* parks with grassy lawns, rustic seats, real shade trees, etc.), the golf course and other delightful features to appreciate just how wonderful and attractive Tudor City really is.

WINDSOR TOWER
5 Prospect Place
Ass'd Val.....$5,250,000
29 Floors.....Built 1927

TUDOR TOWER
25 Prospect Place
Ass'd Val. $3,050,000
25 Floors. . Built 1928

PROSPECT TOWER
45 Prospect Place
Ass'd Val.....$2,850,000
31 Floors.....Built 1927

WOODSTOCK TOWER
320 E. 42nd Street
Ass'd Val.....$3,250,000
34 Floors.....Built 1929

TUDOR CITY IS FOR PEOPLE WHO SPEND CAREFULLY

Large scale production reduces overhead and cost. Tudor City offers people with modest incomes, a home life in beautiful surroundings, magnificent modern buildings, amongst a refined type of neighbors at a price so reasonable that from the very start, additional new buildings have been required to meet the popular demand for space.

Tudor City does not appeal to millionaires, but to the better type of the "middle classes" who spend carefully, and who appreciate the worthwhile phases of good living, free from transportation problems and high rents.

HERE IS A VIEW OF ONE OF TUDOR CITY'S SEVERAL PARKS

ESSEX HOUSE
325 E. 41st St.
Ass'd Val. $1,200,000
12 Floors. . Built 1929

A VIEW OF THE GOLF COURSE

18 HOLES—RIGHT IN TUDOR CITY THE HEART OF MANHATTAN

**HADDON HALL
HARDWICK HALL
HATFIELD HOUSE**
304 to 324 E. 41st St.
Ass'd Val.....$1,500,000
Floors........12 to 17
Built.............1928

A great many young people live in Tudor City—Stenographers, secretaries, book-keepers, salesfolks and others who are in business, as they not only have the advantages of ideal home life but may enjoy the unusual social activities resulting from such a large number domiciled together in such intimate proximity. Bridge enthusiasts, back gammon players and patrons of other games and recreation, have grand times in Tudor City.

THE CLOISTER
321 E. 43rd St.
Ass'd Val...$1,000,000
12 Floors...Built 1928

THE MANOR
333 E. 41st St.
Ass'd Val...$1,900,000
12 Floors...Built 1927

271

BEEKMAN PLACE————→

East of First Avenue from 49th to 51st Streets.
Extending to East River.
Mitchell Place at 49th St. & First Ave., adjoins Beekman Place.

Beekman Place is another ideal home section where a taste of suburban life with its green grass, growing trees and song birds may be enjoyed.

Beekman Terrace and Beekman Manor—the two beautiful modern buildings shown in picture below, are at the extreme end of Fifty-first Street overlooking East River. An artistic iron fence capping the high stone wall at the streets-end, provides safety for both motorists and pedestrians. An artistic stairway leads down to the beautiful little park on the river's edge where green lawns, flowers and shade trees constitute a most delightful breathing spot for the fortunate inmates of these delightful apartment homes. Both of these modern palaces are cooperative owned and enjoy the cooling river breezes in summer and exceptional sunlight in winter.

The above picture shows the mansion erected in 1763 by William Beekman on the sunny bluff commanding a view of East River for miles, which during the Revolution served as headquarters for General Howe, Clinton and Carlton of the British army and which was also used as a courtroom for the trial of Nathan Hale.

The corner of First Avenue and 51st Street marks the site of the famous old building in honor of whose owner "Beekman Place" is named.

BEEKMAN MANSION
and
BEEKMAN TERRACE

439 and 455 E. 51st Street at East River.
(Note description above)

The plans for the Beekman Mansion and Beekman Terrace were drawn by Treanor & Fatic in collaboration with J. E. R. Carpenter. These two twin buildings are conceded to be two of the most picturesque in the East river section. T. E. Rhoades Co. Inc., are the builders—thus insuring high grade construction.

No. ONE BEEKMAN PLACE

At foot of 49th Street & East River.

Sloan & Robertson, Architects.

This enormous and sumptuously appointed apartment building looms up in 49th Street's skyline like a "huge lighthouse at sea." Has commanding view of river, modern throughout and enjoys a particularly high type tenancy.

NOTE—There is not one line of paid advertising in this entire volume and no one has been required to buy a single copy. When we have said "nice things" about folks or their properties, we are simply extending credit where we deem credit due.

SUTTON PLACE

52nd St. to 59th Streets on the banks and adjacent to East River.

MRS. WILLIAM K. VANDERBILT IS LARGELY RESPONSIBLE FOR THE GREAT POPULARITY OF SUTTON PLACE

Only a short few years ago, this whole part of town was largely devoted to small stores, small dwellings or tenements.

Today, Sutton Place is one of the most popular residential sections in the city. Whole rows of fifteen to eighteen story apartment houses similar to "25 Sutton" line the streets—most pretentious buildings with luxurious appointments, quite away from the noise and din of business, yet only a few squares removed.

Sutton Place has many appeals—East River with its cooling breezes, a superior class of residents, and a most Bohemian social life.

With the many improvements all along East River from this point north, the famous old stream is being beautified by private docks and landings with grassy parks, growing trees and other improvements which in time, should result in making East River developments among the most attractive and desirable residential quarters in New York.

The East River Parkway now in course of construction, promises to be a rival of famed Riverside Drive. Judging from the number and quality of the many palatial buildings recently constructed and in process of construction, Sutton Place and other sections developing along East River should solve the housing problem which has so insistently been advanced that New York's entire area would be required for business needs alone.

RIVER HOUSE

ON THE BANK OF EAST RIVER
Extending for full block—Between 52nd and 53rd Sts.
CO-OPERATIVE OWNED.
Apartments—$37,000 to $275,000.

COST $10,630,000

300 ft. high.....30 Floors.....Built 1931
Architects....Bottomly, Wagner & White
Builder..............Jas. Stewart & Co.
Selling and Managing Agent
DOUGLAS L. ELLIMAN & CO.
15 E. 49th St., N. Y. City

THE CAMPANILE

Foot of 52nd St. and East River. Across the street from RIVER HOUSE shown above.

Reminiscent of Venice and its colorful Grand Canal—on the shore of East River. Note boat landing and beautiful park.

ONE SUTTON PLACE

Cor. 58th St. at SUTTON SQUARE.

Cost $1,170,000
17 Floors.......Built 1927
Archts.....Rosario Candela
Cross & Cross

25 SUTTON PLACE

Cor. 54th Street

ONE OF THE 50 MAGNIFICENT APARTMENT BUILDINGS RECENTLY ERECTED IN THE SUTTON PLACE SECTION.

CO-OPERATIVE OWNED
Apartments Cost $50,000 to $65,000
T. E. RHOADS & CO., Builders
DOUGLAS L. ELLIMAN & CO.
Selling and Managing Agents.
Completed in 1930.

OTHER MIDTOWN HOME CENTERS

Enterprising real estate operators have purchased property in *neglected* sections in various parts of Midtown of late years and transformed what was formerly ramshackle tenement districts into beautiful and desirable residential quarters.

Here are a few of the "seven figure" buildings recently erected—

235 E. 22nd St.
N. W. Cor. 2nd Ave.

301 E. 21st St.
N. E. Cor. 2nd Ave.

161 W. 16th St.
N. E. Cor. 7th Ave.

200 W. 16th St.
S. W. Cor. 7th Ave.

235 E. 22nd
Cost close to $2,000,000
19 Floors....Built 1931
Has beautiful private park.
J. H. Taylor Construction Co. Owners & Bldrs.

301 E. 21st, cost close to $1,250,000
18 Floors...Built 1930
Owner....301 E. 21st Corp.
Bldr. Baker Lavine Co.

Nearly a block and a half of old shacks and cheap tenement buildings were demolished to make way for these two beautiful and modern apartment houses—only two to three squares below delightful Gramercy Park.

These are only two of a number of imposing new buildings erected during the past two years in the section lying between 14th and 20th Streets on the west side, replacing small stores or dwellings. This area is developing into one of the most attractive residential sections of the city. The Henry Mandel Co. are investing millions in this neighborhood.

TOWN HOUSE
108 E. 38th St.
Only a stone's throw from business.

Cost
$2,000,000

26 Floors

141 Apartments

Year Built
1930

A sumptuous building for refined people who want a luxurious home right in the heart of activities and yet away from the city's noise.

Owner.....Town House Construction Co.
Architect............Bowden & Russell
Builder..Wm. McKinley Construction Co.
Agent......R. M. Dinsmore & Co., Inc.

PARC VENDOME
330-360 West 57th Street
Extending three blocks to 58th St. near 9th Ave.
Est. Cost
$4,500,000
20 Floors
Built 1931

ANOTHER HUGE HENRY MANDEL DEVELOPMENT

Another small city within itself.
600 Apartments
Swimming pool
Gymnasium

Open air Terrace Dining Hall, Solarium, Terraced Gardens. Shopping Arcade. In fact, the very last word in convenience, comfort, efficiency and modern idealism in living.

ONLY THREE MINUTES WALK FROM BROADWAY

These new home centers are being developed in every part of New York. Many of them are but a short distance from the seething business sections of the city. But New Yorkers are more and more inclined to want to live right in the heart of activities—close to business.

CARL SCHURZ PARK
and GRACIE SQUARE SECTION

ALONG EAST RIVER "IN THE EIGHTIES"

Ever since smart New York awoke to the charms of old East River, wealth to the extent of tens of millions has been invested in land and buildings along its historic banks and property adjacent—transforming whole districts of ramshackle buildings or old landmarks into magnificent home sites and aristocratic neighborhoods.

For many years prior to the Civil War the natural beauty of this section of Manhattan made it most popular with New York's aristocracy for the establishm.nt of country estates, but the rise in land after the war was over swept away the glories of this old stronghold of society. However, "Gracie Mansion," built by the wealthy merchant, Archibald Gracie, still stands and is the big point of interest in Carl Schurz Park which is now owned by the city and used as a museum.

Air view by the AIRMAP CORP. OF AMERICA N. Y.

Society is now reclaiming "East River" and its move to its environments is no mere vogue but is rather a determined desire to take full advantage of its heritage of the past.

Note on this page pictures of four of the palatial apartment homes recently erected in Gracie Square and East End Avenue.

130 EAST END AVE.

Cor. 86th St.

A most palatial apartment building with large airy rooms and every convenience which modern construction makes possible.

120 EAST END AVE.

Cor. 85th St.

One of the regal buildings erected by Vincent Astor. Mr. John J. Raskob, Chairman of the Democratic National Committee has his home here.

**NOTHING CAN BE FOUND IN APARTMENTS
MORE LUXURIOUS THAN THESE BUILDINGS**

No. ONE GRACIE SQUARE

84th St. S. E. Cor. East End Ave.

Ass'd Value OVER A MILLION

Co-operative owned

No. 10 GRACIE SQUARE

Faces both the park and East River

COST OVER $6,500,000

20 floors

Co-operative Owned

Built 1930

T. E. Rhoads Co., Builder

Magnificent Thru-out

For information concerning either of these superlative buildings, address—

DOUGLAS L. ELLIMAN & CO.
15 E. 49th St., New York

275

PARK AVENUE

Lower Park Avenue extends from 32nd Street to 42nd Street, where the New York Central Buildings form a break from 42nd to 46th Streets. Upper Park Avenue extends from 46th Street north.

WHERE MANY OF THE WEALTHIEST FAMILIES IN NEW YORK RESIDE

"15 Park" and "16 Park" at 35th St. (Fred F. French Buildings on Lower Park Ave.)

Years ago the New York Central trains rumbled through the tunnel under Park Avenue, with the smoke and gases from puffing engines rising through the openings right in the center of the avenue (and bridged over only at cross streets). Then, this particular thoroughfare gave very little promise of becoming what it is today—a rival to Fifth Avenue in the wealth and luxury of its lavish living quarters, tenanted by many of New York's smartest and wealthiest families.

But with the completion of the Grand Central Terminal buildings, the electrifying of the underground trains and the closing of the open spaces, Pease & Elliman Co., Douglas Elliman & Co., Brown Wheelock, Harris Vought & Co., and other far-sighted real estate operators and builders, aggressively exploited the avenue. Here, they pointed out, was the ideal residential locality for the aristocracy and wealth of the city who desired to live conveniently near "business" (and yet not actually have their homes on a business street). Magnificent, palatial, exclusive Park Avenue is the result. Today, the mere address "Park Avenue" spells Prestige.

480 PARK AVENUE
N. W. Cor. 58th Street.

Ass'd Val	$5,900,000
Floors	21
Completed	1929
Ownrs	480 Park Ave. Corp.
Archt	Emery Roth
Bldrs	Sam'l Minskoff
Agts	PEASE & ELLIMAN

784 PARK AVENUE
S. W. Cor. 74th Street.

Cost	$2,600,000
oors	23
Completed	1929
Owners	Bing & Bing
Archt	Emery Roth
Bldrs	Bing & Bing
Agents	Bing & Bing

895 PARK AVENUE
S. E. Cor. 79th Street.

Cost	$5,785,000
35 Families	19 Floors
Completed	1930
Owners	Cooperative owned
Archt	Sloan & Robertson
Bldrs	Thos. O'Reily & Son
Agt	PEASE & ELLIMAN

A FEW OF THE SCORES OF PARK AVENUE PALACES

277 PARK AVENUE
From 47th to 48th Streets
Through to Lexington Ave.
Built.........................1924
An August Heckscher Building
Ass'd Val.................$11,500,000
Archt............McKim Mead & White
Bldr................Thompson-Starrett

280 PARK AVE.
48th to 49th Streets
100 % Cooperative
Val..........$5,950,000
18 Floors.....Built 1921
Arch.Warren & Wetmore
Agt.D. L. Elliman & Co

1185 PARK AVE.
93rd to 94th Streets
Ass'd Val......$6,300,000
173 Families....Built 1929
Archt....Schwartz & Gross
Bldr....Bricken Const Co.
Agt..D. L. Elliman & Co.

300 Park Ave. "Sherry's"
49th to 50th Streets
Ass'd Val...........$6,250,000
20 Floors...........Built 1921
Archt.......Warren & Wetmore
Bldr........Thompson & Starrett

580 PARK AVE.
63rd to 64th Streets
$3,250,000...........Built 1923
Archt.......J. E. R. Carpenter
Agt..Douglas L. Elliman & Co.

720 PARK AVE.
100 % Cooperative
$3,250,000...........Built 1929
Archt............Cross & Cross

1070 PARK AVE
S. W. Cor. 88th St.
Ass'd Val...$2,100,000
Archt.......Schwartz
Agt.Pease & Elliman
Built...........1929

1085 PARK AVE
N. W. Cor. 88th St.
$1,660,000..Built 1926
Archt.....Schwartz & Gross
Agt. Pease & Elliman

1100 PARK AVE
N. W. Cor. 89th St.
$2,000,000..Built 1930
Archt.Depace & Juster
Agt.Pease & Elliman

1220 PARK AVE
N. W. Cor. 95th St.
$1,500,000. Built 1930
Archt........ Rosario
Candela
BrownWheelock H.Co.

FIFTH AVENUE
MOST FAMOUS RESIDENTIAL THOROUGHFARE IN THE WORLD

Wealthy and aristocratic old New York families, who formerly occupied their palatial homes on this world-renowned street, have one by one gradually succumbed to changing conditions, and abdicated in favor of enterprising real estate operators who have been so aggressive in erecting towering apartment buildings on Fifth Avenue. The result during the past few years is an almost completely transformed and *NEW* Fifth Avenue.

Massive white marble residential skyscrapers now replace the old brownstone and granite-fronted dwellings. Thirty, forty and even sixty and seventy families now live on a plot of ground that formerly accommodated less than half a dozen individuals and servants.

New York has grown so phenomenally, real estate values have increased so rapidly, and taxes risen so steadily, that even New York's multi-millionaires found housekeeping on Fifth Avenue "a bit expensive" and finally capitulated to the new order of things.

Words convey but a faint idea of the luxury, the regal grandeur and the superb magnificence of many of these palatial apartment buildings which for over two miles face Central Park in almost unbroken continuity. It is estimated that from 59th Street to 110th St. (the length of Central Park) the actual value or amount of money invested in these fifty short blocks is over

Louis H. Dreyer

$250,000,000

The interior decoration and furnishings of many of these homes beggars description. Rare paintings and tapestries costing a ransom, blend with oriental rugs, and costly draperies which cannot be excelled in even the old palaces of Europe.

There are three sections of the city recognized as the outstanding residential districts of New York's aristocracy and greatest wealth:

FIFTH AVENUE and vicinity
PARK AVENUE and vicinity
EAST RIVER DEVELOPMENTS

Pease & Elliman Co., Douglas L. Elliman & Co., and Brown Wheelock Harris & Co. have been most active in this district. New York owes a great deal of its indisputable supremacy in the way of both its commercial and residential palaces, to the promotive genius and aggressiveness of these three enterprising firms.

834 FIFTH AVE.
N. E. Cor. 64th Street.

Cost............$7,000,000
230 feet high......16 Floors
Completed.............1931
Arch........Rosario Candela
Bldr.....Anthony Campagua
Sell. & Man. Agents.
Brown Wheelock Harris & Co.
CO-OPERATIVE OWNED

ONE OF THE MOST REGAL
RESIDENTIAL PALACES IN
ALL THE WORLD

278

AMERICAN KINGS

live on Fifth Avenue in a grander and more sumptuous manner than even the mighty potentates of olden days. Comforts, conveniences, luxuries and delights which many of the world's most powerful monarchs never knew are enjoyed daily in a thousand Fifth Avenue homes. Our modern building methods these days are based on results of constantly new inventions and discoveries, which make it possible to provide for the gratification of every desire in the way of gorgeous surroundings, personal comfort and ideal living. There are no more magnificent homes in all the world than can be found on Fifth Avenue.

1040 FIFTH AVE.
N. E. Cor. 85th Street

Another gorgeous cooperative owned apartment palace housing some of New York's most wealthy families.

Cost Nearly $5,000,000

182 ft. high.........19 Floors
Built....................1930
Archt.......Rosario Candela
Builder...Anthony A. Paterno

Selling and Managing Agent
DOUGLAS L. ELLIMAN & CO
15 E. 49th Street
New York City

Guild Photo

Guild Photo

Guild Photo

Howard Cox

907 FIFTH AVE.
S. E. Cor. 72nd St.

Ass'd Val.....$2,550,000
14 Floors....23 Families
Built.............1912
Cooperative owned.....
Arct.J. E. R. Carpenter
Bldr..J. E. R. Carpenter
Agt.Pease & Elliman Inc.

912 FIFTH AVE.
Bet. 72nd & 73rd Sts.

Value.......$2,000,000
Floors............16
Owner....Truly Warner
Agent..Schwartz & Gross
Builder.Solomon & Kahn
Agt.Pease & Elliman Inc.

920 FIFTH AVE.
S. E. Cor. 73rd St.

Ass'd Val....$1,850,000
15 Floors....26 Families
Built............1922
Ownr.J. E. R. Carpenter
Archt..Schwartz & Gross
Bldr..Realty Mgrs. Inc.
Agt.Pease & Elliman Inc.

960 FIFTH AVE.
Cor. 77th Street

Cost.........$2,750,000
14 Floors....Built 1928
Ownr.963 5th Av. Corp.
Arct.Warren & Wetmore
Bldr.Anthony Campagna
Agt..Doug.L.EllimanCo.

Guild Photo

Guild Photo

Guild Photo

1136 FIFTH AVE.
S. E. Cor. 95th St.

Ass'd Val....$1,450,000
16 Floors....45 Families
Built.............1925
Owner.Albert Solkowski
Arct..Geo. Fred Pelham
Builder.Albert Solkowski
Agt.Pease & Elliman Inc.

1158 FIFTH AVE.
Cor. 97th Street

Ass'd Val....$0,000,000
16 Floors....Built 0000
Ownr.Houston.Propert's.
Archt................
Bldr................
Agt................

1165 FIFTH AVE.
S. E. Cor. 98th St.

Cost........$2,250,000
17 Floors....54 Families
Built.............1926
Cooperative owned....
Arct..J. E. R. Carpenter
Bdr.D. P. Robinson Co.
Agt.Pease & Elliman Inc.

1170 FIFTH AVE.
N. E. Cor. 98th St.

Ass'd Val....$0,000,000
Floors.............16
Built.............1927
Cooperative owned.....
Arct.J. E. R. Carpenter
Bdr.D. P. Robinson Co.
Agt...Brown Wheelock
           Harris & Co.

CENTRAL PARK WEST

A continuation of Eighth Avenue (at Columbus Circle)
—from 60th Street to 110th Street. Bordering the west
side of Central Park for a distance of fifty blocks.

"IT WAS SURE TO COME:"—Thus reasoned farsighted real estate operators who realized that "Central Park West" had exactly the same right to be an ideal home center as Fifth Avenue. It was the prestige of wealth that made Fifth Avenue property many times more valuable than Central Park West property. Both avenues faced the park—neither one having any better view, better air, or better vantage points than the other. But the aristocracy of the city long ago selected Fifth Avenue as the location for their show places. However, New York has grown and grown. So has the aristocracy of wealth. They couldn't *all* live on Fifth Avenue—thus Park Avenue, Sutton Place, the East River developments and Central Park West. Central Park's beauty, wonderful light, air and sunshine, the song birds, the restful quiet and the many other appeals of Central Park West are becoming more and more appreciated.

55 CENTRAL PARK WEST
S. W. Cor. near 66th Street.

573 Rooms........20 Floors
Completed............1930
Ownrs..55 Cen. Park W. Cor.
Archt...Schwartz & Gross
Agents....Earle & Calhoun

101 CENTRAL PARK WEST
69th St.

The beautiful apartments of this palatial building would satisfy even the royalty of Europe.

With a full block frontage facing Central Park a more ideal home site would be difficult to find.

Value $2,250,000.
20 Floors.
103 Families.
Completed 1930.
Owners:
1081 Park Ave., Inc.
Architects:
Schwartz & Gross.
Builders:
Bricken Const. Co.
Agents:
PEASE & ELLIMAN

Photo by Guild Warnick.

75 CENTRAL PARK WEST
67th to 68th Streets.

Ass'd Val.........$1,500,000
17 Floors....Completed 1929
Cooperatively Owned.......
Archt......Rosario Candela
Builders..Fred T. Ley & Co.
Agts...PEASE & ELLIMAN

BERESFORD APARTMENTS
Central Park West
81st to 82nd Sts.

This magnificent structure has a full block frontage facing Central Park and an equal frontage on 81st Street —opposite the park on which the American Museum of Natural History is built.

Cost Over:
$10,000,000
22 Floors.
Built 1929.
Owners:
Manhattan Square
Beresford, Inc.
Architect:
Emery Roth.
Builders:
H. R. H. Const. Co.
Agents:
H. R. H. Mgmt. Co.

CENTURY APARTMENTS
Extending full block on Central Park West. Between 62nd and 63rd Sts.

Est. Cost	$15,000,000
32 Floors	Completed 1931
Owners	Chanin Organization
Archt	Chanin Organization
Bldrs	Chanin Const. Co.
Agents	Chanin Organization

SAN REMO TOWERS
Central Park West—74th to 75th Sts. Built on the site of the old San Remo Hotel.

Cost	$7,500,000
28 Floors	Built 1930 401 ft. high
Owners	San Remo Towers Inc.
Archt	Emery Roth
Builders	H. R. H. Const. Co.
Agents	H. R. H. Mgmt. Corp.

In addition to these enormous and regal buildings shown here, there are

OVER 100 OTHER

magnificent apartment buildings already erected, or in course of construction on Central Park West and its immediate vicinity.

CENTRAL PARK WEST

is rapidly becoming one of the great show streets of the city.

MAJESTIC APARTMENTS
Central Park West—At 72nd St.
Built on the site of the famous old Majestic Hotel. Another Enormous Chanin Achievement.

Est. Cost	$14,000,000
30 Floors	Built 1931
Owners	Chanin Organization
Archt	Chanin Organization
Bldrs	Chanin Const Co.
Agents	Chanin Organization

ELDORADO APARTMENTS
Central Park West—90th to 91st St.

Est. Cost	$8,500,000
30 Floors	1,300 Rooms
Ground Area	42,000 sq. ft.
Built	1931
Arct.	Margon & Holden & E. Roth
Agent	L. J. Phillips

WEST END AVENUE

A continuation of Tenth Avenue beginning at 59th Street, extending north to Broadway at 105th Street.

Albert Rothschild

Over 150 magnificent apartment buildings and apartment hotels line both sides of this beautiful residential Avenue for a distance of approximately two miles housing thousands of most superior type of New York's citizenry.

450 WEST END AVE.
S. E. Cor. 82nd St.
Boak & Paris, Archt.

685 WEST END AVE.
N. W. Cor. 93rd St.

PARIS APARTMENT HOTEL
752 West End at 97th St.
Cost $3,500,000

CROSS STREETS

CROSS STREETS BOTH EAST AND WEST OF CENTRAL PARK AREA

Below are shown a few of the *hundreds* of magnificent apartment buildings on Cross Streets.

There are fully 2,000 beautiful apartment buildings in New York scattered all through both the residential and business districts.

Hundreds of these are in cross-streets.

Here are a few of the *scores* ranging in height from 18 to 25 stories, between 57th and 90th Streets.

Peter A. Juley & Son

Louis H. Dryer

400 EAST 57th ST.
Fronting on 1st Ave.
Douglas L. Elliman,
Agts.

315 EAST 68th ST.
Near East River
Gus & Edwd. Blum Arch.

205 EAST 78th ST.
Near Lexington Ave.

15 W. 81st ST.
thru to 82 ST.
Near Central Park W.

Albert Rothschild

Louis H. Dryer

12 EAST 86th ST.
Near Fifth Ave.

200 AMSTERDAM AVE.
S. E. Cor. 86th St.

40 EAST 88th ST.
S. E. Cor. Mad. Ave.

21 EAST 90th ST.
Just east of 5th Av.

282

BEAUTIFUL RIVERSIDE DRIVE

Riverside Drive has been proclaimed the most beautiful thoroughfare in the world. Commencing at 72nd Street and Hudson River, this magnificent Drive winds along the stately old stream for approximately seven miles, finally turning into Broadway at Dyckman Street.

Commencing at 73rd Street (extending to 74th) is the $3,000,000 palace of Charles M. Schwab—Note extreme right in above picture.

22 RIVERSIDE DR.
Cor. 74th St.
Val. $1,100,000

Most of the grand old mansions on Riverside Drive have given way to regal apartment buildings. Two of the most recent of these are shown herewith. Since the above picture was taken most of the structures facing the Drive have been demolished and sky scraping apartment towers have taken their place. No. 22 Riverside (note cut at left)—directly opposite the Schwab residence, is unique in that the owner has built a complete private house on the roof of the 20th story!

Boak & Paris—one of New York's most outstanding architectural firms, drew the plans for both of these imposing buildings.

The picture below shows how the $20,000,000 tract of land reclaimed from the Hudson River is being utilized to extend and beautify Riverside Park—one of the swimming pools for "kids."

230 RIVERSIDE DR.
Cor. 95th St.
Val. $1,875,000

The New York Central Tracks are to be covered over—thus extending the Park to the water's edge.

We are indebted to the Manhattan Post Card Co. and the City Administration for pictures of Riverside Drive.

HARLEM

Harlem is the name given to that section of the city north of 106th St. between East River and 8th Avenue. The particular pride of Harlem is 125th St. where the enterprising citizens operating the mile or more of business institutions lining the thoroughfare have aggressively developed their precinct into a city by itself.

In the Negro Section of Harlem

Most imposing furniture stores, department stores and almost every type of merchandising concern in the commercial line has given to Harlem a marketing area that rivals many of the big downtown houses.

The Harlem Business Men's Association hold carnivals, festivals and parades which attract New Yorkers from every part of the city borders, and their old time slogan "Watch Harlem Grow" seems to be most appropriate as it is doubtful if in any section of Greater New York, there has been manifested a more enthusiastic local pride and healthier growth than in the business district of Harlem.

Harlem enjoys the unique distinction of having the largest negro population in the world. Over 250,000 live in one neighborhood—many of them being extremely wealthy. New York is proud of its negro element. In no city of the world are there more reliable, highly educated and more cultured colored men and women than in New York. Thousands of positions of trust in banks, law offices and big corporations are held by negroes and a number of them have palatial homes and live in the same refinement as many millionaire white men.

JACKSON HEIGHTS

About fifteen years ago a coterie of live real estate operators selected a tract of vacant land beyond 59th St. Bridge crossing East River (only half an hour's travel from Broadway) and started a "development." They built whole rows of up to date four, five and six story apartment dwellings and advertised extensively that "Jackson Heights" was the ideal home center for young married couples who wished to raise their children in a community free from the confusion and danger of city congestion. They adopted the cooperative idea and advocated buying one's own home.

From this beginning of half a dozen squares of more-or-less modest dwellings, the present and imposing "city" of Jackson Heights has grown. Today, palatial apartment buildings, beautiful schools, parks, clubs, a golf course and a population of close to 35,000 constitute one of the most popular of New York's residential areas.

Electric buses and Elevated extensions of New York's subway system etc., make it possible for "Jackson Heighters" to reach Times Square in less time than those living in many parts of Manhattan.

GOVERNORS ISLAND

This 173 acre island is only half a mile or so distant from the Battery and is the headquarters of the U. S. Second Corps Area.

Its history dates back to the Dutch occupation of N. Y. in 1634 when it was purchased from the Indians by Gov. Von Twiller.

But at that time there were less than 100 acres to the tract. Over 80 acres have been added by filling in land from Manhattan's subway excavations, etc.

This island has been an important army headquarters since 1803.

Government boats ply from the Battery to Governor's Island hourly.

CONEY ISLAND ~

Coney Island forms the most southern part of the Borough of Brooklyn—the great play ground district of New York famed for many years for its "Sea Gate," "Brighton Beach," "Manhattan Beach, etc. Coney Island has been famous the world over for its $2,000,000 Luna Amusement Park, its 10c. side shows, its merry-go-rounds, its professional "barkers," and above all, its ideal bathing beach where upwards of 400,000 bathers go in the water on most every pleasant Sunday.

At a cost of over $3,000,000 the City of New York a few years ago, erected the present Boardwalk extendiny along the ocean front from the City Bathing Pavilion, down past Cortelyou's Steeplechase. Every sunshing Sunday during the summer season, over half a million people stroll up and down its planked floor or ride in roller chairs, enjoying cooling sea breezes and viewing the crowd of bathers.

"Coney" has been undergoing a very marked metamorphis, however, in late years. Since the days of the old beer halls and clam bakes, there has been a general and steady improvement in the buildings, the amusements, and the personnel of the crowds themselves. The "three shell" fakers are gone, the scarlet women have become less in evidence, the "side shows" do not attempt to "sting" so brazenly and the streets are clean, well officered and a very much higher toned atmosphere pervades.

Showing the great "pool" in Luna Park

Many beautiful and modern structures have been built facing the Boardwalk. Really high class amusement is now offered and Coney is commencing to take on an Atlantic City tinge. Those who visited Coney Island in days gone by would hardly recognize the famous old place today.

NEW YORK'S FAMOUS "BOWERY"

Begins at Cooper Union on 8th Street at which point Third and Fourth Avenues merge.

Away back in the Dutch period, this thoroughfare was called "Bowerie Lane" and on it were located the country homes of the wealthy, but later the saloon, the dance hall, sporting, and tougher element gradually took possession, and night life became so strenuous the city had to clean up the district. Today, the Bowery is a busy shopping street and the center of a section given over to small manufacturing and jobbing houses.

CHINATOWN ~

Chinatown is that section of the lower East Side extending from Bayard Street to Chatham Square, where the majority of New York's Chinese reside. The buildings are old, but kept in good repair, and many Joss Houses are open to the public and in Pell, Mott and Doyers Streets, are many stores and shops catering to tourists and visitors.

THE GHETTO ~

The Ghetto is comprised of about thirty to forty squares in the Mulberry Bend district of the lower East Side, where over a hundred thousand of the poorer classes of Italian and Yiddish folk are huddled together in tenements and live over stores and shops catering to about the shrewdest and most conservative buying public in America—The Ghetto is well worth visiting as here will be found the *real* "Sidewalks of New York."

We are indebted to the Manhattan Post Card Co. for pictures on this page

• INDEX •

Note Classification of Business Buildings, Hotels, Theatres, Churches, Civic Buildings, Etc.

STORIES OF NEW YORK'S INSIDE LIFE, ITS ACTIVITIES, ITS STREETS, ETC., ETC.

By consulting these classified listings, it will be easy to find any building, person or subject that may be desired.

THE GALVANOTYPE COMPANY
424 WEST 33rd STREET, NEW YORK CITY

THIS IS **NOT** AN "ADV."
There is not a line of paid advertising in this entire book.

When anything "nice" is said concerning an individual, firm, or property, we are simply extending credit where we deem credit due—thus acquainting our readers with *facts* as we find them and placing them in a position to do business and enjoy relations with responsible people.

The Galvanotype Co. is such an institution. Established fifty years ago (1881) they have learned how to produce the best.

Words mean little. It is *evidence* that counts. The 851 half tones shown in this book were all made by the Galvanotype Co. As a general thing coated paper must be used to bring out the best results from half tones, and yet, these Galvanotype cuts speak for themselves on the ordinary "machine finish" stock used in this book. The general excellence of them is all the more remarkable when it is taken into consideration that fully 200 of the lot were made from ordinary newspaper prints, or impressions from circular matter, brochure covers, etc.